THE STIGMATIST

THE STIGMATIST

A novel of mysticism and international intrigue

HURD BARUCH

MYSTIC PUBLICATIONS

TUCSON

For more information, visit *thestigmatist.com.*

Cover design by Ben Hatke (*househatke.com*),
based on original artwork by Roxolana Armstrong.
Typesetting by Bill Powell at Wineskin Media (*wineskinmedia.com*).

ISBN: 978-0-615-41983-1

To My Wife

Who patiently and lovingly critiqued each version,
to transform my straighforward prose
into a living work of fiction.

Author's Notes

This book is a work of fiction, set five years in the future and peopled with fictional characters not based on specific individuals. Any resemblance to actual persons is purely coincidental, except, unavoidably, for the person of Pope Benedict XVIth, whom I hope will still be exercising the Petrine Office in 2015. As is evident from the text, I hold him and his conduct of the Papacy in the highest esteem. His thoughts, words and deeds at that future time, under the unprecedented circumstances described herein, are products solely of my imagination.

The reported apparitions of the Blessed Virgin Mary during the 1960's at Garabandal, Spain, which form the starting point for this novel, are still under investigation by the Church, and they have neither been approved nor disapproved by it. Priests are permitted to celebrate Mass and administer the Sacrament of Reconciliation there for pilgrim groups. The author expresses his unconditional submission to the final and official judgment of the Magisterium as to whether the apparitions were of supernatural origin.

Acknowledgments

My friends Arnold Gough, Jr. and George L. Holley helped considerably with their critical comments on early drafts of the manuscript, and I am especially indebted to Fr. Greg Adolf, a learned and devout priest, for his meticulous review of the manuscript toward the end of the process. Of course, I alone bear the responsibility for the final content.

The resourcefulness and contacts of my Roman guide, Alessandro D'Ausilio, proved invaluable in gaining behind-the-scenes access at the Vatican and San Giovanni Rotondo.

The syntax, vocabulary and spelling of the dialogue in Part IX between the Stigmatist and his interrogator, an uncultured Russian with only rudimentary knowledge of the English language, were expertised by Jessica E. Mattix, a lady with long experience teaching English as a second language to Russian-speakers.

Contents

PART I

The Pilgrimage

December 2014

A pilgrimage is a journey, assigned by God. It brings
the pilgrim not only to a physical place, but out of himself, and into the presence of God. All else falls away.
There is only the child, his Father, and eternity . . .

Fr. S. Kraljevic, O.F.M., *Pilgrimage*, 67 (Paraclete Press 1991)

— 1 —

Spain

"Thirty-three, thirty-four, thirty-five . . ." Gloria Sanchez moved down the aisle of the *Saints, Signs & Wonders* tour bus, double checking the count she had made as the pilgrims boarded. There was indeed one missing. Again. "Who do you know that you don't see on the bus?" she called out.

This time, the missing sheep was Betty Mangone. Señora Sanchez hurried back into Oviedo's cathedral and found her still browsing in the souvenir shop.

Once she was herded aboard, the group was off for an early lunch before they continued on their journey. The next leg would take them eastward along Spain's northern coast and then south into the interior, for a brief visit to San Sebastián de Garabandal. It was not a customary stop on the Portugal to Spain to France pilgrimage route that Señora Sanchez worked, and she was a bit apprehensive. Not that she expected anything untoward would occur, but there was really nothing special to see or do there, and, more important, the little mountain village was not a pilgrimage site approved by the Church—a fact which made the stop there suspect in her mind.

The pilgrims read or took afternoon catnaps until the bus reached Pesues, and turned off the main road to head up into the mountains. Then, it was time for Fr. Martinez' talk. Holding onto the overhead luggage rack with one hand while he gripped the microphone with the other, the priest began to give an explanation of the significance of Garabandal. For the most part, his charges gave him their attention, though from time to time they turned to enjoy the beautiful Cantabrian mountain scenery they were passing through.

"We are heading now for the humble mountain village of Gara-bandal. It is at the other end of the spectrum from the two great shrines we have just seen, Fatima and Santiago de Compostela, and also from Lourdes, where we will conclude our trip. It has neither a constant stream of visitors, nor a huge basilica, nor even a holy relic to venerate as we did in Oviedo."

"Why then are we going there? What prompts us to spend a few hours in Garabandal is what happened in the early 1960's: four young children reported that Mary, the Mother of Jesus, appeared to them a number of times, and gave them portentous messages, parts of which they were to keep secret until they were told to speak."

"It all began on a summer night in 1961. Four girls—not close friends, by the way—were playing outside in a *calleja*, an alleyway, when a brilliant and beautiful figure appeared to them. He was small, dressed in a blue robe, and had rose colored wings. Obviously, he was an angel, but they didn't know his name for he didn't speak. At a later date, they learned that he was the Archangel Michael. When he vanished from sight they went home and told about what they had seen. Their parents were more surprised than pleased."

"Why was that," Mrs. Mangone wanted to know, "weren't the parents religious?"

"Oh, by all means, Betty," replied the chaplain, "but that is precisely why their parents were upset. After all, if *you* had a 12 year old daughter who came home with a story that she had just seen an angel in the street, would *you* believe her? And wouldn't you be angry if you thought that she might be telling a fib about such a matter?"

She nodded in assent.

"It seemed prudent to summon the village priest the next day— you see he lived down the mountain a bit in the town of Cosío— and he examined the girls separately. To his surprise, their stories were in exact agreement, yet there was no one there with either a motive or the ability to invent the story and coach them. The priest made no judgment, but asked them to report immediately any further unusual occurrences. In the next few weeks, the girls saw the angel a number of times in the same alleyway, each time after being alerted by an unspoken interior call to come together there. At last he spoke and told them that on a certain day he would return with the Blessed Virgin Mary—which he did. The girls said that they talked at length with Our Lady about their lives, and that she was as sweet and natural as a mother to them. The next day she came again, with the infant Jesus."

"Did their parents believe them, then?"

"Yes, and no," Fr. Martinez said, in answer to Mrs. Mangone's follow-up question. "Their parents were ordinary people—just like you and me. They *wanted* to believe, but no one other than the girls saw the heavenly figures. So, their parents went back and forth in their own minds, believing when they saw the girls in an ecstatic state, and then doubting when it was over."

"To make a long story short, the visions continued frequently, off and on for four years, and before they ended, the girls were told about three extraordinary events which would happen in the future: a Warning, a Miracle, and a Chastisement."

"Now, keep in mind that many Marian apparitions have included a warning to mankind. A warning that Jesus is displeased and about to unleash a punishment unless people amend their ways. You will remember from our visit to Fatima that the second of the three 'secrets' given the little shepherds during World War I was a warning that, unless people reformed their lives, an even worse war would break out, one heralded by a night illuminated by an unknown light. As we know, people did not reform their ways, and an eerie light appeared one night in the skies over Europe twenty years later, in January of 1938. The surviving visionary, then a nun, saw the light and wrote to the Holy Father to bring it and its significance to his attention. World War II started the next year."

"The Warning which the Garabandal visionaries were told to expect in the future will be a very different sort of caution. Although they didn't describe it in detail, we understand that, instead of it being the same general message for everyone of a future calamity, it probably is going to be an individualized internal vision of the state of that person's own soul. *People who are living in sin will learn how defective their spiritual condition is—how God views them, and maybe how what they have done has harmed other people. They will be terrified at what they see, and, hopefully, moved to repentance.*"

A passenger raised her hand. "When is this supposed to happen, Father?"

"I really don't know," Fr. Martinez admitted. "I'm not sure that even the visionaries themselves know, though the three who are still alive believe they will see it. They're only in their late sixties, so it could happen twenty years from now—or it could be tomorrow!"

*   *   *

At Garabandal, Fr. Martinez slowly led the group to the spot where the angel, and later the Blessed Virgin Mary, had most often appeared. It was, to say the least, intrinsically unprepossessing, and the cold, gloomy weather made it seem even more forlorn.

"If you can imagine it," said the chaplain, "fifty years ago this scene was even drearier. The little street was just rocks and dirt which turned into mud when it rained or the snow melted. There were only about eighty structures in the whole village, including those for the animals, all made of stone. The people had a very hard life as farmers and shepherds, and it was common to transport produce and such things between the village and the town below on the back of a mule. I might mention that Our Lady seems to have a preference for this sort of out of the way place. She could have quite an audience if she would only appear on the steps of St. Patrick's Cathedral in New York, or St. Peter's in Rome, but that's not how she goes about spreading her message. She uses humble people in humble locations, just as her Son did."

"The four girls used to come right here and kneel on the stones, waiting for her to appear. When they went into an ecstatic state, doctors would test them—pinching them, sticking needles into them, shining bright lights in their eyes, even picking them up and dropping them on the ground. The conclusion of the experts was that their trances were real, and not brought on by hypnosis or some sort of fakery ... Now, let's say the Glorious Mysteries as we walk to the pines, another site where Our Blessed Mother appeared to the visionaries."

Up the path leading out of the village they went, toward the dark pines visible in the distance. Here too the path consisted of jagged stones with gaps filled in by dirt, meandering like a river channel through the scruffy vegetation which grew unchecked everywhere else. They reached a fairly flat area with a stand of nine trees over 100 feet tall, whose branches extended almost too far out for their height. The base of each tree was surrounded by a circular wall of stones, which afforded a place to sit for those who needed to catch their breath after their walk in the thin and frigid mountain air.

The spot itself was part way up a giant natural amphitheatre formed by mountain slopes, forested here and there, and capped with snow. Lower down were the villagers' fields and red-tiled houses and sheds, and the few grander buildings which had been built in recent times as inns for the occasional pilgrims. Still further down, far in the distance, was the town of Cosío. Humans had made only very small marks on nature's immense canvas there.

Whatever spiritual magic had been worked for the visionaries was not evident to the pilgrims, and Mr. Merrill, the unchurched husband of a pilgrim, grumbled about being dragged out into the cold. Fr. Martinez tried to leave them with a good memory. "Look around you and remember this scene," he said. "When the great Miracle occurs, no doubt there will be pictures in all the papers, and you'll want to say, 'I was right *there.*' . . . Now, why don't you make your way back down at your leisure? Just be sure to meet me in the village church in half an hour."

*   *   *

The group reassembled in the stone church, more like a chapel in size. Attached to it was a square, three-story bell tower from whose upper story one could see the pines. The rough exterior gave no hint of the nice features inside, including stone-ribbed vaulting. The *retablo* of dark wood and marble behind the altar was surprisingly ornate, with the town's patron saint, St. Sebastian, depicted at the center, and Christ and the Blessed Mother on either side. Under a high window on the right wall, there was a statue of St. Michael, holding his spear at the head of the Devil, in the form of a crouching, man-faced dragon.

Although there were wooden pews, the pilgrims mostly stood, huddling together for warmth, as the church was unheated and damp. With the group around him, Fr. Martinez pointed to the statue of St. Michael in his warrior costume. "Just one more point— you can see that the girls could not have contrived the description which they gave of St. Michael, from the figure of him here that they were familiar with—the two are totally different. All in all, I find their accounts credible, and I wouldn't be at all surprised, some day in the future, to see events unfold as they predicted!"

As the group filed out of the church, Fr. Martinez stood by Señora Sanchez at her station outside the bus by the door, counting the people climbing aboard. The last one had gone up the steps when, all of a sudden, the priest fell to his knees with a loud cry—"Oh! Jesus!"

The tour director was startled. At first she thought he was going to say a prayer, but then he started talking, though not to her.

"I don't know you." ... "What are they?" ...

Then he screamed: *"No, I don't want them!"* ... *"Keep away!"* ... *"JESUS!!!"* Still kneeling, he started to sob.

"Father—what's wrong? Are you ill?"

His eyes were open but they weren't focused on her, and he made no response. Kneeling there, he was rigid.

She knew she had to get him inside the bus, so she grabbed his jacket and tried to get him on his feet. Seeing her struggle, the bus driver came out and together they raised him up. Nothing like this had ever happened on one of her tours before, and she had no idea of what to do next.

Now the priest was moaning. *She had to do something.* It occurred to her to look into the capacious tote bag which she carried wherever she went. There she found her small flask of holy water, and without further thought, she splashed it in the priest's face. That seemed to bring him to his senses, at least to the point that he fell silent and allowed her and the bus driver to ease him up into the bus and back to the wide last seat, where they loosened his collar and helped him to stretch out.

The passengers on the bus had noticed the commotion and had been looking out the windows with concern. What on earth had happened? A stroke? A seizure? The priest looked like a man stricken—so ashen-faced it must be serious.

The pilgrims were an unusually quiet group on the hour ride down the mountain and into the city of Santander, their destination for the night. There, Señora Sanchez got the group into the lobby of the Hotel El Cid Santander and stayed with them until their baggage had been brought in and they had received their room keys. Then she went back to see about Fr. Martinez. He was sitting up by then, still pale and not speaking.

Being a very practical woman, as all tour directors are, she asked the name of the private clinic to which the hotel directed guests who took ill, and she sent him off in a taxi.

However, as the taxi left the hotel grounds, Fr. Martinez leaned forward toward the driver and countermanded her directions, "I

don't need a doctor. Please take me instead to the chancery of
your Bishop. I must see His Lordship."

— 2 —

Spain

According to the receptionist for His Lordship Alonso de Alvarez y Garcia, the Bishop of Santander, the American priest downstairs at the entrance to the chancery office, who humbly begged an audience with him, was in great distress.

Whatever his problem was, surely it could wait until Monday, said the Bishop. He was not about to have his plans for Friday evening interrupted by this unwanted visitor. Before he could have the man turned away with his regrets, the receptionist mentioned that the priest had just come from Garabandal, where something strange had apparently happened to him.

Garabandal! He groaned inwardly at the mention of the name of that tiny part of his diocese. Of course, he had nothing but fatherly love for his those of his flock who lived there. Still, the *supposed* apparitions troubled His Lordship's otherwise serene existence. He was ruefully aware of the aphorism that, when the Blessed Virgin Mary appears in a diocese, the Bishop there doesn't get a good night's sleep until either *she* leaves or *he* leaves.

He was not against apparitions and pilgrimages to holy sites. Far from it!—as long as they were approved by Holy Mother Church. In his considered judgment, until Rome had rendered its decision on a claim that the Lord or his Blessed Mother had appeared somewhere, it was suspect, and credence should be withheld while awaiting developments. There were enough approved sites that there was no need for pilgrims to go to unproven ones such as Garabandal, where there was a risk of injury to the Faith if no supernatural cause was truly at work.

Bishop de Alvarez' sentiments on this matter were fully in accord with the instructions he had received from the Curia in Rome when he was appointed Ordinary of the Diocese of Santander the year before, namely, that inasmuch as the apparitions not been approved as genuine by any of his predecessors, unless and until he was prepared to render a positive judgment on them, pilgrimages and devotions at Garabandal were not to be officially encouraged. However, in a spirit of charity, he allowed those who wished to come, to do so, and even to have their chaplains offer Mass. Thus, Garabandal had remained the site of an occasional pilgrimage, more than a half-century after the last reported sighting of the Blessed Virgin Mary.

It was his hope that nothing would occur on his watch to disturb the status quo. It was bad enough that the public order in the city of Santander was still strained because the civil authorities had removed the statue of *El Caudillo* on horseback—a memorial to Franco's victory in the Civil War—from the city square. Old wounds from that conflict had been reopened. Now, it appeared from what the receptionist was relating, something had happened at Garabandal that could become a new cause for public agitation, and he had best look into at once, if only to nip rumors in the bud. And so, His Lordship greeted Fr. Martinez at the doorway to his study, albeit with a formal air.

His Lordship was an imposing figure, especially in contrast to the priest. A lover of fine paintings would have recognized the Spanish prelate as a double for a countryman of his, the seventeenth century Cardinal Nino de Guevara, the feared Grand Inquisitor, whose portrait, painted by El Greco, hung in the Metropolitan Museum in New York. He was bald, with a thin face into which dark eyes were set. These features, together with a full, dark moustache and a black beard, gave him the bearing of a man to be reckoned with. Martinez, by contrast, was a nondescript fellow, of medium height and weight, the sort of person one can see a hundred times over without ever noticing him. To make his appearance worse, his eyes were red from crying.

If the Bishop had been an American, Fr. Martinez would have shaken his outstretched hand, but he knew that it was not being offered for that purpose. Observing the European custom, he went down on one knee and kissed the Bishop's ring as a sign of respect.

Standing there awkwardly, Fr. Martinez apologized at once for the intrusion and his own evident agitation. The Bishop politely made a dismissive gesture, and invited him to come in to his study and be seated. The priest quickly explained that he was the chaplain of a tour group visiting Marian shrines, and that he had taken his charges up to Garabandal that afternoon. He wished to emphasize that no one had seen anything out of the ordinary in the *calleja*, at the pines, or in the church.

His Lordship breathed an inner sigh of relief, and asked, "What, then, Father, is the cause of your distress?"

"Everything was perfectly normal, as I said, until the pilgrims had boarded the bus. *That's when I was struck down! It was the Warning!*" he said, and choked up for a moment.

When he could talk again, he added, "Just as the girls said it would be." Another pause. "I saw how I stand with God. *Oh God— forgive me!* Your Lordship, please excuse the added imposition on you, but I must go to confession at once!"

Since his elevation to the purple, His Lordship had chosen to leave hearing confessions to ordinary priests. "Surely Father, you can find a priest to hear your confession at your next stop. You are not in danger of dying are you?"

"I don't know. I thought I *would* die when I was having the vision. If it comes back and I die in mortal sin . . . " The thought caused him to start crying.

The Bishop rose, went over to a sideboard where he poured his visitor a glass of calvados, and then came over to sit near him. *"Tell me about what you saw." That* was what the Bishop was concerned about, and he needed to hear about it *outside* of the seal of confession. As a concession, he added, "I will hear your confession after that."

Fr. Martinez took a few sips of the fiery liquid before he began. "What I saw was all about my sins. I can't tell you about one without the other.—*Please, Your Lordship, I beg you in the name of Christ, let me confess!*" Fr. Martinez got down on both knees, pleading, before the Bishop.

The Bishop of Santander found this development distasteful, but so be it. He retrieved a stole from his closet, put it on, and said, "Very well, Father, proceed with your confession."

"Bless me, Your Lordship, for I have sinned. I have not made a good confession in the past ten years . . . "

"Start with today, Father," the Bishop broke in, not caring to hear a long litany of irrelevant misdeeds.

"Yes, Your Lordship.—In the village, standing at the door to the bus, I saw a flash of light, maybe not even through my eyes. It was more like I felt it. It blinded me. That must have been when I fell to my knees—I'm told I did, but I don't really remember that happening. When the bright light faded, it seemed like I was in a mist. It lifted a bit, and I could see barren ground and then a man coming toward me. As he got close, he said, 'Welcome, friend.' I looked at him, but I didn't know him and I told him so."

"What language did he speak? How was he dressed?"

Fr. Martinez thought about it. "I can't say what language he used. I'm not sure I heard it with my ears. I just knew inside what he was saying. As for what he was wearing, it was a robe, a dirty white robe, with sandals on his feet. He looked a bit scruffy, and there was something strange about his lips, like they were partly eaten away—leprosy maybe—I don't know."

"Take another sip and continue, if you will."

"He came right up to me and said he knew me—I was so much like him, because I too helped myself to money from the common purse. *Oh, I do confess that sin! I stole from the collection plate at my church. Even now I steal alms given to me by pilgrims! I have to struggle constantly against that temptation.—May God forgive me!*" Fr. Martinez started to cry again.

The Bishop did his best to conceal his revulsion at what he had just heard, but his voice was cold as he asked, "What happened next?"

"He showed me a purse he had. He took out some coins and offered them to me. 'Here, take some, my friend,' he said. I asked him what they were ..."

Fr. Martinez forced himself to look the Bishop in the face as he repeated the answer he had received: "'They are the thirty pieces of silver I got for betraying *my* master—and *your* master. I threw them away once, but they came back somehow. I have wandered for so long, trying to give them away but no one will take them. Surely *you* will, my friend? *You have earned them in your own way* ...'"

With that, Fr. Martinez collapsed, prostrate.

Those searing words affected the Bishop too. For the first time, he felt a spark of compassion for the wretch at his feet. Seeing that the priest could not rise by himself, he helped him back up to a kneeling position. "Is that all, Father?" he asked, this time without coldness in his voice.

Fr. Martinez was weeping, but managed to continue. "I must have screamed at that point—they tell me I was screaming before they got me on the bus. That's all I remember, until I came to my senses. May God forgive me for these sins and for all my sins and failings as a priest!"

His Lordship sat in silence, contemplating the extraordinary tale of sin and woe. Yes, a measure of compassion was in order. "Your sins are indeed very grave, Father, but I can see the sincerity of your confession. You have need of much help, and for that reason, the penance I am assigning you is to choose a holy and experienced spiritual director, and to reveal *everything* about your life to him, including what you have divulged to me. Even before you find a director, many sins which you have not confessed today will come to your mind, and you should seek out the opportunity to confess them. And now, with the authority of the Church, I absolve you of the sins which you have confessed and I grant you pardon in the name of the Father, and of the Son, and of the Holy Spirit. Amen."

After the Bishop made the Sign of the Cross over Fr. Martinez's head, the priest got unsteadily to his feet. *"Thank you, Thank you, Your Lordship,"* he said. *"It was the Warning. I know it was."*

The Bishop now took off his stole, and poured a brandy for himself. He sipped it, while considering his dual obligation to the penitent and to Holy Mother Church. He was convinced that the priest had seen what he claimed to—no one could have feigned the message the American had received or his contrition. Especially because he judged the vision to have been supernatural, it was necessary that he make an official report of this incident. However, what he had learned was under the seal of the confession and could never be divulged. Of course, if the penitent were to talk freely about it outside of confession . . .

"Father, your confession is ended, and I cannot discuss it. But, if you are willing to repeat your story again, outside the seal, I will make some notes and attempt to help you to come to grips with your experience." Somehow, Fr. Martinez found the strength to tell his story a second time, much more calmly, and without any change in the details.

Having listened to the account again, the Bishop rendered his opinion. "I would not be prepared to say that the Warning you refer to has occurred. After all, St. Paul suffered a blinding light conversion experience on the road to Damascus. Similar events have happened at other times to a person here or there. We must wait and see before we generalize about this."

Fr. Martinez waited for the Bishop to continue. "That means— and here I must ask you to observe my counsel as you would in obedience to a superior—you must not discuss the substance of what you have just told me with anyone in the media and most certainly not with the pilgrims on your bus, for they could easily be scandalized, or terrified, or both." Concern to prevent disturbing rumors from being spread by the pilgrims was uppermost in the Bishop's mind. "And so, I strongly advise you to try to put this experience out of your mind until your spiritual director can help you to understand it. In the meantime, when you feel temptation coming, ask Our Lord and His Blessed Mother to strengthen you."

Having imparted all the advice that occurred to him, His Lordship asked the receptionist over the intercom to call a taxi to take the priest back to his hotel. With Fr. Martinez out the door, the Bishop poured himself another glass of brandy. He sipped it slowly, with melancholy, fearing that this singular happening might engender much unwelcome notoriety for his diocese and prompt a surge of pilgrims to the unapproved apparition site.

*   *   *

Fr. Martinez sank down in the back seat of the taxi, greatly relieved and so emotionally exhausted that he could not think.

"*Be at peace!*"

The first time he heard the words, he ignored them, not quite grasping that they were meant for him.

"*Be at peace!*"

He looked around. He was alone in the car except for the driver in the front seat, who was listening to music, not paying attention to him.

"*Be at peace!*"

It was like the experience he had had earlier that day—hearing but yet *not* hearing—at least not through his ears. Despite the content of the thrice repeated message, panic started to rise in him at the thought that Judas Iscariot was somehow returning.

"*Do not be afraid. It is I, the Lord, who am speaking to you!*"

"Sir—Lord," said Fr. Martinez, "*I'm no good . . .* " These words came forth without thinking. He truly meant them.

"*No!*" said the voice. "*Weak and unfaithful—like those I chose to begin with—but not worthless. I still want you to serve Me, and now I will strengthen you against temptation.*"

At these words, Fr. Martinez could not help crying, this time with relief. He forced himself to ask: "What am I to do, Lord?"

"Do not worry about that. When the time comes, you will be given to know what you are to do and say. Freely give the forgiveness you freely have received . . ."

Fr. Martinez waited for the voice to resume, but it did not. Back at the hotel, to avoid seeing anyone from his group, he went directly to his room and ordered a bowl of soup from room service. He phoned the front desk clerk to leave a message for the tour director, thanking her for her assistance, and saying that he was already very much improved. He turned his telephone off, and, after eating, dropped into a deep sleep.

— 3 —

Spain

It was three o'clock in the morning when the pounding on his door awoke the chaplain. Groggily, he staggered to the door. Looking through the peep hole, he could see the tour director standing on the other side in her bath robe. Opening the door a crack, he could only mumble, "Señora Sanchez?"

"Father—I'm sorry to wake you like this—I couldn't reach you by phone. Mr. Merrill is screaming, just as you did this afternoon. His wife called and asked me to bring you to him. Would you mind going to their room?—If *you* are all right, that is."

His head was starting to clear. "Shouldn't you call a doctor?"

"I don't know.—She asked for you.—Please . . ."

Fr. Martinez said he would throw some clothes on and be right out.

Señora Sanchez waited in the hall until he was dressed and they went off together to the Merrills' room, where they found him lying on the bed in his pajamas, flopping back and forth like a fish out of water, in some kind of altered state and crying out.

"*No!—Don't touch me!*" . . . "*Butchers!*" . . . "*Let me out of here!*" . . .

The priest felt totally inadequate. The two women were looking to him for help and he had no idea what to do about Merrill's ravings. At that moment, an inner voice spoke to him—the one he had heard a few hours earlier: "*Have him look directly at a crucifix.*"

"Where am I supposed to find a crucifix in the middle of the night?" he wondered. Then he remembered the small one at the end of his rosary. He was dubious that a crucifix could have an effect on anyone in such a disoriented state, especially an agnostic, but he dutifully did as he was ordered. Kneeling down beside the bed, he held it up and said, "Howard! Listen to me. Look here at your Savior!"

To his surprise, Merrill immediately calmed down. They propped him into a sitting position on the bed and put cold washcloths on his head. "Drink this!" said his wife, holding out a glass of water. The Alka-Seltzer tablet she had dropped in was already beginning to fizz.

Fr. Martinez was thinking he could leave now, but the voice insisted, *"Ask him what happened."*

"Howard! What happened to you?"

Merrill replied slowly, "I died. Things dragged me down through the ground. They put me in something like a hospital operating room. Said I was in their care and I'd be there forever."

"Who were they?"

"Devils! Dressed like doctors. I saw they weren't—they had tails sticking out behind them."

"What did they do to you?"

"They butchered me! Kept on doing it! They cut my foot off! My right foot! There was nothing wrong with it. They put on an artificial foot. The devils were laughing. Said they did it wrong—they'd have to cut me up higher next time and put on a new leg too. Then, they took something out of my stomach. They didn't put me under—it hurt so much! I heard them talking about taking out my liver next. Said it was going to be terribly painful for me, but that's what their boss wanted them to do. On the walls, all sorts of things like body parts were hanging from hooks—they were going to fit me with all of them."

"Why didn't you get out of there?" Fr. Martinez asked.

"They wouldn't let me go—anyway, I couldn't go in that condition."

At this point, Fr. Martinez thought to ask Ruth what her husband was hallucinating about—had he had surgery recently, or was he in the medical field? No, she said, her husband had never had an operation in their married life, and he had nothing to do with doctors or health care. He owned three car dealerships outside Philadelphia. She couldn't make any sense of his ramblings.

"Hear his confession," came the inner voice.

Fr. Martinez almost answered "What???" out loud, but caught himself in time. The man on the bed was not a practicing Christian, let alone a Catholic. Going to confession was not something he had ever done, or likely would ever consider doing.

"Hear his confession. I will give you the words you are to say."

The women couldn't guess what Fr. Martinez was about to do, but they acceded to his request that they leave the room and let him be alone with Merrill. Fr. Martinez sat by the bed and gripped one of Merrill's hands in both of his. Merrill said nothing, but seemed to be completely over his altered state.

Fr. Martinez repeated out loud words that only he could hear: "Howard, you have piled up gold on earth, but none in heaven. For years you have cheated the customers at your auto dealerships. On your orders, your mechanics replace perfectly good parts, and damage what they work on, so the cars have to come back for more repairs—until you persuade their owners to buy new ones from you. *Howard, you have been going down the road to Hell, and you're almost there."*

Merrill was chagrined. No one had ever called him to account before. Sure, he had been sued several times by disgruntled customers, but they had not uncovered his scheme. He had regarded the litigation as a nuisance, and continued to do business in the same old way. How did this priest, whom he had never seen before this trip, know what he was doing?

When Merrill didn't respond, Fr. Martinez' inner voice prompted him to persevere. "Howard, listen to me! If your life were forfeit tonight, you would be dragged screaming down to the pit by devils. The horrible visions you had were only a mild taste of the punishment you would receive there by the decree of God. The Lord referred to Hell as a fiery furnace where sinners would be in unquenchable fire, and the worms eating them would not die. Your vision showed you a *special punishment* tailored to your own sins. *Those things with tails were devils and they would operate on you forever.* Think of that, Howard—every organ you have would be replaced time and time again, your arms and legs would be amputated, and you would be in constant pain, knowing there was no escape. Is that what you want?"

An explosive *"No!"* came out of Merrill.

"Jesus is fighting for your soul, Howard! Give it to him now, or the Devil will take it at your death! Repent and confess your sins!"

Fr. Martinez could hardly believe that *he* was saying those things. He had never given anyone a "come to Jesus" talk before. But that was when he was acting on his own; now, he was acting as the voice directed. The Warning vision and his genuine repentance of his own sins had opened him up to experiencing a dimension of his priesthood that he had never known before.

"I don't know ...," Merrill hesitated, trying to calculate whether he could run his businesses honestly and still make money.

Fr. Martinez shook Merrill by the shoulders. *"Forget the dealerships, Howard! Do you want the butchers to come back for your liver?"*

That did it! There was no way that Howard Merrill wanted his liver taken out once, much less again and again forever. *Anything but that!*

"What do I have to do?" Merrill asked, uncertainly.

Fr. Martinez was given the answer, which he repeated. "God has already exposed one wicked scheme of yours. There may be more to confess in the future, but for now He wants to hear you acknowledge this sin in your own words. And then He wants to hear you're sorry, and that you promise to change the way you do business ... "

In a halting voice, Howard Merrill did as he was told. Thus, without knowing quite what he was doing, he came to make his first confession.

*   *   *

It was 4:00 a.m. when Fr. Martinez returned to his room. He decided that there was no point in trying to get back to sleep, which was just as well, for no sooner had he finished his shower and shave, and put his clothes back on, than Señora Sanchez appeared again at his door, this time with Claudia Peterson in tow. Somehow, when he had attended to Mr. Merrill he hadn't thought about the Warning—perhaps because of what the Bishop had said. Now, it was clear to him what was happening. As a priest, he would be on the front line of the action.

Wanting to speak to Ms. Peterson alone, but not in either of their hotel rooms, Fr. Martinez led her down to the deserted hotel lobby, where they sat down facing each other. She had been crying for some time, judging from the condition of her eyes, and she continued to do so, drying her eyes and blowing her nose occasionally as she told of her vision.

She had seen herself visiting an ASPCA shelter, going past interminable rows of dogs and cats, in cages stacked from the ground to the ceiling. They were adorable, and made wistful sounds to her as she passed by. Pointing to one, a woman in a white smock, who was taking her around said, "This one has your name on its collar."

"It must be a mistake," Ms. Peterson answered. She protested that she really had no desire to have a pet—she had wandered in the shelter by mistake. "That's all right," the woman said, "you don't have to keep it if you don't want to."

Ms. Peterson couldn't continue with her story, she was so upset. Fr. Martinez was afraid she wouldn't think it proper if he put an arm around her shoulders, so he merely got up and sat down right next to her, hoping it would help her over the difficult part of her tale.

She blew her nose again and continued. "The shelter woman walked over to a computer and said that the time had come to destroy all the unwanted animals. She typed in something on the keyboard."

"I turned back to the cages. Now, I saw that they contained tiny human babies, not dogs and cats! I yelled at her, 'Stop it! Stop it! They're babies!'"

"The woman acted like she didn't care. She said, 'It's too late, you had your chance before to take yours,' and she left the room."

Ms. Peterson was sobbing, so Fr. Martinez finally put his arm around her shoulders. "Tell me how it ended, Claudia," he said, gently.

"The next thing I saw was that a blade like the one on my kitchen blender had come out from the back of each cage. It started to turn. The babies cried out for a few seconds. Then the screaming stopped. They all were a bloody pulp. I saw in some of the cages little arms and legs, and heads.—Then, the woman came back and said I could have what was left of the one the collar said was mine, if I wanted it."

Fr. Martinez kept repeating, "I'm sorry, I'm *so* sorry," until he felt she had calmed down.

"*Oh, Father,*" she moaned, "*it's been five years since I had my abortion. I've never been able to bring myself to go to confession.*"

"*You just have, Claudia,*" said Fr. Martinez, and he gave her absolution then and there.

✳   ✳   ✳

Sylvia Watkins was sitting across the lobby, out of earshot, waiting to speak to the chaplain. When Claudia left, she approached, not crying, but looking frightened.

"Father," she said, "I think I just received my Warning—I may have seen myself in Hell. I'm not sure it was Hell because there was no fire and I didn't see any devils.—It was some kind of a nursing home—that's what it looked like. I was lying strapped onto a gurney in a dark hallway. There were other people there with me, who couldn't move. I needed to relieve myself so badly. I tried calling out for someone to assist me, but no one came. It was like that for everybody—they were all crying and yelling for help. It was bedlam.—Finally, I had to go in my bedclothes. I smelled so bad. I was thirsty and cold, and no one came around to check on me. *I just knew that I'd never get out of there and no one would ever come to help.*"

Fr. Martinez was sympathetic. "Sylvia, from my own experience, I would guess that what a person sees in his vision can be traced directly to something he's done in real life. I'll be glad to hear your story in confidence, if you'd like to go to confession now."

She did. It turned out that her aged mother had been in an assisted living facility for years until her Alzheimer's became too bad for them to keep her. Sylvia, who had power of attorney over her mother's finances, had arranged for her to be moved into a nice facility for patients with that malady.

"The problem, Father," Sylvia said, "started with my son and his wife—though I'm as much at fault as they are. They came to me one night and said that Nana's care—that's what he called her— was so expensive it would eat up everything she had left, maybe even before she died. They asked me, what about transferring her to a less costly facility? After all, she didn't know which end was up, and the money could be used far better 'by the living,' as they put it."

"I knew it was wrong, Father. I never should have let them persuade me. But, I did what they suggested—I drained her accounts, and left her with nothing, so she could go on Medicaid. The facility I let them transfer her to was just a warehouse for the dying. I saw that when I went to visit her the first time."

Sylvia choked up and couldn't continue for a few minutes. Fr. Martinez waited patiently for her to resume her tale.

"I couldn't bear to go again, and face what I had done. *She was my mother and I let her die all alone. I can never make it up to her now . . . "*

Sylvia had kept her emotions under control until she finished. Then came a flood of tears—and the absolution—and more tears. When she was sufficiently calm, Fr. Martinez returned to his room. Suddenly, he realized that he had heard the confessions of the two ladies on his own—the inner voice had been silent.

*   *   *

After two additional incidents with pilgrims before breakfast had been handled successfully by Fr. Martinez, there was no doubt in the tour director's mind that the prophesied Warning was at hand. Always the practical one, she presumed that if people would go to confession before it hit them, there would be far less commotion, and therefore less disruption of the tour, especially while they were still traveling around on the bus. Accordingly, while the waiters were clearing the breakfast tables in the hotel, Señora Sanchez conferred with Fr. Martinez, and then made a surprise announcement.

"This is turning out to be an especially fruitful pilgrimage," she said, "because members of our group are finding their way back to God. *Saints, Signs & Wonders Tours* has provided Fr. Martinez as a chaplain, not just to take you around the holy sites, but also to make the sacrament of reconciliation readily available to you. I expect that many of you might like to be reconciled at this time. It would be an especially fine present for you to give Our Lady, whose solemnity of the Immaculate Conception we will be observing tomorrow in Lourdes as the highpoint of our pilgrimage. Therefore, I've decided to delay the departure of the bus by one hour. During that time, since we have had to vacate our rooms, the bus will serve as a confessional booth, with no one on it other than Father and the penitent. We'll leave when everyone who wishes to go is finished."

The bus actually left two hours late. Meanwhile, the sight of the American tourists standing in line in the parking lot to go to confession proved to be an engaging, even edifying, spectacle for the hotel's staff. Added to what had been heard by the night shift workers, it gave them much to talk about those strange *Nortre Americanos*.

Once they were on their way, Father Martinez sank back into his seat on the bus. He was exhausted not only by his own traumatic experience of the day before, but also by hearing confessions—so many, and so profound. Nothing like that had happened in his year of pastoring, when aside from the children making their first communion, the penitents who came to him for confession were mainly elderly ladies with only a peccadillo on their conscience. Why did the Holy Spirit not blow like this all the time? Or, at least, occasionally? *What if he had had such an experience when he first had dipped his hand into the collection plate?* Might not his disgrace and years of exile have been forestalled?

It was no use to think of what might have been. The past was what it was, and the wound had been cauterized by his own confession. It was up to him to make a new future, and he resolved it would begin by his distributing in Lourdes the funds which Mrs. Mangone had given him for alms. *All 500 euros*—money he had been counting on to sustain him until his next contract assignment as a tour chaplain. Now that his pilfering days were over, like the Israelites in the desert he would have to trust in God to provide his daily bread.

PART II

The Visions

January 2015

No apparition is indispensable to the faith; Revelation terminated with Jesus Christ. He himself is the Revelation. But we certainly cannot prevent God from speaking to our time through simple persons and also through extraordinary signs . . .

Card. J. Ratzinger with V. Messori, *The Ratzinger Report*, 111 (Ignatius Press 1985)

— 1 —

Rome

After the Christmas holidays, the report of the Bishop of Santander wound its way slowly but surely through the Vatican bureaucracy to the desk of the junior member of a most august Curial Congregation, the one for the Doctrine of the Faith. Pope Benedict XVIth, in his previous status as Cardinal Joseph Ratzinger, had put his stamp on the Congregation during the decades he had headed it, and he continued to work closely with it now that he was Pope and Cardinal Latoya was the Prefect. Indeed, it was the new Pope who had drawn John Ireland into the Congregation and bestowed upon him the rank of Monsignor, an Honorary Prelate of His Holiness, ranking just below a bishop, due to the scholarly friendship they had formed years before.

If truth be known, Msgr. Ireland read the Bishop's account with as much reluctance as the Bishop had felt in writing it, for while the Monsignor was expert in many areas of theology, the mystical branch was not one of them. During the years when he had been a Professor at the Pontifical Gregorian University in Rome, his specialty had been "eschatology," and he had taught Catholic seminarians and clerics about the "Four Last Things"— Death, Judgment, Heaven and Hell. His courses concerned not just the particular judgment of individuals at their death, but also the expected general judgment of all of creation at the end of the world.

As a new member of the Congregation, Ireland felt at home in reviewing the books, articles and speeches written by academics and clerics, to make sure that they held to the Church's doctrinal line on eschatology, but he felt inadequate to assess the significance of the recent developments in Garabandal, in particular whether they called for doing more than merely continuing the Church's watchful waiting for stronger evidence that the long ago apparitions, and their message, were of divine origin.

Ireland had always found it difficult to credit reports of appearances by the Blessed Virgin Mary here and there throughout the world—much less the messages purportedly given by her, which were announced from time to time by self-proclaimed visionaries. The only Marian apparitions which he took to be genuine were two which, after rigorous investigation, had been approved by the Church for public veneration by people who chose to believe in them. These had been experienced a century before: one by a French peasant girl at Lourdes, and the other by three little Portuguese shepherds at Fatima. He knew that events confirming the supernatural nature of those two visions had occurred very shortly thereafter—a spring with healing waters began to gush from the cave at Lourdes where Our Lady had appeared, and at Fatima, tens of thousands of people, drawn by a visionary's prophecy, had seen a prolonged dancing of the sun.

The Garabandal apparitions supposedly came with a somewhat dire message from Our Lady, one about future events. The problem for true believers in that sort of phenomena was that, from the background material the Monsignor was reading, he could see absolutely no confirmatory events in the fifty-odd years since the apparitions had appeared. True, the visionaries there had never claimed that the events they prophesied would occur *soon* or on a future date certain, but he could think of no reason why they had been delayed for more than a half century—or, alternatively, why the apparitions and the prophecy itself hadn't been put off until just before confirming events occurred. His skepticism was held in check only by the Parable of Wise and Foolish Virgins, which the Lord taught concerning a wedding feast, where the bridegroom had been delayed in appearing. So, the mere fact that no signs had previously been seen was not conclusive proof that the promise of them was a delusion.

Pondering what to do next, the Monsignor happened to think of his prize pupil, now back in the States, whom he had not seen or heard from in five years. Every teacher hopes to have at least one student who will surpass him, standing on his shoulders, as he himself stood on the shoulders of his predecessors in adding to the store of the world's knowledge. Professor Ireland expected that student to be Anthony Santorelli.

Tony Santorelli had a first class mind, earning a doctorate from the Gregorian in dogmatic theology with honors, and, more important, he was well read in mystical theology. These apparitions would be right up his alley! He would be the perfect man to send to Garabandal for an unofficial look-see, if he could spare a week or two from his duties back in the States. Besides that, involving him in the project would be a good excuse for them to have a reunion—and the Monsignor would be able to find out about the detour his pupil's career had taken.

Following conferral of the Doctor of Sacred Theology degree, Fr. Santorelli had been called back to Topanga, California, to assume a post at the Chancery Office, under the city's Cardinal Archbishop, Thomas O'Melveny. Not long after that, the Monsignor was surprised to receive an e-mail giving a new address for Fr. Santorelli at a diocesan mission church, without any explanation. Although the members of the "Old Boys' Network" tried to stay in touch with each other, Tony had not.

And so, Msgr. Ireland picked up his phone and called the Chancery Office in Topanga to get a phone number for Fr. Santorelli. After a delay, the answer came back. "The number we have for him is area 661, 729-2000. He's in the state prison in Lancaster."

— 2 —

Lancaster, California

*"Out of the depths I cry to thee, O Lord. Lord, hear my voice! . . . I
wait for the Lord, my soul waits, and in His word I hope."*
Father Anthony Santorelli had made those words of the
Psalmist his own, praying them nightly, without any apparent
effect. He was indeed in "the depths"—the bowels of the state
prison system in California, where he had been working in the
lowly and unenviable position of a chaplain for almost two years
at a maximum security facility.

It was a most undesirable full-time assignment for a priest,
debilitating in mind, body and spirit, because it was mainly the
dregs of society who were kept there, and the chances of their
conversion were small. Not surprisingly, there were bishops who
assigned their worst priest-screwups to such a correctional facility
to get them out of sight. Priests who had taken advantage of a
parishioner who sought counseling about her marriage, or who
had fathered a child or gambled away church funds on junkets to
Las Vegas, might find themselves exiled there.

Of course, there were holy priests among the ranks of prison
chaplains, and Fr. Santorelli was one of them. He had committed
no outrage or crime, nor caused a public disgrace to the Catholic
Church. His only fault lay in greatly antagonizing his religious
superior, the Cardinal Archbishop of Topanga.

Not long after he had arrived back in California, in looking
over a program for an upcoming Catholic Charities awards dinner,
he saw that the keynote speaker was a politician known nationally
for his support of *Roe v. Wade*. And an award was going to the head
of a local Catholic hospital—which, the Topanga Times noted in
a news story, allowed abortions to be performed. Fr. Santorelli
sent a memo to the Cardinal, urging him to block both the speech
and the award, in order to send a Pro-Life message that would be
heard throughout the diocese.

This prompted an immediate summons to the Cardinal's office
and a discussion of his memo, which led His Eminence to conclude
that the priest was not well suited for chancery work. Before the

day was out, he found himself assigned as pastor of a small, mission church. Three years after that, when he again aroused the ire of the Cardinal, he was summarily stripped of that pastorate, and sent off to the place of the living dead. That was how, not four years after having earned a prestigious degree in Rome, he came to find himself ministering in the penal facility at Lancaster, California, 70 miles north of Topanga.

The plight of the prisoners he was among reminded him of the description given by one of the little visionaries at Fatima who had supernaturally been shown a glimpse of Hell by the Blessed Virgin Mary. It was one of many brief spiritual insights which he had pasted into a notebook he kept:

> Our Lady showed us a large sea of fire which seemed to be beneath the earth. Plunged in this fire were the demons and souls, who were like embers, transparent and black or bronze-colored, in human form, which floated about in the conflagration, borne by the flames which issued from it with clouds of smoke, falling on all sides as sparks fall in great conflagrations, without weight or equilibrium, among shrieks and groans of sorrow and despair ... (Sr. Lucia dos Santos, *Third Memoir*)

Such was the Hell below, and such was the Hell he was in the midst of—though still alive. Demons and souls, shrieks and groans of sorrow and despair—it was all there at the "CSP," even the conflagration.

An aerial infrared picture of the facility would have shown 4,000 bright spots of barely contained fury, inside maximum security cages built for only a fraction of that number. These angry hot spots were the most vicious and depraved of men, constantly on the verge of exploding into fights between Hispanic and Black gangs, homosexual rapes, stabbings with shivs made in the prison workshop, and other assaults on each other and on the guards. The correction staff knew that if they suffered a lapse in control, there would be a full scale riot, in which hundreds of men would be injured, some fatally, and cell blocks would be torched.

No one could doubt that the Devil was alive and well and living in that prison—but God was there too, at least as a daily

visitor, in the person of Fr. Santorelli and the other prison chaplains. They were overworked, and underappreciated by the prison
administration, which saw them as a headache, because of the
work entailed in pulling prisoners out of their cells or workshops,
for counseling sessions or worship. Petty harassment of chaplains
was usual, such as the time when the Warden cracked down on
contraband coming into the prison—including alcohol—and the
guards interpreted that as a warrant to prevent Fr. Santorelli from
bringing in the wine he needed to offer Mass in the tiny chapel.

"Look at the size of the vial," he protested, "it's only two
ounces! And I'm the one who consumes it all."

" 'No alcohol' means 'no alcohol'," he was told. It took a week
and a written appeal to the Warden to get the decision overruled.

Surviving in that jungle required Fr. Santorelli to be mentally
tough and to affect a stern demeanor. The "love" he was obligated
to give the sinners there had to be "tough love," and each day
his insides churned as he saw how entrenched sin was in the
prisoners. He had experienced occasionally the joy of hearing an
honest confession, and seeing a behavioral change for the better.
However, most were proudly unrepentant, and not interested in
anything he could offer them that was spiritual. They tolerated
him because he provided a break in their monotonous routine,
and, perhaps more, because he treated them as something more
than human trash.

He did everything he could to bring Christ within the walls,
consistent with the restrictions he worked under, yet nothing he
did seemed to make much of a difference. A recurring analogy
in his mind was of the child's game of 'Whack a Mole'—if by
counseling he prevented a fight in the morning, it broke out in
the afternoon; if he got a prisoner's shower rights restored one
day, they were taken away again the next day. And so it went, in
the daily struggle to bring some measure of mercy to lighten the
scale of justice.

His sense of failure in being of real spiritual assistance to the
prisoners was augmented by his sense of guilt that his fine education was totally wasted. He had begun his career in a position
which other priests coveted, right in the Chancery Office, visible
to the Cardinal. Now, after two demotions, he was condemned
to what could justly be called the American equivalent of Devil's
Island. In spirit, he was in solitary confinement, alone with his

regrets and his guilt. The passage in his spiritual notebook that most resonated with him was Milton's depiction of Satan in Hell as being "unrespited, unpitied, unreprieved." That was exactly how *he* felt at times!

In his rented room in an old motel, converted by the state to house those making below the poverty level, he often recalled happy days in Rome, when God had been readily accessible to him, and he had experienced spiritual ecstasies. He had felt the love of God as a warmth. Unlike that from a hot shower, it had spread over him from the inside out. The warmth was not merely physical—it uplifted him spiritually. He had known that he was loved and secure, like a child held by its parent. And he had reveled in the sensation, wanting to keep it going forever, and disappointed each time it had faded away. But, when he returned to the Topanga Diocese, prayer had become difficult and he no longer experienced an uplift from celebrating Mass. At times, as he looked down at the consecrated host in his hands, strange thoughts and doubts crept into his mind, quite contrary to everything he had just said in his homily to the congregation.

And then, when he became a prison chaplain, night had fallen. He felt that Jesus had abandoned him. At first, he had thought to blame his fall on the Devil's machinations. It was an intriguing and comforting analogy—*he was a latter-day Job,* and he could paraphrase the Biblical words to apply to his own situation—

The Lord had said to Satan, "Have you noticed my servant Anthony Santorelli, and that there is no one on earth like him, blameless and upright, fearing God and avoiding evil?" But Satan answered the Lord and said, "Is it for nothing that Anthony is God-fearing? Have you not surrounded him with your protection? You have blessed the work of his hands. But put forth your hand and touch anything that he has, and surely he will blaspheme you to your face." And the Lord said to Satan, "Behold, all that he has is in your power; only do not lay a hand upon his person."

Could not the hand of the Devil be seen in his demotions? Were not his travails in prison the work of the Devil's disciples? However, he was too honest to believe the fantasy that the Devil was to blame for all his misfortunes. Could he *really* say that he was "blameless and upright," as God had judged Job to be? *No—that didn't ring true.* He knew he was a sinner.

Was he, then, being punished by God for his sins? *No—that explanation didn't ring true either.* It showed the same conceptual error that the very ancient Hebrews made in believing that one's earthly misfortunes, such as being born blind, were a divine punishment. Jesus had made it clear in the Parable of Lazarus and the Rich Man that there was to be another life beyond death, and *that* was when God would punish evil deeds. So, Fr. Santorelli felt justified in not seeing his woes as retribution sent by God.

What then was he to make of his predicament? During his student days, he had read, in treatises on mystical theology and stories of the lives of saints such as Padre Pio and Mother Teresa of Calcutta, that periods of spiritual aridity and of the darkest night were *normal* in the life of a mystic. These were periods when God would deliberately absent Himself, not to punish, but to make the soul long for Him. It was such stories, and passages copied into his spiritual notebook, that pulled him back from the brink of despair, especially the counsel of Fr. Tauler, a 14th century Dominican theologian, which he reread many times: "The demon will leave all else, if only he can unsettle your confidence . . . confidence in God's love during the time of desolation of spirit."

And, an unforeseen occurrence the year before, on Good Friday, had shown him that God still loved him and had plans to make further use of him. Although this brought a ray of light into his spiritual dark night, simultaneously he was made to suffer greatly physically, and so he continued his anguished cries from "the depths."

Finally, the Lord judged the time was ripe to answer him, through a telephone call from Rome.

— 3 —

In flight

Father Santorelli had known he was depressed, but not how deeply, until the prospect appeared of escaping from Hell. The offer of a week's expenses-paid vacation in Rome sounded to him like a brief reprieve in Heaven.

He was now on the long leg of the trip, the flight from LAX to Amsterdam, where the plane would make a two hour stopover before continuing on to Rome. At six foot three, he could scarcely fit his long legs into the allotted space, and when he did, he found his knees locked in place by the reclined seatback of the passenger in front of him. He settled in as best he could with his breviary, a few unread issues of the New Oxford Review, and his many thoughts.

Why in the world had his old mentor called him? He had no real idea, other than it involved a short mission to check out something in the mystical realm, something which the Monsignor didn't feel free to talk about over the phone. And it must require him to speak Spanish—which he had learned out of pastoral necessity—for the Monsignor had asked if he was able to do that, when he called. The mystical bit was intriguing, as it was the then *Professor* Ireland who had steered him away from his particular interest, mystical theology, when he was trying to plan his doctoral studies, on the ground that there was no "market" for academics with expertise in *orthodox* religious mysticism— only for New Age gurus with their crystals and Tarot cards, Ouija boards and horoscopes, and the energy of the universe delivered by the touch of a reiki master.

Yet, he could still remember an incident years ago when he and his Professor had briefly discussed the greatest mystic of the past century. It had begun with the Professor's casual inquiry as to whether his pupil had been to San Giovanni Rotondo to visit the shrine to Padre Pio, a 20th century Capuchin friar, whose supernatural feats were known throughout the world while he was still alive. "St. Pio"—for he had been canonized—had been one of the small number of men and women over the centuries whose bodies were divinely marked with the five wounds of Christ—bleeding openings in the flesh of their hands and feet, and the right side of their chest.

The wounds were called "stigmata," and those who bore them were called "stigmatists." St. Francis of Assisi was a noted one—perhaps the first. Artists often depicted him in the act of receiving the wounds through rays shooting out from a Seraphim. Another noted stigmatist was the 19th century German nun, Anne Catherine Emmerich, whose detailed visions of the life of Christ were the subject of Fr. Santorelli's licentiate thesis.

The priest was embarrassed, now, recalling the immature response he had given to his Professor's question. He had said that he was going to visit the shrine that summer, and added that he was fascinated by some of Padre Pio's charisms such as bilocation, the reading of souls in the confessional, and the healing of physical ailments.

Professor Ireland had astutely noted that he had omitted the charism of being a *Suffering Servant*. "*That was his most important charism*, Tony," the Professor had said. "The stigmata weren't merely *flesh wounds*, you know, they were *holes* in him—it's hard for anyone even to imagine the agony he was in constantly. Despite that, he wasn't lying in a sick bed, moaning, and looking to have people pity or admire him. Instead, every day he was saying Mass, sitting in a confessional for hours, answering a flood of correspondence, and advising his spiritual sons and daughters. Not to mention supervising the construction of the enormous hospital he raised the funds for, there in San Giovanni Rotondo. *He was heroic.*"

Fr. Santorelli had mumbled something about not seeing why his pains were necessary, since Jesus had suffered once for all.

That had drawn a quick retort from his Professor, reminding the priest of what St. Paul had written in his Letter to the Colossians, about finding joy in the suffering he was enduring for his spiritual children—and explaining that he was doing it to fill up what was lacking in the sufferings of Christ for the sake of His body, the Church. Professor Ireland had then put it to him: "Tony, was the *only* act of redemption Christ's death on the Cross? Or is the Church even now participating in the redemption of the world?"

"Well, I'm aware that John Paul II wrote an apostolic letter about that, *Salvifici Doloris*, so, yes, I'd have to say that the work of redemption is ongoing."

"That's right," Msgr. Ireland had replied. *"And suffering with Christ is part of that work.* Jesus said that a disciple of His must pick up his own cross and carry it. *So, if you love Jesus, you'll carry the Cross He gives you."*

"But, I haven't been able to reconcile that concept with the words of Jesus that 'My burden is easy, My yoke is light.'"

Professor Ireland had given him a word of counsel then, counsel which the priest had thought about many times in the past year: "The reconciliation, Tony, is that when you love someone, the burdens you bear for that person, no matter how heavy they would be to someone else, are light to you."

At the time, he had been almost dismissive: "I'll think about what you've said Professor, but I expect to have my hands full just trying to be a good priest, without having to suffer also!"

As it turned out, he did have his hands full with his priestly duties when he returned to America, but suffering came too. During his dark night of the soul, he began to have disturbing visions. Visions—not dreams—he could tell the difference, because the visions came when he was awake. Actually, it was only one vision, but he had it frequently in his room. It came unbidden and left when it would. Usually, he saw it when he was kneeling and saying the evening office from his breviary, facing the crucifix on the wall, one done in traditional Hispanic style—bloody wounds and an agonized look on the face of Christ.

The crucifix would grow to life size, and he would lose his visual perception of all else around him. The distorted corpus of Christ would morph into a different, but similarly gory and naked male figure—*that of himself.* There seemed to be two of him, both full and complete, not merely one divided in half. Yet, he felt himself to be only the observer, not sharing in the pains reflected on the face looking down at him.

A strong white light from an unseen source made it impossible to see any surroundings which might have given him a clue as to where he was. The image, however, was clear. He found himself staring with morbid fascination at the triangular iron nail through each hand, not centered in the palm but near the base of the thumb, and the one pinioning both feet to the wood. They were large and sinister looking, more like spikes than nails, protruding out about two inches beyond his flesh. Blood dripped down from the three holes in him—the other him.

He had never made sense of this bizarre experience, though three possibilities occurred to him. Most likely, it was an elaborate projection of his own mind—his subconscious was reifying the anger and despair he felt daily in a traditional image, that of a crucifixion. On the other hand, since what he saw was a vision and not a dream, it could be the work of the Devil—tempting him to self-pity, discouragement and the abandonment of his vocation. *There was yet a third possibility, much more unsettling than the other two: the image might be one sent by God, as an intimation that martyrdom was awaiting him.*

Though he *did* love the Lord, he was not about to volunteer for the five wounds of Jesus! If physical ills came his way, he intended to follow the prescribed course of uniting them in spirit with the sufferings of Christ, but it was hard enough walking into the lions' den every day, without walking in wounded and dripping blood. Surely, if the Lord wanted to be consoled by a man's suffering, He could pick a victim who had nothing else to accomplish in the world, someone without other obligations, who could withdraw and suffer in seclusion. And if Jesus absolutely wanted *him* to suffer, well, there was no shortage of everyday ailments that could be sent to accomplish that purpose.

Such was his mindset as the night of Good Friday began, the year before. As was his practice, he had knelt on the floor of his room, looking at the crucifix and praying for help, for guidance, and for a renewed awareness of God's love. In sympathy with Jesus' Passion, he had expressed his sorrow for the sins of mankind, the crimes and daily blasphemies of the convicts he was among, and his own sins. Then, without any forethought, he was moved for the first time to offer to suffer in atonement. That night, when the vision took over his mind, *he was the one nailed to the cross,* looking down at his other self. And he was in agony. Each of his wounds bombarded his brain with acute cries of distress. *"Help!!! Get me down!!!"* he called out. But his other self seemed not to hear, and just looked on without acting. Finally, the vision faded, and he saw the familiar sights of his room again. However, the pains persisted, fortunately diminished, though when he sat on his bed and examined his hands and feet, he could see no visible marks.

In the days following that initiation into physical agony, he was barely able to drag himself through his daily shift at the prison. He spent his nights and weekends recuperating—and praying that the scourge be lifted from him. He would not admit to himself the possibility that his condition had been permanently altered. After all, he had not volunteered for the life of a *stigmatist*, and he knew he could not live that life and still accomplish the plans *he* had made to be of service to God.

Naturally, he had told no one at work of his painful condition. Thinking about it now, if he were to tell Msgr. Ireland when they met, his mentor might—just might—believe what he was going through, though it was more likely that he would suspect a psychosomatic origin for the pains. On balance, Fr. Santorelli thought it better not to mention his condition to his mentor if he could avoid doing so. As of now, it was still a secret between himself and the Lord, and if the Lord wanted it known, let Him be the one to reveal it.

— 4 —

Rome

Once Fr. Santorelli had cleared passport control and customs at Fumicino, he called Monsignor Ireland for instructions. It was too early for a restaurant to be open for dinner, so the Monsignor suggested that he check into the room arranged for him at the Vatican's hotel for priests, the Domus Romana Sacerdotalis, on the Via della Traspontina. He didn't mind that the room was small and spartan, for the building was perfectly located, just steps from St. Peter's Square, with a chapel on the third floor where he could offer Mass, and a dining room.

Later, a taxi took him to the Via dei Soldati, a narrow street near the Ponte Umberto I, where he found the restaurant chosen by the Monsignor, *L'Osteria dé 'Memmo' i 'Santori'*. The interior proved to be as unprepossessing as the entrance, but given his mentor's gourmet tastes, he was sure that the food would be special. The Monsignor was already seated, sipping his favorite *Montalcino* red wine while awaiting him—and itching to ask how in the world he had wound up in prison. It was certainly not a fitting post for a priest with a doctorate from the Gregorian!

When the waiter ushered in Fr. Santorelli, the Monsignor rose to greet him. Standing there together, they were a Mutt and Jeff combination. The priest was half a foot taller than Msgr. Ireland. That wasn't the only obvious difference. Santorelli was on the thin side, while Ireland was stout. Santorelli had a full head of black hair, with some premature white streaks, while Ireland was bald. And, the prelate looked the picture of health, while the priest, fifteen years his junior, looked worn to a frazzle—and acted it, as he very gingerly shook the Monsignor's hand.

Salutations exchanged, they sat down and turned their attention to the extensive menu. "This brings back memories of some good meals we had together, Monsignor!" said the priest. "You know, a few days ago, I had no idea I'd *ever* see you or Rome again. It's *quite* a change for me! I feel like Lazarus emerging from the tomb at the call of Jesus!"

After the waiter had taken their orders, they were able to talk freely, as it was still unfashionably early for dining, and the regular patrons had not yet come to fill the adjacent tables. "Did you have a good flight over last night, Tony?" the Monsignor inquired.

The priest nodded. "Yes, thank you, Monsignor—as much as anyone who's over six feet can, on that long a flight, in seating configured for midgets." He took a sip of mineral water, and added, "The plane was full, but I didn't feel crowded—nothing like being in prison."

Msgr. Ireland picked up on his reference. "Tony, I have to say that in tracking you down last week, I had quite a start when the Topanga Chancery Office gave me a phone number and said it was for the California State Prison. That's not where I expected my best student to wind up!"

"Nor was it where *I* expected to wind up then," Fr. Santorelli admitted with a wan smile. "I hope someone at the Chancery Office had the decency to tell you that I was there as a chaplain, and not for some horrible offense."

The prelate shrugged. "They just gave me the number, period—but I knew you too well to suspect you of doing anything improper."

"I treasure your good regard, Monsignor. Hopefully my being here today confirms what I told you on the phone about my being at the institution as a *chaplain*, and not a criminal . . . "

"It does," said the prelate with a laugh. "Of course, I'm curious about how you got there—that is, if you wouldn't mind talking about it."

On the flight over, Fr. Santorelli had thought about what he should say about that and how he should say it. While he trusted his former professor completely, he felt constrained in how he spoke of the man who was still his religious superior, Cardinal Thomas O'Melveny.

He was about to answer when a plate of bread was set before them, along with their first antipasti: big chunks of cantaloupe melon, sizeable slices of prosciutto, and firm balls of buffalo mozzarella. He took as little of each as he could, compatible with politeness.

"In retrospect, Monsignor, it was unfortunate that I started at the top of the ladder, with a job in the Chancery Office. That was His Eminence's choice, not mine. It turned out that I had learned both too much and too little over here. Too much about the Faith; too little about what was happening in the diocese back home." And he related the story of his memo and his criticism of the Cardinal's support of pro-abortion public figures.

"I can't believe that he bounced you all the way to prison just for the one memo, Tony," his mentor said.

A new round of antipasti arrived, temporarily interrupting them: grilled zucchini, eggplant, mushrooms, bits of calamari, onions, artichoke hearts, and meatballs. Fr. Santorelli put the tiniest possible portions of several of these on his plate, while the Monsignor helped himself generously and refilled his glass of wine. Fr. Santorelli's remained untouched.

"No, he didn't," the priest continued. "My next assignment was as pastor of a struggling mission church. I figured that the Cardinal wouldn't be visiting me there, so I was free to run things the way I thought best. I'm sure you wouldn't be surprised if I told you that Eucharistic Adoration, the Rosary, and Stations of the Cross hadn't been observed there or in certain other parishes in that diocese for years. When I started them, it was like I had turned on a magnet. In three years, people were driving in from all over to attend them, and also a Tridentine Mass on Sunday, with a choir that made an effort to sing plainchant."

"That *was* a problem for His Eminence, wasn't it?" asked the Monsignor, grinning.

"Not until it showed up on his radar scope. He didn't know about it until I did something stupid without thinking. A cantor who came once from the outside said she had a connection at a newspaper. I figured it would help to have a story run about what we were doing—it might attract more parishioners. We needed to increase the Sunday collection to make repairs on the church building. Well, the reporter added a piece of her own, beyond what I had told her—it contrasted the growth in Mass attendance at my mission church with the decline at a number of big, well known parishes."

Msgr. Ireland cut in: "And, *their* pastors were jealous of your getting coverage, not to mention they weren't thrilled at the comparison—and neither was His Eminence.—So, he made sure you wouldn't embarrass him again, by sending you into total obscurity as a prison chaplain.—Enough said. Let's eat."

The next course was a specialty of the restaurant—*spaghetti all' amatriciana*—spaghetti with a ragu of Italian bacon from the jowls of the pig, tomatoes and pecorino cheese. They took it as a signal that it was time to change the subject for something lighter, and they reminisced about people they had known in the old days at the North American College, where Fr. Santorelli had resided while he was a graduate student at the Gregorian. The priest then asked to be filled in on his mentor's elevation to the prelature and his assignment to the Curia.

In a conversational lull, Fr. Santorelli pulled out of his pocket a folded, four-page flyer, with a picture on the cover of a mushroom cloud arising from an atomic explosion. Handing it over to the Monsignor, he said, "Here, this is for your extensive collection of 'End Times' prophecies. I don't expect you'll be teaching eschatology any more, but maybe someday you'll deliver another lecture on the subject. I found this in the seat pocket of the plane when I was rummaging for something to read."

"Oh, not another of these stupid things," the prelate groaned as he scanned it. "A few years ago, they were expecting doomsday because the Mayan calendar was coming to an end.—What's *this one* based on? An asteroid striking the earth?"

"Why, I thought you'd *love* this one," said Fr. Santorelli, in a mock tone, "because it's based on the Jewish calendar.—It's put out by an outfit called The New Age Church of Biblical Prophecy down in Texas. The pastor begins with Peter's speech in the Acts of the Apostles about the last days—the speech where Peter quotes the words of the Prophet Joel, about young men seeing visions and old men dreaming dreams, when the sun is turned to darkness and the moon into blood. At that time, according to the Prophet, the Lord will show signs in the heaven, and on earth—blood, fire and columns of smoke. The pastor says that the reference to blood moons is to those during lunar eclipses, when they do look reddish in color, and of course the sun turning dark happens during a solar eclipse. He uses the eclipses to establish a date certain."

"Eclipses happen all the time," said the Monsignor, unimpressed.

"True, but not on key dates *in the Jewish calendar*, which is the one Joel would have known. It just so happens that there was a total lunar eclipse during the Jewish holy days last fall, and there'll be another one during Passover this Spring. Plus, a total solar eclipse is coming up soon, in between the lunar eclipses. Using NASA's astronomical tables, and stringing the three together, *the pastor arrives at a pseudo-scientific prophecy that the End Times are at hand this year!*"

"I guess we'd better eat our lunch quickly!" joked the Monsignor, with a smile. "It certainly is *novel!—*That's about all I can say in favor of it. Thank you for giving it to me—I'll add it to my files."

Finally, halfway into the main course of *spigola alla griglia—* grilled sea bass—which only the prelate ordered, Msgr. Ireland broached the matter on his mind. "It's time I explained why I sent for you, Tony. You know how highly I regarded your work. Not just your doctorate thesis—your licentiate thesis as well, the one you did on the Blessed Anne Catherine Emmerich. In fact, it was your appreciation of her visions that made me think that you'd be the right person to help me with an unusual project. Of all the students I've ever had, you were the one most attuned to the *mystical* aspects of our Faith. I'm hoping you can make some sense of this file."

Handing Fr. Santorelli a dossier, Msgr. Ireland added, "This must be kept in the strictest confidence. Frankly, I don't have authority to show it to you, but I don't know how else to proceed. It was given to me by the Secretary of my Congregation. I'm supposed to draft a response."

Intense interest and concern showed on the young priest's face as he studied the report from the Bishop of Santander. The report mentioned that the Spanish monarch was interested in all things having to do with Garabandal, and it ended with the Bishop's plea for instructions as to how he should deal with any report of additional visions, and whether he should issue an order barring further pilgrimages to the area.

When Fr. Santorelli had finished reading and handed the material back, Msgr. Ireland said he had a question to pose.

"I have to confess, Tony, that I've never been particularly attuned to Marian apparitions, and Garabandal was not one that I'd heard of before. I pulled up a brief account of those visions on the Internet after I read this report. I gather that there is supposed to be a warning, followed by a miracle, and possibly a chastisement. Tell me, have you heard of that prophecy before?"

"As a matter of fact, yes, Monsignor," the priest replied. "I once did some research on the apparitions at Medjugorje, and was led by that to books about the Garabandal visions. There is a marked similarity between them."

"Do you have any feel for Garabandal's authenticity?"

"Some feel, I suppose, but no certainty—and, as I should, I await the definitive judgment of the Church with a readiness to accept whatever that may be."

"Well, it's time for you to sing for your supper. Tell me what you think of Garabandal."

"There have been many claimed Marian apparitions in recent years, Monsignor—you might say they've been coming thick and fast. They all strike the theme that Our Lord is angry and threatening to unleash a catastrophe on mankind for its sins. It's very hard to tell which, if any, visions are real and which are imagined or fabricated. As I'm sure you know, that's why the Congregation for the Doctrine of the Faith, years before you became a member, put out a warning about accepting them uncritically.

"Garabandal is typical in that respect. Some think that time has passed Garabandal by and has disproved the seers' claims, since they were made back in the 1960's. The bishops there over the years have been mainly hostile, though some, including the present Ordinary, have kept an open mind. I've never been there myself, but I can't dismiss the claims, because they've been given credence by two saints: Padre Pio and Mother Teresa. Personally, I think it's very possible that Our Lady did appear there and that there will be, in sequence, a warning, a miracle, and a chastisement, with the latter marking an end—to use the words of a visionary."

At that, the Monsignor arched his eyebrows, and put down his fork. "*An end? Do you mean THE END, in capital letters?*"

The priest opposite him sighed. "I don't think so. That's how the popular press often treats it, but nothing's that clear when you're dealing with visions. As the Holy Father has said, supernatural impulses like visions are translated by the subject according to his or her own capabilities for seeing, imagining and expressing. So, there are questions of whether the seer genuinely saw something and perceived correctly what she was shown. Also, whether she understood what she saw. This is especially crucial if the vision or apparition had mystical aspects or obviously symbolic aspects. Then, there are questions of whether she later accurately described what she had seen, and so forth. *I can say this—when pressed on the exact point you raise, the girl with the clearest recollection indicated that it would not be the end of the world as at the time of the Second Coming of Our Lord, but rather the end of the age we live in.*"

Msgr. Ireland was growing impatient. "That's interesting, but what's meant by 'the end of the age'?"

"The visionary didn't know, and you would be in a better position than I to speculate, Monsignor, since *you* taught the course in realized eschatology.—Perhaps it will be something like the destruction of Jerusalem by the Romans, which had so many major implications for the Jewish people and their religion, especially the end of the cult of Temple worship. Or it might be like the Christian millennialists once speculated. You had us read some of the unorthodox theorizing of the Calabrian Abbot.—It was too turgid for me to remember much—although I seem to recall that he made a threefold division of time into the Age of the Father, which lasted up till Jesus, then the Age of the Son, lasting at least the millennium after Jesus appeared, and finally the Age of the Holy Spirit, which he hoped had already started with the birth of the Franciscan Order. As a matter of fact, didn't our present Holy Father write a thesis on the theological problems which St. Bonaventure saw with Joachim's tripartite schema?"

The Monsignor nodded in recognition. "You're right! Your memory is pretty sharp, Tony! That class was half a dozen years ago. As a matter of fact, I got to know Benedict because of our common interest in that heresy." He paused, reminiscing, before continuing. "Well, to get back to the visions at Garabandal, was there any projected *beginning* date for the Warning?"

"No, but *if* it's going to happen at all—and that's a big *if*—it's likely to happen soon. And before you ask me what I mean by 'soon,' I'll say probably during this papacy."

"All right, then, Tony, *what do you think is happening now over in Spain?* Do you think the incident reported in detail by the Bishop concerning that tour chaplain, and the incidents involving other pilgrims on that tour, which the Bishop learned about from his housekeeper, are the first instances of the Warning?"

"I don't know, Monsignor."

The prelate felt frustrated. *"I know you don't know, Tony. I asked you what you think ... "*

He received something less than a direct answer. "The sky has grown dark, the wind has kicked up, and a few large drops of water have fallen from the sky. It could just blow over—or it could be an ordinary rain.—*Or ...* "

"Or what?" the prelate asked.

"Or it could pour so strongly that it becomes a deluge."

"If you had to bet me a lunch on which one of those this will turn into, which would you bet on?"

Fr. Santorelli thought about it, and with great reluctance answered the question: "I couldn't afford to lose that bet, Monsignor, but if you'll make it a gentleman's wager, *I'll bet on the deluge.*"

Msgr. Ireland pushed his plate away and gave his undivided attention to his guest. "Why is that?"

"Because people in the countries of what used to be called 'Christendom' appear to have lost their sense of the *vertical dimension* of 'sin,' *sin as an offense against God*. The courts deal with sins which are also civil wrongs or crimes every day. But, while the harm to the fabric of society caused by these acts is recognized, few people seem to realize that they also injure their relationship with God. It's a failing of long standing. In a used book store I once found a volume with the title, *Whatever Became of Sin?* You'd think it was by a clergyman, but it wasn't—the man who wrote it was a nationally famous psychiatrist, and he was lamenting what had already taken place before I was born."

"And you attribute the loss to what?" asked his mentor.

"To secular governments forcing religion out of the public square, to the media's hostility against everything sacred and their disparagement of the Church and sacramental confession, and, also, I hate to admit it, to some misguided members of our clergy."

"Our clergy? I find that hard to believe," Msgr. Ireland replied. "The Church's teachings about *sin* haven't changed in centuries. They aren't preaching heresies are they?"

"The official doctrines haven't changed, Monsignor, but how often is *sin* discussed in a typical pastor's homily? From complaints I've read in conservative periodicals, the answer in many parishes would be, not very often, perhaps *never*. And when it is, the priest's approach is likely to be 'God hates the sin, but loves the sinner.' "

"What's wrong with that?" asked the prelate, becoming a bit heated. "It's *very pastoral*."

"What's wrong with that," said Fr. Santorelli, "is that, *unless much more is said*, it detaches the sin from the sinner, and gives the impression that sinning doesn't really matter, since God loves the sinner anyway. I know we're supposed to be sorry for our sins primarily because they offend God, who is all love—but for people that aren't motivated by that thought, a dread of the loss of Heaven and a fear of the pains of Hell provide a useful backup prod—or at least they would, if people still believed in Hell. Which brings me to a pet peeve—the word 'Hell' doesn't even appear in the New American Bible—the one we use in church in the States. 'Hell' has been replaced by six different words, like 'the netherworld'—none of which has *any* emotional impact on modern man. Does anyone fear being sent *there*, or to Gehenna or Sheol?"

That drew a pointed retort from Msgr. Ireland. "Let's say that the Faithful *have* strayed, Tony—how would *you* go about winning them back? The Church has been seeking to assure people that it's like the father of the Prodigal Son—eager to welcome them back. Would you substitute harsh condemnations? And if you think that preaching hell-fire and brimstone is the way to go, have you seen any notable success on the part of fundamentalist preachers?"

"I'm not calling for that kind of preaching, but please recall what the Prodigal Son said when he was welcomed home—'*I have sinned against heaven and against you, father.*' It's precisely that sense of sin—and its confession—that is lacking today on the part of Prodigal Sons and Daughters, perhaps because priests don't make a point of it." Fr. Santorelli was primed to say more along that line, but the steely look in his mentor's eyes warned him that he'd better not, so he shifted gears.

"Well, I'll get off my soap box, Monsignor, and just say a final word about the Garabandal prophecy. In the old days, when the people needed to be shaped up, God sent them a prophet. All I can guess is that with us, He's decided to send individual visions instead. I may be wrong, but I think they will soon be raining down—on everyone and everywhere."

Msgr. Ireland was mollified by the abrupt end of the priest's peroration. "You may be wrong, as you say, *and I hope you are*. Still, the views you've expressed confirm my hunch that you could be of help.—Tony, you'd be doing me *and the Church* a service if you would go to Garabandal as soon as possible and make some discreet inquiries as to what's going on there."

"Exactly what do you think I should be looking for Monsignor?"

"*I* don't know—but *you* will, when you see it, *or don't see it.* I think that my superiors on the Congregation would be especially worried about having false claims about visions spread about, deceiving the Faithful."

Something about the way Msgr. Ireland said that made the priest ask, "That hasn't happened—or has it, Monsignor?"

"Well," he admitted, "since I received the Bishop's report, I've made it a point to check the Internet daily for anything to do with visions, figuring that if this *is* something from God, it's bound to spread like an epidemic. So far, there have been only a handful of stories, about an individual here, another there, having an encounter with devils—that sort of thing. The media haven't made anything much of them, probably because there are a lot of crazy people in this world who see strange things all the time.

"I thought *you* might be able to get to the bottom of exactly what happened in Garabandal, Tony, especially looking to see if you can find any indication of fakery. If so, that would give us comfort that we don't need to be too concerned about the reports popping up elsewhere."

"Wouldn't you be better able to size up the situation there if you went yourself, Monsignor?"

"Unfortunately, that's not possible. Given my position in the Curia, I'd have to tell the local bishop that I was coming, and word would appear in some newspaper that the Congregation was taking an interest in the apparitions. You can imagine the uproar that would cause here! They'd probably find some Italian jail for *me* to be a chaplain in." The prelate was only half joking. "No, I can't go. Besides, I need *your* judgment about what's going on there, to begin with."

"You weren't prepared for my guess about the future, Monsignor.—Have you thought of what you'd do if I came back with the report that there *is* something brewing of major concern? Would you shoot the messenger?"

"Heavens no!" said Msgr. Ireland. "I'd need you all the more, Tony. In fact I'd try to have you transferred over here to help me figure out what to do. From what you've said, I'm sure His Eminence in Topanga would be relieved to be rid of you ..."

The waiter came over to clear their entrée plates and bring them pineapple for dessert. When he had done so, Fr. Santorelli addressed the prelate's proposition.

"Your wish is my command!" He said it with a smile. "I took a ten-day leave from my prison assignment, and I'm willing to make a quick trip to Spain if you can supply me with the ticket and money. In fact, Monsignor, it would help if you'd pick up the tab at the hotel you booked me into for tonight. I'm close to broke. As to joining you here, I'd like to do it, but there's a personal situation which I would need to discuss with you first."

Msgr. Ireland looked greatly relieved. "You don't know how much I appreciate this, Tony! You can rest up tomorrow here in Rome, and go on Thursday. I'll arrange to have what you need, including some euros, delivered to you. You won't have to worry about accounting to anyone for it—the money will come from my own personal funds, as your flight here did. Just remember what you're doing is strictly unofficial. It's OK to wear your collar, but let everyone think you're on a pilgrimage of your own. Call me on my cell phone when you return to Rome, and we'll work out where to meet at that time."

The prelate paid the check and blessed Fr. Santorelli before they went out. Msgr. Ireland noted a flash of pain in the priest's eyes as they shook hands. He had seen it also when they met. Perhaps his "personal situation" was a medical problem? In any event, the prelate had more important things to worry about at the present, including the possible ending of the age he was living in. These could be exciting times!

*   *   *

Fr. Santorelli entered his small room at the Domus Romana Sacerdotalis and made for the bathroom, where he threw up his dinner. He had known this would be the result of overeating at the restaurant—not gorging, but eating small portions of rich foods. These days, he normally subsisted a whole day on a couple of boiled eggs, or a bowl of prison stew, and some coffee. He hadn't wanted to call Msgr. Ireland's attention to his eating habits by refusing to share in the repast which the Monsignor obviously intended as a treat for him. As it was, he had to fluff over the reason why he ate so little—attributing it to his fatigue from traveling. If he was going to stay in Rome for a while after his return, he would have to have a better excuse the next time he dined with his old mentor, who obviously remembered his past relish at downing a trencherman's portion of food.

— 5 —

Spain

After morning flights from Rome and Madrid, Fr. Santorelli arrived at the Santander Parayas airport, picked up a rental car, and headed for the Hotel El Cid Santander—the place where the tour group had stayed. He didn't feel like eating lunch, but he visited the hotel's dining room anyway, ordering a cup of coffee, hoping to pick up some information from his waiter, whose name tag identified him as Emilio. He mentioned that he was wondering whether it might be worth driving up to Garabandal, since he had heard of apparitions of Our Lady there 50 years before. "Have you seen any pilgrims here recently?" he asked.

"¡Si, Padre, muchos peregrinos en Diciembre!" The waiter gave a little giggle.

"Did they do something to make you laugh?"

"¡Si, si!" Emilio chuckled. "In the night, they go from room to room. Much knocking on doors. Very early, they come down to lobby in—," he scratched his head, unsuccessfully trying to think of the words in English, "sus camisones y albornoces."

"In their night clothes and bathrobes? Why did they do that?"

"They want see their padre. I think then he mejor."

"Was he sick, Emilio?"

Emilio nodded. "Padre es muy enfermo—very sick—when the bus it comes from Garabandal. They say he have—un desmayo. He go off in taxi. See doctor. In morning, he OK!"

"So, he fainted at Garabandal? How did that happen?"

The question momentarily stumped Emilio. Then an answer occurred to him, and he gave it with a smile: "It must be Our Lady did it to him!"

"Really? What happened next?" asked Fr. Santorelli, fishing for anything more Emilio might know.

"After breakfast, we see peregrinos in line outside hotel. They go to confesión, in bus! One hour. Two hours. We watch them. So much time they stand there!" Emilio could not suppress another giggle. "We make jokes. Ask, '¿Who are they—grandes pecadors?—o grandes santos?'"

Now, *that* was interesting. It strongly supported the hypothesis that the whole pilgrim group had experienced a Warning vision! They probably could be tracked down in the States, and questioned if their stories turned out to be important. The priest paid the check, telling Emilio that he had decided to go have a look around Garabandal for himself, and might want to chat with him further, upon his return.

With his rosary beads hanging on the rearview mirror of his little Fiat, the priest headed the car southwest toward Garabandal. The highway was good, but the driving was physically taxing, as the route twisted and turned for 50 miles along the Pena Sagra ridge of the Cantabrian mountains.

The priest could not help thinking again about Good Friday night, when he had experienced the agony of transverberation—the inner piercing of his hands and feet. Please God! The "test" or the "penance" or *whatever* it might be, would come to an end now, and the added pains of this trip would be the last drops Jesus would ask him to drink from the Chalice of Suffering!

*   *   *

At the village, he parked his car and walked with great difficulty up the uneven path to the pines. One day, according to the visionaries, a great miracle would be visible from there. At present, there was only an uninteresting vista of low mountains. Feeling absolutely no inspiration there, he hobbled even more slowly down the path to the little church, wishing that he had thought to rent a cane for the excursion. Finding the church empty, he knelt on the step before the altar and tabernacle and said the Chaplet of Divine Mercy. He had deliberately tempted lightning—"*the Warning*"—to strike again in the place where the tour group chaplain was overcome, and apparently it was not going to do so. Somewhat relieved, he was about to rise and go out, and see if he could contact the parish curate and some of the villagers, when he was—*Zapped!!!*

He felt the strength go out of his legs and he found could not get up off his knees. Simultaneously, he lost all awareness of his surroundings. It was as though his five senses were shutting down, leaving his mind without sensory inputs. A fleeting thought occurred to him—now I'm going to have a Warning vision—but that did not happen! Instead, he heard a voice speaking to him interiorly in his head, without any sound passing through his ears.

"*Anthony* . . . " It had a rising tone, calling, and requesting a response.

He had last heard that unmistakable voice four years before, during his student days in Rome. He almost cried out with joy and relief at hearing it again now, and he quickly gave the desired acknowledgment: "Speak Lord, your servant is listening . . ."

"*Are you truly My servant, Anthony?*" the voice asked in a tone indicating it doubted his answer. "*You are bearing only a sliver of My Cross, and that only with reluctance. Will you not accept your role in the redemption of the world?*"

He hesitated in answering.

The voice insisted upon an answer. "*Will you not accept My pains?*"

"Lord," he replied, "I don't think I'm strong enough for *that.*—I couldn't do my job in prison."

That was met with silence.

"What if I have to quit my job and the Cardinal forces me out of the priesthood?"

Still hearing no response, Fr. Santorelli said, finally, "*I can't refuse you, Lord.*—*Give me the strength I need, and do with me as you will.*"

Unexpectedly, the voice spoke again.

"*Anthony*—*I drew you here to carry to My Vicar on earth a message illuminating the future. My Church has much to suffer, but it will prevail and it must then proclaim the Good News to all, as on the day of Pentecost. I will now send visions to convict men of their sins and turn them back to Me. And through your mouth many will be given the choice of life or death.*"

He then both saw and heard the message, which was divided into separate parts—seven citations to Scripture. He recognized each one as it flashed at him, but the whole sequence came far too quickly for him to attempt to understand how any portion might be realized, much less make sense of the aggregation.

Even as he was attempting to firm up the passages in his memory, he was beginning to wonder how he was supposed to get the message across to the Pope. What could he say or do to make his fantastic story plausible?

Before he could voice his query out loud, the Lord spoke to him again interiorly, telling him that his wounds, previously only internal, would now be visible to all as a sign that his mission was from God.

Fr. Santorelli was given no time to question or object. All at once, his sensory awareness returned, and a movement off to his right drew his attention to the church's small statue of St. Michael the Archangel.

It seemed to come alive—the little figure lifted his spear from the dragon's head, and thrust it five times towards him.

Immediately, the priest slumped face down by the altar, unconscious from the pain.

When he came to his senses and raised himself to the kneeling position, he saw his skin beginning to tear open in the palm of each hand, and drops of blood forming. He screamed, not from the sight, but from the pain of the happening. He could feel the wounds in his side and feet opening too. Good God! He had to get out of there and get medical help. And something for the pain!

No!—On second thought, he *couldn't* get medical help—he would become a spectacle. And a pain killer was out, too. The Lord *wanted* him to suffer. But, he couldn't make do without bandages, as the blood was steadily dripping out of him. He had to drive down to the nearby town of Cosío. As fast as he could!

And even before he started the car, he had to write down the message citations so he wouldn't forget them. He didn't need to be exact about the chapter and verse—he could look those up later, if he just memorialized right now what each part was about. It proved to be easier in contemplation than in deed—he could barely scrawl words on a notepad that became smudged and wet with blood.

Driving down, out of Garabandal, was excruciating. He could grip the bloody steering wheel only with his fingertips, and work the pedals of the car only with his heels. Finding the farmacia, he went in after wrapping his right hand with his handkerchief. He knew from reading about St. Pio that antiseptics were unnecessary for his wounds; they would remain open and uninfected indefinitely. For them, he just needed non-stick bandages of different shapes and sizes, and rolls of tape. He also thought to buy a pair of cheap clogs to wear after he had bandaged his feet. Fortunately, the clerk was engaged in a cell phone conversation, and paid him no attention even as he paid for his purchases with a bleeding hand. Sitting there in his car, he attended first to his hands as well as he could, then he slapped a large bandage on his chest. His shirt was already showing a dark stain, although it was black. During the tortuous drive to Santander, he allowed himself the luxury of groaning and crying, since there was no one to hear and give him sympathy.

*   *   *

Back in his room at the hotel, he took his time bandaging all five wounds carefully. His shoes were soaked with blood, which he rinsed out in the washbasin before slipping on his new footwear. Then, he sat down on the bed and called room service for two oranges—already peeled, for he knew his hands were not up to that task—and a liter of bottled water, asking that Emilio be the waiter assigned to bring up his order.

"*¡Madre de Dios!*" exclaimed Emilio, dropping the serving tray he was carrying as he came near Fr. Santorelli.

An American waiter wouldn't have given a second thought to the thick bandages on the hands and feet of the priest. But Spaniards have long lived with religious mysticism. They know the lives of their saints such as Teresa of Avila and John of the Cross, and from their childhood they are surrounded by gory crucifixes of Christ and icons of martyrs too numerous to number. Coming on top of the previous week's events, it was apparent to Emilio that he was in the presence of a holy man. Without even thinking, he knelt down to kiss the priest's hands.

That act showed Fr. Santorelli he would have a real problem unless he kept his bandages covered in public. "Emilio! Emilio! Please don't do that," Fr. Santorelli begged. "You don't understand. I'm a sinner like everyone else." That failed to get Emilio off his knees. "Look," he said in desperation, "I will have to leave the hotel right now if you treat me this way."

That got through to Emilio. The waiter stood up and apologized profusely, backing away toward the door. Fr. Santorelli called out, "Wait. Don't go. Pick up what you brought, if you will. I'd like to talk with you for a minute—I do believe now that something wonderful has happened at Garabandal!"

His credence opened the way for Emilio to confide further in him. It turned out that, in the two weeks since the pilgrims had left, a number of members of the staff had been experiencing "dreams" which came while they were awake. These were described as strange and terrifying, but no one chose to reveal exactly what he had seen.

"Emilio, that's *very* interesting!" said Fr. Santorelli. "If you can find out anything more tonight, please let me know in the morning at breakfast," and he took his wallet out of his pants pocket.

Emilio put his hands up in a gesture to forestall a monetary tip, but he said "Padre, with your permission, I will take these,"— pointing to the bandages which the priest had put on in the car and which now, covered with dried blood, were on his night-table, ready to be thrown away.

Fr. Santorelli's heart sank. Was this how he was going to be treated from now on—with people clamoring for his soiled bandages and toe nail clippings as relics? In refusing Emilio's request, he graciously asked him if there was anything else he might do for him. Emilio begged the favor of hearing his confession, and when Emilio convinced him that otherwise he would not go to a priest, he agreed.

The waiter's urge to confess was prompted by his own experience with a daytime "dream" which had struck him that very afternoon, while he was relaxing for a moment with a cigarette outside the hotel on his break. He had seen himself hiking in the mountains near his home, with his wife and three children. His wife wanted him to rope all of them together for safety, but he would not hear of it—there would be time enough for that further on, he said, if the climb became difficult.

Up he went easily, leading the way. When he finally stopped to look back, he saw that his children had taken different paths up the rocks and were now widely separated from him and from each other. His wife, near the bottom, was in no danger, but his children were half-way up. While he was still watching them, one by one his children worked themselves into positions from which they could neither advance nor retreat. Trying to get down to the nearest one, he missed a hold and he himself slid down to a ledge barely big enough to stand on. He realized that he and his children could not save themselves from falling to their death. It was at that point that his terrifying vision ended.

After getting this story out. Emilio was silent, so Fr. Santorelli urged him on: "Emilio, what grave sin of yours did this vision reveal to you? Can you tell me?"

"My children, Padre—I do a bad thing to them. God knows. Their mother, she try—she go to Mass Sunday, all the year. But I no go. I tell her it not something *for a man.* My sons, my daughter, no go anymore, I think because they see what I do."

"Didn't you care you were setting a bad example?"

"I think it not matter. I think they decide about church when they grow up—go if they want."

"What has become of them, Emilio?"

"All three of them, they leave the Church. One is a Jehovah's Witness now." Tears were forming in his eyes. "*Oh, Padre!* Now I see they go fall. I go fall too. The Devil he take us!—*It all my fault.*"

Fr. Santorelli reflected on what he had heard. "In a moment, Emilio, I will absolve you of this sin, but first I want to explain the very hard penance which I am going to give you. You must call a meeting of your family—your wife and your children. You must relate to them the vision you had, just as you have told me, and you must explain its meaning. Then, you must beg their pardon for failing them in your fatherly duty to guide them spiritually. And *you* must return to the Church! If you do those things, you will live, and, if God so wishes, their lives will be changed too . . . "

After completing the rite of reconciliation, the priest walked the waiter to the door of his room. Despite what he had said earlier, he was prompted by an inner urge to go back and retrieve a bloody bandage. "Here, Emilio," he said with a smile, "you can take this, if you promise me solemnly you will show it only to your own family—no one else—as a sign that I will hold you and them in my prayers."

*   *   *

Alone, he lay down on his back, deeply troubled. He felt that he had not progressed spiritually since the day when Professor Ireland had lectured him about St. Paul suffering to fill up what was lacking in the sufferings of Christ, and he had responded by questioning the need to do so. He had accepted, *intellectually,* Pope John Paul II's teaching that *everyone* was called to share in that suffering through which the Redemption was accomplished, but he had considered it to be an undesirable impediment to the pursuit of the vocation to which he had felt called.

Why had he not embraced the Cross after he received the wounds of Christ internally? Digging down as deeply as he could, he concluded that it was because he had sensed that there was a more painful sacrifice coming further down the road—and he had wanted to limit his suffering to what he was already dealing with. His avoidance-response had not worked. The pains he had thought might be 'further down the road' were even now upon him—brought on by the full manifestation of the stigmata that afternoon.

A new and worse fear came over him. After he delivered the message to the Pope—then what? It had been difficult enough carrying on his prison ministry with five *invisible* wounds; it would be impossible with *visible* ones. He was going to have to resign his chaplain's position, by phone, and Cardinal O'Melveny would naturally be notified of that. The Cardinal would assuredly react badly to the news, probably withdrawing his faculties to act as a priest.

He forced himself to focus on the immediate task of delivering the Lord's message. Knowing what was in it, he was not looking forward to being the one to relate it to His Holiness. It would be in keeping with protocol if he simply gave the message to Msgr. Ireland and let *him* hand it over at a Papal audience. But, if the Lord had wanted to arrange matters without Fr. Santorelli interacting with the Pope, *He* could have dictated the message to the Monsignor—or, indeed, given it directly to the Pope—leaving Fr. Santorelli out of the picture and his wounds invisible. No, for a reason unknown to Fr. Santorelli, the Lord clearly wanted *him* to be the one to deliver it, in person. And he could foresee that when he did so, the Monsignor, if not the Pope, would be asking him how the phenomenon of the Warning visions was related to the message—assuming they believed his story.

The first two parts of the message seemed to relate specifically to the Warning visions. Either the sixth or the seventh part of the message might relate to the Miracle, but they also might not—all seven parts might only relate to the visions. The obscurity of the Lord's communication was as in olden times, he thought, recalling a passage he had copied into his spiritual notebook from the writings of the great mystic, St. John of the Cross: "a person cannot completely grasp the meaning of God's locutions and deeds, nor can he determine this by appearances without extreme error and bewilderment. The prophets, entrusted with the Word of God, were well aware of this. Prophecy for them was a severe trial because the people observed that a good portion of the prophecy did not come true according to the literal meaning."

In any event, he would be reporting his conclusion that a "deluge" was on its way, and the Church had better prepare for it . . .

— 6 —

Rome

As instructed, Fr. Santorelli contacted Msgr. Ireland when he landed at Leonardo da Vinci Airport. "Monsignor, it's Tony. I just got off the plane. There's been a development I need to see you about urgently."

"By all means, Tony! I can't wait to hear your report! I expect you'll take the express train in to the Termini Station and a cab from there. Let me give you directions to my office."

There was a silence and then a strained reply. "I'm sorry, Monsignor—I'm just not physically up to taking the train right now. If you can give me the name of a place to stay very near the Vatican, I'll take a cab straight there. I don't want to check back into the priests' hotel, because there are too many knowledgeable eyes there. When you see me you'll understand. What I'd like is a pension run by an order of nuns who can be trusted to be silent."

Well, well, well! Whatever did he mean about *knowledgeable eyes*? the prelate wondered. "I'm sorry to hear you're not feeling well. By all means, take a cab in and go—let me think—to the Procura Generale Suore Missionaries Pallottine. It's on the Via della Mura Aurelie, just south of St. Peter's. I'll call the Mother Superior and make sure a room is waiting for you. You can let me know when you're ready for a visitor, Tony."

*   *   *

In the afternoon, at the pension, a sister accompanied Msgr. Ireland to the third floor on the elevator, and flicked the hall light timer-switch on, then left him alone to visit the new guest. The prelate saw at once how pale Fr. Santorelli's face was as he opened the door to his room. Noticing how gingerly the younger man walked back inside, and then the bandages on his hands, he blurted out, "Tony! What the *hell* is wrong with you? Do you need a doctor?"

"A doctor wouldn't be able to help, Monsignor," the priest replied. "I feel awkward talking about my condition, and I don't want to blow it out of proportion, but after what happened on the trip, I can't conceal it any longer." The priest sat down on the single bed, against the wall opposite the door, and ever so carefully unwrapped the bandage on one hand.

The prelate looked at the bloody wrappings and Fr. Santorelli's hand. *"Oh my God! ... ,"* he exclaimed. There was a moment of silence in which he thought furiously. *"Don't tell me!—Your feet and side, too?"*

"I'm afraid so ... "

Msgr. Ireland was stupefied—*his former pupil was a stigmatist!* He was aware that there had been a very small number of such people over the centuries, with Padre Pio being the first priest among them. But, he knew Anthony Santorelli as his pupil Tony, and *Tony was no Padre Pio—Padre Pio had been recognized as a saint while he was still alive!* In the years Ireland had been together with Tony, he had never suspected the younger man of exceptional sanctity, nor had he ever imagined that Tony's mystical bent would one day be crowned with the wounds of Christ.

He blurted out, "Tony, please forgive me! I would never have asked you to go to Spain if I had known about this. I can't believe I missed it the other day when we dined together ... "

"No apology is called for, Monsignor," the priest was quick to reply. "There was no reason for you to know—I had the wounds, but they weren't visible then. They were opened at Garabandal. And the Lord told me that *He* had called me there, so please don't blame yourself.

"In any event, my wounds are secondary. I need to fill you in on what I found out. If you don't mind, I'll just lie down here on the bed while I'm talking. I'm feeling a bit weak at the moment. Maybe it's the loss of blood. I'm going to have to get used to my new condition ... "

Msgr. Ireland sat down on the only armchair in the room and listened as Fr. Santorelli proceeded to relate what he had learned about the pilgrimage in December, and described his experience with the hotel waiter as being further evidence that the Warning was real and was spreading, though of course he refrained from revealing what the man had said under the seal of confession.

Msgr. Ireland was dismayed because he felt powerless and at a loss to know what he should be doing now—and he said so.

"Well, Monsignor," replied the priest, *"I can suggest the first step—please take me to the Holy Father—I have a message for him."*

The prelate sat looking at him in silence for a minute. His mental circuits were overloaded. *"You have a message for the Holy Father? . . . From whom?"*

"From the Lord . . ."

Again a pause while Msgr. Ireland tried to process what he had just heard, before he spoke. *"From—the Lord???"* He hoped that he'd heard wrong.

"Yes, Monsignor—from the Lord. That's why my wounds were made visible—so that the Holy Father will credit the message I must give him."

That was too much! One bombshell after another!

He had to ask. "What's the message?"

Fr. Santorelli's tone was apologetic, as were his words. "It's in seven parts, and I have to deliver it to him in person. With due apologies, Monsignor, I think I should reserve it for the Pope's ears first, and let him decide whom to share it with."

A longer silence followed before the prelate spoke again. The frustration was evident in his voice.

"Tony, do you have any idea of how hard it is to get in to see the Pope, in his condition?—Do you?— He's really not in good shape. Only two Cardinals—Malapensa and Latoya—have ready access to him. I'm just a junior monsignor. There's no way I could get a private audience for myself on *official* business. How am I supposed to get in on an *unofficial* matter with a *prison chaplain from America?"*

Fr. Santorelli sympathized with Msgr. Ireland's problem, but he had faith that if the Monsignor knocked, the door would be opened.

"I wish I didn't have to hit you with all this at once, but I would ask that you call the Holy Father's personal secretary and explain the situation. Think of it this way: would I have been given this message if I were going to be stopped from delivering it?"

That point made sense to the prelate, and he decided to make the call from the room there, while Fr. Santorelli was with him to supply information if asked.

The Pope's personal secretary, Anton Waldheim, was not a mere amanuensis but a monsignor himself, not yet 50, from Austria, who served as Benedict's trusted personal assistant and gatekeeper. He and Msgr. Ireland were not personally acquainted and so they addressed each other with formality.

Msgr. Ireland explained that he was seeking a very urgent private audience on behalf of a priest, a valued former student of his at the Gregorian, who had just returned from the site of Marian apparitions in Garabandal, Spain, with news that the first part of a prophecy, concerning a Warning to mankind, was being carried out even as they spoke. More than that, the priest had a message which he had to give to the Pope personally.

"Who is it from?" Msgr. Waldheim asked.

Msgr. Ireland mustered his courage and answered, "From the Lord, Monsignor."

"I see . . . ," said the Pope's personal secretary. "May I suggest, Monsignor, that you have this priest write out the message, seal it in an envelope, and give the envelope to His Eminence, Cardinal Malapensa? If the Secretary of State thinks the matter important, he can notify me."

It was a polite brush off, but Msgr. Ireland persisted. "Monsignor, please do me one personal favor—go and tell the Holy Father what I told you, and that I am at this very minute sitting in a room in a nearby pension with the priest, who is bleeding profusely from stigmata which were opened yesterday at Garabandal. These markings are genuine. I will lay my purple on the line that what he has to say is worth the Holy Father's personal attention right away."

The prelate heard the phone being put down at the other end. Several minutes later, the response came. "The Holy Father will see you and the priest at four o'clock this afternoon in his private apartment, for five minutes. As you understand, Monsignor, your career may depend on what you bring forward to justify this *extraordinary intrusion* on His Holiness."

*　　*　　*

A visitor to the basilica of St. Peter's, with his eyes fixed on the church ahead of him, might never notice that at the western end of the north colonnade, there is an opening for a set of marble steps leading up into the Apostolic Palace. Atop the steps is the imposing doorway of the Bronze Doors, designed by Bernini. Perhaps a dozen feet wide and more than twice that tall, it is flanked by a colossal marble pillar on each side, holding up sculptures of angels and a tympanum of the Virgin with Child. The huge doors, made of wood and bronze taken from pagan temples, are guarded by Swiss Guards in their colorful uniforms. It was through this entrance that the two clerics entered the palace, an immense structure, with more than 1400 rooms, including separate apartments where the Pope and his second in command, the Secretary of State, lived and worked. They were escorted from the doors by a Gentleman of His Holiness, on their ten minute walk up many stairs and through corridors to the Papal Library. There they were met by Msgr. Waldheim, who asked them to avoid greeting the Pope ceremonially when he entered, and to state their case directly.

Fr. Santorelli was completely distracted, going over in his mind what he needed to say to the Holy Father, while Msgr. Ireland had the luxury of being able to indulge his interest in fine art by taking in the surroundings for a few moments while Msgr. Waldheim went for the Pope.

The room was large and beautifully appointed. Sunlight flooded in from three windows on the long side of the room, looking over the Square to the south, opposite the door through which they had entered. At that end was the focal point of the decorating scheme, a striking painting of the Resurrection of Christ by Perugino. He had heard of it, but never seen it in the museum's Pinacoteca gallery, as it had hung in the Papal quarters for more than fifty years.

Christ floated triumphantly in mid air with a pennant of victory in His left hand, the staff symbolically pointing down to the now empty tomb beneath Him, while His right hand pointed upwards. Angels on either side adored Him, and three guards down below drowsed as a fourth, awakened, gazed up at Him. The tempera and oil painting was on a vertical wooden panel, oval-arched at the top, that had been framed in a rectangular gilt frame, with the empty spaces in the top corners filled in and brilliantly gilded. The gilding went well with the pale yellow figured silk velvet wallpaper, and the wide landscape friezes which ran all around the room at the top of the walls, set off by moldings below and above them. And the ceiling too was a blaze of color, intricately carved and gilded, with illustrations.

It could not have been a working library, for although there were a number of outsized cabinet-type bookcases, the uniformity of the bindings of the books betrayed the fact that they were sets, present for decorative effect rather than use. A large, reddish oriental rug covered most of the white marble floor, which was inlaid with black marble squares set at right angles.

Movable chairs, covered in a gold fabric, had been set out for the Monsignor, Fr. Santorelli, and Msgr. Waldheim at the other end of the room, on one side of a long wood table. The table was out five feet from the end wall, on which hung a large painting by Antoniazzo Romano, *Madonna and Child enthroned*. On the table were only a lamp, a clock in a brass case, and a small standing crucifix.

This was where the Pope greeted the famous of the world and exchanged ceremonial gifts with them—presidents and prime ministers, and bishops on their *ad limina* visits. Msgr. Ireland, duly awed, uttered a silent prayer that Fr. Santorelli would have something to say that would truly be perceived as justifying their presence there. He did not doubt that his own career was on the line, as he had so rashly placed it by his phone call to the Pope's personal secretary.

Msgr. Waldheim returned, wheeling in the Holy Father to a place between the wall and the desk. The two visitors stood and bowed their heads as he raised his right hand and made the Sign of the Cross in blessing them. He was leaning slightly to one side in his wheelchair, but his face radiated intelligence and interest. The three clerics sat down and Msgr. Ireland began with an introduction, speaking in fluent Italian.

"Holy Father, may I present to you Father Anthony Santorelli, who was a prize pupil of mine years ago here in Rome. Earlier this week, I asked him to come from America to assist me temporarily, and then I sent him on a strictly unofficial trip to Garabandal, the site of Marian apparitions 50-odd years ago. While he was there, he found proof that one of the prophecies was coming true at this very time—namely that there will be an internal warning from God given to everyone individually, convincing him of his sins. According to the visionaries, the warnings are supposed to be followed by a great miracle, showing God's great mercy to mankind. The effect of the warnings and the miracle cannot help but be extraordinary for the whole Church, and we need to start taking account of it immediately."

Msgr. Ireland was not through, but unexpectedly, the Pope interrupted him. "Thank you, Monsignor. Our Blessed Mother sends her children many warnings and messages. It is difficult to assess their validity and significance without a thorough investigation by the proper authorities, which, I believe, has *not* been done in the case of the Garabandal prophecies."

From the curtness in the Pope's voice, it sounded like he would cut the audience short right then. Instead, he continued. "At the moment, my concern lies with Father, here, since I am informed that Father has received a message from Our Lord."

Turning to Fr. Santorelli, the Pope said, gently, "Father, I have also been given to understand that you bear His wounds. May I see those in your hands?—Of course, if you have no objection."

Fr. Santorelli immediately knelt by the Holy Father and with Msgr. Ireland's help removed the bandages, showing both sides of his hands, all the while trying not to bleed on the Pope's white cassock. The wounds were gruesome—triangular, about a centimeter across on the palm side and half that on the back side, and fresh, deep and oozing blood, with no scab or evidence of infection. Surprisingly, a sweet odor came from them—like a rose perfume. Neither Msgr. Ireland nor Fr. Santorelli himself had noticed that before.

"Thank you, Father." The Pope's tone indicated he was satisfied with what he had seen, and Msgr. Waldheim seemed to relax somewhat. "You may re-bandage your hands. Please tell me how you came to receive those marks."

As Msgr. Ireland was helping with the bandaging, Fr. Santorelli told his story. "The wounds first came internally, last year, Holiness, in California. I was grateful that they were concealed, so that I could continue to work. Yesterday, in the church in Garabandal, I had a locution in which the Lord gave me a message for you. He said that my wounds would be opened to validate that message— and so they were!"

"As to the message, Father . . . ?" the Pope inquired.

"Yes, as to the message, Holiness. It wasn't like you might expect, with words forming sentences of a paragraph. Instead, it took the form of seven citations of Holy Scripture. As each verse was cited by Him, the text appeared to me visually in red letters—I guess, to make sure I would not forget or mistake it. As soon as I got in my car, I wrote down the citations on this piece of paper."

Fr. Santorelli drew forth a sheet of notepaper smeared with dried bloodstains. The pencil marks on it looked liked a child's scrawls, bearing witness to his difficulty in writing.

"Was there any explanation given along with the verses— anything which would help us understand how they may be applicable?"

"No, Holiness. Just the words of the verses."

"Well, then, what were they, Father?"

"First came, Luke 12:2."

Msgr. Waldheim went for a Bible, and when he returned he opened it to that verse. *"There is nothing concealed that will not be revealed, nor secret that will not be known."*

"The second," said Fr. Santorelli, "was 1 John 1:9." Again Msgr. Waldheim read the verse: *"If we acknowledge our sins, He who is just can be trusted to forgive our sins and cleanse us from every wrong."*

"The next one was verse 2 of Psalm 2." *"Kings on earth rise up and princes plot together against the Lord and His anointed."*

Fr. Santorelli hesitated before continuing. "The fourth citation, Holiness, I regret to say, was John 21:18." Msgr. Waldheim looked it up and recited the words of the resurrected Jesus to St. Peter. *"Truly, truly, I say to you, when you were young, you girded yourself and walked where you would; but when you are old, you will stretch out your hands and another will gird you and carry you where you do not wish to go."*

The Pope seemed to sag. "So it will come to that . . . ," he said, somberly, nodding his head. The other clerics did not know what to say to him.

The Holy Father seemed to grow tired. "If you will leave with me your notes, Father, I will consider the remaining parts later. For now, you have given me enough to think about. I take it you have no special knowledge what any of these passages refer to?"

"No, Holiness. However, the Lord did tell me that He was sending the visions to convince men of their sins, and that the Church had much to suffer, but it would prevail and it should proclaim the Good News to all as at Pentecost."

The Holy Father nodded and said, "Monsignor Ireland, Father, I thank you for bringing this matter to my attention." And with that, the papal audience was over.

*   *   *

Fr. Santorelli was already walking down the steps when it hit him—
*he had been to see the Holy Father and had actually spoken with
him in person!* He couldn't remember a single detail of the Papal
Apartment he had just left, so focused had he been on delivering
the message well and convincingly. And he had done so! Even in
the years he had spent in Rome as a graduate student, when he
had attended papal general audiences and ceremonies and Papal
Masses here and there, he had never gotten up close physically
to the Holy Father. Today, he was right next to him, so close that
he was worried he would stain his cassock. And Benedict XVIth
was not just *any* Pope, but one of the greatest ones in the whole
2,000 years of the Papacy! What a thrill it was to think that he had
actually been of service to the Vicar of Christ on earth by bringing
him an important message! And maybe he would be of help in
the future too!

    Thus pride raised its ugly head, and he fell prey to it. For-
tunately, Fr. Santorelli's vice did not survive for long, as Msgr.
Ireland brought him down to earth with a broadside when they
were back outside the Bronze Doors.

    *"Tony, are you bloody crazy? Telling the Supreme Pontiff he's
going to die a martyr? Were you trying to end both our careers?"*

    Fr. Santorelli was surprised by these harsh words, which came
at him out of the blue. "What were you expecting the message to
be, Monsignor?" asked the priest, defensively.

    The Monsignor stopped walking for a moment to think. "I
don't know—I suppose something like 'Prepare for a large number
of conversions.' Or, 'Well done, thou good and faithful servant!'—
Would there have been anything *wrong* with you bringing him
that message, Tony?"—He glared at Fr. Santorelli.—"Certainly
nothing like what you brought him! I'm surprised he didn't stop
you, and have Msgr. Waldheim usher us out after you dropped
your bomb!"

    "My bomb? It wasn't *my* bomb, Monsignor," said Fr. Santorelli.
"I was just delivering a message.—And, didn't you tell me you
wouldn't shoot the messenger?"

    Msgr. Ireland and his slow moving companion had just passed
out into the Square when their conversation was interrupted by
the ringing of the prelate's cell phone. It was the Pope's personal

secretary, who had gotten instructions from the Pope after they had left. "Monsignor, the Holy Father wishes to have his own doctors see Fr. Santorelli as soon as possible. If he has no objection, I will call over and arrange for him to be admitted at the Gemelli Clinic right now."

Fr. Santorelli readily agreed. Msgr. Ireland, somewhat mollified by this development, accompanied the priest in a taxi to the Catholic University of the Sacred Heart, where the world famous Policlinico Gemelli had a modern 2,000 bed facility. Once there, Bishop Ireland went to the chapel to restore his tranquility by kneeling before the tabernacle housing Jesus in the Eucharistic sacrament. The priest was taken up to a suite reserved for the Pope's use, to be subjected to a battery of physical examinations, including MRI's and a full body CAT scan, despite it being after hours on a Friday.

Fr. Santorelli had no illusion that he was at the clinic to be treated, and he wasn't. He was a specimen—and a *suspect* one at that—almost like a corpse on which the medical examiner was performing an autopsy, to draw out its secrets. Still, the staff dealt with him very respectfully. The nurses tried as best as they could to minimize the pain from repeatedly unwrapping and re-wrapping his bandages, and when they had finished, they were good enough to give him a supply of the right kind of dressings and show him how to cleanse his wounds, if needed, with alcohol. Finally, they fitted him with gloves whose fingers had been cut off near the palm.

The examining physician, Dr. Augustini, was interested in the fact that the entry wound in the chest was triangular, rather than being a slit, as a knife blade would have made. Also, the perforating wounds in the hands were not in the center of the palm—the location favored by artists, but in the exact position where a forensic pathologist researching the Shroud of Turin had postulated they were in Christ's case. For the record, Dr. Augustini wrote up his observations in standard anatomical terms, noting, with respect to each hand, that an entry wound was found at a spot in the thenar furrow of the upper palm, three centimeters from where the furrow began at the wrist. Whatever had made the wound had proceeded at a 15 degree angle toward the wrist and slightly toward the thumb, through an area created by the metacarpal bone of the index finger and the capitate and lesser multangular bones of the wrist, before exiting the wrist.

For the Pope's consumption, the verdict he promptly phoned to Msgr. Waldheim was more simply stated: "The wounds are what they appear to be: stigmata with no evident natural cause. Any attempt at deception is ruled out."

While eating a late supper at the facility before they headed back toward the Vatican, Msgr. Ireland was called again by the Pope's personal secretary, this time asking him to thank Fr. Santorelli for submitting to the inspection, and passing on the Pope's request that they both consider the meaning of the different parts of the message and how the Holy Father might respond publicly to the Warning if that phenomenon became widespread.

On the taxi ride to pension where Fr. Santorelli was staying, they were silent, thinking their separate thoughts. When the exhausted priest was back in his room and had lain down on his bed, Msgr. Ireland spoke. "It's an honor to be asked for advice by the Pope—one I hoped someday I might have—but not on a matter I know nothing about. Maybe if you tell me your story again of what happened in that church, something will pop out that you haven't remembered up till now."

Fr. Santorelli groaned involuntarily as his throbbing pains increased. "Monsignor," he said, "I'm just too exhausted to work with you tonight. Is it O.K. if we resume in the morning?"

"Tony—I've been thoughtless." The prelate was contrite. "I intended to leave you alone when we got back here, but my good resolution was lost in worrying over our assignment. Give me a call tomorrow morning when you feel like it. I'll accommodate my schedule to what you're able to do."

After Msgr. Ireland left, Fr. Santorelli held off sleep just long enough to say the Divine Mercy prayer: "Eternal Father, I offer you the Body and Blood, Soul and Divinity, of Your dearly beloved Son, Our Lord, Jesus Christ, in atonement for our sins, and those of the whole world."

*   *   *

Back in his apartment, Msgr. Ireland sipped a nightcap of amaretto liqueur as he reviewed the events of the day. The religion to which he had dedicated his life was built on belief in purposeful miracles, beginning with the very creation of the universe out of nothing by an all knowing and all powerful eternal being, and continuing with the loving creation of mankind, and its redemption through the Incarnation, Passion, Death and Resurrection of the Son of God. And he accepted without a doubt that the divine intervened daily in the present day world—so why did he find it so difficult to credit what he could see was happening now to and through his former pupil?

Why? Because it was improbable that God would send a detailed prophetic message for a Pope—that wasn't how God customarily dealt with his Vicar on earth. More to the point, because there were far more credible persons who could have been tapped to act as God's spokesperson. Many holy members of the hierarchy, some even brighter and more learned than Tony. It made no sense to the prelate that Anthony Santorelli, a junior and most obscure priest, had been chosen to be the messenger, instead of the Ordinary of a diocese or the prefect of a Curial congregation—*or, come to think of it, even the Monsignor himself.* He would have to find out what he could from Tony, delving into his past, to try to understand this mystery of faith.

— 7 —

Rome

As on the night he had spent in Spain, Fr. Santorelli was able to
sleep only between two and five a.m., and then was awakened by
pains that assaulted him from all directions—hands, feet and side.
He could sense that there would be no getting back to sleep. In
the contest between fatigue and agony, the latter would win out.

For almost a year, he had been nauseated by the smell of food
and his intake had been drastically reduced, without any loss of
weight or sign of malnutrition. Now, it was looking like he would
be foregoing the comfort of sleep. The repasts, he *did* miss. Sleep,
he probably wouldn't—but what was the use of being able to do
without sleep, if the consequence was just more hours spent lying
awake in pain? 'Stop it!', he told himself. It was useless to weigh
pros and cons—he had no say in the matter.

Light was now seeping into his room at the pension through
tiny slit-like openings in the articulated metal shutter outside the
window. Inside, there was only a sheer curtain, so the shutter had
to be let down at night for privacy, and then rolled up by a stout
strap in the morning.

There was neither a TV nor a radio in the room, so he was
alone with his thoughts. And a craving. A craving for a shower. A
long, hot, steamy, refreshing one. That was the only pleasurable
physical sensation which had been left to him in life after he had
received the wounds of Christ internally.

In Santander on Thursday, and last night in Rome, he could
do no more than sponge away some of the dried blood, and dab
himself here and there with a washcloth. He couldn't figure out
a way to shower without soaking all his bandages. He thought
of asking Msgr. Ireland to buy him a pair of rubber dishwashing
gloves. That would at least enable him to dip his hands in a basin
of water to wash the other parts of his body. And, if his mentor
was willing to be his personal shopper, he could very much use a
couple of changes of clothes, good sandals, and gloves or mittens—
something to put on his hands over his bandages—the largest
size available. He could explain wearing them in public, if he

needed to, by vaguely referring to a "skin condition"—which was somewhat true.

Long before it was time for the early morning Mass, he took the elevator down to the floor below the ground floor, to begin saying his daily office in the chapel used by the Pallottine Sisters and their guests. It was really quite beautiful. Even apart from the Mass, when Jesus would be present in the priest, in the assembly, and in the Word, He was present or represented there in the chapel at all times in three ways, most tangibly in the form of the Eucharistic hosts, which reposed in the tabernacle set into the front wall. It had a circular silver cover which had been worked into a design of grapes and wheat. An arc of red marble, matching that tiling the floor, was inset in the wall around most of the cover, thereby directing one's eyes to that holy spot as a sort of bulls-eye.

To the left of the tabernacle on the wall was a lit red votive light, and further left, Jesus was depicted in human form. A three foot tall picture of Divine Mercy hung there—Jesus with red and white rays emerging from his Sacred Heart, and underneath, the words *Gesu Confido In Te* (Jesus I Trust In You). The altar nearby rested on a marble base which showed Jesus in yet another traditional form—as a fish swimming in the sea, under a cross. Along the side wall opposite the door, there were stained glass windows which picked up the scanty light below street level, and a small wooden statue of the Virgin and the Christ Child holding the orb of the world. Fr. Santorelli knelt down on a pew next to them.

After Mass, he went across the hall into the smaller of two breakfast rooms, where he found a table for one with his name on it. Two large hard rolls were set before him, with pats of butter and little containers of jelly. He ate one roll slowly, with black coffee, observing the pilgrim groups in the larger room. The sisters in their grey habits moved around quickly and quietly with coffee and tea, as their guests chatted happily about their coming visit to St. Peter's. When he was alone, he wrapped the other roll in his paper napkin to take to his room, in case he became hungry before breakfast the next day, for the Sisters served no meal but breakfast and he was not of a mind to leave the pension that day if he did not have to. There was certainly no sightseeing he needed to do, and good reason not to appear in public, where his condition might be noticed and remarked on.

Back in his room, with difficulty he raised the shutter and looked out the window. Between the front of the building, where his room was, and the street, a driveway descended sharply, and the ground dropped off further between the driveway and the building, with the result that a small bridge was necessary to connect the front door with the driveway, like a drawbridge over a castle moat.

The scene he faced was of two brick walls—one running downward from the road, which was at his eye level, and the other, much more massive, extending from the road up to the high reaches of the steep Janiculum Hill. These were not just any old walls—they were part of the extensive fortifications built centuries before to protect the Vatican and its dependencies from brigands and invaders. At one time, they were linked with the high walls which still surrounded most of the Vatican City State, and which ran all the way to the Castel Sant'Angelo on the bank of the Tiber.

On top of the hill, with a commanding view of the Vatican and the City, was the North American College, where he had lived for four years. He was now rooming well down below it—which he perceived to be an allegory of the decline in his prospects since the days he was an outstanding graduate student. So many future achievements had seemed possible then . . .

And now? His career was at a dead end in the States, as long as he remained under the thumb of the Cardinal of Topanga. Was the Lord calling him to a new mission in Italy? Possibly, but doing what? Hopefully, it would not be to enter a friary and suffer heroically there for fifty years, like Padre Pio at San Giovanni Rotondo. His depressing thoughts were dispelled by a phone call from his mentor, who readily agreed to purchase all the new clothing he needed, and bring it to his room on Sunday.

After the call, he made out an accounting of the funds he had expended on his trip to Spain, and then took up his diary to record the events of the past two days, omitting nothing, including, when he came to set down what the Lord had told him, the words that through *his* mouth, the Lord would offer many the choice of life or death.

That statement had puzzled him at the time, and it puzzled him now. It seemed to mean either too little or too much. When he had been a pastor, he had, in a sense, put that choice before his flock, weekly. He doubted that the Lord was telling him that he would again be exhorting a congregation to choose good and not evil. He did not expect to be restored to being pastor of a church back in Topanga, not even another missionary chapel. And surely he was not destined to be a bishop, with a flock in the tens or hundreds of thousands. Then, the idea came to him that maybe he was destined to have an evangelistic ministry through the medium of television, like Bishop Sheen. That, he would be *thrilled* with! Lying back down on his bed, he took comfort in the thought that there might be a light at the end of his tunnel.

— 8 —

Rome

Having rested and prayed on Saturday, Fr. Santorelli was ready to receive Msgr. Ireland in his room at the pension on Sunday. The prelate handed over the purchases he had made for the priest, and took the armchair, while Fr. Santorelli sat up on the bed with pillows behind him. The Monsignor was still dazed by Friday's unprecedented events.

"Tony," he said, "I have to admit I never would have imagined *anything* like this happening to *you*. And sitting there, you seem so—*blasé*—about it. There are lots of priests who would give their *eye teeth* to receive the Lord's wounds as you have!"

"If so," Fr. Santorelli replied, "they'd be wanting them for the wrong reason. Maybe they'd be thinking of them as a badge of distinction, something that would elicit the admiration of the Faithful. You know, people saying—'*Look! There goes a living saint!*' It would be awfully hard to avoid the sin of pride, with a capital 'P.'"

"And you," the Monsignor asked, "are *you* avoiding that sin?"

"I'm *proud* to say that I am!" replied the priest, and they both laughed at his jest.

"The fact is, Monsignor, I feel like an imposter—like a soldier who's had a medal pinned on him that he hasn't earned. It brings him respect that he isn't entitled to. And that isn't the only reason I feel *ashamed* to bear these marks."

"*Ashamed?*—I'm shocked that you would say that," said the prelate.

"I'm ashamed because I was reluctant to receive the stigmata. The Lord Himself called me 'lukewarm.'"

"*You* lukewarm? I'd never have guessed that! Well, then, Tony, do you have *any* idea why *you* were chosen to receive the stigmata?—Maybe, if you don't mind, you could give me a brief rundown of your spiritual life?"

Fr. Santorelli nodded. "As to your first question, the answer is, 'No.' I'm in the position of the man in Cardinal Newman's prayer for trust in God—the man knows that God has created him to do Him some definite service, and realizes that in *this* life he may never know exactly what it is. I really don't know why I was chosen or what He expects of me now.

"As for my spiritual life, since you've asked about it, I'll try to give you a summary, though I don't think you'll find any reason there for what's happened to me. I guess it could be divided into three periods, the first being growing up and going through seminary. My Mother's parents were traditional Catholics when she was young. They drifted away from the Church after Vatican II, and she did also. When I came along in the 80's, she wanted to give me the religious experience she remembered fondly from her childhood. She found us a parish where the Tridentine Mass was said. I grew up with a feeling of awe for what went on at Mass, and was very proud when I was allowed to be an altar boy.

"I would have liked to attend Daniel Murphy High School, the junior seminary. My father, who wasn't Catholic—he couldn't be bothered to go to any church—put his foot down and insisted that I go to the public high school. The CCD class proved to be worthless, so my mother, God bless her, gave me instruction using the Baltimore Catechism and a bookshelf of home study materials from an outfit in Front Royal, Virginia. Anyway, during those years I felt a stronger calling to the priesthood. It was funny later to hear my classmates in seminary reminisce about what had made *them* think about a vocation—for a number of them it started with a nun who told them she could see they were *special*. Of course, not attending parochial school, that didn't happen with me. I know others in the seminary who felt called when they did a social service project. Me—I was hooked by Bishop Fulton J. Sheen."

Msgr. Ireland was surprised to hear that name from the priest. "Sheen was a truly great evangelist, both on radio and TV, but, he wasn't around any longer by your time, Tony. How did he come into the picture?"

"Our parish church had an audio-visual library with dozens of tapes of him. I thought he was—well—*so cool*, standing up there in his bishop's outfit, explaining everything in life so well. I could see myself doing that."

Fr. Santorelli smiled sheepishly at what he'd just said. "Oh, not the *bishop* part—the explaining part—the reasoning, the persuasive examples. You know what I mean—*proclaiming the Gospel in a convincing way*. And that's what I still think is the highest and best use of my talents—what I was called to the priesthood to do."

The prelate nodded for him to continue.

"Anyway, when I was 18, and out of high school, there was nothing to stop me from attending St. John's Seminary, just outside L.A. During my years there was when I had my only real problems with the Faith. The biggest was that I became put off by the doctrine that I'd been created to *serve* and love God in this world, and be happy with Him in the next.—As you know, it's not in our nature as Americans to think of ourselves as *servants*."

"That's exactly where the Devil went wrong too," interjected the prelate, "with his defiant cry, *'Non serviam!'* That's what led to the fall of the angels!—I'm glad you got over your objections."

"Yes. I was able to reason my way out of the problem. I began by trying to imagine what *I* would do if *I* were an all powerful Creator who wanted to be served. I figured I'd create servants whose only function was service—essentially they would be inanimate objects like robots. Robots that were completely controllable, and disposable if they failed or wore out."

"*Not angels?*" asked Msgr. Ireland, with a smile.

"No, not angels," came the reply, with an answering smile, "at least, not angels with free will, angels who would be free to disobey and even turn against me. And, Monsignor, *the very last thing I would do would be to create a race of humans with free will—hairy bipeds who were incompetent, unfaithful, unproductive, troublesome and needy*. In short, servants whose shortcomings were magnified to the point where they required more of my attention and care than any benefit they rendered me by their service.

"My conclusion was that we were a totally ridiculous type of creature for God to create if he really was after service of the kind *we* think of when we use the words 'service' and 'servant.'

"That conclusion was strengthened when I considered the glories which God had built into human nature. The capability of creating and enjoying music and art, stood out. Again, if *I* were making *things* to serve *me*, I would not even think of building into them a capacity for pleasure on *their* part, much less a capacity for joy. And finally, it would never enter my mind to make it possible for the *servants* I created to become adopted members of my own family—*especially to do so at the cost of my suffering for them.*

"You can see, Monsignor, why that reasoning persuaded me that, assuming we were created beings and God was omniscient, He didn't create us to receive service from us. He created us out of love for us. He—the Trinity, that is—*wanted us to exist* because the dynamic love of the Trinity is so expansive it had to be shared with beings that could, however poorly, reciprocate that love."

The priest's explanation drew an immediate objection from the prelate: "Father—you're not denying the Church's doctrine that we were created to *serve* God, are you?"

"No, not at all, Monsignor. I'm just trying to put the word 'service' into proper context. And the context is this: *The purpose of having us human beings serve the Creator, is to give our lives meaning.* Our service consists in doing something that He requests—or at least trying to do so. Especially doing the acts mentioned in the parable of the sheep and the goats—feeding the hungry, clothing the naked, and so forth. It's not a service that He requests because He wants to be 'served'—as we use the word. *Rather, the reason he creates the opportunity for us to do something for Him is because it enables us to grow into our potential role as members of His family. By serving Him, our wills become aligned with His will, and, if all goes well, we become fit to enter into His eternal life.*"

Fr. Santorelli paused, and asked, "Does that make sense?"

"I guess so, Tony," Msgr. Ireland replied, a bit unsure, because he had never tried to put himself in the mindset of the Creator, but relieved that his star pupil had not turned into a heretic. It was time to get the priest's story back on track. "Didn't you run into serious problems in the seminary?" the Monsignor asked.—"I mean, *it was in California* . . . "

"You're right, there," Fr. Santorelli acknowledged with a sigh. "The personal lives of some of my fellow seminarians were—disordered—to put it charitably. But you know all about that from the visitations that were conducted of the seminaries in America. They were accepting candidates they never should have, possibly thinking that the process and the grace of ordination would turn them around. I survived by minding my own business, and keeping my nose in the books. I found out what the professors wanted to see by way of answers and that's what I gave them. Period."

He thought for a minute. "Oh, yes, and there was even a temptation—of the normal kind. I went home for a vacation with a classmate who happened to have a sister who was everything I could think of wanting if I had been looking for a wife. We had some long talks, but that was the extent of it. Or, at least it was insofar as anything passed between the two of us. I confess that my subconscious brought her up again in a dream once, but I haven't thought about her in years."

"To finish up that chapter of my life—I also had a problem with God when my mother died of cancer. My father was already dead, of a heart attack. I still feel guilty that my reaction to the two deaths was so different. He went quickly, in his sleep—just the opposite of my mother. He was unchurched, as I said, while she was a devout Catholic. I didn't feel much at *his* death—it was quick and painless, but I sure was angry with God for letting *her* suffer—*despite my prayers*. I guess I felt entitled to special consideration for her because I was dedicating my life to the Lord."

"If it's any consolation, Tony," offered Msgr. Ireland, "that's not an uncommon feeling among priests and religious. A feeling of a sort of *entitlement*—not for us personally, but for special treatment of our loved ones. In most cases, it doesn't work out that way—insofar as matters go in this life—and we just have to get over it. *Which requires forgiving God . . .* "

"*It took a while . . .* ," Fr. Santorelli said, and then fell silent.

"O.K., I think we're up to your studies here in Rome . . . ," the prelate prompted.

"Yes, Monsignor.—I came here nine years ago, happy and in love with God, and pleased that He had chosen me for the most intimate type of service to Him. During my first year of graduate study, I had a locution—a reproving one, I might add—and in my second year . . . "

He was about to continue, when the prelate interrupted. "Would you mind telling me about hearing the supernatural voice? I've never had anything like that happen *to me* . . . " There was a trace of envy in his voice.

"It was on the first Friday of Lent. I went to spend a little time at the 40 Hours devotion in the chapel at the College. I prayed for a while in front of the Blessed Sacrament, and then opened my book of visions of the dolorous Passion—those were visions recounted by Sister Emmerich. I remember that I was reading her description of the scene of Jesus remonstrating with His three sleepy disciples in the Garden of Gethsemane. I placed myself there in the role of one of the disciples, and tried to imagine their physical and emotional exhaustion, and then His disappointment with them.

"Well, when the half hour I had allotted was up, I prepared to leave the chapel. Right then, I heard the words: 'So, *you too* could not keep watch with me for one hour?'

"It was a man's voice. I looked around, but there was no one within five pews of me. Again I made ready to leave, and again I heard that question, only this time I was conscious of hearing it internally, rather than through my ears. It was obvious to me that the voice must have been the Lord's, and that He wanted me to stay there with Him the full hour."

"What did the voice sound like? Was it a deep bass?"

"No, Monsignor. It was higher than that—in the tenor register, but different from any human voice I had ever heard—no matter who the speaker and no matter what the language."

"Different? How do you mean it?"

"I've thought about that myself, and I can't explain it, really— you'll understand if you ever hear it. The best I can do is give you an analogy. There are Tibetan monks who can make musical sounds which we can't, because they've learned how to employ cavities in the head that we don't make use of. I'm not saying that that's what Jesus did—but somehow there were resonances or maybe overtones in his voice that made it unique. It was ineffable."

Msgr. Ireland saw that was all the description he was going to get. "You must have been excited, Tony!" he commented. "Why didn't you ever tell me about it?"

"Yes, it was exciting—but also unnerving—to think that, with the entire universe to keep track of, God was observing what *I* was doing. Before that happened, I had occasionally been having moments of what I thought might be spiritual ecstasy. I didn't talk to anyone about these mystical experiences for fear that they would stop. They were like a secret shared between two people. I just decided to keep the locution a secret, too.

"To shorten my story, let me turn to the third part of my spiritual development," Fr. Santorelli said. A negative tone of voice signaled a change in his mood. "All the *good* experiences stopped abruptly when I was called back to the States. As I told you the other day, I lasted only a few months at the Diocesan Chancery Office. Then, when I was the pastor of a mission church, I became personally acquainted with a downside of mystical occurrences— what the spiritual masters refer to as 'spiritual aridity.'

"I've heard something like that described in some confessions of married men and women who were no longer in love and said they got nothing out of their mutual relationship, yet weren't willing to make a break. Their problem was different though, in that both partners generally ceased to have much to do with the other, sort of drifting away, whereas in *my* arid period, I chased God harder than ever. I kept thinking—'Maybe I can attract His attention if I double my prayers, or my devotions, or my penances.'—As you might guess, nothing worked for me. I received no spiritual consolation from anything I did, and God remained hidden. I hate to admit this, but I didn't really *know* I had a soul before that happened—I mean, know it in the sense of feeling it as an organ physically present inside of me, aching, longing for God.

"Working in prison was much worse for me. There, I went from a feeling of aridity to a feeling of desolation. I tried to tell myself that I was going through what the masters call the 'dark night of the soul'—and now I know that I was—but at times while it was happening, that intellectual insight was less powerful than the emotional waves that swept over me. I began to doubt myself and my faith, and I thought that God would never come to me again because I was so sinful, although I kept confessing and trying to make amends. It wasn't as bad as Martin Luther's scrupulosity affliction, but you get the idea, Monsignor. At my low point, I thought seriously of killing myself to stop affronting God. And I might have done it, too, if I could have convinced myself that I would be sent to Purgatory, and not Hell."

"Purgatory is a pretty bad place too, from what I've read."

"Yes," the priest responded, "but the primary torment there is an unsatisfied longing for God, and I was already feeling that, so, in a way, I was already there, without the prospect that the way to heaven was assured, in time."

"It sounds like you've been through a lot, Tony," said Msgr. Ireland, compassionately. "It's too bad you had to experience all that, but it looks like you've bounced back well."

"You know, Monsignor, maybe having to undergo the dark periods was for the best. The spiritual treatises I've read say that the first stage of the ascent of the holy mountain is disillusionment with the world and detachment from it. Obviously, that's not how I started off in my vocation. When I finished graduate school I thought I was already half way up the mountain, yet I'd never been disillusioned or felt detached from the world. It turned out that I had only been climbing in the foothills. Now I know better, and having gone through those two stages, I feel much stronger and able to resume the climb—if God is ready to have me do it."

"I take it you feel that you're out of the 'dark night of the soul' stage?"

Fr. Santorelli nodded. "I think so, given what happened to me in Garabandal, which completed a process that started last year, when I had my first visions of a crucifixion—with myself on the Cross instead of Jesus. And ... "

Msgr. Ireland gasped. He held up his hand to keep the priest from going on. "Let me get this straight: *You saw yourself being crucified?*"

"Yes, in a split vision—both looking up at myself on the cross and looking down at myself standing there. No way was I going to tell anyone about *that*! I couldn't figure out how it came about or what it meant. I guess, now, it was a test—I was supposed to understand that the Lord was inviting me to fully accept His Cross—not just as an observer, but as a participant. But I didn't want to go there."

The prelate found himself saying, "*You didn't want to go there?* ... What *were* you thinking?"

"I'd never been one for suffering, even as a penance. I'd read about those ancient anchorites who whipped their back until it was bloody—even some recent saints did that—but that sort of thing never appealed to me. If *I* had a headache, I took an aspirin— I didn't grin and bear it, offering it up to the Lord. So, on Good Friday last year, knowing my recalcitrance, the Lord moved things along—He sent me the pains of His wounds without the visible markings. You'll recall that you didn't see them when I had lunch with you a few days ago.

"The pains were so great that right away I found myself walking in a queer way across the prison exercise yard, trying to put my weight on my heels, and avoiding using my hands if I could.

The cons were quick to notice. A few related to me more easily, guessing that I must be suffering from some malady. Most of them mocked me, and a couple of the worst ones deliberately stepped on my feet if they got the chance. It was *torture* for me to drive a car, because of the foot pedals. I had to sell my old heap, and pay a guard to pick me up in the morning at my rooming house, and drop me off there after work. I had no choice but to rent a car to get to Garabandal, but I hope my driving days are over."

"And in Garabandal—you had another locution. What about a Warning vision?" the prelate prompted. "Have you had one yourself?"

"Not exactly, Monsignor," the priest replied, "but as I just mentioned, He expressed disappointment with me. Hearing that from Him was worse than seeing pictures of my sins could have been. Then, He asked me explicitly to embrace His Cross with all its pains.

"I didn't just say, 'Yes, Lord!' I thought about it. I couldn't imagine how I could function that way, and I told Him so—*but, in the end, what could I do but say yes?*—Well, I think that's my whole life story, up to date. I'm sure it was more than you bargained for . . . "

"That *was* quite a tale!" Msgr. Ireland admitted. "And now? How do you feel *now*?"

"*Terrible!—but I'm relatively happy!* Would you believe?"

Seeing the prelate's look of confusion, he quickly explained. "Oh, I'm in bad shape, all right, on a purely *physical* level. The wounds are always throbbing and they can be excruciating at times. There's no way I can get comfortable for long, and I'm able to get only three hours sleep a night. I'm sure I'm not supposed to take anything to relieve the pain, so I don't.—Having said all that, I have to add that my suffering is balanced by the perception that the Lord hasn't given up on me! *I'm getting spiritual endorphins right now to help with the physical pain!*"

Msgr. Ireland still looked dubious, so Fr. Santorelli added a further explanation.

"Remember the parable Jesus told of the wedding guest who started out sitting at the highest banquet table, and then was reseated lower, twice?—Well, after my demotions, the host has now asked me to come up higher. *He's rehabilitating me!*"

The Monsignor thought about all that he had heard. "Tony," he said slowly, "even with that explanation, what you're going through is beyond me. As you know, I've always been a bit skeptical about mystical happenings.—Still, if you say that's the way it was, I accept it. And, I want you to know that *I* believe your account of what happened at Garabandal ... "

They sat there in silence, until Fr. Santorelli asked, "Now, *what about His Holiness?* Do you think *he'll* credit the message I gave him? Or will a memorandum of our audience be filed away in a secret Vatican archive, and the whole matter dropped?"

"My guess, Tony," said the prelate, "is that it depends on what happens in the outside world. I scanned the Internet before I came to see you, and I picked up a number of brief news reports of people seeing strange visions or dreams. Evidently the media received some of these reports on Saturday, but wanted to check them out before posting them. Today, they apparently feel confident enough that it isn't a gigantic hoax, like UFO sightings, that they're willing to run the stories. It's clear that the phenomenon has already spread beyond Spain. Of course, if instances of the Warning remain few in number—just curious, isolated anecdotes here and there—what you've reported will be forgotten. And you— *and I*—will quietly be reassigned to a monastery high in the Alps as punishment for upsetting the Holy Father with your tale.

"On the other hand, if matters develop as *you* expect, I don't doubt that the two of us will be called on again by the Pope." Msgr. Ireland gave a sigh before continuing. "Frankly, I'm more concerned about the reaction of the Prefect of my Congregation *tomorrow morning*. It's bad enough that I brought you into this without his approval. He's going to be furious that I went over his head directly to the Pope, without even so much as a 'by your leave' for him. I'm sure I'll get a severe dressing-down when I go into the office in the morning ... "

— 9 —

Rome

It was Monday morning, and it was already clear that reports of strange visions were multiplying by the minute. Msgr. Ireland drove over to the pension to pick up Fr. Santorelli, and quickly related what was on the Internet. Meanwhile, after the Pope's morning Mass, the Pope's personal secretary was similarly brought up to date by the Vatican Press Officer, Juan Gariega. People all over Europe were claiming to have had disturbing visions of their past, sometimes followed by scenes of them undergoing torments by strange creatures. A few let slip the fact that the visions had reminded them of their sins.

The press naturally wondered whether this phenomenon was spreading in the same fashion as a medical epidemic, so they dug into who the people were and whether there was any common nexus—a place they had all been to, or a food they had all eaten, or a group they all belonged to, and whether they knew each other in any way. No common connection emerged, other than when questioned about their religion, they identified themselves as Christians, of one denomination or other.

Msgr. Waldheim was able to put the news into context for the Press Officer, by explaining about the Garabandal prophecies and what the Pope had been told on Friday about the recent occurrences there.

The Vatican's press man was experienced and able, but he admitted that he had never heard of such a development. "Apparitions—yes, especially of the Blessed Virgin. We have a standard form response for dealing with them when they occur. We say that the matter must be viewed cautiously, and examined in the first instance by the local bishop, and so forth. Usually we don't need to say anything specific, and if we do, it pertains only to a very localized situation."

"But," said Msgr. Waldheim, "*these* visions appear to be widespread over countries, maybe soon over continents, and so we're dealing with an unprecedented situation. We need to think carefully before making any response."

"Carefully, *but quickly!*" replied the Press Officer. "I can hold my friends in the press corps at bay for only so long. As you know, we take a long view of such events and we try to harmonize what we say today with what the Church has said over many years, but the media want a sound bite—a quick fix on every situation, no matter how complex. In this case, Monsignor, I see dangers on both hands. If the Holy Father says nothing or if he simply disclaims knowledge of whatever is happening, the visions will be dealt with on the local level by each bishop. No doubt, that will entail many different responses, some contradicting others, and they might not be spiritually helpful to the Faithful."

Msgr. Waldheim agreed. "You're right, Juan. And what if the Holy Father *does* speak out?"

The Press Officer answered with reluctance, choosing his words carefully. "For action by the Holy Father to do the most good, he will have to get out in front of the wave, so to speak. Obviously, he won't be speaking in a binding way, because this isn't a matter of faith or morals that calls for an infallible definition. Still, whatever he says will set the direction and tone for the response of the Church. I have to point out that doing so will make him the target of criticism of those who routinely express the view that Rome is too controlling. And—if he goes so far as to characterize the events favorably—there may be people who will blame him for somehow *causing* the visions."

"I'm not sure I follow your last point, Juan," said the prelate. "What kind of stories would you expect to see in the media?"

"You know better than I, Monsignor, that not every sinner is open to acknowledging his faults, much less correcting them. Any cleric who welcomes this development will find himself the scapegoat for the fury of sinners. It will be easier for critics to blame the Pope than to blame God."

*　　*　　*

Msgr. Ireland arrived at the office of the Prefect of the Congregation for the Doctrine of the Faith, in the Apostolic Palace, that morning with Fr. Santorelli in tow, to see Cardinal Latoya as soon as it was convenient. The Cardinal called for him to enter first, alone.

He could see from the Cardinal's look that his worry had been justified. He was in for a dressing-down, and so he said immediately, "Your Eminence, I owe you an apology and an explanation for how I came to see His Holiness without your prior knowledge and approval."

The Cardinal's voice was as stern as his face. "Yes, Monsignor. I would appreciate both."

Msgr. Ireland made his case as best he could, beginning with the report from Santander, his reaching out to Fr. Santorelli for help, Father's thoughts, and his own request for some unofficial and low-key probing in Garabandal. He continued by relating his shock at the priest's physical condition upon his return from Garabandal, and the tale of a message from the Lord meant for the ears of the Pope. He had felt the circumstances precluded him from involving the Cardinal before the Papal audience.

Cardinal Latoya was only partly assuaged. "I accept your explanation as demonstrating a lack of willfulness or an intent on your part to subvert the proper procedures. However, Monsignor, your judgment was not as good as I would have expected from a member of this Congregation. Those who have been selected to serve the Holy Father in the Curia must accommodate themselves to the formalities which have grown up over a long period of time to protect him from being besieged by people who think they have information or a proposal so extraordinary that only *he* can appreciate it. Never forget—you are only one of *thousands* of prelates. If every one of you were given a private audience whenever you had something you wanted to tell the Holy Father, he would have time for nothing else."

The Cardinal was not finished. "Moreover, the Holy Father depends on *me* to advise him about many matters, and I cannot carry out my responsibilities to him if my own subordinates are acting in a way which I know nothing about. *If you desire to continue working for the Congregation, Monsignor, we need to have an understanding that what happened will not be repeated.* Whatever message you wish to give His Holiness pertaining to matters under the jurisdiction of this Congregation are to be brought to my attention first. *I did not appreciate having to learn of this matter second hand, through the Pope's personal secretary this weekend.*"

Msgr. Ireland accepted his dressing down without demurring, apologized effusively, and gave the Cardinal the assurances he demanded. With that out of the way, the Cardinal softened his look and his tone.

"I would like to meet this former pupil of yours, especially since Msgr. Waldheim has suggested you might like to have him transferred here to the Congregation as a Consultor. You must consider whether he might find himself overwhelmed by our work. We can't make a place for him simply because he's a stigmatist, as you can well understand."

"I would be very grateful if such a transfer could be accomplished, Eminence," the Monsignor said. "If you have time, please call Fr. Santorelli into your office right now, and take his measure yourself."

*   *   *

The Cardinal was not one for small talk. Fr. Santorelli had no more than sat down beside his mentor when the young priest found himself faced with a difficult question—perhaps asked more to test how he handled himself than in the expectation of receiving an enlightening answer: 'What, if any, insights did he have to share with the Congregation for the Doctrine of the Faith concerning the message from the Lord?'

"It seems to me, Eminence, that the most important question for His Holiness to decide is whether the visions are coming from God, for if they are, he must support them in every way he can. Personally, *I think it is indisputable that they are of divine origin—no power on earth has the technical capability to create and transmit the visions, but for the sake of the discussion, I would like to add two significant proofs. The first is that the Warning so far has been addressed only to baptized Christians—a great miracle in itself.*

"Eminence, please think of the tenth plague in the Book of Exodus, the one which struck down the first born of the Egyptians. A plague is not a discriminating evil, but in that instance it was divinely made such: it did not strike *all* the Egyptians, or kill them randomly, but rather it discriminated among them on the basis of a *hidden* characteristic, namely, whether the man or beast was the first born. *Similarly in the case we are dealing with, according to the news reports Monsignor has told me about, the visions are being seen by Christians—and they are not externally marked as such. There is no way any human agency could pick them out and deliver a message only to them. Only God himself, and the angels he empowers, can look at a person and know whether he or she has been marked with the baptismal sign!"*

The Cardinal and the Monsignor looked at each other in amazement. That was a profound insight which had not occurred to either of them.

"The second additional proof, Eminence," Fr. Santorelli continued, "can also be seen clearly in the light of the last plague in Egypt. *While it picked out its targets deliberately, all it fell upon died—they were treated equally in that regard. Here, the Warning has been individually tailored not only to the sinner, but also to the sin—each one is treated separately. It is as though God called each person on the telephone, individually, and spoke to them words which showed that He knew the secrets of their own life! That is precisely what the first part of the message from Our Lord was about: nothing is hidden from God that will not later be revealed."*

Again, the prelates nodded in appreciation of Fr. Santorelli's insight.

"As to the next part of the message, Father," asked the Cardinal, "how do you read it?"

"I see the second part as posing a significant problem for the Church, Eminence, one that I would hope could be dealt with this week. If I am right in believing that the whole world will see the Warning, a very large number of people will be forced to confront their own sinfulness, and they'll be looking for some form of reconciliation with God. I think the Holy Father needs to come to a decision and address how that is to be done—preferably in his very first pronouncement on the subject of the Warning, as the problem might overwhelm the existing penitential system."

Cardinal Latoya was satisfied with that answer and asked whether the priest had any further thoughts to share.

"Yes, Eminence, in particular, I would like to mention something else for possible prompt action by the Holy Father. Over the years, His Holiness has considered issuing an Apostolic Constitution on Our Lady's role in assisting her Son in the redemption of the world. He may wish to make that the capstone of his pontificate, and the time may be growing short for him to do it. We need to try to persuade Protestants, in particular, of her powers of mediating grace."

The Prefect of the Congregation for the Defense of the Faith was impressed with the prison chaplain in spite of himself. What the young priest had said was not something which he could have learned from his studies or been coached to say by his mentor. It was original thinking applied to a challenging and novel problem. In fact, Cardinal Latoya had on his desk right now the Pope's latest draft of just such a Constitution about Mary as the spiritual mother of all humanity. Fr. Santorelli had demonstrated to the Cardinal's satisfaction that he had a keen mind to go along with his supernatural "gifts."

"Monsignor," said the Cardinal, no longer stern, "your former pupil has justified your confidence in him. I can see how he could be of assistance to you here. I will discuss with Cardinal Figlio, the Prefect of the Congregation for the Clergy, whether he can be transferred here. In the meantime, he can remain with you.— And now, perhaps the two of you can help me with a task the Holy Father gave me this morning—drafting an Apostolic Letter responding to the Warning." ... "You see," he added, "our Press Officer has suggested that the Holy Father issue something by way of guidance to his fellow bishops and the Faithful as quickly as possible, and I'm trying to have a first draft for him in the next few days. I would be pleased to consider any thoughts you could give me at nine o'clock tomorrow morning about what should be covered—including how *you* would propose to handle the first situation you mentioned, a strong demand for confessions, prompted by the Warning."

Msgr. Ireland and Fr. Santorelli left the Prefect's Office energized and thanking God for the positive outcome of the session.

*   *   *

They walked over to the cafeteria of the Vatican Museum, for a coffee and talk.

"Tony," said Msgr. Ireland, "it's fantastic to be right here at the Vatican during these events, isn't it?! I feel like this is the center of the entire universe—spiritual energy is flowing all around us! Don't you feel it too?"

Without waiting for a reply, the prelate handed over his cell phone, which he had used to pull up the latest stories on the Internet. "Here—look at this report about lines forming for confession at churches right here in Rome! . . . When we had our luncheon before you went to Garabandal, you were much too *negative* in your thinking! Remember? You described what might happen in terms of a *deluge. Instead, it looks like the sun is beginning to shine!* This could be a great development for the Church! I think evangelization is going to take off like a rocket—you know, like it did in Mexico after the appearance of Our Lady of Guadalupe to Juan Diego! *How can anybody ignore what's happening now?*"

— 10 —

Rome

Fr. Santorelli rested as best he could the remainder of Monday in his room, with short visits to the chapel, and was ready with suggestions when he and Msgr. Ireland returned to the Prefect's office on Tuesday morning. "I don't know what themes you and the Holy Father may already have decided to pursue, Eminence, but the quickest and clearest way I know to give you *my* suggestions would be to lay out how I would write this Apostolic Letter— unless you think that manner of presentation too presumptuous."

"Under other circumstances, it would be," said the Cardinal, "*unacceptably so*, but the time we have is short. You may proceed." And he took up his pen to make notes.

"Eminence, I would like to propose the following as the first sentence, which would set the tone for the whole work. Quote, '*A period of grace has been given to all those baptized in the name of Jesus Christ!*' End quote.

"*The single most important point to be made in the letter is that the Warning itself is not a punishment. Rather, it is a grace, a gift, intended to make us realize that the most important personal relationship in our life—that with God—has been damaged through our own fault, and that God very much wants us to repair the injury.*

"*Indeed, Eminence, the fact that God has sent the Warning to all the baptized Christians—and not only to Roman Catholics—leads me to make the recommendation that His Holiness should address his letter to all Christians of every denomination, and that he should prescribe the healing medicine for all.*"

The approving look on the Cardinal's face was gone, replaced by upraised eyebrows of incredulity.

Seeing that, Fr. Santorelli said, "Eminence, please recall how His Holiness responded to the criticism he received years ago when he removed the excommunication of the schismatic bishops. He said that a logical consequence of the fundamental priority of the Church—leading men and women to God—was that we must have at heart the unity of all believers.

"Next, I think it's absolutely necessary for the Holy Father to discuss the concept of 'sin' once more, because that has been lost sight of in today's world. He could remind all of God's abhorrence of sin, perhaps by quoting Our Lord's words that 'out of the heart come evil thoughts, murder, adultery, fornication, theft, false witness, and slander,' thereby defiling a person. And, of course, I would mention the many sins which the Holy Father himself has decried in the past."

Cardinal Latoya laid down his pen and asked, "And the remedy for these sins is to be *what*, Father? The sacrament of Reconciliation and Penance, I assume?"

"Yes—with a modification I would propose, Your Eminence," Fr. Santorelli replied. "If you had asked me a week ago, before the Warning began, whether I would approve of a new penitential rite, I would certainly have said 'No'. The change in my thinking has been caused by a factor which I believe is of overriding importance—the second part of the message I received from the Lord in Garabandal. I ask you to think about it this way: that part *could* have consisted of a citation to John 20:23, which, as you know, was the commission of the risen Christ to the Apostles: 'if you forgive the sins of any, they are forgiven; if you retain the sins of any, they are retained.'—Eminence, do you see how profoundly that passage differs from the citation actually given me from the First Letter of St. John: 'If we acknowledge our sins, He who is just can be trusted to forgive our sins and cleanse us from every wrong.'?"

"I'm afraid I don't, Father," said His Eminence. "Tell me what you have in mind."

"John 20:23 empowers *priests* to give *or withhold* absolution for sins—and that decision obviously can be made only on the basis of the circumstances related by an individual regarding his own acts, and his own contrition and willingness to amend his life. *If that verse* of Scripture had been cited, I would have had no doubt that *individual confession* was being called for in response to the Warning.

"*But the citation actually given to me, the verse in the First Letter of St. John, merely calls for the acknowledgment of sins—and then it leaves it up to the Lord to forgive and cleanse us from them.* Eminence, I beg you to consider how appropriate this solution would be, given that so many Christians are not in communion with us and would not be availing themselves of our sacrament of Reconciliation and Penance in any event . . . "

His Eminence was surprised by the tack which Fr. Santorelli was embarking on. He had expected that the priest would propose one of the nostrums constantly being urged by the dissidents in America—including dealing with the shortage of priests by returning to good standing the married priests who had been laicized—but what he had just heard was a novel idea. It was worth at least exploring what Fr. Santorelli had in mind.

"Exactly what are you proposing, Father?" the Cardinal asked. "What is it you would have sinners do?"

"I suggest that the Holy Father quote the Scriptural passage which was cited to me, and say that there are a number of ways in which sins could be acknowledged. The one ordinarily of most benefit to the penitent would be through individual confession to a priest, because the priest could help the penitent to understand the nature of his sin, and could tailor a penance to the circumstances. Naturally, the Holy Father should present that as the best alternative. However, where that was not possible, some form of a *communal* penance service should be the next choice."

"When even that was impossible a *private* acknowledgment of sin would suffice, *provided that three elements were present.* First, unless he was physically unable to do so, the penitent must go to a Christian church—*any Christian church*—and there must honestly search his conscience and call to mind his sins, especially those shown him by the Warning vision. Second, he must resolve to avoid those sins in the future. And finally, he must look upon or touch a crucifix, or at least a picture of Jesus on the Cross, and repeat the following words: '*Jesus, I trust in you. Have mercy on me, a sinner.*'"

That was quite a proposal for Cardinal Latoya to ponder! He knew that the Pope had struggled against the current for years to preserve the requirement of individual confession in cases of grave sin. He had supported the Pope in turning back suggestions by many in the hierarchy for adoption of general absolution as an equally acceptable alternative rite. Now, he was being bearded in his den by a priest half his age—one who had been a lowly prison chaplain in America only the week before. Yes, auricular confession would be preserved in theory by the proposal he had just heard, but he could foresee that it would quickly be eliminated in practice, just as the Tridentine Mass had been forsaken when the new, vernacular Mass was introduced.

The Cardinal tried to put aside the battles of the past. To be fair, Fr. Santorelli was not arguing that centuries of practice should be set aside for the oft-voiced, pragmatic reason that people had all but abandoned the confessional booth themselves. Rather, he was proposing it to meet a totally new circumstance—the objective reality of the Warning—in the light of what he believed God now wanted. And it was evident that he had drawn up his proposal with great care. "*Jesus, I trust in you*," was the phrase famous for accompanying the image of the resurrected Jesus with rays of white and red emanating from his breast, an image venerated by the Church on Divine Mercy Sunday. And, everyone would recognize the words from St. Luke's Gospel, "*have mercy on me, a sinner*," as those of the tax collector whom Jesus had observed as he stood in the Temple, beating his breast, not daring to raise his eyes to heaven.

"*He went away justified!*" Those words came to Cardinal La-toya's mind and would not go away.

Was that the key? wondered the Cardinal. Jesus himself had said that the tax collector had been justified by acknowledging his sins in the sight of God, and begging for mercy! Why would that not do for the present? Particularly when the verse from John's letter said that "he who is just can be trusted to forgive our sins *and cleanse us from every wrong*." So, if there was acknowledgment of sins, there would be a cleansing, however that might be brought about—whether by the instrumentality of the Church or by the Holy Spirit acting directly.

Moreover, there was a great benefit to what Father was recommending—it was open to Christians of all denominations. No one could complain that the Pope was prescribing medicine which only a Catholic pharmacy could dispense!

Cardinal Latoya decided that he needed to pray over the suggestions he had heard, and he dismissed the two clerics with his thanks.

*   *   *

Msgr. Ireland was walking on air as they left the Prefect's office. "Whichever way the Pope goes on the reconciliation rite, it's going to be a terrific letter! *This is a time of grace, and by God, we're going to capitalize on it!*—Tony, I'm so glad I thought of asking you to come help me! I owe you something—something better than another gourmet meal which you only nibble at. Is there anything you'd like me to do for you?"

Fr. Santorelli didn't take long to respond. "I'm thrilled that His Eminence is willing to transfer me here to assist you at the Congregation. If there comes a time when I'm no longer needed, I'd love to teach at the Gregorian, as you did! That may be the real reason why God arranged to have you call me back to Rome.—Do you think you could pull the necessary strings for me?"

The prelate's face fell.

"Tony, I'd love to say, 'Yes,'—but we have to take account of your stigmata.—It's one thing to be buried away in the Curia as my assistant, out of the limelight. It's another to have to deal with dozens of other faculty members, maybe hundreds of students, and who knows how many journalists, members of the public, et cetera, all curious about you and your charism. You wouldn't be able to have the ordered existence which I found so important to scholarly life.—Don't forget that Padre Pio was tucked away in a remote friary, and access to him was limited. Other stigmatists that I've started to read about, such as Therese Neumann and Marthe Robin, also were secluded.—Of course, I'm not saying you *couldn't* pull off teaching in a university—just that we need to think the problems through thoroughly before I try to arrange it."

Fr. Santorelli was hard put not to show his disappointment. He felt that he was entitled to unqualified support from his mentor.

"I'm not as concerned as you are about the stigmata, Monsignor," he managed to say, in an even tone. "Now that the Holy Father has accepted the message I brought from Garabandal, my hope is that they'll shortly become invisible again. My guess is that they've served their purpose. Only a few people have seen them, so if the marks do disappear, even if I still bear the wounds internally, the public will never know about them . . . "

Left unmentioned by the priest were the Lord's words to him, that *he* would be used to offer the choice of life or death to many. He had been praying that it would come about through the teaching ministry that he so much desired. With that intention in mind, after they parted he began his daily recitation of the Rosary, as he slowly walked back to the Pallottine Sisters' pension.

The easy part was crossing St. Peter's Square and taking the pedestrian tunnel under the Via Porta Cavalleggeri to the base of the Janiculum hill. There he began a steep climb, one made considerably more difficult for him by the broken and uneven pavement and sidewalk. Thirty minutes later, he arrived at the beginning of the driveway that served three similar apartment buildings, including the pension, below road level. The way down was hard on his wounded feet as his weight was thrust off his heels and onto his soles. Halfway down, he turned and went down the rest of the way sideways.

The sister who buzzed him in the front door came out from behind the reception desk. "Ah, there you are, Father," she said. "You ran out this morning before I could catch you. We require that our guests pay every day, and you are *four* days behind."

"Didn't the Monsignor who arranged for my stay agree that you could charge it to him?"

"No, Father, and we only accept cash—no credit cards. That will be 260 euros, please."

He pulled out his wallet. He could cover the bill with what he had left over from his trip, but not much more. Only one more night, in fact. And the few thousand dollars he had in his checking account back in California wouldn't last long over here. The incongruity of the situation struck him. Only a few days ago the supreme leader of the Church had granted him an audience in the room where heads of state were received—and now he was wondering if he'd have a place to sleep by the end of the week.

It shouldn't have come as a surprise. None of the stigmatists, from St. Francis on down, had had a cent to their name. Still, financial insecurity was a new experience for him, and he didn't like feeling needy. Perhaps the Lord was teaching him a lesson: "You preached to others that *they* should trust in Me—now it's *your* turn to do likewise."

— 11 —

Rome

One of the few clerics to see the Holy Father almost daily was his second in command, Cardinal Giuseppe Malapensa, the Vatican's Secretary of State. Like other men in their early seventies, he had shrunk in physical stature, to only five foot eight, and retained just a fringe of thin white hair. Yet, he still was a compelling presence, with his parchment-white skin, blue eyes, Roman nose, and high forehead. These patrician features he had inherited from his Milanese mother, along with a generous share of the family's fortune, which he had put to good use over the years in advancing his ecclesiastical career.

His working meetings with the Pope were usually held in the latter's office. The Pope would sit with his back to an enormous open bookcase, crammed with part of his own collection of books, and the Secretary of State would face him, on the other side of the Pope's cluttered desk. Laid out, along with official papers for the Pope to read or sign, there were always new texts of his own which he was working on. That secretly angered the Cardinal. Ratzinger had continued as Pope in the same vein as he had throughout his career—churning out one book after another, as though what people wanted or needed was yet another erudite exposition of platonic concepts like truth and faith, and hope and reason. The Secretary of State often complained to members of his circle that the Pope was a modern day King Canute, foolishly seeking to stem the incoming tide of secular rationalism, which had almost covered the western world, by erecting paper barriers made up of his own writings.

And now, or so he had heard—for the Pope had not discussed the matter with him—Ratzinger was engaged in defining yet another Marian dogma. Malapensa was convinced that its pro-mulgation would doom all the Church's ecumenical projects now beginning to bear fruit, and end any possibility of arriving at a universal religion by consensus with other faiths. The projected Apostolic Constitution had to be stopped at all costs—if only Malapensa could figure out how!

In the meantime, he had an urgent matter to attend to, which was deterring the Pope from responding publicly to the visions. After finishing his other business with the Pope, Malapensa brought them up. "Holiness, no doubt the media will be asking the Church's view of these reports of perverse visions, and I would hope that you would not keep the matter alive by giving the reports any credence."

It was a longstanding practice of Benedict XVIth, dating back to his years as a seminary professor, to listen courteously to views he disagreed with, so he asked, "Do you not believe that the reports are genuine, Eminence?"

Cardinal Malapensa did not bother to disguise a sneer. "They strain credulity, do they not, Holiness . . . ? Besides, the purported apparitions at Garabandal never received approval. Indeed, the Bishop at the time they occurred did not believe that there was any supernatural occurrence. Out of nothing, nothing comes."

"Then, how do you think it happens that the reports are coming in from all over, Eminence—not just from the recent group of pilgrims to Garabandal? I've seen accounts which speak of thousands of people having experienced visions in different countries."

The Cardinal had a ready answer. "The media also publish reports of flying saucer sightings from time to time. Perhaps, Holiness, this so-called Warning began with someone's nightmare. Once that was given publicity, many other people decided to seek a bit of attention with their own imagined accounts, each one more lurid and fantastic than the previous one. You know how many spurious reports there are all over the world of appearances of our Blessed Mother, and how they confuse the gullible little ones. This may be one of those situations where it takes us years to sort out the truth, and in the meantime, Holiness, nothing will be lost by telling the Faithful to ignore the reports. Indeed, it would be beneficial to do so because it would put their fears to rest that such visions might be real."

"Have you considered, Eminence, the possibility that the visions might truly be a warning from God?"

"I cannot even *begin* to imagine that possibility, Holiness," replied the Cardinal, with disdain in his voice.

"Why is that, Eminence?" the Pope inquired.

"Because there is no record in the entire history of the Church of any visions being given to a multitude of *ordinary* people. If you go back through the Old Testament all the way to Adam, you will see that God has *never* acted in such fashion. *Divine visions have been experienced only by a few, especially enlightened, souls."*

The Pope was not pleased by the Cardinal's dismissive attitude, but he replied with more mildness than he felt. "Are not the common people worthy of such enlightenment, if God chooses to grant it? After all, did not Moses express the wish to Joshua that all the people of the Lord were prophets?"

Those questions were left unanswered, as chagrin replaced haughtiness on the Cardinal's face. "Holiness, permit me to express my concern at your willingness to consider that these so-called visions come from God. *If I may speak frankly, one of the reasons why people who are baptized Catholic leave the Church when they grow up is that they regard our Faith as one unduly shaped by mysticism rather than reason."*

That brought a pointed retort from the Pope: *"Eminence, our Church was not built upon reason. It was built upon revelation— revelation of mysteries which reason could never have arrived at."*

"The revelation of which you speak is *public revelation*, is it not, Holiness? And that ended with the Age of the Apostles."

"So it did, Eminence," replied the Pope, "but private revelations have continued. And in some cases, the Church has expressed its judgment that the private revelation is worthy of belief, and it has even canonized the visionary."

Cardinal Malapensa had yet another comeback. "Of course, as I hope you would agree, if the purported 'revelation' is only a bad dream, or is the product of some mass hysteria, it needs to be promptly rejected."

"Yes, I agree with that, Eminence. That is why what we need now is to discern accurately the source of these visions. And if they are genuine and come from God, then we must not deny them."

Cardinal Malapensa had become increasingly alarmed by the Pope's firm stance. *"Holiness, I beg you not to comment on this novel phenomenon at this time!* You would greatly discredit the whole Church if you were to be seen as authenticating the visions—and then some sort of chicanery or manipulation were revealed to be behind them ... "

"Your prudential concerns are duly noted, Eminence, and I will reflect upon them. As always, I am grateful for your advice," said the Pope, unmistakably bringing their conversation to an end.

— 12 —

Tehran, Iran
8 Bahman 1393 Anno Persico; 28 January 2015 Anno Domini

The visions had spread beyond Europe, to the greatly oppressed Armenians and Assyrians living in Iran. Unfortunately for them, their contagious joy and encouragement at this manifestation of God's grace quickly came to the attention of the secret police, and thence to the Revolutionary Guards Corps. The Ministry of Intelligence and Security had several Christian priests from each community brought in to Evin Prison, where they were interrogated without constraint in the infamous Ward 209. The priests did not deny having seen visions, and they readily admitted these bolstered their faith in Isā, whom they called Jesus, but they went to their death claiming they had no idea of how the visions had come to them and their people, or who had sent them. This left an unresolved mystery and a menace, which required the personal attention of General Ali Hashemi.

*   *   *

Allāhu Akbar!
Yes! A feeling of power surged through Ali Hashemi as his grey blue eyes went from his country's flag, where the exultation, "God is the Greatest!" was repeated twenty-two times in stylized Arabic lettering, across his office to the map spread out on his desk. He moved his index finger slowly, tracing once again the outline of the Persian Empire of old. It spread out from Iran itself, east to Pakistan and Afghanistan, north and then west to Tajikistan, Kyrgyzstan, Uzbekistan, Turkmenistan, Azerbijan, Georgia, Armenia, and Turkey, down to Syria, Iraq, Jordan, Lebanon, and Israel. Here, his finger paused while he uttered a malediction, before continuing the great loop to include Egypt, and parts of Libya, Greece, and Bulgaria.
Ali was a doer, not a dreamer, but he did have one dream. It was that those countries, whose boundaries and whose very names were chosen by unbelievers, and the other lands on the

Arabian peninsula, would all be folded into a new caliphate under Iran's Supreme Leader! *Ali was confident it would happen one day, through his own hand on the Sword of Allāh*—the sword represented on the Iranian flag, with a tashdid over it, doubling its power!

He did not mourn the fate of the ancient Empire. It was the will of Allāh that it had fallen. The people had worshipped false gods—Ahura Mazda, Mithra and Anihita. Gods made of silver and gold, iron and clay, whose statues were merely curiosities in Tehran's Archaeological Museum. When the Islamic Revolution totally achieved its goal, throughout the entire region the only worship would be that of Allāh, the one true God, who had been proclaimed by the Prophet Mohammed (Blessed be he)!

It seemed to Ali that he had been born to be a warrior. His father had been killed in Saddam Hussein's genocidal war against Iran, and he had been raised by his uncle, Muhammad, a cleric, who didn't quite know what to do with the scrappy little boy. After his enlistment in the Army was over, with Muhammad vouching for his revolutionary ideals, Ali had joined the Qods Force of the Revolutionary Guards Corps. He was strong, but no stronger than others, and modestly intelligent, certainly not as smart as some. But he had a certain charisma, a fierce, almost animal wildness. If anyone was going on a dangerous mission and had the choice of who would go with him, it would be Ali. And he had no compunctions about firing rockets at civilian targets and planting car bombs in the marketplace. Eventually, he was rewarded with command by his superiors because they saw that he was a perfect role model for the men in the Force.

As the head of the Qods Force, Ali was in charge of forcibly exporting the Revolution throughout the Middle East, undermining the efforts of the United States to bring about secular societies friendly to the west, and fomenting the struggle against the occupation of Palestine by the "Zionist pigs." Through its own military operations, and by training, arming and financing foreign jihadists, the Qods Force had extended Shiite rule beyond Iran itself, to the Afghani province of Herat in the east, and to parts of Iraq in the west—with far flung islands of influence in the Levant and Bosnia.

He knew that many guerilla operations lay ahead of his men in the Gaza Strip and the West Bank, before a full scale assault on Israel could be mounted. He himself had been in the forefront of that fight until he was wounded by a missile from an Israeli Air Force helicopter, which struck the building where he was meeting with Hezbollah leaders. While the long term struggle against the Zionist state would have to continue, Ali was developing a new and surprising conviction that there was an even more important target requiring the attention of the Qods Force.

The Jews, as loathsome as they were, were not idolators: they too believed in only one God. And, the Jews did not proselytize. Once the Zionist entity had been crushed, the individual Jews who had survived could safely be allowed to live in ghettos within the ruling Islamic society, as they had done centuries ago in North Africa and Spain.

It was Christians who were the greatest enemies of the Islamic Revolution, there being no more resolute and powerful obstacle to the spread of Islam than the Roman Catholic Church. The Church was still the defender of Europe's alleged "Christian identity" and claimed a special place for that faith. Worse yet, it had the temerity to seek converts throughout the world, even in Muslim countries, while it was engaging in a "dialogue" with representatives of Islam to divide the Muslim world.

Ali had been steeped since his childhood in tales of the humiliations which the forces of Islam had suffered at the hands of the Church. How could he help but think now of the Crusades, which the Roman Catholic Church had sponsored to take away lands claimed for Allāh? Or of the reconquest of Spain by Catholics from the Moors, or the decisive victory of the Holy League over the Turks in the great naval battle of the Gulf of Corinth, which prevented Islam from dominating the Mediterranean Sea? Although these wars had taken place centuries ago, they were wounds deliberately kept alive in the collective memory of Muslims.

A man whom Ali revered as a hero, Mehmet Ali Agca, had acted out of just such a sense of past humiliations inflicted by Christians. In November 1979, Agca wrote to a newspaper in Turkey protesting the then forthcoming visit of the Pope to that country: "Western imperialists ... are sending to Turkey at this delicate moment the Commander of the Crusades, John Paul, disguised as a religious leader. If this visit is not called off, I will definitely kill the Commander-pope." Agca did not strike on that visit, but he did less than two years later in St. Peter's Square. It was a plot formed in Tehran as an act of jihad, and Agca trained for it in Iran, before his masters routed him through other countries in an effort to prevent the world from discovering who was behind the assassination. His shots would have killed the Pope, but for what John Paul II believed to be a miracle brought about by the virgin Marium, the mother of Isā.

Thinking of that brought Ali back to the bedrock of his faith, the Qur'an. There, in the fifth Sura, the Prophet (Blessed be he!) had written:

> And when Allāh will say: O Isā son of Marium! did you say to men, *Take me and my mother for two gods besides Allāh*, he [Isā] will say: *Glory be to Thee, it did not befit me that I should say what I had no right to say* . . .

But, Catholics did not accept the teaching of the Qur'an that there is no God but *Allāh*, for they worshiped Marium's son as "God"— and they worshiped her too, or so he mistakenly thought, as "the Mother of God."

Putting all this together, it was obvious to Ali—*Who but Roman Catholics could be responsible for the blasphemous visions which had forced their way into the Islamic Republic of Iran?* To be sure, Ali was not afraid of what they might inspire the Christian minorities to do, for these were unarmed and insignificant, and forbidden to make converts upon pain of death; they could easily be driven into exile, or exterminated if need be. Rather, the danger he foresaw was that similar visions could be sent to proselytize and unsettle the followers of the Prophet (Blessed be he!). Perhaps such affronts were even now being planned!

It was up to Ali to wield the Sword of Allāh against the idolators!

— 13 —

United States

At last! Christians who previously had not seen a vision were caught up in one in the early morning hours. Each vision lasted only seconds in terms of time off the clock, yet time was elongated for the person seeing one. It seemed to last several minutes, and then the vision vanished without a trace—other than the person's indelible memory of the experience. What they saw, and how they came to see it, was enough to leave most people shaking.

One of them called the Vatican—a cousin whom Msgr. Ireland rarely heard from.

"Johnny—it's your Cousin Frank—in Beantown.—*I just had to call you about what's happening here!*"

"You sound like it's the Second Coming," replied the prelate, with a chuckle.

"Sure, and maybe it is! Maybe it is! The visions, Johnny!— They're here! Just like what we've been reading about over where you are."

"What did you see, Frank? Maybe some devils?"

Frank hesitated in answering. "Things I really didn't want to. Things I'd done I'd forgotten about.—That's what's happening to everybody—and they're scared out of their minds."

"Who says?"

"They do. I've been listening to talk radio—you should hear what people are saying! I've never heard anything like it! And, I have to tell you, Johnny, they're mad as hell! They want the government to do something to stop the visions. They've been calling 911 for help—the lines are jammed."

"Good luck on that!" said the prelate with a laugh. "The emergency people are useless—they should be looking for a priest to confess to."

"Yes—you *would* say that, Johnny.—Well, I don't think *that's* in the cards for them."

"How about *you*, Frank?" the prelate inquired gently.

There was an awkward silence, but Frank did respond. "It's been too many years, Johnny. I'd be embarrassed to go to one now."

"Would you be embarrassed to confess to me?"

Another silence. "I guess maybe not, but you're over in Rome."

"I know you and I can hear you loud and clear over the phone—and I'm sure the absolution I'll extend will wing it's way to you. Why don't you start out by telling me what you saw in your vision?"

Hanging up a half hour later, Msgr. Ireland was elated. What he had done was unorthodox, but it had worked. Why not call all of his other relatives in the States to see how *they* were doing . . . ?

*   *   *

Televangelists were in their glory talking about the wrath of God—the coming fire and brimstone! This was the culmination of their life's work—a time when God himself was validating their preaching through the visions He was sending. The TV pastors would have liked to have a parade of sinners trotting before the cameras to tell their own poignant stories of sin and redemption, but the first penitents, who indiscreetly blurted something out, soon learned just how many people they knew had been tuned in. An employer, a friend—or perhaps a spouse! Very quickly, it seemed that no one wanted to confess *their* particular sins in public. While it was commendable to give witness to the Lord, it wasn't worth exposing one's secret shame. So, the preachers had to be content with euphemisms referring to unsavory conduct.

Religious fundamentalists who were enamored of the *Left Behind* series of novels were thrilled at the apparent corroboration that the visions gave to their expectation that sinners would meet a gruesome end on Judgment Day. They went to their bookshelves and pulled out their copies of the *Glorious Appearing* novel, to revel again in the scenes of non-Christians being splayed and filleted in the streets, eyes melted and tongues disintegrated, at the word of Jesus at his Second Coming. Come Lord! *Marana tha!*

A glimmer of light came from the Eternal Word Television Network. Its lead news anchor was interviewing a noted grey-robed friar about the phenomenon. Could he explain it? Yes, he could, and he did. It was, he said, *"The Warning,"* sent in fulfillment of what had been told four little girls at a Marian apparition in Garabandal, Spain, back in 1961. The Warning would be followed by a great Miracle, and very possibly a Chastisement. From that hour forward, the visions were always referred to in the media as *"the Warning."* Better and better, thought the television producers, and they promptly sent camera crews out to hunt down the three surviving original visionaries, who were forced to go into hiding.

*   *   *

The editors of the N.Y. Times, while eager to blame someone, were still of mixed mind about who that someone was, and they chose a safe target for their barbs:

What Homeland Security?
The deficiencies of the Department of Homeland Security are plain for all to see. It is unable to protect us from unwanted intrusion in our homes and offices. The inmost core of our being—our mind—is being invaded by a so-called "Warning." Yet, this huge bureaucracy, which spends more than 60 billion dollars a year, is next to useless. It has no clue as to who is causing the assaults, how they are being transmitted, or what can be done to stop them. We do not buy the explanation being floated by some Administration officials that the visions are simply a product of mass hysteria. Rather than viewing mass hysteria as a *cause*, we worry that it will be a *result* of the visions, as people grow frustrated at being forced to watch them.
The Administration's failure extends beyond this one hapless agency, for surely a weapon of this sort, wielded on a global basis, must have been developed over a period of years, and there must have been clues which the CIA and other intelligence agencies could and should have picked up. That is, unless they are still focused on searching for weapons of mass destruction in the Iraqi desert . . .
Not a single agency of Government has acknowledged responsibility for getting to the bottom of this

dire situation. Mr. President—this buck stops with
you!

*   *   *

The public's agitation—and the N.Y. Times editorial—put pressure
on the White House to address the issue, hopefully with a solution.
Not having one in hand, President Gardiner could see the wisdom
in keeping himself distant from the problem, so he directed the
smartest man in Washington, his Chief of Staff, Bernard Cohen,
to take charge. Bernie quickly named a working group comprised
of the Secretaries of Defense and Homeland Security, the Director
of National Intelligence, and the Attorney General, and he invited
them to the White House. It was an invitation they could not
decline.

When they were all together in his office, Bernie cut to the
chase, asking three questions:

"Is there any domestic group that could possibly be sending
out the visions?"

"Is there any foreign group or country that could possibly be
doing it?"

"Are you aware from electronic surveillance of any message
from anyone, anywhere in the world, which indicates any knowledge of who is causing this, or how it's being done?"

None of the four officials answered any of the questions in
the affirmative. Bernie hadn't expected that they would, but he
needed to ask them for the record, to document that the President was keeping himself fully informed and that these men had
been given the opportunity to tell whatever they knew. He could
foresee that Congress would eventually second guess whatever
the Administration did or failed to do.

Bernie then turned to George Haley, the square-jawed head of
Homeland Security, hoping he could pull something—*anything*—
out of his hat. It didn't need to be a *whole* rabbit, even part of one
would do for starters.

"Given *what's* happened and *how* it's happened, I think everybody is straining awfully hard to avoid the obvious," Haley
said.

"And that is . . . ?" asked Bernie.

"That is—these visions are being sent by God, and no power on earth is going to stop them."

There it was, out in the open, the 'God' word—dreaded by politicians and bureaucrats of all persuasions! It was not a word much used in the White House since the Presidency of George W. Bush, because of the politically unacceptable baggage it brought with it. The other four men looked at Haley as though he had let loose an enormous Senate-bean-soup fart.

It wasn't a momentary inspiration on his part. Haley had been brought up in the Bible Belt, and had heard his share of sermons before he had gotten into politics and had no more time to attend church. Seeing their discomfiture, he sought to explain himself.

"I don't see why that should be such a problem. It's as obvious as the nose on your face. We can't disown God—the public refuses to give up the motto we've got on our quarters. And we keep talking about the 'Judeo-Christian tradition of the Founding Fathers.' *Well, damn it—visions from God are part of that tradition, whether we like the ones we're seeing now or not!"*

Damn it, indeed! What Haley said made some sense, but it was unclear where he was going with the idea, and pitfalls abounded. "George," said Bernie, "that's an interesting thought—do you have any suggestion about what we can do, if you're right?"

George rose to the occasion. "I seem to recall that the Bible tells of a great Hebrew teacher giving advice to the authorities about what to do with the Apostles."—"This was after the Resurrection," he added, for the benefit of Bernie.—"Something to the effect that, if what the Apostles were doing was through the hand of God, then they could not be opposed successfully, and fighting them would be fighting God. And, if they were only acting on their own, why, then, they could be left alone safely because they would be bound to fail anyway.—It seems to me that that approach could be taken here."

On first thought, Bernie reacted negatively to this counsel. "George, the problem is that people are worried and angry. They want something done. The President has to say *something!* Didn't you read that New York Times editorial, 'The Buck Stops Here'?"

The others, having no suggestion to offer, sat there in silence.

Bernie then had a second thought. "Unless ...," he said, rethinking fast.

Unless *what?* they all wondered.

"Unless we follow George's suggestion, and take the position that these visions involve matters of religion and the consciences of individual citizens. That being the case, we are precluded from taking any action lest we breach the Constitutionally mandated wall between church and state! Any cure we attempt for the visions might be unconstitutional."

"Bernie, you're *brilliant!*" said George, relieved to be off the hook. It was a sentiment that the President himself would voice when he heard the idea. The longer that his options could be kept open, the better.

"If you take that tack," offered the Attorney General, "you might want to couple it with the thought that even having the Government investigate these visions would necessarily infringe on the right of privacy. You could raise the specter of the FBI going around questioning people about what their visions revealed. If the matters in the visions concerned their misdeeds, maybe even crimes, our questioning them would be like asking people for a confession.—Would we have to read them their Miranda rights before talking to them?"

"Great thought!" congratulated Bernie. "We all know the groups that would go ballistic if they heard we were going to launch that kind of an investigation! But, without ascertaining the facts from individuals as to what they saw, and what they understood it to mean, how could we be expected to take action?"

After the four visitors were dismissed, Bernie called in the White House Chief Counsel, explained the situation, and asked him to craft a legal opinion laying out the problems which precluded President Gardiner from taking action right then. It would be a good handout for the press to accompany the public statement he would draft for the President to make the next day.

Alone in his office again, the smartest man in Washington sat back with relief. 'We might dodge this problem after all,' he thought. 'The Left can't complain about a President who upholds the Right of Privacy, and the Right can't complain about a President who upholds the Freedom of Religion!'

— 14 —

Rome

The Holy Father would have liked another few days to polish his Apostolic Letter, but the Vatican Press Officer had warned him that time had run out if he wanted to shape the Church's response for the media. Already, the secular commentators were using the Warning as an occasion for bashing the Catholic Church, it being the main institution which still pretended that there was a God who cared about the "sinful" behavior of individuals.

Juan Gariega began the morning press conference by issuing, in the Pope's name, a flat denial of any Church involvement in bringing about the Warning, or any control over it. He then handed out copies of the Pope's Apostolic Letter addressed to "All Who Have Been Baptized Into the Body of Jesus Christ." Many of Fr. Santorelli's suggestions had been incorporated, from the wording of the first sentence, to his formula for acknowledging sins. Of course, the Pope had crafted the letter in his own way and added additional thoughts, especially requirements as to what steps a penitent should take to evidence true contrition and a purpose to avoid sin in the future. Specific suggestions were made for those in certain occupations, including politicians and government officials, health care workers, and those required by Canon Law to make the Profession of Faith.

The Apostolic Letter was only four pages long, and it did not take the assembled reporters long to go through it. There were howls of disapproval, totally out of keeping with the decorum traditional at such a gathering, and questions were shouted out imperiously.

Q. Is the Pope telling leaders of other religions how they should act?

A. Not at all. His message is addressed to individual Christians. In Christian charity, he is suggesting to them how they might take advantage of the great grace now being offered.

Q. Is the Pope going to excommunicate Catholics who refuse to go to confession?

A. Of course not, but Catholics already have an obligation to confess serious sins.

Q. Has the Curia approved this?

A. His Holiness did consult with certain members of the Curia, but the views are his own.

Q. Does the Pope believe in the prophecies of Garabandal?

A. He neither believes nor disbelieves. He is awaiting future events, and a future judgment by competent authorities, and the Faithful should do likewise.

Q. Is the Pope going to go to Garabandal?

A. He has no plans to do so.

Q. Has the Pope himself received a "Warning" vision?

A. I have no knowledge about that.

When the press saw that they weren't getting anything further of value by questioning the Press Officer, all but one bolted out of the room to dictate their stories and fax a copy of the Pope's missive. The one who remained was a correspondent for *Inside the Vatican*, a monthly publication which specialized in reporting the inside stories of what was going on there.

She had noted that Msgr. Ireland had been standing off to the side, observing the press conference, and knowing his position in the Curia, she wanted to ask him if he could shed any additional light on the Pope's statement. In particular, what would the Monsignor say to people who had trouble giving credence to visions?

To her surprise, he was willing to give a substantive response.

"I would start out by saying that there is a spiritual realm not found in our space-time universe, a realm which breaks through into our universe in ways which we only sometimes recognize. Often it is by means of apparitions or visions which contain a message from God. They are an absolutely integral part of our Christian religion—because we believe in a God who is constantly involved in our affairs—though of course we must prudently test new visions as they are received to ascertain if they truly are of divine origin.

"There are many familiar examples in the Old Testament— Moses and the burning bush, Jacob's ladder extending to heaven,

Elijah being taken there in a fiery chariot, Ezekiel in the valley of dry bones, the detached hand which wrote on the wall at Belshazzar's feast, and so forth. And the New Testament story begins with Zechariah's vision in the Temple, foretelling the son his wife Elizabeth will conceive. Then, of course, we have the vision of the angel Gabriel coming to Mary, the star of Bethlehem, angels in the fields, Joseph's visions, and the vision which Jesus' closest disciples had of the Transfiguration. And who can forget the visions St. Paul had, or the whole Book of Revelation—which is about one long vision. So, I would say to them that if they are determined to ignore visions as being untrustworthy, they will wind up cutting so much out of the Bible that it will look like a Swiss cheese!"

*   *   *

An article in the next day's edition of *La Repubblica* set tongues wagging in Rome about a mutiny in the Pope's own household. Although the copy bore the byline of a commentator well known for his anti-clerical sentiments, it purported to report the sentiments of a "highly placed Vatican source," who reacted negatively to the Pope's Apostolic Letter.

Among the choice quotes from the anonymous prelate was the judgment that, "If the visions have a supernatural origin, as some say, they should be regarded as the work of the Devil, not God. They encourage people to the vice of *hyperscrupulosity*—an unnatural concern with sin which takes the joy out of the everyday activities of life. It creates among those affected a sort of paranoia, focused on a dreaded god who is always looking over one's shoulder." To give in to the visions and go to confession for what one did not personally consider sinful, according to the secret Vatican source, "would be to turn oneself into a puppet jerked about by strings pulled by an unseen puppet master." A final kick at the Holy Father came in the columnist's last sentence: "With all the real world problems facing the Church, the Pope's diversion of attention to deal with this transitory and ephemeral phenomenon shows that he is losing touch with reality."

— 15 —

Rome

The Pope was continuing to grapple with the message Fr. Santorelli had brought him. In his Apostolic Letter, he had already
dealt with the first two Scriptural passages—the ones which referred to a person's hidden sins, and to Jesus' desire to cleanse His
followers if they acknowledged their sins to Him. The Pope's attention was now focused on the third passage—"Kings on earth rise
up and princes plot together against the Lord and His anointed"—
and he requested another session with Msgr. Ireland and Fr.
Santorelli to get their counsel. Now at ease with them, he had
Msgr. Waldheim show them into the Papal Library again.

"I would be grateful to hear your interpretation of the third
passage," said the Pope. "Do you anticipate there will be a plot
only against me—or a more general one against the Church?"

Fr. Santorelli shot a quick glance at Msgr. Ireland, who nodded
to indicate that he should be the one to answer the question.

"The latter, Holiness. If the impending danger were directed
solely at your person, the fourth passage of the message, referring
to you being carried away against your will, would have sufficed.
It seems to us that the third part of the message, relating to
plotting against 'the Lord's anointed,' refers to plotting against the
clergy or the Church generally. And the hostile action will be not
just by individuals but, from the Scriptural reference to kings and
princes, by governments."

"You don't *really* think there's a threat to the continued existence of the Vatican, do you Father?" the Pope asked.

"Yes, Holiness—both of us do, though in very different ways,"
came the answer.

The Pope frowned. "Since we are only a small island in the
City of Rome, action against us would necessitate an attack on
Italy too, would it not, Father?"

"Not necessarily, Holiness," the priest replied. "Msgr. Ireland
doesn't foresee a war or that type of physical destruction, so much
as a move by Italy prompted by the European Union to finish
the effort begun in the *Risorgimento* to take away all of the Holy

See's territories. You personally, and our Church as a whole, are a reproach and an obstacle to the secular governments of Europe and the new paganism they promote. The continued existence of the Vatican as an international state is a bone in more than a few throats."

His Holiness looked incredulous. Turning to the prelate, he asked, "Monsignor, have you considered that the Republic of Italy has a Treaty of Conciliation with us which recognizes the sovereignty of the Holy See? It took fifty years to negotiate that after the civil war. You aren't suggesting that the Government of Italy would break those solemn promises, are you?"

"Treaties *do* get violated from time to time, Holiness," the prelate replied without hesitation. "That's one of the ways that wars start. The Italian people, of course, are devoted to the Church, but I'm concerned about what that *Bolshevik* they have as their Prime Minister might do.—*I don't doubt that he's thought of abrogating the treaty and annexing the Vatican's territory—and expropriating all the Church's assets he can lay his hands on.* When the Bolsheviks took over Russia, they didn't destroy the churches and seminaries. They took them over and used them for public purposes, whether as museums or stables for their horses. If Italy moved in and seized St. Peter's, the Socialists would probably set up in the basilica the pagan art in the Vatican's collection, while they trashed the precious relics and statues of saints."

The Pope looked at Fr. Santorelli to see if he had anything to add.

"Holiness, I, on the other hand, do anticipate significant destruction and loss of life—that seems to me to be what is foretold by other parts of the message I brought to you. I can't say I see a hostile army marching on Rome, but, as you know, Rome has been sacked more than once by invading forces—including by the Muslims in 846, when they carried away the treasures of St. Peter's. Indeed, the Muslims might even now hold the city if they had not been defeated at the Battle of Lepanto. You can imagine what they would have done to St. Peter's if they had won—they would have turned it into a mosque like the great Santa Sophia basilica in Istanbul. Even in our own times, Hitler ordered his general in charge of the Nazi occupation of Rome to burn the city as he retreated—an order he ignored, thank God!

"I also think that the coming destruction will decimate the hierarchy of the Church—I suspect that's the persecution referred to in the fifth part of the message. However, I can't figure out any precaution to recommend that you take with regard to your people. You probably would be thought mad if you ordered the Curia and staff to evacuate their offices and sit around somewhere else until an 'all clear' was sounded."

The Pope shook his head from side to side. "This is all too much to consider deciding at the moment. But, tell me, do you think I should take steps to protect the sacred relics and the artistic treasures here, at least those that can be moved?"

In the hope that he would be asked that question, Fr. Santorelli had come prepared with a complete answer.

"Yes, Holiness. We both strongly urge you to act now to protect the Church's relics in this vicinity. Specifically, you might send the relics of St. Paul to Athens on loan for a year. This would be an extraordinary ecumenical outreach! Relics of St. Peter, found under the basilica could be sent to a university in Milan or Bologna, or another Italian city, there to be authenticated. The same with pieces of the True Cross and the Crown of Thorns. Also the Lance— and so forth. You know best which ones can be transferred, and where they should go.

"Moreover, Holiness, you can transfer movable objects of Christian art, such as the *Pietà*, and Raphael's *Transfiguration*, and the many priceless manuscripts. Specifically, we propose that you announce that all such works under the Vatican's control are immediately available for loan, for a period of one year, to those recognized museums around the world willing to transport, insure and display them appropriately."

The Holy Father threw up his hands, as if to say, 'How can you ask me to do that?' "Father, do you doubt that there would be a great outcry if we sent such treasures out of the Vatican? And would not the consternation be increased if we explained what we were doing by referring to visions in Garabandal or the message which you brought back from there."

"You have a good point, Holiness," Fr. Santorelli responded. "In explaining this magnanimous gesture, we suggest that you couple it with the announcement of a Year of Evangelization— your intent being that this great art would be used to rekindle devotion throughout Italy and in other Christian countries. If it turns out that the message from Garabandal truly presages a catastrophe here, you will have earned the gratitude of all future generations. And even if there is no catastrophe, you will still have earned the gratitude of the present generation of Christians who will be able to see the treasures for the first time. The citizens of Rome need not fear being left without tourist attractions—there will remain St. Peter's basilica and Michelangelo's Sistine Chapel, and hundreds of other churches, with thousands of murals and precious objects that cannot be moved."

In the silence that followed, Msgr. Waldheim asked a question. "You mentioned *Christian* art, Father. We have many treasures from the pre-Christian era, and also a huge number of ethnological items—collected by missionaries all over the world. What would you recommend the Holy Father do with them?"

"Thank you for reminding me of them, Monsignor," Fr. Santorelli said. "As for the Vatican's sizeable collection of pagan art and artifacts, why should all of it not be sold? It does not radiate the Christian message. Museums and collectors all over the world would jump at the chance to acquire these treasures, and their sale could easily be justified if the proceeds were turned over to the bishops in poor countries ... And I should also mention the Vatican's financial assets. Msgr. Ireland recommends that, if in the Vatican Bank's vault there are securities in bearer form, or other valuables such as bullion, they should be moved to banks in other cities."

Having come to the end of his proposal, Fr. Santorelli paused to hear the Pope's verdict.

"You've given me a great deal to think about, Monsignor and Father. If I decide to deal with the Church's cultural patrimony as you have suggested, no doubt the matter can be handled by the Pontifical Commission for Preserving the Patrimony of Art and History."

Unexpectedly, Msgr. Ireland held up his hand in a cautioning gesture. "Holiness," he said, "while the Commission's help will be needed, I beg you not to refer the matter to them in the first instance.—Leaks about the project probably would succeed in building up overwhelming opposition even before the plan is properly drafted.—Instead, if you become persuaded that these steps should be taken, Holiness, I encourage you to have your decree drawn up secretly by a trusted advisor, and then announced

publicly as soon as you've signed it. I would expect the decree to
unleash powerful economic and political forces *in favor of your
actions*. They will prevent critics in the Curia from nullifying what
you have ordered."

The two guests had already exceeded their allotted time, and
Msgr. Waldheim signaled to them that they should leave. After a
word of thanks, but no commitment, from the Pope, they were
ushered out with his blessing. As they were walking toward the
door of the Papal Library, a piece of art on the long wall opposite
the windows caught Fr. Santorelli's eye, and he paused before it.
It was a painted wooden crucifix of the School of Giotto in the
form of a cross potent—a heraldic cross with crossbars at the ends.
At one end of the main crossbar, there was the image of Our Lady;
at the other, the image of St. John. The upright was enlarged to
be the corpus of the dead Christ, with a wound in His side from
which blood and water flowed, and the wounds on His hands and
feet also dripped blood. *That* image Fr. Santorelli could relate to,
in a way unique to him.

Back in his room at the pension, the priest felt spent from his
intense meeting with Pope and the cumulative effect of too little
sleep and too much internal agitation. He pulled his bed out from
the wall, so that lying on his back, he could extend his arms at
an angle over the side. That way, the wound on each wrist was
not touching the bed. Not that it lessened the pain that pierced
his wounded flesh again each time his heart beat, but at least his
sensitive wrists were not chafed every time he moved his arms.

He closed his eyes, but could not turn off his mind, which
alternated between fearing that he was being too bold in his comments and suggestions, and wondering if he should be speaking
out *publicly*, to promote acceptance of the visions and to warn
people what might be coming. It was a test of his judgment—and
also of his obedience, for Msgr. Ireland and the higher-ups had
obviously resolved to keep him away from the media. Reluctantly,
he gave up the idea of holding a press conference of his own. He
was no rogue priest—he would allow his superiors to use him as
they saw fit.

— 16 —

Jerusalem

Shabbat had just begun in Jerusalem when the Warning struck there. Strange visions appeared in the mind of all Jews, religious and secular, men and women alike. They were identical in substance to the ones previously seen by Christians—a replaying of their sins, with or without scenes of future punishments in store for them.

The Israeli Prime Minister, Levi Hertzel, decided that an emergency session of the Cabinet had to be called late that night in Jerusalem, despite it being Shabbat. Given what had already happened to the *goyim*, there was nothing about these visions which indicated that Jews were being singled out. However, he was concerned that these visions might only be the *first* shoe to drop. What if there were a *second* shoe waiting—a shoe full of Christian imagery and proselytism? Better to face up to the problem right away, and call in the country's top intelligence resources.

The first to report was Eli Ereli, the Director General of Israeli's famed Institute for Intelligence and Special Tasks, the Mossad. Unfortunately, the man who was in charge of Israel's spies abroad had to confess that none of them had picked up the slightest indication of who was behind the visions, or how they were being transmitted. As far as his people knew, the governments of all the countries where they had agents were similarly in the dark.

Next came Barak Rosen, the head of the Israel Security Service, better known as Shin Bet, or Shabak. That was the agency in charge of counter-intelligence and internal security. He confessed that he too had been a victim, and he had no idea of how to stop more visions from coming in the future. In his own defense, he noted that his homeland security counterparts in the United States and Western Europe were still struggling unsuccessfully with the same questions about the Warning received by Christians there.

After discussing various proposals, the Ministers who attended displayed rare unanimity in deciding that the Mossad and Shin Bet must redouble their efforts—regardless of cost. They also decided to send a strong message to the Vatican. There was no proof of its involvement, and no discernible Christian content to the visions, but, in view of the Vatican's embrace of the Warning directed to Christians, it was deemed appropriate to demand that it disclaim any involvement with the visions which had just been seen by Jews, and refrain from approving of them in any way.

They did not address the issue of the elephant in the room with them. That elephant was God—*their God*—surely the only power in the universe both concerned about sin and able to parade a man's sins in front of his eyes.

The Orthodox members who attended the meeting could not admit the possibility that the visions were valid—that *they* were sinners—they who had so scrupulously observed the 613 rules of their faith. The secular Jews too could not admit that God existed, because he was not a part of their lifestyle. And the non-Orthodox believers felt wedged between the other two blocs, willing to consider the possibility that the visions were sent by God, but keeping silent because they were uncertain what such consideration might ultimately lead to.

While the uproar was continuing in Israel, the Warning was spreading westward everywhere to all who belonged to the House of Israel. Those in Europe had advance warning of what was coming—and they tried to protect themselves as best as they could. Orthodox men strapped additional phylacteries on their head and left arm. Other Jews sought refuge in Kabbalah spells, or donned earplugs and sleep masks, as if covering their eyes and ears would protect them. No matter what they did, though, the Warning got through to them, as it had to the Christians before them.

— 17 —

Rome

Msgr. Ireland drove over to Fr. Santorelli's pension at nine o'clock on Saturday morning, to pick him up and take him to the Palace of the Holy Office, where they were going to meet. The prelate wanted to discuss the reports he had seen on the Internet of the visions spreading to the Jewish people. When the priest didn't appear at the front door and didn't answer the room phone, the Monsignor went up to his room. Not getting a response to his knock on the door, he had it opened for him by the sister in charge. They found Fr. Santorelli sprawled face down on the floor.

Together, they got him up and into a chair. The priest groaned, but said nothing. "Tony! Tony! What happened?" the prelate demanded, worriedly.

"Black dog," was the whispered reply.

That made no sense to him. The prelate asked the sister if she could offer any information. Had there been any visitors?

No visitors, but she had been told that there was a lot of noise coming from this room in the night. Other guests had complained. "You can see for yourself that the furniture has been pushed around, Monsignor. You can appreciate that we cannot keep your friend here if whatever happened here last night is likely to happen again."

It was undeniable that the bed was against the desk instead of the opposite wall, the Crucifix was under it on the floor, the desk chair was upside down, and the telephone table was lying on its back. The heavy wooden chifforobe had also been moved from its nook into the room.

With a few swallows of water, Fr. Santorelli seemed to come around a bit. "Have her leave," he said in a whisper to the prelate.

When the sister had left the room, Fr. Santorelli slowly tried to give an explanation. "Black dog attacked . . . Mastiff."

He saw that the Monsignor's eyes were uncomprehending. How to explain the inexplicable? He had read many stories of incidents where Padre Pio was beaten in his cell by demons. His fellow friars sometimes heard a ruckus coming from his cell, and they found him lying black and blue, even bleeding, on the floor, with things thrown around in his cell, but the demons they never saw. They just had to take his word for what had happened.

Fr. Santorelli tried again to communicate, hindered by his condition as well as the mystical nature of the event. "Padre Pio called him 'Bluebeard' ... The Devil ... Comes in disguises ... Animals, people, angels ... Raged about message for Pope ... Dragged me around room. ... Expecting him since Garabandal ... First time he's come... Won't be the last ... Birthday present—my 33rd birthday ... Tell Mother Superior I'm sorry ... "

The first thought that crossed Msgr. Ireland's mind was, 'I don't know what I've gotten myself into, and I don't know how I can get myself out of it—but I'd better try.'

Necessity was the mother of invention. "I don't dare repeat what you've said, to Mother Superior," he told Fr. Santorelli. "And we'd better put the room back the way it was. After that, I'll try to get a room for you over at the Domus Sanctae Marthae. It's only a few steps from my office, so that'll cut down on your walking, and the staff may be able to look in on you from time to time and make sure you're O.K.—I'll check that out when I leave."

Walking out of the room, not comprehending anything of what he had been told, the prelate shook his head as he muttered, "*A black dog! ... The Pope better not hear about that one ... *"

*   *   *

Msgr. Ireland succeeded in arranging for Fr. Santorelli to stay at the five-story Vatican hotel next to the Papal Audience Hall. It had been built to house the cardinals during a papal conclave, and at other times was used by visiting prelates. That afternoon, the two of them moved the priest's belongings to a room there, and then went to the Monsignor's office.

The Palace of the Holy Office was a large three story structure within the enclosure of the Vatican's walls and gates, except for its front, which faced the Piazza della Santo Uffizio. The central entrance there was surmounted on the second story by an ornamental balcony, from which the Papal flag flew. The building could claim no distinguished history—being less than a century old—and the rooms lacked the magnificent wall, ceiling and floor decorations of the Vatican properties which had been built many centuries before. Although the rooms had high ceilings and tall windows, the only ornamentation of note inside was art from the Vatican's collection.

The priest looked pensive as he sat down on the other side of Msgr. Ireland's desk.

"A penny for your thoughts, Tony," offered the prelate.

"Only a penny?"

"That's just an expression I picked up from my parents when I was a kid. There's been a lot of inflation since then. I'll be glad to pay you more—if I like what you have to say."

"In that case, Monsignor," replied the priest, "I won't be looking for any reward."

"That bad? Well, let's hear your thoughts anyway," said Msgr. Ireland.

"Do you remember the luncheon we had when I first arrived back here?" Fr. Santorelli asked. "I happened to mention Joachim da Fiore. I'm not buying into the Calabrian Abbott's schema of historical ages, but I have a sense that we're at one of those points in history that people look back on and recognize as pivotal, as bringing about a major transformation in civilization. 'A tipping point,' if you will."

"Well, I hope you're right about that," said the Monsignor, cutting Fr. Santorelli off before he could explain himself. "Of course, *the* central point in all of history has already occurred, in the Incarnation—God entering our world as man. And right now, I'm hopeful that God's open intervention in our affairs through the Warning visions will spark a springtime of belief—a resurgence that will reverse the tide of atheism and secularism in the Western world!"

When the priest did not join in with an affirming comment, the prelate said, with some asperity, "Don't tell me you're still wringing your hands about a possible *deluge*, Tony . . . "

The question put him on the spot. "I'll be thrilled if events bear out your hopes, Monsignor, but I don't want to be like those false prophets that God called to account through Ezekiel's mouth, the ones who prophesied what they thought their audience wanted to hear. You reproached me after our first meeting with the Pope for not giving him an uplifting message. I can't say anything has changed since then."

"Are you sure you aren't letting yourself be overly influenced by the end-of-the-age aspect of the Garabandal prophecy?" the prelate asked.

Fr. Santorelli briefly considered whether he should reveal a part of the personal message he had received from the Lord—the warning that the Lord was going to use *him* to offer the choice of life or death to many—and decided that the time was still not ripe for that disclosure. "No, Monsignor," he said, "my unease now is due mainly to the message I was given for the Pope, especially the last three parts. The Garabandal prophecy does intensify that, and, at the risk of having you laugh, I would add that part of what I'm feeling is the angst of a poetic vision."

The Monsignor could not resist rolling his eyes. "*Angst? . . . A poetic vision?*"

"Yes. Surely you know those lines of Matthew Arnold— '*The Sea of Faith was once, too, at the full . . . but now I only hear its melancholy, long, withdrawing roar . . .*'"

"*Dover Beach,*" said the Monsignor, pleased to have recognized it. "How can you apply those lines now, when the Church has grown significantly in the past century?"

"I can apply them because the Church's growth has come in the underdeveloped world, while in the meantime it has been shrinking at an accelerating rate in Europe, the cradle of Western civilization. It won't be long before Muslims outnumber us here— and take over our church buildings and turn them into mosques."

"Is *that* what has you worried?"

"Yes, Monsignor, but it's only part of the story. Do you also remember Yeats' poem, *The Second Coming*? The imagery begins with a falcon that cannot hear the falconer, and a 'centre' that does not hold, and a 'blood-dimmed tide.'"

"I think so, Tony, though I certainly couldn't quote it now. But, I don't see how it's relevant to our situation. How would you apply it, beginning with—who or what is the falcon?"

"Why, Monsignor, *all of our race*. We're exerting our independence of God more and more, fleeing to avoid hearing His call. *Do you recall that the Holy Father said that we suffer from 'a hardness of hearing God'?* And the 'centre'—which I take to mean Rome— has not held Christendom together. Anarchy has been loosed upon the world by terrorists. Don't many of the 'best' lack all conviction, and aren't the 'worst' full of passionate intensity against the

Church? Surely you're aware of the war the secular bureaucrats of the European Union are conducting against the participation of religions—especially ours—in the public square. I can foresee that the Pope's Apostolic Letter won't go down well with them. And, if they could find some way to outlaw the visions, I'm sure they'd do so!"

Msgr. Ireland took a while to consider the analogies drawn by his former pupil. "I don't know, Tony," he said finally. "Regarding the 'blood-dimmed tide,' as I recall it, Yeats was referring to the millions killed by revolution and the First World War. That would have been what he was facing a century ago, wouldn't it? What makes you think he was writing a prophecy about our situation today?"

Fr. Santorelli saw that he needed to sharpen his point.

"I didn't mean to sound like I was looking to poetry *as a predictor*. I was just trying to indicate that I was feeling the same sense of loss of the old order, and fear of the new, as Arnold and Yeats did in their time. You're hopeful, because you're expecting the visions to lead people to the Christian faith, especially in the once Christian countries of Europe. I, too, am hopeful of a resurgence of Christianity there, and even having it take root elsewhere—but I don't think the visions by themselves will suffice to bring that about. I think it'll take coupling them with the Miracle and the Chastisement—and before that happens, we in the Church will be in for hard times."

When his host continued to look unhappy and did not respond, the priest added, "I hope I did not speak more frankly than you wished, Monsignor. I have trouble putting into practice the lessons I was taught by the Cardinal in Topanga."

"No, no, I asked for your views, Tony. I admit I didn't expect such a negative appraisal from you.—Let me ask you this. There was a stupid sci-fi movie that featured all sorts of calamities all over the world—tidal waves, earthquakes, fire raining down. Are you thinking of that sort of a doomsday scenario?"

"You mean the '2012' movie for real? Not exactly," said Fr. Santorelli with a very thin smile. "If God wants to act through the forces of nature or rain down fire from heaven, obviously He can do so, but as you know better than I, the Bible gives us more examples of Him acting through human instrumentalities—who usually don't realize they're serving a divine purpose. God's way of punishing the Israelites was to allow pagan armies to conquer them and destroy their cities. I think it's more likely He'll just allow Satan to get away with directing the actions of earthly rulers."

Seeing an opening, he continued. "Let me give you an example from our own times, Monsignor. Have you ever pondered the warning at Fatima, where the little children were told by Our Lady that although the first world war would end soon, another, even greater, war would occur if men did not turn back to God? That's exactly what happened! *The forces of evil are always at work, so if God merely withdraws His defensive efforts, His protective shield, all hell will break loose.*"

"You were right not to expect a reward, Tony," said Msgr. Ireland, his enthusiasm now thoroughly squelched. "I withdraw my offer of a penny. I'm not paying you anything for *negative* thoughts like those.—And I guess I'll put off until Monday asking you what you think about the Warning spreading to the House of Israel. You might as well leave now and have a good rest in your room at the *Domus* today and tomorrow—I'm sure they don't allow black mastiffs in there . . ."

PART III

The Plots

February 2015

Against the spirit of the world, the Church takes up anew each day a struggle that is none other than *the struggle for the world's soul.* If in fact, on the one hand, the Gospel and evangelization are present in this world, on the other, there is also present *a powerful anti-evangelization* which is well organized and has the means to vigorously oppose the Gospel and evangelization.

Pope John Paul II, *Crossing the Threshold of Hope,* 112
(Alfred A. Knopf 1994)

— 1 —

Brussels

Fr. Santorelli's premonition that the Apostolic Letter welcoming the Warning visions would provoke a strong reaction from the European Union came true two days later. Archbishop Tedesco, the Papal nuncio representing the Vatican at the EU's headquarters in Brussels, was summoned to appear at the office of Réné du Marais, the EU's Commissioner for Employment, Social Affairs and Equal Opportunities. Meetings in the past between the two had not gone well, as the Vatican had strongly opposed the Commissioner's particularly radical agenda.

Unlike his predecessors in that post, who had focused on policies to improve the lot of workers, such as laws regarding pay and the movement of workers across state borders, du Marais was dedicated to pushing the frontier of civil liberties. He interpreted the various legal documents of the EU in his field as authorizing coercive policies to promote reproductive freedom, sexual education of children, and non-discrimination on the basis of gender.

There was no way he could apply EU legal regulations directly to the Vatican City State, since it was not a member country, but du Marais had been working to force the Vatican's acceptance of his agenda indirectly, through having the member countries adopt joint policies applying pressure on the Holy See.

"I have requested your presence, Excellency," du Marais began, "to protest the *offensive* letter which your leader in Rome issued a week ago."

"Offensive?—Offensive to whom, Commissioner?" the Archbishop asked in his most polite tone of voice.

Du Marais glowered at him. "That should be obvious! To all the citizens of the Union! It violates the basic freedoms guaranteed them by the Charter of Fundamental Rights."

Archbishop Tedesco was not impressed. "Forgive me if I appear to be arguing with you, Commissioner, but *even if* the Holy See were to act contrary to the Charter in some way, I fail to see how there could be a violation. Isn't a violation of the Charter only possible by action of a member state?"

The answer came back almost as a snarl—"Don't try to hide behind technicalities!—The policies set forth in the Charter are ones which the member states wish to extend also to third countries, such as yours."

The Archbishop continued methodically uncovering the Commissioner's position. "How were those provisions violated, in your opinion, sir?"

"You are playing games with me, Excellency!" du Marais shot back. "As you are well aware, these *horrible* visions force their way through the walls of a man's house, and then into his mind. That clearly violates at least *three* fundamental rights: the security of one's person, respect for one's private life, and, freedom of thought. No doubt you are aware that many peoples' visions purported to show that exercising one's sexual freedom is a *depraved* act. *That message is homophobic, hateful, and discriminatory to minorities!*"

The Archbishop guessed that du Marais had already had his own Warning. "You are complaining of visions, without explaining how this all relates to the Holy See. Surely, sir, you do not claim that the Holy Father was responsible for sending the visions, do you?"

"We do not know the extent of his responsibility. What we do know is that your Pope, by his letter praising the visions, and asking people to accept and act on their message, is at a minimum a *conspirator!*"

The Archbishop permitted himself a skeptical look. "A conspirator, Commissioner? May I ask whom you think the Holy Father is conspiring with—perhaps the Holy Spirit?"

Commissioner du Marais seethed at this riposte. Unable to come up with a good answer, he proceeded to deliver his ultimatum: "Enough of your obfuscations! Consider well, Excellency, that your country is a tiny one, landlocked and with no airport, which lies within the territory of a Union member state. Action by the Council could have *dire* consequences, and could be imposed on relatively short notice. In my official capacity, I request that you inform your Head-of-State that unless he withdraws his letter approving of the visions, and, further, acknowledges them to violate the freedoms guaranteed by the Charter, *I will recommend to the Council of the Union that it call for your country to be quarantined!*"

Du Marais' face was flushed with triumph at the thought of bringing about that calamity.

"I will look forward to a response from you within a week, Excellency," he said, in dismissal.

As soon as he returned to his office, Archbishop Tedesco phoned in a report to the Vatican on his stormy meeting with Commissioner du Marais, adding his own view that the Commissioner would do his best to carry out his threat and might find a number of member states receptive to the idea of a quarantine. His superior said he would pass the report on immediately to Cardinal Giuseppe Malapensa, the Vatican's Secretary of State, and obtain instructions as to how Tedesco should respond to the Commissioner's demand.

Rome

Cardinal Malapensa had been infuriated by the release of the Apostolic Letter concerning the Warning visions, the more so since he had cautioned the Pope strongly against taking any public notice of them. It grated on him that he was now forced to approach the Pope to obtain instructions for the Papal nuncio in Brussels on how to respond to the threat which the letter had evoked.

His Holiness was at the moment occupied with editing his planned Apostolic Constitution on the Mother of God as Co-Redemptrix, Mediatrix and Advocate. It was a most difficult theological proposition to define in such a way that it would not diminish the role of Jesus Christ as *the* Redeemer of the World and *the* Mediator between God and man, and the Pope had gone through draft after draft trying to find the right persuasive words. When Cardinal Malapensa entered his study, the Pope reluctantly put his manuscript aside, and listened to a summary of the diplomatic situation.

After relating the development, the Secretary of State gave his recommendation to accede to the demand of the EU Commissioner, and withdraw the Apostolic Letter. The Pope rejected this advice out of hand. "What he asks is wrong and beyond his authority to demand, and we will not agree to it, Eminence."

That was exactly what Cardinal Malapensa had feared the Pope's stand would be. "Holiness, does it not matter that the visions do in fact violate everyone's fundamental rights?"

It was an irrational position for the Cardinal to express, and the Pope did not let it pass. "How can *God*, the ultimate lawgiver, be said to violate rights in a charter *written by human beings*? Are not all of His actions—even sending the visions—indisputably just?"

Cardinal Malapensa should have backed down, but did not. "Holiness, you are basing your decision now, like your Apostolic Letter, on the *questionable* assumption that the visions are from God. How can you justify that assumption, when in the two thousand years since the coming of Our Lord, He has never before violated a person's conscience? If God were willing to override men's consciences and infuse His own moral judgments into their minds, why hasn't He been doing so ever since He created mankind? *Holiness, has it not occurred to you that these visions are most likely a trick of the Devil?*"

The Pope was growing annoyed with Malapensa's persistent, perhaps willful, obtuseness, but he patiently explained what should have been evident to the Cardinal.

"Eminence, do you not see that if the Devil knew each person's sins, he would do his best to make the person forget them or ignore them? And he certainly would not be showing anyone what their fate in *his* kingdom would be. No, Eminence, there is simply no way to avoid the conclusion that the visions come from God, and, that being so, we must encourage everyone to take them to heart.—As for Commissioner du Marais, have Archbishop Tedesco try to talk to him personally. Beg him to open his heart and his mind to the Warning. Surely, he must have received his own vision by now. Invite him to cleanse his sins and put off his old ways. We can do nothing else." With that, the Pope resumed his editing, and the Secretary of State could only withdraw in frustration.

Cardinal Malapensa could hardly wait until he was out of the Papal apartment to utter a few choice oaths: "*Senile old fool! . . . Bumbling incompetent!*"

To his way of thinking, Benedict XVIth had lost touch with reality. A minor bureaucrat in Brussels was threatening catastrophe to the Holy See unless the Pope backed down, as Malapensa thought he should—and the Pope's only response was to try to save the man's soul!

The Pope's muddled handling of this important affair was just one more example of his increasing incompetence. He had committed major gaffes with the Muslims, the Jews, and the archconservative Lefebvrists. Now, his uncompromising attitude toward the European Union, an attitude which, to Malapensa's way of thinking, was *so unnecessary*, was exacerbating a long standing problem. It was up to the Vatican to back down from its lofty perch of claimed moral superiority, and accept the will of the people as reflected in the laws which the countries of the European Union had passed, and in the EU Charter adopted by their governments. *They* saw nothing wrong with complete freedom for reproductive rights—contraception and in vitro fertilization and abortion. *They* saw nothing wrong with same sex unions, or with euthanasia, or with stripping public places of all religious symbols, or enforcing anti-discrimination and hate-speech regulations against religious institutions.

This Pope, though, had never yielded an inch to the will of the people and the secular authorities, and he was not going to surrender now—which no doubt would soon lead to a confrontation which the Holy See could not win.

There was, however, a bright spot in this for Malapensa which assuaged his anger: the imposition of a quarantine against the Vatican just might light the fire of open rebellion in the Church's hierarchy. It could provide the cause for rallying the cardinals to remove Ratzinger as Pope, and then elect a Pope who would bring about a grand accommodation of the Church with secular society—*and who better for that task than himself?*

— 2 —

Brussels

The Holy Father's instruction to Archbishop Tedesco was relayed to him the following day—albeit without the assistance of Cardinal Malapensa, who washed his hands of the matter. Faithful diplomat that he was, Archbishop Tedesco accepted his assignment without complaint and prepared for what he knew would be an unpleasant meeting with Commissioner du Marais. He had no expectation that he could bring the man around either to repenting of his sins or to refraining from carrying out his threat against the Holy See, but he would try his best.

"Commissioner," the Archbishop began, "as you have requested, I have returned with a response from my superiors. But before we talk officially, may I, Gaetano Tedesco, speak to you, René du Marais, as one human being to another?"

Without waiting for the surprised bureaucrat to reply, Tedesco plunged on. "Surely, you can see that no power on earth could be responsible for sending the visions, as you yourself put it, through the walls of people's homes and into their very minds. And surely you can see that any power which could accomplish this, and do so even without leaving an external trace, could just as easily have struck the recipients of the visions stone dead.

"I suspect that you have received a vision, just as I myself did, and I am thankful that it came and went, leaving me alive and able to respond. The visions are acts of love on the part of our heavenly Father, who wants us to restore ourselves to His good graces through our giving a most simple sign of love for Him. In welcoming the visions, the Holy Father did not condemn anyone in his Apostolic Letter. Indeed, he referred to the present time as a period of grace—*grace which is available to you just as it is to me!*"

Archbishop Tedesco would have liked to go on with his soft words of persuasion, but the Commissioner cut him off by raising his hand.

"That will do, Excellency!" he said. "*You are not here to try to convert me!*"

"Now, it is my turn to talk to you. So, you want me to be penitent, do you? Very well, you're a priest. I will begin my confession with when I was an altar boy at the church of St. Thérèse of Lisieux. Fr. LeGrande, the curé, saw that I was a lonely child, since my father was dead, and he favored me with his affection and caresses."

There followed a short and sordid account by the Commissioner, which the Archbishop wished he could close his ears to, ending with these fiery words: "My confession to you is that I still love him for awakening my sexuality so tenderly. He never made me feel an outcast because of my sexual orientation. It is *your Church* that fosters disapproval and hatred. *And so I also confess that I have long hated your Church and everything you stand for, for ruining that sweet old man—defrocking him and throwing him out into the gutter like garbage, just because some nasty little boys didn't understand his way of showing them love!*"

The Archbishop sat stunned and horrified. But for his being there on a diplomatic mission, he would have fled from the room.

Du Marais studied the dismay registered on the Archbishop's face, with great satisfaction. Then, he broke the silence to say, "Now that we each have spoken person-to-person, Excellency, I ask for the reply of your Government to my démarche."

As he left the Commissioner's office, after delivering the negative response rejecting any change in the Pope's position, the Archbishop crossed himself three times. Tedesco had long suspected that du Marais was possessed by a devil, and the look in du Marais' eyes, and the tone of his voice, as he related his unholy alliance with a former priest, convinced the prelate that his suspicion had been correct. There was also no doubting that the man would proceed with his evil scheme to cause the Holy See to be isolated like a coral atoll in the middle of the ocean.

— 3 —

Rome

In view of the adverse developments in Brussels, the Pope redoubled his efforts to follow up on the suggestions of Msgr. Ireland and Fr. Santorelli regarding the material treasures of the Holy See.

A wealth of stelae and clay figurines, bronzes and cuneiform tablets, from Egypt, Mesopotamia, and Syria-Palestine, dating back to 2600 B.C., were on display in the Gregorian Egyptian Museum. None of these objects, even the Roman copies of Egyptian art made in the first or second centuries A.D., related to Christianity. In the Gregorian Etruscan Museum, there were objects from closer to home, but still pre-Christian—the Etruscan civilization in Etruria. Heretofore, there had been no reason to dispose of them, but if one accepted that the Garabandal prophecies were genuine, as the Pope had by now, a program of deaccessions made good sense.

The Ethnological Missionary Museum housed about 80,000 objects of a religious nature from Asia, Oceania, Africa and America. These objets d'art could be very useful in evangelizing, and obviously could be spread out on loan to museums throughout the world. There were also items from the British School of Archaeology in Jerusalem, and Judaica, which the Israelis would like to display. Although relations with the State of Israel were at the breaking point, he was sure that his officials could deal with individual Jews in other counties who would step forward to seek objects from their own history.

There was never a thought in the Pope's mind to dispose of the treasures of Christian art, the 500 or so paintings in the Pinacoteca, most of them by Italian masters. This collection was one of the sights, like Michelangelo's ceiling in the Sistine Chapel, which had to be checked off on every guidebook's list. For many of the tourists to the Vatican, they were something of great beauty observed only for a moment and lodged in memory, but making no lasting impression on the soul. For others, who had the time and knowledge to unpack and meditate upon their artistry and religious sentiments, the paintings brought the soul closer to God. They stood as witnesses to the faith of the Church through many centuries, and to epiphanies of the glory of God breaking forth into the human condition, as it did with the Incarnation.

These works, the Pope decided, should be kept together in a display which would remain in Italy, traveling to Milan, Venice, Florence and Naples. After all—the people in Italy were in no less need of re-evangelization than the Christians in other countries. He embodied his decisions in a *Motu Proprio* decree, a type of order which the Pope could issue on his own authority. As suggested by Bishop Ireland, he had it drafted in secret, without consultation with the Curia, and now he was ready to read it in a broadcast by the Vatican's own television station, originating from one of the *Sale dei "Foconi"* in the Papal Apartment.

"Dear Brothers and Sisters! The great period of grace we are now living in should be not only a time when we reconcile ourselves with the Lord, but also a time of evangelization and re-evangelization. When my predecessor of happy memory, John Paul II, met with the Pontifical Commission for the Cultural Patrimony of the Church in the Holy Year 2000, he told the members 'to spare no efforts to see that the works of culture and art turned over to the care of the Church are always used more efficaciously in the service of authentic human progress and the spreading of the Gospel.' I wish to speak to you now about two of the ways which I have directed that this be accomplished."

"In the words of a poet, 'truth is beauty, beauty truth.' Great works of religious art are, at the same time, sublime religious truths, and a shining sign of God. In Christianity, the heart and reason come together, beauty and truth touch. That is why, for many centuries the Vatican has sheltered masterpieces of Christian art. My predecessors in the shoes of Peter have done well in commissioning and accumulating these treasures, and protecting them against the ravages of time."

"Now, the time has come for the masterworks in the Vatican collection to be shared more widely, so that the clergy of other cities may use them to instruct their congregations in the beauties of the Faith. For that reason I have made provision for temporary loans of significant artistic treasures, as I will shortly reveal. At the same time, I have directed that a program of deaccessions be undertaken immediately with regard to the pagan art and artifacts in the Holy See's collection, with all the proceeds being allocated to evangelization, primarily in mission countries, but also in the cities of Europe which have forgotten their Christian roots."

The Holy Father's voice was showing his fatigue in his tone and occasional stumbles, so his personal secretary took over the recitation of the remaining sentences, with the Holy Father nodding to show his approval.

*   *   *

Sacrilege! Infamy! Madness! These were the first words that came to mind among the citizens of Rome when the Italian media picked up the story. There seemed to be only two points of view—either the Pope had gone mad, or he had been bribed by foreign interests. When it came to defending the cultural patrimony of the Church, even people who cared not a whit for the Church itself proclaimed their outrage.

The Italian Prime Minister, who routinely attacked Benedict XVIth at every opportunity, saw this as a chance to solidify public opinion against *the German Pope.* When the TV cameras were ready, he thundered: *"This is perfidy! ... Treason! ... The work of a foreigner! Tomorrow I will ask the Parliament to pass legislation expropriating the treasures of the Vatican for the benefit of the Italian people."* Overlooked in the heat of his passion was the inconvenient fact that the Vatican City State was a separate country whose sovereignty Italy had formally recognized by treaty.

Editors of newspapers of every political persuasion began to draft news stories and editorials for the next morning's editions, using strong words to protest the Pope's decree.

Then, a funny thing happened. Words like "imprudent," "profligate" and "reprehensible," started being deleted from the texts on their word processors. No invisible hand was erasing them. Rather, wealth and power and civic pride were raising their voices in public *in support of the plan.*

Giotto! Perugino! Raphael! Leonardo! Caravaggio!

These blue chip artists were red letter drawing cards for any museum. The mayors and the civic leaders of Milan, Venice, Florence and Naples rushed to give out statements of praise and thanksgiving to the Holy Father that such treasures would be coming to their cities. They knew that not only was the Vatican collection in the Pinacoteca an attraction by itself, it would also bring forth loans from other museums and private collections around the world for special retrospective exhibits. Raphaels from elsewhere would be paired with those from the Pinacoteca. Tourists would come from all over Europe and America for these once-in-a-lifetime shows. Happy days and many, many euros would be on their way! The same was true for the parts of the Vatican collections which would be sent out on loan to other museums—for example, the dons at Cambridge University were ecstatic at the thought of seeing firsthand the Vatican's medieval manuscripts.

And as for the collections to be sold, there was enormous interest in the Vatican's projected sale on the part of dealers and private collectors in America and Europe. Patrons of the arts in Los Angeles began to call around their circle to form a syndicate to buy the Etruscan collection as a whole for the Getty; Berliners wanted the Egyptian collection for their museum; and so it went. This would be the most important sale of antiquities since the adoption of the UNESCO Convention to stop the international trade in objects which had been stolen or illegally exported. Collectors and museums had no worry that their purchases would be snatched away from them by the authorities—all of the Vatican's items were freely saleable because the Vatican could prove that it had acquired them long before the 1970 date of the Convention.

— 4 —

Rome

The Pope's surprise announcement offering the Vatican's artistic treasures for immediate loan and sale found one museum official fully prepared to facilitate that great project: Fr. Justin Casey, S.J., one of the few Christians who had experienced no warning vision. If anyone had known that, and asked him why he had escaped, he might have replied modestly that perhaps it took longer for the Warning to reach down into the mines where he labored. He was a troglodyte, like one of the early Christian priests condemned by a Roman emperor to dig copper ore, out of the light of the sun, until he died. In Father's case, the condemning authority was his own brothers in the Society of Jesus.

He was both old and an *old school Jesuit*, one who had seen the decline of his order and the unfaithfulness of some of its members to its special charism of loyalty to the Pope. He had made no secret of his support for Pope John Paul II in removing Fr. Arrupe as the General of the Jesuits in 1981, and as a result he had been ostracized by Fr. Arrupe's successors. Forbidden to publish or speak in public, he was thankful that at least they allowed him to continue to work in his field of expertise. With a Ph.D. in Greco-Roman antiquities, he found employment in the bowels of the Vatican Museums.

Tens of thousands of items in the Vatican's collections were stored in boxes and crates. Many were uncatalogued, and some were unknown treasures which nobody would miss if they vanished in the night. It brought to mind a line from Browning's famous poem, *The Bishop Orders His Tomb at Saint Praxed's Church*: "So much was saved if aught were missed." Browning's bishop was reminiscing that he had saved many priceless objects from a fire at his church, and then kept them for himself because nobody remembered them afterwards. Fr. Casey, however, was scrupulously honest. He had never taken advantage of the opportunity he had daily to walk out with a gold necklace, or small marble statue or ancient scroll for sale to a complaisant dealer in antiquities.

For years he had been working his way methodically through the vast underground storerooms of the Vatican, like a caterpillar munching its way through the leaves of a tree. His explorations were briefly noted each day on his laptop computer, and at the end of the month he researched his entries and used them to update the official catalogue.

It was his custom to emerge from his labors at the end of the day and board a bus for the Pantheon. There, he would relax at a trattoria with a Cinzano and a cigarette, before retiring to his pension nearby, a seedy one befitting his vow of poverty.

One night a year or so before, his routine had been briefly interrupted when a man had unexpectedly sat down at his small table. Explaining that he was a dealer in Judaica, he expressed an interest in buying any significant pieces that Fr. Casey turned up in his work. Seeing the expression of shock on the priest's face, the man hastily added that, of course, he meant he would like to buy them from the Vatican authorities—not from Fr. Casey himself.

That only slightly reassured the priest. "Why are you coming to me directly about this?" Fr. Casey wanted to know. "I don't handle such negotiations myself."

"As you above all know, Father, not all the items in the Vatican's collections have been catalogued. I have heard that you are working on updating the records, and I thought if you ever came across an important piece, you might let me know. There is *so much* in storage that will never see the light of day.—And, I don't need to remind you, Father, that the Vatican always runs at a deficit. Surely there must be opportunities to make arrangements of mutual benefit ..."

Probing him, Fr. Casey came to the conclusion that the man was not really a dealer in antiquities as he claimed, for in trying to find out what sort of pieces the man had in mind, Father could tell that he did not have the knowledge necessary for one in that trade. Perhaps the imposter was a thief, trying to find out what to steal? Father rejected his overture out of hand.

Six months later, Father happened to see the same man, this time inside the Vatican, with an acquaintance whom he knew to be on the Vatican's internal security staff. The next day, he made an inquiry about the man, expressing concern about his occupation.

His acquaintance had a good laugh. "A thief? Well, maybe, Father.—But what he steals, or at least tries to, is not the kind of objects you deal in. *It's secrets!*"

"Secrets? Who is he?"

The security man shrugged. "You can call him Signore Finzi. That's the name he goes by. He's a *Mossad* agent. We deal with him on matters of mutual interest."

"I don't understand," said Fr. Casey. "Why would he be making a contact with me, of all people?"

"Think, Father—," was the answer. "He's hoping one day you'll turn up their precious Menorah."

Of course! How stupid of him! That was *exactly* what the man must have been after. That was the one religious artifact of their Second Temple that the Jewish people were still looking for, hoping anxiously that it had survived.

When their revolt against the Roman Empire was crushed and the Temple destroyed, the Jews' holy vessels were carried off from Jerusalem to Rome as spoils of war. The huge, seven-branched candelabrum was such a prize that it was sculpted in bas-relief on the triumphal Arch of Titus, near the Colosseum. This particular lamp of gold had been fashioned for the Hasmonean kings in the second century B.C. after they had driven out the Syrian Greeks and rededicated the Temple. It was one of the glories of the Temple when Jesus worshipped there, something which never had been forgotten.

A number of different theories had sprung up about what had become of it. One was that the Vandals had carried it off when they sacked Rome in the Fifth Century A.D., another, that it had survived the Vandals but then was sent to Constantinople by a Roman emperor—in either case, the Menorah was supposedly lost in a shipwreck. Yet, many Jews still hoped against hope that it had somehow been preserved in Rome all along and now was stowed away in the Vatican's basement. If it ever turned up, the Government of Israel would certainly be willing to pay a king's ransom to get it back.

Only Fr. Casey knew for sure whether the Menorah still existed, for he had actually found the prize three weeks before, in a forgotten and completely mismarked crate. At that time, he held back news of his discovery so that he could, in seclusion, go through all the similarly marked crates to see whether they might contain any other Second Temple treasures.

He was of mixed mind as to whether, and how, to reveal his great secret. Years before, the Israelis had sent a mission to the Vatican, begging the Pope's help in having the Menorah returned—assuming, of course, that the Vatican had it. Fr. Casey realized it could be a valuable bargaining chip in diplomatic negotiations. But, given the strained relations between the State of Israel and the Vatican, most recently concerning the first Warning visions, he doubted whether the Vatican officials would have any interest in seeing the Menorah returned to Jerusalem, no matter how many euros were offered for it. Rather, they would prefer to leave it buried in the basement, if necessary for centuries more, until the time was ripe to announce its existence. Indeed, he was convinced that the crate had been deliberately mislabeled long ago, as containing Egyptian antiquities, for the purpose of hiding its contents.

Right now, the Menorah was not at the forefront of his mind. He was totally preoccupied, thanks to the Holy Father's unexpected Motu Proprio, in supervising the shipment of portions of the Vatican collections from the storerooms. The years he had spent in quiet explorations were paying off—his knowledge of what was there and precisely where everything was located enabled him to readily direct the moving crews as to what to dispatch to each museum. He had dealt with the staffs of many museums over the years, usually when they were looking to see what could be borrowed for their special exhibitions bringing together artifacts from a number of institutions to illuminate a particular theme in art or history. He had proven that he knew what was what among the tens of thousands of different items in the storerooms, and that the shipping manifests he made out were absolutely correct. Having built up trust over the years with the recipients of the loans, they now did not think it necessary to see the crates being packed—Fr. Casey merely prepared the needed documents on his computer, listing what items were in a crate, and a museum representative would sign a receipt, and then see to its shipment.

After work on the day following the Pope's announcement, as he pondered the dismemberment of the Vatican's collections, drink and cigarette in hand as usual at the café, he was accosted by "Signore Finzi."

"Father," the *Mossad* agent said, as he sat down without asking permission, "forgive the intrusion. I will be brief. You know that times of turmoil are often fateful for works of art—they get stolen, or destroyed, or even melted down, if they are gold. Many important works known to have existed have vanished in this way over the centuries."

Fr. Casey readily agreed. That was very true—and the current period was unexpectedly turning out to be a time of turmoil. No doubt, some treasures would be lost here and there.

Finzi had a request to make. "While the Vatican's collection was all here together, we had hope that your efforts would one day identify absolutely everything, and what was important would be brought to light. But, if the crates are dispersed all over, we won't know where to turn. *I beg you*—if there is anything you know to be of particular importance to the Jewish people, tell me now, while there is time to do something about it. We are not asking for anything that is not rightfully ours, and we are prepared to pay well to get it."

This time, Fr. Casey did not ask his uninvited visitor to leave. He signaled to the waiter to bring him a second Cinzano, and Finzi ordered a Campari to be companionable. Fr. Casey took his time thinking about how to respond to the man's plea.

Finally, the priest said, "Your Government has created great difficulty for itself by the way it conducts relations with us. I don't see how any of my superiors could deal with you at present, even if there were something to talk about."

"Government to Government is impossible, I agree," said Finzi, "but not person to person. Individuals can change the course of history in small ways, Father. That is why we recognize righteous gentiles ... "

"Your people should have recognized His Holiness as one of them! He has wanted to have a rapprochement with our 'elder brothers,' but they have attacked him repeatedly over the years," Fr. Casey snapped back.

Finzi took the reproach in stride. "Yes, I cannot deny it, that *is* what *my Government* has done, as well as certain rabbis here and there. But, Father, you know *our* history—when we had kings they made many mistakes. And we know *your* history—your Popes have made mistakes too. What can you expect of governments? Please keep in mind that their bad deeds don't relieve us as individuals of our responsibility to do good."

Fr. Casey decided to keep the conversation going. "I know that you are in the business of gathering information, Signore. Perhaps you would share your view of what is happening in the world these days with me, over dinner?" Finzi was delighted to accept the suggestion, and knew a restaurant in the Jewish district where they would not be recognized.

Speaking only as an individual, he said, his personal view was that the world situation was ominous. "It's obvious that something beyond the normal—*something climactic*—is happening. I feel sure that the world hasn't seen the end of 'interventions' such as the visions, whatever their source or purpose might be. As for your own little country, have you considered that it may be torn apart?"

"What do you mean by that?" Fr. Casey asked in surprise.

"We've gathered from contacts in various countries that some princes of your church are preparing for the most divisive battle for its control since the times when the loser in a papal election would continue his struggle as an anti-pope. Those on the losing side this time may be anathematized and dismissed from the clerical state. Apart from that internal strife, strong action against the Holy See is being talked about in Brussels. I realize, Father, that you have not expressed an interest in anything for yourself, but if you help us now, we will not let you drown later should flood waters sweep you off your feet."

As they continued to talk about this and that, without ever mentioning the Menorah, the Jesuit crossed the Jordan in his own mind. When they finished, Fr. Casey insisted on paying his share of the check. They stood outside the door of the restaurant for a moment to say good-bye.

"There is in Warsaw a Museum of the History of Polish Jews, is there not, Signore Finzi?"

"Yes, Father, there is. The previous Pope sent a congratulatory message when it opened."

"I thought I remembered that. Our current Holy Father, too, has always had great sorrow about the fate of the Polish Jews."

Finzi made no response, sensing that Fr. Casey was weighing saying something more.

"If someone with authority to sign a receipt on behalf of the Polish museum were to show up tomorrow morning at my office, Signore, I could identify a crate which was labeled many years ago as containing Egyptian artifacts from the dynasty of Thutmose II. *Despite its markings, I expect that the museum would find the contents—enlightening,*" said Fr. Casey with a smile. "I only have the authority to lend them for a year. Perhaps someday, if the diplomatic situation improves, a permanent loan might be arranged ..."

As "Signore Finzi" walked away, he felt sure that one day Justin Casey's name would be added to the list of righteous gentiles.

— 5 —

Rome

Msgr. Ireland was looking glum when Fr. Santorelli arrived at his office for a morning meeting. He launched right into what was on his mind. "Tony, the media back in the States have been taking stock of the results of the Pope's Apostolic Letter—and from their reports I can't say it's been a success. It looks like the Pope has ruffled the feathers of a lot of churchmen by the ecumenical outreach you proposed."

"Has he gotten *any* support?" the priest asked as he sat down.

"There are some evangelicals who see value in having a common penitential rite, but that's about it. The mainline Protestant denominations haven't formulated their response, and as you might expect, there's been a chorus of negativity from the churches that teach that the Pope is the Antichrist."

"What can they possibly have against the words, 'Jesus, I trust in you; have mercy on me, a sinner,' Monsignor?"

"They haven't been challenging the words as such—what they're objecting to is saying them while looking at or touching a *crucifix*." The Monsignor poked around his desktop and picked up a newspaper clipping. "The leader of the Irish Protestants came out with a statement blasting use of a crucifix as, and here I quote, 'the sort of abominable Popery that was abolished in the glorious Reformation,' end quote. A number of fundamentalist pastors in our own country have adopted his line."

Fr. Santorelli's face showed his exasperation. "That's exactly why the Pope proposed the alternative option of having the penitent look upon a picture of Christ on the Cross! They can't possibly object to that—they have those pictures in their own churches . . . "

"They've just conveniently ignored that option—so they can give the Pope another kick."

"Leaving aside the Apostolic Letter, the success of the Warning itself has been *what*, Monsignor?"

"In general, Protestants haven't been moved by the visions. *Older* Catholics are going to confession—mainly in communal penance services—but the *younger* ones don't seem to be taking the Warning seriously. They still aren't attending Mass, much less going to confession. For the life of me," he said, dispiritedly, "I don't know what it's going to take to shape them up."

"What does a cook do if the soup isn't getting hot fast enough?" replied the priest. "He turns the heat up!"

"Turns the heat up?" the Monsignor asked, with a puzzled look.

"Intensifies the visions. You know, like a parent warning a child not to do something. He doesn't say 'No' just once. If the child continues to disobey, the tone of his voice changes, and he may add the threat of a spanking . . ."

*   *   *

The first type of Warning vision continued to spread worldwide, and a new type of Warning was sent to those Christians who had previously received a vision, but had paid little or no attention to it. The worst sinners saw Hell *up close,* far more real and frightening than any glimpse of it they might have had in their first Warning vision. Those who received that vision did not have a placid, museum picture-viewing experience. Rather, they found themselves naked in the middle of a three-dimensional arena while sinners were being tortured all around them, with attendant gore and foul smells, curses, cries and inhuman sounds.

There were flaming pits and icy lakes, and swamps and cesspools crawling with giant snakes, spiders and scorpions which looked as though they had come straight from a prehistoric age of monsters. As if all those terrors could not provide sufficient punishment, there were *demons*—not the tame little red imps marking a can of Underwood's deviled ham—but horrid shapes that were at the same time part human and part animal. These were busy employing all the ingenious cruelties which men have inflicted upon each other over the centuries, as well as some not possible on earth. It was as though Hieronymus Bosch's *Last Judgment*, a grotesque, phantasmagoric 15th century altar triptych, had been painted from real life, or rather, from real death.

Just as the demons turned their attention to the person having the Warning vision and made ready to grab him, he felt the ground giving way under him and he fell down through the air toward what looked like a huge central fire pit far below, where bodies were cooking on coals and being tossed aloft by jets of fire and smoke. In his vision, the sinner tumbled uncontrollably as he fell, like a jumper from the top of the World Trade Center on 9/11. A split second before he plunged into the coals, his vision came to an end, and he found himself in his familiar surroundings. *No one* went through that experience without screaming, not even Cardinal Malapensa.

After he got over his fright at his vision of himself in Hell, the Cardinal Secretary of State grew very angry over what he had been put through. He assumed that the Pope was somehow involved, at the very least by petitioning God to continue sending the visions. His anger had a second focus, for the day before a subordinate of the Cardinal's had passed along information which suggested that Cardinal O'Melveny might share in the blame. Well, he would call the Cardinal of Topanga, and give him a warning of his own! Time zone differential be damned—let him be awakened by this call!

He was brusquely imperious with the American. "Eminence, *I am very displeased by these so-called Warning visions*—in particular at finding myself a target. I don't know yet how they are being transmitted, *but I want you to understand that when the whole machination has been exposed, I will see to it that those who are parties to it are stripped of their offices and dismissed from the clerical state.*"

Cardinal O'Melveny was totally unprepared for this sneak attack. "Eminence," he said, doing his best to respond in a calm voice, "*I have no idea what you are talking about!* Believe me, I find these visions as intrusive and offensive as you do. I can't imagine how you could think *I* would have anything to do with them."

"Is that so, Eminence?" Malapensa replied sharply, "do you not have a priest under your jurisdiction by the name of Anthony Santorelli?"

O'Melveny thought for a minute. "Yes, I regret to say I do. He was a real troublemaker, so I buried him alive. He's in a state prison as a chaplain. I haven't heard a peep out of him for years, now."

"*In a prison?*" The sneer in Malapensa's voice was obvious over the phone. "Well, you might be interested to know that he's been here for a week, meeting privately with the Pope. The visions started when he came, and he's been leading the Pope around by the nose in responding to them. I also suspect that he was the one who persuaded the Pope to dispose of the treasures in our museums. There's some secret about him which I haven't yet penetrated—some mysterious hold he has on the Pope. *Tell me, if you will, Eminence, how a lowly prison chaplain in America even gets in to see the Pope, let alone become his Rasputin, if he does not come with a very favorable personal recommendation from his Ordinary—meaning you, Eminence.*"

This allegation was so ludicrous that O'Melveny wondered if Malapensa was drunk. That would have been surprising considering it was morning in Rome, but it would explain why Malapensa was so inconsiderate as to awaken the Cardinal in the middle of the night.

"I can assure you, Eminence," said O'Melveny, "that I had no knowledge that he had left his post at the prison, much less that he was in Rome. If you think he had anything to do with those damn visions, I'll withdraw his faculties. Just send him back to me, 'in obedience,' and I'll make sure you never hear from him again."

"Very well, Eminence," said Cardinal Malapensa, "I will speak to Cardinal Figlio and make sure he is ordered to return to you immediately." And he hung up, still in a fury.

The Secretary of State lost no time in sending for Cardinal Figlio, the Prefect of the Congregation for the Clergy.

"Eminence," he said, "there is a plot underway to control the Holy Father. It is being masterminded by Cardinal Latoya, with the aid of Msgr. Ireland, and an American priest, who is exerting a mysterious influence over the Holy Father. You know Ratzinger's weakness for the mystical? Well, this priest is posing as a stigmatist, and has been guiding him, contrary to my best advice, in all matters pertaining to the visions and the sale of the patrimony of the Holy See. *The man is a Rasputin!*"

"That is news to me, Eminence!" replied Cardinal Figlio, in stunned surprise. "Who is this priest, and by what right is he here?"

"His name is Anthony Santorelli."

Cardinal Figlio gave a start at hearing that name, and turned away, as casually as he could, pretending to look out the window, hoping that the Secretary of State had not noticed his reaction.

Apparently Malapensa had not, for he continued right on. "He is incardinated in the Diocese of Topanga, in California. His repeated acts of disobedience there caused our brother, Cardinal O'Melveny, to demote him to the post of prison chaplain. Despite that, his one time mentor, Msgr. Ireland, summoned him over here and somehow managed to introduce him to the Holy Father. Since then, he has often been seen in the corridors of the Palace of the Holy Office and even in the Apostolic Palace."

"His own Ordinary was naturally outraged when I apprised him of these developments, and he asked that we see to the priest's return to his diocese immediately, *in obedience*. Once he returns, His Eminence has resolved to deal with the scoundrel in a way which will ensure that he never again disturbs the Holy Father's equanimity—or ours!"

Cardinal Figlio was in a state of confusion. He knew he had to respond—affirmatively—yet without making a commitment he would later regret.

"I will look into the matter at once, Eminence," he said smoothly, "and see what can be done! Thank you for bringing it to my attention."

Back in his own office, Cardinal Figlio sat pondering the difficult position he had been put in. Cardinal Latoya had already been to see him, asking that the priest be transferred to Rome, as a Consultor to Latoya's Congregation. Cardinal Malapensa outranked Cardinal Latoya, and so *his* direction to send Fr. Santorelli back to California posthaste should prevail. But, from what they both had to say, the Holy Father himself was making use of the priest, and if Figlio had him peremptorily shipped back to California, the Pope might be furious with Figlio!

This was clearly a situation where he should make haste, but slowly—*very slowly*.

— 6 —

Tehran, Iran
16 Bahman 1393 Anno Persico; February 5, 2015 Anno Domini

The accursed visions had now been seen by the Jews as well as the Christians—all blessed by the Pope, the German one who had insulted the Prophet (Blessed be he!). Would such visions be long in coming to Muslims? And where might they be coming from, if not the large broadcasting antennae within the Vatican's own walls?

Such were the thoughts that had led Ali to the conviction that it would be pleasing to the one true God to eliminate not merely the Crusader-Pope, but the entire Roman Catholic Church—a thought which was not original with him. A number of Protestant sects in Europe had come to the same conclusion, though for different reasons, at one time or another in centuries past, and a few had actually tried to do so but failed. Still, from what he had read, some Christian sects even now regarded the Pope as the *Antichrist*—the evil one known to Muslims by the name *Masīh ad-Dajjāl*.

Knowing that much, but little more, Ali's emotions and revolutionary fervor had swept him along to the inspiration that it would be possible to deal a fatal blow to Catholicism by wiping out a single target, the cobra's den itself—the city of Rome—with an atomic bomb. After all, what was the use of the sacrifices which his country had made to develop nuclear weapons in the face of western sanctions, if they were not to be used to advance the Revolution?

It was a breathtakingly simple, bizarre and ridiculous concept, yet one which was consistent with his having been promoted to a position of leadership because of his revolutionary zeal and personal bravery, rather than any cogency of reasoning, much less mastery of geopolitical strategy. Ali's logic would not have commended itself to a westerner; indeed, one might have questioned whether Ali's brain had recovered from the shaking a near hit by an Israeli missile had given it. But then, western minds find it hard to imagine the consequences that crackpot ideas can have when they are advanced by a man willing to commit genocide to see them implemented, as witness the careers of Vladimir Lenin and Adolf Hitler, among others in the last century.

Despite his prominent position as the Brigadier General commanding the Qods Force, Ali did not have authority to mount an attack on Italian soil, and he doubted that he could obtain it by going through the ordinary channels. Fortuitously, he had a back channel to his country's Supreme Leader, the Grand Ayatollah. He had never had occasion to use it before, but he would now try to put it to good advantage, by driving to the holy city of Qom, there to pay a call on his uncle, who was one of six senior clerics on the twelve member Council of Guardians of the Constitution. If it was the will of Allāh, on the next occasion when his uncle met with the Supreme Leader, his uncle would put forth Ali's plan to destroy Rome and the Catholic Church!

— 7 —

Rome

Cardinal Latoya wondered what Fr. Santorelli had on his mind in asking for a meeting on Monday. It turned out that he wanted to discuss the first Warning visions sent to the Jewish people, at the end of January.

"Eminence, I've been looking for some indication that the Holy Father has taken note of that development, but I haven't seen one. Have I missed some remark in an address that he's given?"

"No, Father, you haven't. His Holiness is aware of the visions, of course. However, Cardinal Malapensa strongly cautioned him against saying anything publicly, so as not to cause a breach in diplomatic relations with Israel."

"Well, I realize that you haven't asked my opinion," said the priest, "but I would like to express the view that it's very important for the Holy Father not to let this event pass without comment. *Carpe diem! That's my advice for him. Carpe diem!*"

"Oh? And just *how* should the Holy Father be *seizing the day?*" asked the Cardinal. "Hopefully you have in mind something not quite as provocative as the Apostolic Letter you persuaded His Holiness to issue."

Fr. Santorelli noted with relief that the tone in his voice was one of wariness, not anger.

"It's something which I think needs to be said by him, and can be directed to Catholics rather than to the Jewish people."

"You may proceed, Father," said the Cardinal, ready to make notes.

"Please forgive me for presuming once again to dictate the language of the first sentence. It is this: 'We rejoice that Our Father in heaven has extended to the House of Israel the same period of grace as He has offered to those who bear the mark of Jesus Christ, for the purpose of making right their relationship with the Father!'"

"*Father,*" said the Cardinal with exasperation, "*what makes you think it's any business of ours what the Jewish people do or don't do about what they're seeing?*"

"With all due respect, Eminence," replied the priest, "I think that it *is* our business, because, as your Congregation stated in *Dominus Iesus*, all salvation ultimately comes from Jesus Christ. Wouldn't He want His Vicar on earth to lend a needed hand here so that the Jewish people at least *consider* the offer of salvation being extended to them?"

"That's not the point, Father," Cardinal Latoya said. "If the Holy Father went near this subject in public, I don't doubt that the fears of the Secretary of State would come true—the Israelis would break off diplomatic relations with us. As it is, they have a long standing grievance with us, about our saying prayers for them."

"They shouldn't, Eminence. Just as we shouldn't be offended if they prayed for us."

That piqued the Cardinal's interest. "What do you mean, 'if they prayed for us,' Father? What sort of prayers are you thinking of?"

"*Prayers for our conversion, Eminence. Prayers that we no longer believe in the false Messiah, the blasphemer and sorcerer, Jesus of Nazareth. That would be an act of love on their part.*"

Seeing the shocked expression of the Cardinal, Fr. Santorelli hastened to explain.

"You see, Eminence, we both worship the God of Abraham, Isaac and Jacob. There is really only one issue between us: was Jesus of Nazareth the Messiah and Lord, the God of God, Light of Light, True God of True God, as we believe—or was He not? If He was *not*, then *we* should be Jews, and if He *was*, then *they* should be Christians."

"*Now, what I'm saying is that, if we really loved one another, we both would pray that the other group would see the light and convert. They need to understand that it is love that inspires us to pray for them. If we didn't love them, we wouldn't care if they got their theology wrong, and were not saved.*"

"I must admit, I've never had that thought, Father. Most interesting!" said the Cardinal. "I'll pass on your proposal to the Holy Father, but don't be surprised if Cardinal Malapensa's cautionary counsel, and mine, to the contrary, prevails on this issue."

Fr. Santorelli thought that the meeting was over, and started to rise, when Cardinal Latoya motioned him to remain seated.

"The visions sent to the Jewish people certainly make me wonder what is supposed to happen, in general, as a result of all these visions—what is it that God wants to accomplish? Do you have any insight into that, Father?"

"Eminence," Fr. Santorelli replied, "please don't think I'm quibbling about the wording of your question, but I think there's an ambiguity, which I'd like to deal with by breaking your question down into two separate questions and answers—What will God *actually* accomplish with the Warning? And, what might God have *wanted* to accomplish different from what He actually will accomplish?"

The Cardinal was a bit put out at the priest's suggestion that his question was defective. "I'm not sure I understand what you're driving at, Father. By definition, God has the power to accomplish anything He wants to."

"Yes—but as you know better than I, Eminence, He doesn't always do so, on account of allowing our free will to prevail. For example, you know that when He told the Chosen People to enter the Promised Land, they held back for fear of the inhabitants—and He was so angry with them that He condemned them to wander in the desert for forty years."

Cardinal Latoya sighed. "All right, Father, then answer my question as you will."

"I would analogize the Warning visions to John the Baptist's call to repentance, leading to acceptance of the Good News. I assume that God very much would prefer the visions to succeed, and so *we* must do all *we* can to get people to receive them favorably and act on them—and be saved. That's why I've been so insistent in urging the Holy Father to take the lead in promoting them through his public statements.—But, we know that Jesus Himself, the preeminent sign of all signs, was contradicted. So, I expect the visions will *not* succeed in many cases, at least not merely through their own persuasive force. The Lord told me that the Church will suffer—and that suggests to me that the visions will lead to strife, even wars."

"*Wars*, Father?"

"Well—yes, Eminence, *wars*. I expect the visions will greatly sharpen the divisions in society between good and evil people. The good ones will strive to reorient society to embrace Christian values, while the evil ones—especially government officials who do not repent of their evil ways—will resist and persecute them. And, in the non-Christian areas of the world, I expect religious pogroms and wars, as the Devil seeks to keep those areas in thrall to him . . . "

The Cardinal looked very unhappy with what he had just heard. "An unremittingly bleak forecast, Father, is it not? Where is your Christian virtue of hope?"

Fr. Santorelli had a ready response. "It lies in a promise God made—the covenant sealed with a rainbow—never to wipe out mankind again. So, sometime before we've made the earth unin-habitable and we're all done in, I expect the Lord will step in and put an end to the destruction. Also, I'm relying on the fact that He told me that the Church would prevail."

"By asking another question, Father, I don't mean to imply that I accept what you've said so far—but, I *am* curious. *Why* do you think all this is happening *now*? I mean, we're not wickeder or more in need of correction than past generations—*or are we?*"

"I've asked myself that, Eminence," the priest replied. " '*Why then?*' is a question that could be asked about everything from the 'Big Bang,' to the creation of man, to the coming of the Messiah. I really can't accept that pivotal events occur as a matter of chance at random moments in time. We can't *know* God's '*why*,' because God foresees all the consequences in the future of an act done today. It may be a consequence well down the road—even long after we're dead—that His action today is intended to bring about. So, the only answer I can think of to your question is that it's *now* that He's got all the parties and forces lined up the right way to achieve His purpose, sort of like a planetary conjunction that astrologers consider powerful, or the critical mass for a nuclear chain-reaction that physicists attempt to create."

Cardinal Latoya shook his head in puzzlement. "Is it a matter of there being a time when certain world leaders are on the scene, Father?"

"Yes, I think so, in part, Eminence. Political leaders, military commanders, religious figures, and so forth, but also certain indi-viduals of no consequence in the world's sight. Think of Peter the Fisherman—and Judas Iscariot—were their roles not vital in sal-vation history? Did God not select both of them?—Even more so think of the Blessed Virgin Mary. Did not God make our salvation wait for ages until *she* was born and of an age to conceive a child?

God is a patient master choreographer who uses unheralded players as well as kings to achieve His purposes.—Who knows? We may be among them ..."

— 8 —

Rome

Discouraged by the apparent rejection of his suggestions by Cardinal Latoya, and feeling drained by a loss of blood from his wounds,
Fr. Santorelli decided to go to the chapel in the building where
he was now staying. As soon as he entered, he could tell that, in
contrast to the chapel at the pension, it was not the sort of place
where he would find peace. All the elements were very modern in
design, beginning with the ceiling, which was in the form of an
A-frame—but not a simple one of bare wood as in many churches.
Instead, in between the ribs were diagonal members forming pro-
nounced crisscrosses which imparted a busy, commercial look to
the room. The lighting was built into two sets of square modern
pillars running down each aisle. Movable wooden chairs on the
polished marble floor furthered the cold and antiseptic appearance of the room. He forced himself to say a short prayer, and
left.

Searching for a more tranquil place to meditate, he walked
over to the Vatican Museum, where he wound up in a quiet
gallery, Room XII of the Pinacoteca. There he sat unmoving but
not unmoved, absorbed by Caravaggio's *Deposition from the Cross*.
One of the masterpieces in the Vatican's art collection, it merited
and was accorded a wall all by itself.

While in the seminary years before, he had sat through an art
appreciation course—a cursory slide show of religious pictures
and sculptures—which had succeeded in making him realize that
an enormous amount of skill and science went into creating a
work of representational art, and that he would never perceive or
understand the half of it.

In this canvas, though, he could not have failed to notice
that an unseen source of light illumined the principal subjects
in a way which sunlight could not have done. Christ's almost
naked body, temporarily supported horizontally by Nicodemus's
arms under His knees, and John's arms under His back, was
rendered in a luminous white—whiter than the bloodless hue
of a corpse—ensuring that it would be the center of attention.

The effect reminded him of two other Caravaggio paintings he had seen in the Cerasi Chapel of the church of Santa Maria del Populo—the Conversion of Saul and the Crucifixion of Peter. The most striking feature of the *Deposition* was the contrast between the illumination of the figures in the foreground, apparently by a "divine light," and the darkness of the background. It led the priest to meditate on Jesus' prophecy that darkness would fall after the Light of the World was taken from it.

That gave way to a second meditation: there were only five people left around the Son of God at the end of His life on earth. Two relatives—His Mother and Mary Cleophas (a first cousin), one of the 12 disciples—John, and two other disciples—Nicodemus and Mary Magdalene. The Messiah had crisscrossed the country, top to bottom and side to side, for three years. Three years in which he had instructed and healed thousands of people—maybe tens of thousands. *Where were they all now?* Indeed, where were the remaining ten apostles, men who had been closer to Him, and better understood who He was, than Nicodemus? The scene spoke to him in a way which prompted Fr. Santorelli to offer up his own loneliness in *his* ordeal, in union with that of his Lord.

Late in the afternoon, the priest was roused from his reverie when a guard approached. "Excuse me, Father, but it's almost closing time. Better have your last look—Fr. Casey will be boxing this painting up soon, along with the rest of our collection. The Pope is sending it elsewhere, as you've probably heard."

'Fr. Casey'—hearing that name brought to mind a memory from his first days in Rome as a graduate student. On a hunch, he enquired, "The Fr. Casey you mentioned—would he happen to be a Jesuit, an old Irishman with blue eyes?"

"Yes, Father, that's him. He works in the basement."

"I do believe I met him once, years ago. Could you tell me how I'd go about finding him?"

"He leaves every day when we close, so if you stand by the main exit then, you'll catch him passing by."

Fr. Santorelli felt a little thrill of excitement as he stationed himself by the front door. As he recalled it from their brief and accidental meeting, Fr. Casey was adept in spiritual matters. Any insights he could offer about Fr. Santorelli's condition would be appreciated.

Thinking back to when they met, he recalled the comical incident at a trattoria. It had been a searingly hot September day, and, newly arrived in Rome for post-ordination study, he had not realized the difficulty of running errands after class in its unfamiliar streets. They trapped him like the fabled Minotaur in a maze. His map did not reflect the irregular sizes and shapes of the smaller blocks, which ran off at all angles, while the straight main streets confused him by changing their name after each short distance. He smiled, now, as he recalled the uncomprehending looks he got when he sought directions from passersby in phrase book Italian, and, when that didn't work, in his relatively good Church Latin.

And so, back and forth and round about he had trudged, awkwardly carrying his purchases and his books, until he found himself enmeshed in crowds of people getting off work. Sweating profusely in his black, clerical suit, he had thought of a consolation not available to the Minotaur—sitting down with a cold beer. A cold beer in a *frosty glass*, if the Italians had such a thing.

Happening by chance upon a trattoria down a side street from the Pantheon, with its outside tables partly screened off by shrubs and canvas panels, he had entered with a feeling of relief, only to find all the tables taken. At one of them there was only a single person, an elderly man in a clerical collar. He would not have disturbed an ordinary stranger, but since the man was a fellow priest, he had walked over, pulled out his pocket Berlitz, and asked politely whether he might share the table.

Sizing him up quickly, the priest graciously responded, in English with a tinge of Irish brogue, "Of course, Father."

As he sat down, Fr. Santorelli thought to introduce himself, but the priest seemed to be otherwise absorbed, looking into the distance while sipping his Cinzano, and then lighting a cigarette. Fr. Santorelli ordered a *birra Peroni*, hopefully adding the words for 'glass' and 'ice,' and gesturing to indicate that the glass should be cold. The beer arrived at the table in a cold bottle, accompanied by a tall glass full of ice. The ridiculous sight struck the fancy of his table companion, who put out his cigarette and took a look at Fr. Santorelli and the treatises on mystical theology which he had placed on the table.

They were the subject of the conversation, while his beer lasted. The old priest had a number of comments to offer, comments which showed that he had read the books himself. Finding by happenstance a stranger who was familiar with these tomes, which dated back all the way to the 14th century, made an impression on the young priest, who thought to introduce himself as they parted. And that was the one and only time they had met.

Now, Fr. Casey looked around to see who was calling out his name. Eyeing Fr. Santorelli up and down, he smiled and said, "Aren't you the young man who wanted his beer *ice cold*?" They both had a laugh at that, and quickly agreed to have another drink together, in the trattoria where they had met—the old priest was a regular there.

After they had ordered, Fr. Casey asked with interest, "You must have finished your studies here long ago. What are you doing?"

Not wanting to blurt out everything at once, Fr. Santorelli made a non-committal answer. "Right now, I'm on a sort of extended vacation. My assignment is back in California, but I'm hoping maybe to be transferred here."

"Still interested in mystical theology, are you?"

"Still interested," Fr. Santorelli acknowledged. "It's so much easier to read about it than to do it, if you know what I mean."

"Yes." Then, pointing to the coverings on Fr. Santorelli's hands, he said, "You weren't wearing those when I saw you last."

"You're right, Father—the gloves are new—only two weeks old, in fact. I never dreamed I'd be needing anything like them, one day."

"If they're what I think they are, I didn't think you would either," said Fr. Casey. "As I recall it, you hoped to follow Jesus while avoiding suffering. If you don't mind my asking, what happened to change your mind?"

Fr. Santorelli saw it was no use trying to hide his situation. "In a nutshell, Father, I was brought low. I guess it's easier to accept a bit of suffering when you have neither comfort nor success to lose by it."

After telling Fr. Casey a bit about his career, Fr. Santorelli posed a question. "One of the things I don't understand is why I don't have any of the same feelings about being a stigmatist as Padre Pio did. I've read his letters to his spiritual directors, thinking they should prompt certain emotions and reactions on my part, but they don't. I've tried forcing my feelings—and I can't. I'm sure I'm responding to God's graces inadequately, and I don't know what to do about it . . ."

Fr. Casey had listened patiently, without interrupting. Now, he had some words of counsel. "Tell me, if you can, what other saint was like Padre Pio? Each saint is unique, even those with the same name. St. Teresa of Calcutta was not another St. Thérèse of Lisieux, who in turn was not another St. Teresa of Avila, and so on. *You know that.* You can't expect to be like St. Padre Pio just because you share the gift of the stigmata."

"If God wanted a clone of Padre Pio," the old priest continued, "He would have cloned him. From what you've told me, Father, it seems clear that God had a different role in mind for you. Padre Pio had the gift of reading souls, so he spent many hours in the confessional booth. I gather that you don't have *that* charism, but you're able to give advice to the Holy Father and the Curia—which Padre Pio never did. So, stop kicking yourself around for what was not meant to be."

"On the other hand, I do feel the need to mention two areas where you might consider improvement. First, you say you feel detachment from the world, but I detect a note of pride in your comments about your fine education, especially your lament that it's been wasted. That's the *old* you talking—the *you* that is still thinking of an academic career, now that you're back in Rome. Your education *was* a success. It brought you to the attention of Professor Ireland, and it's enabled you to advise him and others now. *God is aware of what you know. Forget how you want to use that knowledge—and let God steer you and your vocation where He will, without regret or complaint.* In that regard, you say that the Lord told you He would use you to present the choice of life or death to many. Who can you think of in the Bible, other than the Lord Himself, who had such a task?"

"Moses," Fr. Santorelli immediately replied. "He put the choice to the Chosen People twice."

"Yes. But you're no more a Moses than you are a Padre Pio. Who else?"

Fr. Santorelli thought, coming up with "Jonah."

"Yes. Exactly. That's more like it," said Fr. Casey. "God could send you someplace to convey that stark choice. And if He did, I don't think he would be relying upon your knowledge or your persuasive abilities to get the message across, any more than He did with Jonah. He would give you the words to say at the time. So once again, do not look to a teaching career or your learning as being determinative of your path or how you are to fulfill your mission."

"Even more important," Fr. Casey continued, "if you don't mind my saying so, it sounds like you're failing in a critical respect. You say that you wish the stigmata would close up because they greatly slow you down, and they're unnecessary now that you've given the message to the Pope. It seems to me that you're thinking of your stigmata as only being for the purpose of validating the message you were given, to the exclusion of their marking you out for heroic suffering."

"*A holy priest-theologian said that when a soul suffers out of pure and disinterested love without regard to itself, it is more useful to the Church militant and to the whole world than when it is engaged in a most brilliant and successful apostolate . . .* I suggest that you take those words to heart."

Fr. Santorelli had been listening without interruption, but at that advice, he demurred. "Forgive me, Father, but I don't see how that can be. Isn't that contrary to what St. Paul taught about the different parts of the body all having their different roles to play, but all being necessary? Is not one fitted for the apostolate, another for a different service, and a third fitted for suffering?"

"Taking your example of St. Paul," Fr. Casey replied, "no one ever was better fitted for the apostolate than he—yet he suffered greatly all the while from scourgings, stonings, and shipwrecks, not to mention the 'thorn in the flesh' which he begged the Lord to take away. And then at the end of his life, he was called upon to suffer martyrdom.

"All those sufferings came about in the course of his fulfilling his mission as an apostle," Fr. Santorelli pointed out. "It ties in exactly with what Our Lord said: 'If they persecuted me, they will also persecute you.' Physical suffering is just something that comes and has to be endured."

Fr. Casey tried a last approach. "*You need to think more deeply about the nature of suffering, Father. If you willingly accept it in union with the suffering of Christ, you transform it from being merely an irritant in your daily life, to being an instrumentality of your participation in the redemption of the world and in your own glorification.* Look, Father, at some point you must have expressed a willingness to suffer—*God wouldn't have given the stigmata to you otherwise*—but seems to me that you aren't identifying yourself with Christ with regard to His suffering. It was part of His mission to suffer, and like it or not, it's part of yours too. *In that regard, forgive me if I'm misjudging you, but it seems to me that, up till now, you have only been a servant who is suffering—as opposed to being a Suffering Servant. There's a crucial difference in attitude—and usefulness to the Lord—between the two.*"

Fr. Santorelli thought about that remark for a while, then said, "Well, you've given me a lot to think about, Father. Maybe that's what Jesus Himself was trying to make me understand at Garabandal. But, as long as I have a role to play right here at the Vatican, I think that apostolate takes precedence."

Recognizing that he had led Fr. Santorelli as far as he could along the Way, the old priest brought their conversation to an end. "Then, that's all I can think of for now, Father. If you ever want to talk with me again, you know where to find me."

"Are you sure about that, Father?" asked Fr. Santorelli. "Given the dispositions of the various collections ordered by the Holy Father, are you going to have anything left to do in the Vatican storerooms?"

"Probably not in the storerooms. Next week, I plan to go back to Ireland for a visit. After that, I'll return here. If there's nothing left for me to do working on the catalogue, I might go to Zurich to help take care of the collections of antiquities while they're awaiting sale. The Museum will always know how to get in touch with me. I assure you, it wouldn't be an imposition—I really would be interested to hear from you as you continue your ascent of the holy mountain."

— 9 —

Qom, Iran
22 Bahman 1393 Anno Persico; February 11, 2015 Anno Domini

In Iran, it was a day for rejoicing, and also for mourning. *Revolution Day*—the annual anniversary of the first Supreme Leader's accession to power in 1979—was celebrated by one and all, albeit in different ways. Mothers, dressed in black, held up pictures of sons martyred defending their country against Saddam Hussein's army, or in the many attacks which Iran had itself launched elsewhere. Other citizens, dressed in their finery, paraded down the avenues holding aloft the Grand Ayatollah's portrait. Students participated by leading a donkey draped with the American flag, or hoisting effigy balloons of Uncle Sam, which were later to meet a sorry fate. Fired up by the general revolutionary enthusiasm, Ali Hashemi drove to Qom to hear from his uncle how his plan had been received.

Muhammad Hashemi warmly welcomed his nephew Ali into his home. A servant brought a dish of pomegranates, which they ate while engaging in small talk about the family and drinking their black tea, piping hot and strong. After the table was cleared, it was time for Muhammad to speak.

"Nephew, our Supreme Leader was pleased with your initiative. Your objective is indeed a worthy one—he congratulates you for your ingenuity! However, it is far too risky to undertake."

"No!" Ali would have protested more had his uncle not motioned him to be silent.

"Naturally, the head of the Foreign Ministry was consulted. His opinion was that the entire international community would be *outraged* by the destruction of Rome. Everyone would say that jihadists must be behind such an act, and that only *our* country could have supplied them with such a weapon. The Italians would invoke the NATO Charter, and the Americans would be only too happy to retaliate with a devastating attack on us—*perhaps even on this holy city!* We cannot allow that to happen!"

Ali could contain himself no longer. "That's just what I expected of the Foreign Ministry! Tell me, Uncle, are we going to let the unbelievers trample on us for another thousand years?"

Muhammad responded calmly to the rant. "Hear me out, my great warrior! I have much more to relate, and it is good news! Our Supreme Leader believes that the *Mahdī* is ready to return, and that your plan, *if modified*, might even hasten his coming! And so he has given your project a code name—'*The Cleaving.*'"

Ali jumped right up, his eyes ablaze at the mention of the Awaited Savior.

"*The return of the Mahdī at last? Oh, Uncle, I would die a thousand deaths to bring him back now!*" Both of them fell silent, contemplating the prospect of the glorious return of the One who would purge the world of its injustice and corruption, and fill it with peace!

Ali broke their reverie. Sitting down, he inquired, "All right, then, Uncle, tell me what I *can* do!"

"Although, as I said, destroying *all* of Rome is out of the question, to achieve your objective, you need destroy only a small area of it. Within the city itself is a small country, the Vatican City State. It does not belong to NATO, and has many enemies of its own. The worldwide headquarters of the Catholics is there, as is their main church, which is filled with idolatrous representations of Allāh—images which must be obliterated."

"So, am I to come up with a new plan to do that?" Ali asked.

"Indeed you are, consistent with the conditions I will tell you about. First, the bomb you will use will have to be the smallest in our arsenal—one that can fit into a large suitcase. It will be a surprise 'package' for the enemy! Even so, it will have the power to destroy all life and all the buildings in the immediate area of the Vatican, without much damage to the rest of the city. That will spare the great mosque in Rome, which one day we shall be in charge of. Besides that, limiting the area of destruction will greatly lessen any international pressure for retaliation."

"What about my plan for delivering this 'package'?"

"It was ingenious, but a simpler one is possible because the suitcase will not be heavy—less than 50 kilograms. It will be disguised as the diplomatic pouch, which you will be able to carry right into the Vatican itself."

"And the Foreign Ministry does not oppose *this* plan?"

"Once it was clear that the Supreme Leader favored the plan as modified, the head of the Foreign Ministry did not dare to object. Indeed, he noted the fact that what he referred to as 'low yield, suitcase nuclear bombs' were made during the Cold War by Russia, and that several of these are known by the West to be unaccounted for at this time. That will make our denial of responsibility much more plausible. And, as you have said, al Qaeda will certainly claim to have been behind the exploit."

"Then, do I take it that my project is approved, with those revisions?"

"Yes, as to planning. No as to operations."

"I don't understand, Uncle. Didn't you just say that our Supreme Leader favored it?"

"Again I ask you to be patient, Nephew, let me finish. Our Supreme Leader has decided that so long as none of the followers of the Prophet (Blessed be he!) are receiving visions about Isā, the execution of the project should be put on hold until there is a gathering of leaders of the Catholic Church at the Vatican, when a thousand or more of them will be there together.

"You see, an attack at any time would kill the Pope, but another would take his place. One such serpent has succeeded another for two thousand years. Just as I and the other Guardians function under the Grand Ayatollah, and many thousands of clerics function under him too, so under the Pope there are more than a hundred clerics of the first rank called cardinals, and several thousand of lesser rank, called bishops, all of whom have a share in running the Church. It would be well if we could eliminate many of these too. And we believe that there will be a gathering of them all in the near future."

"Why would that happen, Uncle?" Ali asked.

"There are times when the enemy holds a great council with all of its highest leaders present at the Vatican, especially when one leader dies and his successor is chosen. The current Pope is old and ill, and under attack from many quarters. Therefore, we will wait in the expectation that you will soon be able to send the whole lot of them to the eternal fires of Hell!

"So, take heart!" added Muhammad Hashemi, smiling at last. "The Supreme Leader has given you approval to perfect your plan at this time with the various ministries, and when you are allowed to carry it out, your martyrdom will win a great victory for the Revolution! As you can understand, there can be no public acknowledgment of your role, Nephew. But, I will erect a lasting monument in the courtyard, and plant red tulips around it, in tribute to your sacrifice. And I will be overjoyed for your sake, for *martyrs are especially loved by Allāh—Glory be He, the Most High!"*

— 10 —

Rome

The Latin Mass was concelebrated as usual by the Holy Father and his personal secretary at seven in the morning in the private papal chapel on the third floor of the Apostolic Palace, with a few of the consecrated women who assisted in the papal household in attendance. Afterwards, the Pope said that he would like to remain there in adoration for a few minutes, and so Msgr. Waldheim left him alone in his wheelchair, facing the altar and tabernacle, and the life-size metal crucifix which hung high above them on the concave red marble panel forming the middle of the back wall. A grey-white panel sculpted in bas relief on either side depicted how the two great leaders of the Faith had met their death— the crucifixion of St. Peter, and the beheading of St. Paul. The stained glass panels on the side walls were a blaze of color, as was the whole ceiling, which was given over to a modern version in stained glass of Perugino's *Resurrection of Christ*.

Half an hour later, Msgr. Waldheim returned for the Pope, and found him out of his seat, lying sprawled on the marble floor, not moving.

His first thought was, "O My God! He's dead!"

He felt for a pulse—and there was one! Thank God!!!

After he turned the Pope on his back, he was rewarded with a word—"*Anton.*"

"Holiness, just rest. I'll summon the doctor and Malapensa."

With an obvious effort, the Pope managed to speak two more words. "*Not Malapensa!*"

"All right, just the doctor. What about Latoya?"

Benedict XVIth nodded 'Yes.'

Msgr. Waldheim's emergency call brought the papal doctor on the run from the nearby Vatican hospital. The Pope seemed to improve even as the doctor bent over him, beginning to speak more. The two men picked him up and reseated him in his wheelchair.

His secretary left the Pope to the physician's ministrations, while he greeted Cardinal Latoya, who had just arrived. When the doctor was finished, he wheeled the Pope over to them and gave them his report, which was encouraging, but did nothing to dispel the mystery. It did not appear that the Pope had suffered a heart attack or a stroke or seizure, and there was no other major medical emergency that the doctor could detect on the basis of his quick examination. He wanted the Pope to enter the Gemelli as soon as possible for comprehensive tests. Since the Pope was not disposed to accept that recommendation, there was nothing further he could do at the moment. Warning them to keep an eye on him, the doctor left.

"Holiness . . ." It was just one word, but the way it was spoken conveyed the Cardinal's deep and genuine concern.

"Eminence . . ." The Pope stopped right there, as if too fatigued to continue.

"Don't tire yourself. Please! We can talk tomorrow. Let us help you to bed!"

"No—I will be all right now . . . *It was the Miracle—I had a vision of it!* I felt the urge to kneel. I tried to do so—that's when I fell down."

"The Miracle?"

"*The Garabandal prophecy.*" Again the Holy Father stopped abruptly.

Cardinal Latoya accepted what he said without hesitation. Benedict XVIth was incapable of lying, and he was still mentally competent. The Cardinal knew that many other Popes had had visions, including Pius XIIth, who on four occasions in 1950 had seen the same type of dancing of the sun in the sky as had been witnessed by pilgrims at Fatima decades previously.

In a minute, the Pope seemed to grow stronger, and he went on. "*You* will see it one day, too. *The whole world will!*"

"See what, Holiness?"

The Pope shook his head, refusing to answer. "It will be time enough when it comes . . ."

"When will that be, Holiness?"

"I don't know. I think soon. It may be that I was given this special gift now because I will not be alive when it comes."

The Cardinal was touched by that thought, but there was nothing to be gained by giving in to maudlin sentimentality. "How can I help you now, Holiness?" he asked.

The Pope knew exactly what he wanted. "I would like you to insert language concerning the visions seen by Jewish people—

something along the lines proposed by Fr. Santorelli—into a script I will be using tomorrow at one of my public audiences. You can choose the most appropriate audience for that purpose, but, be sure to add language about coercion not being acceptable in religious conversions."

"Holiness," protested Cardinal Latoya, "surely you remember the concerns which Cardinal Malapensa and I expressed about the effect of your endorsing the latest visions, on our relations with Israel."

"Yes, Eminence, I have been well warned. The situation has changed even since yesterday. In light of what I have seen today of the coming Miracle, *I am persuaded that we must seize the day*, as Fr. Santorelli advocated! We must not allow the visions to fade from the scene, ignored, in silence."

*   *   *

The next day, the Vatican Press Officer called the press corps to a conference at which he released the Holy Father's remarks that morning, stating that the visions offered a period of grace not just to Christians, but to the Jewish people as well, for the repentance of their sins. The media gave his words great publicity, and almost all of the commentary was hostile. Overlooked or ignored was this strong caveat:

> *"While we welcome visions sent in an exercise of divine power, we condemn as sinful any human attempt to convert people to the Faith by coercion, whether physical or mental, and regardless of the motivation of the actor.* It is the Most High himself who will put faith into the hearts and minds of those who are receptive to such a great gift, which brings with it the promise of eternal life!"

The immediate result was a perception that a "truce" between Christians and Jews which was part of the social compact had been broken. Calls started to pour into the office of the Vatican Secretary of State, who had received a courtesy copy of the remarks only after they were given. Cardinal Malapensa was furious with the Pope, and incensed at receiving calls from his fellow Cardinals who assumed he must have had some responsibility for the release. The more he thought about it, the more significant this whole incident became in his mind. He had begun working behind the scenes to ease Ratzinger out as Pope, and this public relations debacle would furnish powerful ammunition in his conversations with other Cardinals about the need to replace him immediately!

— 11 —

Jerusalem

Once again the Israeli cabinet felt compelled to meet although Shabbat had begun. The Mossad and Shin Bet chiefs knew no more than they had when the visions started, other than that Jews all over the world had been "penetrated," as one Cabinet member put it. The purpose of the meeting was to consider how to respond *politically* to the Pope's brief remarks earlier that day.

The Cabinet members were united in the appraisal that they must be seen by the public as doing *something*, and the easiest measure was the strongest one—ending diplomatic relations with the Vatican City State. That was agreed to quickly, but it was not all. Lev Meier, an ultraorthodox member, called for approval of legislation which had been proposed repeatedly from time to time over at least a 20-year period, but killed by the Government each time. It was a law to make it a criminal offense to disseminate anything in which there was an "inducement to conversion" to any religion other than Judaism. He argued it was needed, "because whoever is behind *these terrorist messages* must be brought to justice in our courts!"

Dr. Tova Rabinowicz, the Health Minister and only female Cabinet member, said, under her breath, "assuming *they are* terrorist messages." It wasn't quite *enough* under her breath. Meier, sitting next to her, overheard it.

"What do you mean by that?" he demanded to know.

"I mean that we live in a world of very smart and very inquisitive people. Nobody has been able to figure out any way these visions could be sent with any technology known to man— even a theoretical technology that hasn't been tested. And nobody has been able to figure out who is responsible. Not just our own security people are in the dark—but those of every country in the world, as far as I know. So, why can't we at least *consider* the possibility that the visions are being sent by the Lord God?"

The elephant in the corner which they had ignored at their last meeting was now becoming visible in the Cabinet room.

Meier glowered at her. "That's ridiculous! It shows just why *we* don't let women speak in *our* services. *You don't have any idea of what you are saying . . . !*"

"Oh, don't I?" she retorted. "Isn't everything in our religion based on visions and supernatural events—from Moses and the burning bush to the visions of the prophets? The God of Israel has *always* made Himself known in visions. Just because there haven't been any for two millennia, do you think He's lost the power to do so?"

Meier, incensed by her taunt, was about to escalate the personal confrontation, when the Prime Minister stood up and called for order. In the momentary silence, an orthodox member of the Cabinet started to speak in a calm but pedantic tone.

"Tova," he said, "our ancestors had to deal with an untutored rabbi from Galilee, who went around stirring up the people with the false hope that he was the Mashiach. Even worse, he was proclaiming himself to be the divine son of the Most High. The Sanhedrin properly had him punished him for his blasphemy. They weren't taken in by his magic tricks, because they recognized them as works of the great deceiver."

"*I'm telling you—these visions we are seeing now are cut out of the same cloth—they are the work of Satan. He's trying to bring our people to apostasy. We must have a law to stop anyone from trying to induce conversions!*"

Dr. Rabinowicz chose not to do battle over the assertion that the visions were from Satan. She knew that there was nothing she could say to dissuade him of that view. Instead, she contented herself with asking, sarcastically, "Do you really expect that your law will stop the visions?"

"No," he admitted, "but it will prevent the heretics and apostates from following them up—saying a few words about the visions to get their foot in the door, and then leaving their pamphlets and Bibles to further their deception."

The proposal to ban Bibles set off alarm bells with the Prime Minister. He was a secular Jew, whose administration was continually being entangled in the snares and schemes of his religious fellow Israelis who sought to have their beliefs reflected in the laws of the Jewish state. This was, to his way of thinking, one more instance of how their "meddling" in secular affairs would lead to bad policy.

"Look!" said the Prime Minister to the orthodox member, "we're already using a group of your people to harass the Jews for Jesus so that they will leave our country—the authorities turn a blind eye when the *haredim* seize their pamphlets and Bibles, and trash them. But, what you are asking for now goes too far!

"*Do you have any idea,*" he asked rhetorically, "*of how much grief it would cause us in America if we banned their Bibles? Think of our Christian friends in the Government there. They're vital to our defense. Do we want their Bibles? Of course not! But, if we say 'No' to their Bibles, we run a great risk of them saying 'No' to making available the weapon systems we need to defend ourselves, like their Patriot missiles. I beg you—let's not be so righteous that we cut off our nose to spite our face . . .*"

His wise counsel defeated the resolution, but only narrowly, and the minority served notice that they would keep bringing it up again until it was approved.

— 12 —

Rome

The next day, as soon as the Pope's private morning Mass was finished, the Vatican Secretary of State came to the Papal Apartment looking somber.

"Holiness, the Israeli Cabinet met last night. I am here to inform you that the Government of the State of Israel has broken diplomatic relations with the Holy See on account of the comments *you* made yesterday about the visions received by the Jewish people."

Seeing no reaction from the Pope, he commented, acerbically, "I gather that you are not surprised."

"Disappointed, Eminence, but not at all surprised. The Prefect of the Congregation for the Doctrine of the Faith warned me that this would be a consequence."

"*So, you acted notwithstanding that advice, Holiness?*" There was reproach in his voice, which he did not bother to hide.

"That was my prerogative as Supreme Pontiff, was it not, Eminence?" The rhetorical question, though delivered in an even tone, was an unmistakable reproof. "I did what I believed the situation called for. The Israelis did likewise for their part. Time will show where righteousness lies."

Cardinal Malapensa proceeded grimly to his second topic. "That was not the only unfortunate repercussion of *your remarks*, Holiness. Permit me to read an editorial, which will appear in the New York Times this morning." And, without waiting for the Pope to grant permission, he proceeded to do so.

King Benedict XVI

Benedict XVI has now proved himself a worthy successor to the Bourbon Kings who once ruled in Italy. Their reactionary intransigence was memorialized in the saying that over the years, "they have learned nothing and forgotten nothing." We confess we were misled by the steps the Vatican had taken to enter into relations with the State of Israel and the international Jewish community, into believing that Benedict was

leading the Catholic Church to accept the choice of
Jews as to whether and how to worship.

We now see that that was a masquerade. The Bourbon King has exposed his true agenda—conversion—
by praying that the Jewish people will "arrive at the
fulness of redemption." *As if Judaism were not sufficient to accomplish that goal.* We have no doubt that
Jews will stand firm in their faith, as they have done
for 2,000 years in a hostile world, but, we believe,
individual courage is not enough.

The Holy See may seem puny to the point of in-
significance, but it has frequently shown itself capable of enlisting its members in mass political action,
from the Crusades, to the religious wars in Europe, to
the massive rallies of Solidarity in Poland in our own
times. We believe that the best way to prevent the
Vatican from mobilizing its adherents to proselytize
the Jewish people against their will is by having the
countries of Europe isolate it through diplomatic mea-
sures. It should not be allowed to spread its poison
freely in countries where there is already much la-
tent anti-Semitism left over from centuries of Church
teachings reviling Jews. We saw the warning signs
when Hitler published *Mein Kampf*, but the world did
nothing. This Pope frightened us when he welcomed
back into the Church a Holocaust-denying bishop. The
warning signs in the latest comments of King Benedict
XVI must not be ignored. *We call upon the world to act
at once!*

Having read the offensive piece aloud, the Secretary of State
augmented the insult with his own commentary. "Holiness, this
piece will strike a responsive chord in the foreign ministries of
certain countries. You will recall that Archbishop Tedesco reported
the rather petulant actions of a European Union Commissioner
following the Warning received by Christians. Your approval of the
vision seen by the Jewish people, is sure to fuel consideration of
his recommendations by various governments. Short of a complete
about face by you, by retracting your comments and publicly

apologizing, it is highly likely that other nations will follow the example of the Israelis and end relations with us."

The Pope did not react with surprise at this prediction, either. "Wisdom is not to be found among the rulers of the Earth," the Pope replied mildly. "I trust that you are already in the process of drafting instructions to our nuncios in the European Union countries on how to deal with this matter, Eminence."

Cardinal Malapensa reacted sharply. *"I hardly know what to tell them*—perhaps your Secretary for Relations With States would have a better idea of what you wish. I am *supposed* to be your second in command, but you did not even consult me regarding either the Apostolic Letter or those inflammatory remarks. Had you done so, I would have strongly urged that they never see the light of day. Obviously, I have lost your confidence. *Indeed, it seems to me that you have fallen under the influence of a Rasputin!"*

"A Rasputin? Whatever are you talking about, Eminence?" asked the Pope in amazement.

"From what I have heard, you are taking guidance these days from a young American *prison chaplain* who has been disobedient to his Ordinary, the Cardinal Archbishop of Topanga. I have just learned that his supporters even put him in for transfer to the Curia so that he can have continued access to your ear. How do you think that makes those of us with years of experience in matters of state feel, Holiness?"

Cardinal Malapensa did not pause for an answer.

"It is even whispered, Holiness," he continued, "that the man claims to be a *stigmatist*. Don't you remember the last one to make pretensions about having stigmata? A Father Gino, here in Italy? Quite a mess *he* caused! We had to take action severe action, stripping him of his priestly faculties for violation of the seal of the confessional and sexual abuses. The last thing the Holy See needs now is for you to become involved with another *mystic* who may bring disrepute on the Church—and on you for your credence of such questionable phenomena."

"I see," said the Pope, angry and dismayed. He thought briefly of informing Malapensa that he had had the American priest thoroughly checked out medically—and cleared—at the Gemelli immediately after first meeting him. But it was obvious that Malapensa's mind was closed, and there was nothing to be gained by arguing with him. He merely asked a question. "It would seem that you came prepared to speak your mind, Eminence. Is there anything further you wish to say?"

"Yes, though I deeply regret having to say it. *I and many of my brother cardinals believe that you have done grave harm to the Holy See, and that your continuance in the office of Supreme Pontiff will only deepen the wound. We hope that upon prayerful consideration of this matter, you will see your way clear to give up the burdens of your office now, and go into retirement . . . "*

His own chief lieutenant was leading a rebellion and calling upon him to resign!!!

Such treachery—such an insult to the Vicar of Christ—was unthinkable. Except that it had just happened . . .

He had been aware of Cardinal Malapensa's disaffection, but the virulence of this attack shocked him to the core. By rights, he could have taken great offense at the unprecedented tongue lashing from his subordinate, and replied in kind, dismissing him from office on the spot. But, that would be a useless gesture, he realized, in view of the fourth part of the message which the American priest had delivered to him.

And so, he only said, with deep emotion, "Eminence, I am truly sorry you and others feel this way!—I will pray about the matter, as you suggest, and in turn, I ask *you* to pray about whether *you* should resign as Secretary of State, since it appears that you are no longer willing to carry out my instructions . . . "

*   *   *

Cardinal Malapensa returned to his quarters in the Apostolic Palace in a state of high dudgeon. More and more often in his daily meeting with the Pope his frustration increased to the point that he had to look away in an effort to hide his anger. On such occasions, his eyes usually traveled around the corner of the room, past the antique life-size statue of the Virgin and Christ child, and came to rest on a casement window opening onto the Square. *That* window was the one which the Pope traditionally appeared at to bless the crowd on special occasions.

Obviously, the Cardinal could not get up and walk over to it in the Pope's presence. But, back in the dressing room of his own apartment, he could draw himself up before a full length mirror in a gilt rococo frame, and admire himself in a cassock and zucchetto changed by his imagination from cardinal red into papal white. With his left hand, he fingered the pectoral cross on his chest, pretending that it was embellished with diamonds. And he practiced slowly turning from side to side, making the Sign of the Cross with his right hand as though he were at the famed window, solemnly bestowing his Papal blessing on those looking up at him from the Square. It was only a fantasy, but one which he expected would soon become real.

Given his family's wealth and prominence in Milan—he counted several cardinals and one Pope on his family tree—and his own talents, he had aspired to the highest ranks of the clergy even before becoming a priest. As he rose over the years in the Vatican's diplomatic service, he had suffered a twin disillusionment. The Church no longer had any interest in exercising temporal power in society, and the nation states which did exercise such power had shown themselves unable to assure safety and sufficiency for their citizens.

The solution, or so he came to believe, was a universal government, one with a universal religion at its command to help unify all peoples under a common ideology. The beginning framework was already being formed through the European Community, the United Nations, and similar international organizations—as well as private groups unknown to the public, such as the Cavour Lodge of freemasons in Rome. The latter group, which he was secretly inducted into after he was made cardinal, were convinced that the masses would willingly surrender their freedom to a government that could enforce a universal peace and assure everyone of enough food to live on. Malapensa agreed with that, and with their further belief that to be successful, such a government would need—and deserve—a citizen's total allegiance. No competing claim to loyalty by a religion could be tolerated.

It was obvious that these views were antithetical to what Ratzinger held to, for he had openly refused to accept the Zeitgeist of the 21st century. And so, Ratzinger had to be pushed aside as Pope by Malapensa and his powerful friends, which numbered among them the Prime Minister of Italy. After that was done, his assignment in the New World Order would be to bring the Church under the government's control. It would be a most difficult task, but Malapensa had assured his new found Masonic friends that he would be able to accomplish it, once he was crowned Pope and had populated the College of Cardinals with men of his own selection.

Invoking Jesus' words to Peter that whatsoever he loosed on earth would be loosed in heaven, as his master stroke, Malapensa would promulgate the dogma that all moral judgments were relative and that an individual's conscience was the ultimate guide and the test by which a man or woman should live and would be judged by God. Therefore, whatever was permitted by one's conscience would be considered "loosed" by the Church and ipso facto would not be "sinful."

He foresaw that the masses would be grateful that the sense of sin which now weighed upon them had been lifted. At the same time, his enemies would be hoist with their own petard of orthodoxy. By declaring the primacy of conscience "ex cathedra" in his capacity as pastor and teacher of all Christians—a doctrine of faith which must be held by the universal church—those in the hierarchy who accepted the dogma of papal infallibility would be forced to accept the new dogma or be excommunicated as heretics!

— 13 —

Miami

As soon as he saw the Pope's remarks on the visions seen by the Jewish people appear in a posting on the Internet, the Cardinal Archbishop of Miami, Seymour Lazard, called his mentor, Cardinal O'Melveny. Lazard had been given his red cardinal's hat the year before by Benedict XVIth, despite being in the Pope's disfavor. In truth, as a bishop, Lazard had done nothing to commend himself to anyone other than O'Melveny, for whom he had done many deeds which the Cardinal was too devious to involve himself in directly. However, O'Melveny had threatened that the bishops in America might choose to end the annual Peter's Pence collection which was sent to Rome unless Lazard were elevated to the cardinalate. Great pressure had been put on the Pope by the head of the Vatican Bank, who painted a dire picture of the Holy See's finances if the Americans withheld their financial aid, and this had forced the Pope to capitulate despite his low regard for Lazard.

Lazard's past was such that he had received more than one Warning vision. In the first, he had seen the many sins he had committed in his prior diocese in California. That vision showed him visiting the Sisters of Hildegard of Bingen at their mother house fifteen years before. To his way of thinking, the nuns were neurotic, repressed, and obsessed with ritual. Their "hyper-scrupulosity" drove them to confess trivial faults and thoughts week after week. To liberate them and finally usher in the Spirit of Vatican II, he arranged for them to have psychotherapy. It was given by a humanistic institute, and paid for by the diocese. There were lectures, workshops and encounter groups. The idea was to rid the nuns of their "encrustations," including the habits they wore, and their ridiculously pietistic way of walking and talking. They needed to be opened up so that they would express their emotions freely.

The Cardinal wasn't fazed as in his vision the scenes progressed to the aftermath—sexual experimentation, out-of-wedlock births, abortions, mental breakdowns, even suicides of some of the ex-nuns, and the total collapse of their religious order. Why should *he* feel responsible for such developments? He had done nothing against *his conscience*, and nothing against *their wills*; they had chosen their lot, just as he had chosen his.

In the second Warning vision, he had seen Hell up close, and it did frighten him, but only momentarily. He had long ago lost his faith, and bet his soul that of the Four Last Things, the only one which was real was Death.

In response to Lazard's plea for instructions as to how he should respond to questions about the Pope's comments, O'Melveny expressed his great satisfaction with the development. "I couldn't be happier, Sy!" crowed the Cardinal of Topanga. "Now all the media will be attacking Ratzinger. He should have kept his thoughts to himself. It's clear he's incompetent to run the ship of state. Support for him must be at a tipping point, if he hasn't already lost most of the cardinals."

"Then, what can *we* do to take advantage of the situation, Eminence?" asked Lazard unctuously.

"I think I'll arrange for you to be interviewed by Barry Prince on CNN, Sy. Your job will be to cast aspersions on Ratzinger's remarks. Then, why don't we work with the various interfaith groups we belong to, like the Conference of Christians and Jews, and the Anti-Defamation League? Let's reach out to our Jewish and Protestant co-chairmen and have them take the lead. Encourage them to arrange protests—picketing at the Vatican Embassy in Washington, university conferences, or whatever they can think of. As invited participants at their events, we will be free to support *their* attacks on the Pope. The more condemnation we can stir up on the outside, the more evident it will be to our wavering friends that Ratzinger has to go!"

— 14 —

Miami

If he had his druthers, Lazard would have liked to avoid the TV interview which Cardinal O'Melveny had readily arranged. He was sensitive about his personal appearance, which he knew was not telegenic. The 300 pounds on his short frame looked even heavier when he had on his ordinary clerical suit instead of his red robe, which at least tented over his figure. His large bald head, with small black eyes, sat on too short a neck. He tried to disguise the latter anatomical defect with a full black beard, one he fancied gave him a "patriarchal" look. In any event, despite his physical deficiencies, his mind was sharp enough to generate mocking disdain of the Pope's comments on the visions, as he had been tasked to do by his patron.

Barry Prince's soft tone and conversational style belied the very well planned questions he asked, designed to bring out a maximum of information. "What is your overall reaction to the Pope's statements welcoming the Warning visions, Eminence?" the show's host asked.

"I find them very—," Lazard paused theatrically, as if searching for the right word, and stroked his beard, before settling on "unfortunate."

"*Un*fortunate? Why was that?"

"As you know, the Pope is the Bishop of Rome—only one bishop among thousands with respect to matters other than faith or morals. On a novel and far reaching matter such as this, it would have been better had he taken the time to consult with his fellow bishops before making a pronouncement. By not doing so, he reinforced the misperception that the only view that counts in the Catholic Church is that of one man in Rome. Added to that, he insulted our brothers of the House of Israel."

Barry followed up on the hint. "Suppose he had consulted *you*, Eminence, what advice would you have given him?"

"I would have cautioned him not to assume that these so-called 'Warnings' were something sent by God."

Barry found that surprising, coming from a cardinal. "What makes you think they might *not* be a warning from God?"

"The visions present a person's experiences from a very *judgmental* perspective."

"And so . . . ?" asked Barry.

"And so, I don't believe that they could have come from God. Our religion isn't about making people feel bad for what they've done. Jesus didn't even condemn the woman caught in adultery."

The host continued feeding questions which the Cardinal could answer any way he wished. "Some people claim to have seen pictures of Hell. Why do you think that was, Eminence?"

"We've all seen such images in cartoons and movies. They're firmly entrenched in the popular imagination. I regret to say they can be traced to teachings of the Church in times past. To stop such nonsense, when I became head of the Miami Archdiocese, I instructed my priests that they were never to preach about Hell."

"Is there any other aspect of the Pope's comments you object to, Eminence?"

Lazard stroked his beard again before replying. "I'm sorry to say there is. Once more, the Bishop of Rome has tried to tell people how their consciences should operate and how they should carry out their religious beliefs. Perhaps he doesn't suffer from a want of an audience because of all the visitors to Rome, but I have to tell you, Barry, that if I tried to give orders to people like he does, the churches here in Miami would be empty!"

There was less than a minute left for this segment of the show, so Barry switched to broader questions. "Do you think the Pope doesn't understand the American spirit?"

"I think he *understands* it well enough. He just won't *accept* it, as he has said a number of times."

"Is anything going to change Rome, Eminence?"

"I don't expect any change until we have a new Pope, Barry. When that happens, we'll see a major realignment of doctrine to match practice—an updating of the theology textbooks to reflect how people actually live their lives in this very complex and nuanced society, where truths are relative, not absolute."

— 15 —

Rome

The point man in the developing diplomatic campaign to isolate the Vatican was not a foreigner, but an Italian—indeed, the Prime Minister of Italy! Ercoli Togliatti Genovese was the leader of the country's socialist bloc, and, beneath his public veneer, a Communist, like his parents. They had both worked for the Communist Party when it was headed by the legendary Palmiro Togliatti, whose pen name was "Ercoli," or Hercules. He had grown up with the dream of stripping away from the Church the territory of the Vatican—the home base it had left after the revolution which took place in Italy in the mid 1800's.

In 2015, all of the major European countries were governed by socialist parties, and this political alignment, together with Genovese's secret connections as a very high level member of the Masonic Order and head of its Cavour Lodge, gave him access to levers of power throughout the continent. He sensed that the time had come for him to pull those levers with all his might! The Pope's enthusiastic embrace of the visions had provided the *casus belli*—the excuse for war—against the Vatican by the European Union.

His first step was to reach out by phone to Geoffrey Hutton, the British Prime Minister.

"Hello, Geoffrey! It's your friend Ercoli in Rome! How are you doing?" ... "Good! Yes, I'm fine! I haven't been plagued with visions of my misdeeds, since I was never baptized, but, *I sympathize with you*. It's just *terrible* when a man's home isn't his castle!" ... "The reason for my call is that I wondered if you've considered whether this is an opportune moment to deliver a knockout blow to the Vatican?—Don't your people call the Pope the Anti-Christ?" ... "Specifically? I was thinking that our representatives in Brussels could coordinate an EU position.—You've read the New York Times editorial, haven't you? The one calling for the Vatican to be quarantined?" ... "Yes, I realize it would be up to us here in Italy to be the primary enforcers. There would be a lot of opposition from the right in Parliament, but I can handle the outcry, provided I'm not on the front line alone. My thought is that if your country, France, Germany and Spain all form a bloc with us, we can ride out the storm together." . . . "You will? Excellent! Excellent! I'll let my Foreign Minister know what we've discussed and have him call your man within the hour. My friend, I thank you! It will be an honor to work with you on this project!"

*   *   *

Archbishop Van Tri, the Vatican's Secretary for Relations with States, tried to keep the Holy Father advised of diplomatic developments in the European Union through periodic phone messages to Msgr. Waldheim. In the evening, the Archbishop briefed the Holy Father in person, with Monsignori Waldheim and Ireland, and Fr. Santorelli present, about the resolution against the Vatican City State circulated that afternoon by the British Government. Papal nuncios in the various EU countries had been alerted to test the waters, and with few exceptions they reported back that there had already been much high level discussion of the resolution, and the Holy See was in deep trouble.

"Paradoxically, Holiness, much of the problem is anti-Semitism," said the Archbishop.

"Anti-*Semitism*, Excellency?" asked the Pope, "Don't you mean anti-*Catholicism*?"

"Actually, no, Holiness. As you know, strains of anti-Semitism have been very strong in countries such as France for many years, and their governments have been severely criticized by Jews domestically and abroad for their failure to deal with that evil. The British resolution gives those governments a chance to do something major to appease those constituents at little cost, by coming down hard on the Pope. In addition, many in their own Catholic populations would welcome it if a quarantine succeeded in forcing your Holiness to make changes in doctrines and policies.—I regret to say that I expect the British resolution to pass overwhelmingly tomorrow."

When the Archbishop was excused, the Pope spoke freely. "The third part of the message Fr. Santorelli brought me was of kings rising up and princes plotting against the Lord and his anointed. Is that not already happening in Brussels?"

"Yes, Holiness, it is," said Msgr. Ireland, "but we don't need to take what's going on in Brussels lying down! You still have great moral authority with many people in Europe. Surely, we could craft a statement chastising those who would seek to stifle your prophetic witness. We could draw powerful a parallel between you and the Hebrew prophets, particularly Jeremiah!"

"*Thank you*, Monsignor," the Pope replied as he nodded in acknowledgment of the compliment, "the comparison is flattering. However, the world appears tired of listening to messages from us. Another one would not have any effect on the heads of state—they need no warning from us to know that what they are doing is wrong . . ."

Fr. Santorelli unexpectedly entered the discussion. "If you think that a message from you, standing alone, would not be effective, Holiness, what about issuing excommunications against government leaders—that is, those who claim to be Catholic?"

"*Excommunications?*—What for, Father?" asked the Pope.

"I'm not expert in Canon Law, Holy Father, but what they are doing is whipping up animosity against the Church, and attempting to intimidate you and the hierarchy from freely proclaiming the Church's teachings. Are those not offenses for Catholics?"

"They are indeed offenses, Father," Msgr. Ireland interjected curtly, "but the Holy Father has indicated that he is not of a mind to pursue canonical penalties against civil leaders."—"Let that be an ended of the discussion," he added, seeing that Fr. Santorelli was preparing to press the issue.

"Yes," said the Holy Father, "excommunication would be the wrong remedy. They would refuse to recognize a decree of excommunication, and draw the mantle of Martin Luther over themselves—which would greatly enhance their popularity. We must leave it up to God to deal with them . . ."

*   *   *

Msgr. Ireland and Fr. Santorelli walked out of the Papal Apartment thinking very different thoughts about what they had learned that evening. The prelate spoke first. "As bad as the news is from the European Union, I'm relieved that the threat is now out in the open. It's only a quarantine—not a military action. So, Tony, your worst fears of some sort of outside forces coming in and causing great physical destruction and loss of life weren't justified!—The Pope won't starve, and the people will become increasingly furious that they are being kept away from St. Peter's. After a few months, the besiegers will have to slink away. *I predict it'll end in a great victory for the Papacy!*—And, I'm not asking you for *your* comments, because I'm sure they'd be *negative.*"

When Fr. Santorelli continued to walk with him in silence, the prelate relented. "Oh, all right, you Cassandra. Tell me what you see."

"I see the quarantine as opening Pandora's box. It will legitimate all sorts of opposition to the Pope, most particularly by those who will claim that *he* needs to go in order for *them* to save the Papacy from his misguided rule. My only hope is that they overplay their hand so badly that it discredits the lot of them—so that *they* don't wind up in control of the Papacy. If one of his critics became Pope, it would be a worse catastrophe for the Church than any physical destruction here."

— 16 —

Brussels

Not since the days of the pagan Roman emperors had Europe been so united against the Papacy. In Brussels, the European Council held a special meeting in the Résidence Palace to consider a resolution put forward by the British Prime Minister, who explained to the assembled heads of state and heads of government why Her Majesty's Government was now formally proposing action against the Vatican City State:

"A new phase has been opened in the campaign of the Vatican City State to change the laws of our countries to suit its backward religious doctrines. It has blessed mental assaults upon innocent people in other countries, men and women who were minding their own affairs, often in their own homes. These assaults, in the form of inner visions, have confused, angered and frightened citizens in each of our countries, and, indeed, throughout the world. Visions purporting to show tortures which will befall people who do not act as the Roman Catholic religion prescribes clearly violate provisions of our Charter of Fundamental Rights."

"In the dark days of our continent, war was readily resorted to when nations opposed one another on such basic principles. With the progress of civilization, we have other, better means at our disposal to handle such disagreements, including joint action to enforce a quarantine of an offending state. *Accordingly, Her Majesty's Government is proposing that, pursuant to Article 11 of the Treaty on European Union, the member states define and implement a common foreign and security policy, in the form of a quarantine, against the Vatican City State, until it shall have renounced its support of the visions and affirmatively brought its social policies into line with those of the Union.* In carrying out this resolution, each member state which approves it will be expected to take whatever actions it deems appropriate."

The historic proceedings in the European Council were broadcast throughout Europe, and there was widespread jubilation as speaker after speaker rose to support the British resolution. It passed with only five dissenting votes—those of Poland, the three

Baltic States, and Greece, whose Orthodox Patriarch had warned against the anti-religious tide in the EU. Europe had resolved to give the Vatican a "bear hug" to bring it into the modern world.

Rome

Italian Prime Minister Genovese's triumph in fomenting the EU's action against the Vatican went to his head. After the vote, Genovese boasted to the French Foreign Minister that next he was going to "give the old kraut the boot." His remark was overheard, and reported by the media.

He quickly learned what a blunder he had made. In the ten years that Joseph Ratzinger had been Pope, the Italian populace had come to respect him as a towering intellect, and a modest and humble man in person. Yes, he was a German, but he had lived for many years in Rome, spoke Italian fluently, and had made clear his love for Italy and for the Italian people. They took umbrage at Genovese's crude disrespect.

What did Genovese mean, anyway, by his threat against the Pope? Caller after caller to daytime radio shows in Italy expressed fears for the Pope's physical safety, some crying as they did so. To quell the growing uproar, the Prime Minister hastily called a late afternoon news conference, without consulting his Cabinet first about what he should say.

To the question, "Do you plan to remove the Pope by force?" he replied superciliously, "That would be a last resort. For now, we are going to put in place a quarantine. I expect when he gets good and hungry, he'll leave of his own accord."

"You mean you're going to cut off his food?"

"Of course. Food, water—everything! What do you think a quarantine is? He has to be taught that the Vatican is not a world unto itself. It's only a tiny island, dependent on our good will."

Instead of scribbling down that answer, as the others were doing, a journalist from the Corriere della Sera flipped through his notes about the Lateran Pacts of 1929. He had done his homework the day before the European Council's vote, and had concluded that isolating the Vatican would not be a simple task for Italy.

Somehow he made his voice heard over the other shouts, with the question, "How do you plan to get around the Lateran Pacts?" Every Italian schoolboy had to learn about *those* treaties. Indeed, just two weeks before, the Prime Minister himself had attended the annual anniversary celebration of the signing of the Lateran Pacts, held at the Palazzo Borromeo. But now, the Prime Minister looked at the reporter blankly, because he had not taken their provisions into account in his maneuverings.

Genovese had been a radical labor leader, the head of the Confederazione Generale Italiana del Lavoro, which had a reputation for calling illegal strikes, a background which indicated a contempt for legal restrictions. And the answer that came off the top of his head was in keeping with his roots: "Mussolini gave away too much to the Church. The time has come to sweep those arrangements into the dustbin of history."

That was an even more serious mistake—calling into question his government's adherence to the settlement of the civil war in Italy between Church and State. The Prime Minister's impetuous answer created the same shock as if an American President in this day and age were to declare that the Treaty of Paris, which ended the American Revolutionary War, was too favorable to Great Britain in allowing it to retain Quebec as part of Canada, and therefore the treaty should now be abrogated.

The Corriere della Sera, the country's most prestigious daily, put a slashing editorial on the wires that evening:

> **"Who's the *Real* Foreigner?"**
> The Prime Minister has expressed his disdain for Benedict XVI as a foreigner. But from observing him closely for a decade, even when we disagree with his policies, we do not doubt that the Supreme Pontiff embodies the same nobility of mind and heart as his greatest Italian born predecessors, and respects our country and its civilization. On the other hand, we regret to say that our native son, Enrico Togliatti Genovese, speaks like an apparatchik of the Marxist-Leninist school from the old Soviet Union when he talks about sweeping the Lateran Pacts into "the dustbin of history."

Perhaps he has forgotten that the settlement of the Roman Question took 50 years to accomplish, and that we have been at peace internally for more than 80 years since then. Or is he deliberately trying to reignite class and religious warfare? And, what other treaties would he reopen? Perhaps the one settling World War II and our national boundaries? Unfortunately, in this matter, Hercules has shown that his muscles are better developed than his brain.

The Italian Prime Minister's embarrassments made him even more determined to drive "the old kraut" out of the Papacy, though he was careful not to say that again out loud! He met with his key Ministers to ask what he *could* do immediately to throttle the Vatican without violating those damn Lateran Pacts.

Was the reporter right, that he couldn't starve out the Pope?—Yes, he had to let the water and food get through in accordance with Articles 6 and 20 of the Conciliation Treaty, and the January 2004 explanatory agreement on the water supply.

What about cutting the phone lines into the Vatican, and the mail service?—No, that was forbidden. Article 6, again. And jamming the Vatican's radio and TV broadcasts?—No, also forbidden by Article 6.

"And if I order barricades put up at the entrance to St. Peter's Square, to keep people out?" he asked.

That was a difficult question to answer, they replied, as they pored over the provisions of the Treaty. It was clear from Article 3 that *the Holy See* could not prohibit the public from coming into St. Peter's Square, except temporarily, for special ceremonies. But there did not seem to be a specific provision requiring *Italy* to give access to St. Peter's Square and the Vatican, other than for ecclesiastics and diplomats, and the small number of people who actually were citizens of that country. And the wording of Article 3, stating that "St. Peter's Square shall continue to be normally open to the public and shall be subject to supervision by the Italian police authorities," seemed to contemplate that the Square could be closed off by police authorities when conditions were not "normal."

Since his Ministers could not tell him that blocking public access to St. Peter's was *prohibited*, the Prime Minister decided to treat it as *permitted*. And so they were tasked to work up a quarantine proposal for Parliament to consider as an emergency matter, to go into effect as soon as possible.

Washington, D.C.

When the State Department learned that the Italians were moving quickly to follow up on the vote by the European Council, the President sought the advice of his Chief of Staff and the Secretary of State. None of the three men who met in the Oval Office was in a mood to befriend the Vatican. Bernard Cohen, a Conservative Jew, and Secretary of State William Howe, an Episcopalian, were simmering about the visions they had had of their sins. And President John Gardiner, a very lapsed Catholic, was still mentally reeling from a vision of himself in Hell.

The President turned to his Chief of Staff. "Bernie, I assume if we do nothing, the Europeans will just handle this matter themselves. Is there any reason for us to get involved?"

"You're right, Mr. President, they can and will handle it. Even the Italians can't botch the quarantine, since they already surround the Vatican. What I think you should consider is whether there's any mileage to be gained by associating us with the EU's action. Bill can speak to that."

"Mr. President," said the Secretary, "I agree with Bernie that we aren't needed, but we would score points with a lot of European governments if we backed them in this initiative instead of sitting on our hands—and at no cost to the taxpayers."

"What do you think domestically, Bernie?" the President wanted to know.

"I've already seen a stinging editorial in The Forward, a prominent Jewish periodical, denouncing the Pope for blessing the visions sent to Jews like me. It calls him a threat to world peace. More than that—it says the international community ought to remove him if his own people don't. That's a sentiment widely shared in my community—and I guess many Protestants and Catholics must have it too."

"I know I do!" the President responded. "Well, Mr. Secretary, what do you suggest? Sending over some sort of note saying 'add our name to the list'?"

Secretary Howe was delighted that the President was willing to strike a blow against the Pope! "We can certainly do that, and if you're willing to be a bit more aggressive, Mr. President, there are two further steps we could take. The first, obviously, is to cut diplomatic relations with the Vatican, as the Israelis have done. The second would be to ask the United Nations to revoke the permanent observer status for the Vatican City State—that, and the special right it has to speak in the General Assembly. That's what enables the Vatican to introduce its doctrines into UN debates. You'll remember how their lobbying has been able to block our reproductive rights initiative making abortion an absolute human right. If we take the lead, we'll easily get a majority for those steps, and it'll be a very strong blow to the Vatican's ability to carry out its foreign policy."

"That sounds good! What do you think Bernie?"

"I think it's the right thing to do under the circumstances, Mr. President, and one which the media will applaud you for."

— 17 —

Rome

Fr. Santorelli was surprised, one morning in mid-February, to be asked to come to the office of Cardinal Pierre Zanier, the Prefect of the Congregation for the Evangelization of Peoples. The work of that Congregation, in directing and coordinating the spread of the Gospel, was so important that its head was by custom informally referred to by Vatican observers as the "Red Pope."

Although Zanier was thus a top official of the Curia who had been appointed by Benedict XVIth, the two men had never been personally close, perhaps due to their widely dissimilar backgrounds—Ratzinger's as a German academic and Zanier's as the head of the Church in the Congo. And their paths did not cross now informally during the day, as the Congregation's offices were not within the Vatican enclosure or nearby, but instead were across the Tiber in a magnificent Italian baroque palace near the foot of the Spanish Steps, the Palazzo di Propaganda Fide.

Given Cardinal Malapensa's open hostility and disobedience, which made it impossible for the Pope to rely upon him, the Pope had reached out for help to Zanier, an efficient administrator who had proven himself to be loyal to the Magisterium and ready to carry out the Pope's directions. Msgr. Waldheim was sent to brief the Cardinal on the many events of importance concerning the visions, and the participation of Msgr. Ireland and Fr. Santorelli in the Pope's actions. It was the latter's role that occasioned the Cardinal's summons to the priest.

Cardinal Zanier got right down to business with him. "Father, Cardinal Latoya has given me a brief summary of recent events concerning the visions and what you've been doing in Rome. I've been given to believe that it was *your* advice that led to the Holy Father issuing his Apostolic Letter and also the comment with regard to the visions seen by the Jewish people. Is that correct?"

"I'm sure there were other considerations, Eminence, but, yes, I think that he found what I had to say persuasive."

"And your advice was in the context of using the visions as an aid to evangelization, was it not?"

"Yes, Eminence. I was attempting to carry out the Lord's instruction that His Church must proclaim the Good News everywhere."

"Did you think about contacting *me*—or any member of my Congregation—in that regard, Father? Or the Pontifical Council for Promoting the New Evangelization, either?"

Fr. Santorelli stiffened. He saw for the first time the error in how he had proceeded. "To tell the truth, no, Eminence. When I returned from Garabandal, the uppermost thought in my mind was to put the message before the Holy Father without delay. And when the visions became widespread and the Prefect of the Congregation for the Doctrine of the Faith asked me for my views, I didn't give a second thought to working with anyone but him."

The questioning continued. "And, then, Father, when the visions came to the Jewish people—*did it occur to you to contact me or my Congregation?* Or did you just run to Cardinal Latoya again with your thoughts on how to deal with that situation?"

"The latter, Eminence.—I see too late that I committed a major blunder in not ensuring that *you* were made a party to the consultations when I was setting forth my thoughts. And I humbly apologize for that. I assure you that my fault was through inadvertence and not design."

That was not sufficient to mollify the Cardinal. "Father, I have to say that while I approve of the advice you gave—insofar as it has been related to me—your mistake was indeed serious, and one which I find very surprising given your years as a graduate student here."

"Yes. I have no excuse, Eminence," Fr. Santorelli replied.

"Father," the Cardinal continued, "I want you to understand that I am not giving you a dressing down over what I believe you call in your country a 'turf war.' Missionaries all over the world look to us for guidance as to how our Faith should be announced to other peoples and inculturated in their societies. I will accept your apology only if you assure me that in the future, I will be consulted when you give advice for the Holy Father on how evangelization should be conducted—especially having to do with the visions."

"You have my assurance on that, Eminence," Fr. Santorelli said quickly. "I am duly chastened."

"Good! Then that's behind us.—Now I'll explain why I've been so severe with you. When the visions first came to Christians, I thought that they might stop there—Christ bracing His followers. Now that they have been seen by Jews as well, it seems to me that they will next be seen by Muslims. Do you agree?"

Fr. Santorelli was glad to perceive that there had been a softening of the Cardinal's tone. "Yes, Eminence—I do expect the Muslims to be next, perhaps followed by the Hindus."

"Let's just deal with the Muslims, Father. The reason I'm interested is that I'm trying to foresee and plan ahead for that eventuality, because the followers of our two religions interact uneasily in so many countries. I wonder whether it might be possible to use the visions as a common experience of divine power to dialogue about. Or, at the other extreme, whether the visions might provoke further hostility against Christians, and the Vatican in particular, as was the case with the Israelis. So, I'd like to know what you think they might see."

"I don't know, Eminence—possibly their sins, if the pattern holds."

"Do you, Father? And what would that entail? Do you expect that a man will be blamed for taking four wives, or beating a woman for showing her face in public, or stoning an adulterer—all done according to the Qur'an?"

Fr. Santorelli could do nothing but shake his head and confess, "I don't know—and I see where you're headed with your questions, Eminence. Next you'll be asking me if a Muslim will be reproved in a vision for killing unbelievers as an act of jihad."

The Cardinal nodded. "Yes. That's exactly the sort of thing I had in mind. *He* thought it was a meritorious act—one which Allāh wished him to commit. Do *you* think it will be depicted in a vision as a heinous crime? And will he be told that Jesus was truly divine—contrary to the words of the Qur'an?"

"I don't know that either," replied Fr. Santorelli, "but I would guess that's likely to happen."

"Do you have any idea of what the outcome might be if that's the case, Father?"

Fr. Santorelli sat there still and silent for several moments, praying for guidance as to whether he should answer the Cardinal's question frankly. Not sensing any internal monition warning him not to do so, he gave a tentative answer. "Eminence, the Lord hasn't revealed that to me, and I doubt that you would want to hear my personal thoughts."

Cardinal Zanier was not dissuaded. "Let me be the judge of that, Father. You've made your disclaimer, now tell me what you think."

"Well, then, I suppose there's a *possibility* that the result of the Muslims seeing the visions would be a nuclear holy war." With that, Fr. Santorelli fell silent again.

"*A nuclear holy war?* Perhaps you were right about my not wanting to hear your thoughts, but you can't just stop there with an *ipse dixit* like that," said the Cardinal. "What do you have in mind?"

"*Insofar as I understand their religion, I believe that the Qur'an specifically commands them to wage war against unbelievers, and to subjugate or kill them.* The surest way for a Muslim to attain Paradise is to die as a martyr to their faith, in a holy war."

"In my personal experience, Father, there are many peace-loving Muslims, and I understand that their Qur'an prohibits forced religious conversions."

"Eminence, there are parts of the Qur'an which would seem on their face to be pacific, but Islamic scholars, recognizing internal contradictions in the Qur'an, have a doctrine that the later suras repeal the earlier suras by implication. Since the authorities determine which ones are earlier and which later, they can and do give precedence to the militaristic ones. The result is that we are seeing attacks by Muslims on unbelievers everywhere, as I'm sure you know better than I, because of the reports coming in to the Vatican from Papal nuncios in many countries—crucifixions and enslavements, rapes of Christian women, forced reconversions, the torching of Christians' homes and churches—all in Muslim countries. The only reason we haven't seen outright war against us up until now is the military backwardness of the Muslim countries. Unfortunately, that's changed now that the Iranians have the atomic bomb ... "

Cardinal Zanier shook his head in disagreement. "I think you're being an alarmist, Father. It's true that the leaders of Iran bluster a lot, as all dictators do, but their audience is their fellow Muslim states, and the Saudis in particular. They want to be supreme in the Muslim world."

"Yes—that and more. They want to rebuild the empire they once had, and extend it to all of Europe. The best that we Christians could hope for would be that we would be allowed to live in ghettos as a despised minority, paying a heavy tax for that concession."

The Cardinal was not persuaded by the priest's come-back. "Father, you Americans see things much differently than we do over here—far more black and white—'good guys' and 'bad guys,' I think you say. I personally have known and worked with many Muslims who wouldn't dream of going on a jihad."

"No doubt, Eminence, *but those are not the ones in control of the Islamic Revolution in Iran.* And I beg to differ with your assessment that is it my *American* perspective that is misleading me into expecting them to launch an attack on the west.—Let me get at the nub of the problem by asking you a question if I may, Eminence—have you ever had the occasion to study the apocalyptic beliefs of the Shi'a?"

"No, Father. Why would they matter?"

"Because those beliefs are driving the rulers of Iran toward nuclear war. The Shi'a believe that shortly before the end of the world, the *Masīh ad-Dajjāl*—the False Messiah or Anti-Christ—will appear and there will be a tremendous battle between the forces of good and the forces of evil. You could call it *their* version of Armageddon. At the same time, *the Mahdī al-Muntadhar—the Awaited Savior—will appear on earth and will destroy the Anti-Christ and his followers. He will bring about universal peace and justice, and Islamic rule, by force where necessary.*"

"Now, the reason I think that this is a matter of life and death *for us* is that they believe that the harbingers of the Mahdī's coming—set forth back in the seventh century—have largely been fulfilled, and . . . "

The Cardinal unexpectedly interrupted Fr. Santorelli at this point with a question: "Harbingers? Like what, Father?"

"There are a number of them, one of which is that barefoot, naked, destitute bedouin shepherds will compete in the construction of tall buildings. In the seventh century, the thought that the Arabs of the Persian Gulf coast would *ever* build tall buildings must have sounded ridiculous. But now, as you know, Eminence, the world's tallest building is in Dubai, and many other skyscrapers have been erected in that region."

"Here's the ominous part, Eminence.—Another one of the key harbingers of the Last Days is supposed to be *smoke covering the world*. Put that together with the fact that the sixth part of the message which the Lord gave me in Garabandal also is about smoke, in words spoken by God to the prophet Joel about the Last Days: 'I will work wonders in the heavens and on earth, blood, fire, and columns of smoke.'"

"*Eminence, everyone knows that an immense column of smoke arises from an atomic explosion. My fear is that the rulers of Iran will be tempted to initiate the end-of-the-world battle with the west in order to hasten the return of the Mahdī and the triumph of Islam—and that they will do so by using atomic bombs.*"

The Cardinal was dismissive. "You don't really think, do you Father, that they could expect to triumph over the West in a nuclear war they initiated?"

"No and yes," was Fr. Santorelli's answer. "'No,' in the sense *we* would use the word 'triumph.' *But, 'Yes,' as they would use the word—for they think that by precipitating the return of the Mahdī, they will bring about the triumph of Islam worldwide. And, they won't be deterred by the fact that they themselves will be incinerated in the process, because they're confident of their personal resurrection, and the reward of martyrdom in the Paradise that awaits them at the End of Time.*"

The Cardinal shook his head. "I wish I hadn't called you over here, Father.—But, now that you've unloaded your fears on me, I'd like you to keep me advised of any further insights you may have as matters play out—hopefully not as you expect . . ."

With that, Fr. Santorelli's first encounter with Cardinal Zanier was over.

*   *   *

The next day, Fr. Santorelli was called on the carpet by his mentor. Msgr. Ireland's angry tone matched his facial expression. "Tony, what the hell did you say to Cardinal Zanier yesterday?"

"I'm not sure what you're referring to, Monsignor," replied the startled priest. "He called me over to his office and asked me a number of questions, and I answered them."

"Your answers went from him to the Pope, and from him to Cardinal Latoya. Msgr. Waldheim was good enough to let me

know. You've sure stirred up a hornet's nest! Wasn't it enough
that you had already speculated about a threat to the Vatican's
existence, and the death of many clerics? Did you have to go and
raise the prospect of Armageddon and a nuclear war?"

"Oh, that.—Well, I tried to avoid answering His Eminence's
question about what I saw likely in the future, but he wouldn't let
me remain silent.—You wouldn't have wanted me to dissimulate,
would you?"

"Not dissimulate, Tony—but there's a time and a place for
everything. Haven't you ever heard of the virtue of Prudence?
I see you really didn't learn anything from your experiences in
Topanga. Speaking with a cardinal who is a leading member of
the Curia is not the time to go off on your own toot.—Exactly
what was it you told him, anyway?"

"I explained a bit about the eschatology of the Shi'a, centering
on their expectation of the return of the Mahdī, and it was in that
context that I mentioned the possible response by Iran's leaders
if the Muslims start seeing Christian visions. What worries me
is that the reference to columns of smoke, by the Prophet Joel,
ties into their expectation of smoke covering the earth in the Last
Days."

"*Tony,*" said Msgr. Ireland sharply, "*did you or did you not
predict a nuclear war?*"

"I said that I was frightened because that's what the signs
were pointing to—*in my own view*. Believe me, Monsignor, I dis-
claimed any divine inspiration on that point, apart from what was
contained in the message I received."

"*Tony, Tony, Tony—what am I going to do with you?*" asked the
prelate in frustration, holding his head in his hands to emphasize
his point. "Don't you realize that because of how the Lord has
marked you out, people think your words carry a special significance? Even when you disclaim divine inspiration, people assume
that there is more than merely human reasoning behind what you
are saying. If you said you thought the stock market would go up,
people would buy just on your say-so. *You aren't just any old priest
anymore . . . !*"

"What would you have me do, Monsignor?" asked Fr. Santorelli
in a subdued voice.

Msgr. Ireland had to think about that.

"Look, Tony—as you yourself said at that lunch we had when you just came over—great care has to be taken in interpreting mystical things like apparitions and locutions. You say you had a vision of yourself being nailed to a cross. Obviously, that was symbolic or allegorical—no one's actually going to nail you to a cross. As for the columns of smoke in Joel's prophecy that have you so spooked—maybe the reference was to the smoke plumes of volcanoes—you know, like the ones in Iceland that disrupted air traffic all over Europe. Why do you have to go and assume the smoke is from nuclear explosions? Is *that* exercising great care in interpretation?—I wish you wouldn't say *anything* that could be taken as a prediction of the future, especially anything about atomic war or a chastisement, unless I'm there with you to cut you off if I think you're going off the deep end.—*Will you do that for me?*"

"I'll do my best, Monsignor," said the priest, meekly.

To his surprise, that promise was not accepted. "Tony, you're going to have to do better than 'your best.' Look—have you ever thought to ask yourself just who you think you are? I mean, were you given a mystical scroll to eat, like Ezekiel?"

"No, Monsignor."

"Were you chosen by any prophet as his successor, the way Elijah chose Elisha?"

"No, Monsignor."

"Did the Word of God come to you the way it did to Jeremiah, announcing that you had been dedicated by God as a prophet?"

"No Monsignor."

"*Well, then, for God's sake, Tony, stop acting like an Old Testament prophet! Especially now that the knives are out for you!*"

"What do you mean by that, Monsignor?" asked Fr. Santorelli.

"Cardinal Malapensa found out about you and called your Cardinal—and then Cardinal Figlio. Malapensa wants to have you shipped back to your diocese in California."

"*Oh, God!*" Fr. Santorelli involuntarily exclaimed.

"Yes, '*Oh, God!*' is right!" said Msgr. Ireland. "So you'd better keep a low profile while I'm trying to save your hide!"

PART IV

The Attack

February 2015

Attacks on the Pope and the Church come not only from without . . . Today we are seeing it in a really terrifying way: that the greatest persecution of the Church comes not from her enemies without, but arises from sin within the Church . . .

Pope Benedict XVI (May 11, 2010)

— 1 —

Rome

Cardinal Giuseppe Malapensa sensed that power was flowing away from Benedict XVIth, who was becoming progressively more isolated as the result of his own narrowing focus on the tasks he felt vital to complete in the time he had left, and due to some members of the hierarchy pulling back from him as they began to concern themselves with a coming papal succession. Having summarily rejected the Pope's suggestion that he resign as Secretary of State, Malapensa was taking advantage of their unrest by attempting to line up support for a palace coup, a coup he expected would put *him* at the head of almost two billion Catholics.

He found the going tough, far tougher than he had expected. Many of the European cardinals still had personal affection for Ratzinger, and were unwilling to join Malapensa in pushing him out of office. The third world cardinals were even more reluctant to abandon the Pope. At that exact moment, Malapensa was sitting at his desk attempting to induce one of them to sign the plotters' declaration of removal, and he was becoming more and more exasperated. The man on the other end of the phone, the Patriarch of the East Indies, seemed not to grasp the generous proposition which Cardinal Malapensa had just made him, and he asked to have it repeated.

Malapensa was provoked into putting aside the careful circumlocution with which he had begun their conversation, now explaining frankly what was at stake.

"As I said, Eminence, we are asking for your support in removing Ratzinger and installing a Bishop of Rome who is suitably in tune with the times, one who will reform outmoded practices and dogmas and bring the Faithful back to empty churches."

. . . "What?—*You* don't have a problem with empty churches in your See? Well, you are most fortunate. Believe me, it's a worry to our fellow Princes of the Church all over the world, and they know they cannot make progress until there is a change in leadership at the top. More than half of them have already signed off on an instrument removing Ratzinger as Pope, and we very much hope *you* will join us."

... *"Yes, of course what I'm telling you is true,"* he lied, his voice rising. "We have signatures from more than half already, but we want as many as we can get in the hope of persuading Ratzinger to go quietly."

If Malapensa had been given to demonstrative actions in keeping with his anger, he would have hurled something across the room. *How dare the man question his veracity? Who did he think he was speaking with, anyway?* As he listened for the man's response, he began to draw a rectangular box around the name of José Maria de Silveira on his "To Call" list.

... "Even if *your* people are satisfied with the status quo, Eminence, think of the money we will be receiving from the sale of the antiquities in the Vatican's collection. Wouldn't you like to have, say, 500,000 Euros, for the needs of your See? We will be distributing the proceeds of the deaccessions to cardinals who need financial help—*naturally with preference to the ones who have supported us.*"

Their conversation was going nowhere. Malapensa wondered why Ratzinger had ever made the little brown man from the third world a cardinal. He was only archbishop of two tiny, former Portuguese enclaves—Goa and Daman—on the west coast of India. It must have been due to Ratzinger's misguided effort to internationalize the governance of the Church—as if there was anything wrong with Italians continuing to dominate its affairs, as they had for 2,000 years.

He tried another tack. "What is it then, that you want, Eminence?—Perhaps a position in the Curia, so you can leave India and enjoy life in Rome in your declining years? Or, if not that, then tell me what we can do to obtain your concurrence in this matter."

Malapensa's doodling had altered the long sides of the rectangular box slightly to form what clearly was a penciled coffin around the man's name, and now he added cross hatching, obscuring the letters inside.

... "Very well, I ask you to think further about what I have offered. *But, if I do not hear back from you today, I will have to inform the others that you have declined to be a part of our group—*

and you can expect to find it very hard to communicate with the new Pope we will be electing. Good day to you, Eminence."

He slammed the phone down hard without waiting for a good-bye from the other end, and then thoroughly blacked out the man's name in the coffin-shaped box on his pad. The Patriarch of the East Indies would find himself a *non-person* when Malapensa succeeded to the Papal throne . . .

— 2 —

Miami Beach

Across the Atlantic, Cardinal O'Melveny was about to begin the same process of soliciting his fellow cardinals to remove Ratzinger, albeit leaving most of that dirty business to his protégé, Cardinal Lazard. They met in Miami's Fontainebleau, where the U.S. Catholic bishops then happened to be holding their annual gathering. It was a mild afternoon, and they settled into chairs on the balcony of O'Melveny's suite in the Tresor Tower, overlooking the ocean. The sun illuminated a steady procession of container cargo ships in the distance, moving slowly toward or away from the port, while O'Melveny laid out the battle plan.

"My sources in Rome tell me that Ratzinger's lost in a mystical cloud, formulating another Marian dogma. It's worse than Nero fiddling while Rome burned. Ratzinger hasn't just been *watching* the fire started by those damn visions—*he's been fanning the flames* by approving of them. Everyone I've talked to thinks the coming quarantine is due to his mishandling of the EU. The good news for us is that *Ratzinger* is getting weaker politically day by the day, and *we're* getting closer and closer to taking power."

Lazard's eyes lit up. "You mean the time's finally come for the Catholic Church of America?" he asked excitedly.

O'Melveny had to restrain a grimace. Lazard could be slow-witted at times.

"*No, Sy, not that,*" O'Melveny said. "I know that's been our long-term goal, but I think another path has opened up to accomplish everything we want without going out on a limb that way." He dropped his voice, though there was no one who could have overheard him. "*There's a good chance that most of the cardinals will join in declaring the throne of Peter vacant! Once Ratzinger is gone, there'll be a vacuum of power, and I'll make my move to take command in Rome!*"

Lazard gasped. "*You mean—you think you have a chance to be Pope?!*"

"*That's exactly what I mean, Sy!*" said O'Melveny with a confident grin. "*And soon, too! Malapensa has as many enemies as he has friends—they'll cancel each other out in the voting. I have a track record of independence, plus the riches of America to offer."*

O'Melveny stood up, went to the railing, and turned around to face Lazard, blocking his view of the sea, the better to have him focus on what O'Melveny was saying.

"The difference between being on the outside here and being on the inside there is like night and day. When I'm Pope we'll represent the official Roman Catholic Church, and anyone who doesn't go along with our agenda will be on the outside looking in! They'll be the schismatics!—The heretics!"

Cardinal Lazard sat there, tugging at his "patriarchal" beard while savoring that unexpected, thrilling prospect. It was beyond his wildest dreams! "I'll do *anything* to help you!" he said, and meant it.

"I knew I could count on you, Sy," said O'Melveny. "Here's the plan. I need you, Sy, to get the signatures of all the Central and South Americans on the removal declaration I'll give you a copy of, while I'm doing the same with the cardinals in this country and Canada. Also, I've prepared a short list of a few others for you to call, including Cardinal Zanier—you know the *African*."

"From everything I've heard of him, he's very orthodox," Lazard protested, fearing that he would fail in that task. "He supports the Pope. He wouldn't dream of going along with us."

"Well, we have to try. He's been on the lists of some of the media as a *papabile*. He has no chance of being elected Pope, of course, but he might draw off some votes away from me in the Papal enclave. It would be good if we could get him on our side before then.—Why don't you offer him the post of Secretary of State?"

Lazard's eyes opened wide. "You wouldn't choose *him*, would you?" he asked in consternation, for Lazard had seen *himself* in that position as soon as O'Melveny had raised the possibility he might become Pope.

O'Melveny had no trouble reading what was in Lazard's mind. "Of course not, Sy," O'Melveny replied reassuringly, sitting back down. "But, *he* doesn't know that. Just dangle the bait and see if he takes it. You'd be surprised what people will do for the chance to be Number Two at the Vatican! We may have to promise it to more than one of them!"

"And once we get their signatures on the declaration, what happens?"

"Then, we confront Ratzinger face-to-face, and if he doesn't leave voluntarily, we pull the trigger and remove him."

"I wonder—," said Lazard, doubtfully. "Won't there be protests?"

"Here and there, maybe, but once we announce our reforms, *most* of the people will back us, and we'll have *all* the media in our corner, because we'll announce that we're calling the Vatican III Council to reform the Church," said O'Melveny in his most confident manner. "So, I wouldn't worry about any opposition."

"One more thing, Sy," the Cardinal of Topanga added, putting his hand on Lazard's arm in a gesture that said *we're in this together*. "I'm planning on you going over to Rome to be in on the confrontation with Ratzinger!"

— 3 —

Rome

Since the Pope could no longer entrust the day-to-day operations
of the Vatican City State to his disobedient Secretary of State,
he asked Cardinal Zanier to join his inner circle of advisors. The
Cardinal promptly requested a meeting with Cardinal Latoya, with
Msgr. Ireland and Fr. Santorelli also in attendance, to discuss a
matter of grave importance.

When they were assembled in Latoya's office in the Apostolic
Palace, Zanier explained his concerns. "I need to speak frankly
about a current of opinion which I've heard expressed by more
than a few members of the Curia.—It's resentment against both
you, Monsignor, and you, Father, because you two now seem to
have the Holy Father's ear, while cardinals and bishops cannot
speak into it themselves . . . *Worse still, I regret to say that there is
a plot underway by some cardinals against the Pope—they wish to
remove him.*"

Fr. Santorelli was stunned. *"They wouldn't dare! It's unlawful!"*

Cardinal Zanier looked at him as if he were naïve. "Father,"
the Cardinal said, "your circumstances in America were very different from those you have been thrust into here. You don't have
experience in the intrigues of Rome."

"Forgive me for challenging you, Eminence" Fr. Santorelli
replied, "but a cabal of cardinals conspiring against the Pope is a
stock element of the plot in paperback thrillers about the Vatican.
It doesn't make sense to me that the majority of cardinals who
elected him Pope, and the ones who subsequently were appointed
by him, would turn on him."

"I hope and pray you're right, Father," responded the Cardinal, "and I feel pretty sure that *most* of them remain loyal. But
some of them are disaffected, and I could mention a number of
possible factors. One is simple ambition on the part of those who
want to hold the highest positions themselves. Such ambition is
unfortunate, but normal, even in the hierarchy. A second factor is
that there are some who want to call another ecumenical council
in order to restructure the Church and its doctrines in ways that

the last Vatican Council stopped short of doing. And there may be one or two undercover *Masons*, fomenting things to accomplish *their* agenda."

"Masons? You say that like you think they're a disloyal threat," said Fr. Santorelli. *"My own father, a Protestant, was a Mason.* I remember one time seeing his little apron and other paraphernalia. He went to meetings with his friends for a bit of relaxation, and he enjoyed the rituals and the pretense that they knew what he called 'the secret wisdom of the ages.' It was all a bit silly, if you ask me, but hardly dangerous."

"Father," said Cardinal Zanier, "the Masons in Europe are not at all like the ones you have in America—at least not like the ordinary ones such as your father. Believe me, on the Continent, going back to its founding three centuries ago, the society of freemasons has been *virulently anticlerical.* The organization is dedicated to establishing a *secular* world order, one controlled by the 'Adepts,' high ranking members of the Masonic fraternity. They realize that to achieve such a *de facto* universal government, they will have to subject and subordinate all religious institutions, most especially the Church. That's why they've constantly tried to infiltrate the hierarchy. They are looking to the day when the cardinals will choose a Pope who secretly accepts the goals of freemasonry."

"Do you *know* there are Masons *on the inside?*" asked Fr. Santorelli, not yet convinced.

"No—it's only been rumored, apart from some circumstantial information we've learned in exorcisms, which, I grant is of questionable trustworthiness. Of course, you'd expect their membership to be buried down deep—they'd be excommunicated if that tie was known. In any event, I don't want to dwell on that possibility, because the factor that seems to be providing the energy now for those who are disaffected is an honest perception that the Pope is leading the Church in the wrong direction with respect to the visions and that the course needs to be reversed. They think what he's done has proven disastrous in bringing about the quarantine and the break in diplomatic relations with Israel. *Now, I don't know how these disparate factors that I've mentioned are coalescing, but I can tell you that only yesterday, I was offered a bribe to sign a declaration that Ratzinger is incompetent and is therefore removed as Pope . . . "*

The others sat there in shock. The menace to the Pope was closer at hand than they had imagined. Msgr. Ireland broke the hush by asking, "Did they offer you money?"

"No, Monsignor," Zanier replied, "it was a promise that if I signed their declaration and I encouraged others to do so, I would be rewarded by the next Pope with the position of Secretary of State."

"*That's simony! Whoever made you that offer has excommunicated himself!*" responded Msgr. Ireland.

"True, but how could it be proved?" asked Cardinal Zanier softly. "There was no witness."

"Who was the traitor?" Cardinal Latoya wanted to know.

"The Cardinal Archbishop of Miami."

"He wouldn't have dared do that except at O'Melveny's instigation!" thundered Latoya. "Have you told His Holiness himself about this?"

"Yes, Eminence," replied Cardinal Zanier. "In fact, he told me that the Patriarch of the East Indies had already reported that *Cardinal Malapensa* had offered *him* a bribe—funding for his diocese if he signed a faxed copy of the declaration. The Patriarch even sent a transcription of the offer, as taken down by his secretary over the phone."

"And what was the Pope's reaction?"

"His Holiness said that now was not the time for a confrontation. When I started to protest, he reminded me that, in accordance with the Garabandal message that Father gave him, his Pontificate is fated to be brought to a bitter end, and he is determined not to widen the divisions in the Church in a futile effort to prolong his reign."

— 4 —

Rome

Fr. Santorelli was so agitated by what he had just heard from Cardinal Zanier that he asked to have a private audience with the Pope—only the two of them—and the request was granted. They met in the private study where the Pope was working on yet another draft of the projected Marian dogma.

"Holy Father," Fr. Santorelli said, "I've just learned from Cardinal Zanier of the treasonous attempts underway to unseat you, and also that you do not plan to oppose them. I'm concerned that your decision may have been influenced by the message I transmitted to you. Now, I related the message exactly as it was given to me—as God is my witness—and I understand what it is pointing to, *but, Holiness, God can accommodate His plans to take account of what we do. Aren't we obliged at least to try to forestall their wicked deed?*"

"What would you have me do, Father?" the Pope asked mildly.

"*Excommunicate them!!!* It's a just penalty under canon law for plotting physical harm against you, and also for offering bribes to obtain ecclesiastical offices."

Fr. Santorelli could see the distress on the Pontiff's face, as he thought about how to respond.

"Subscribing to a decree purporting to remove me from office is not the same as a physical assault on me, Father, and proving the offense of simony would require a canonical trial."

The Pope thought about leaving his answer at that, but decided to explain more fully his thinking. "Have you given any thought to what it would do to the image of the Church if I put a number of cardinals on trial—a trial which could not be kept secret? Consider, Father—do you not think that Our Lord's parable of the wheat and the weeds is applicable? *He will deal with the weeds in His own time.*"

To the surprise of the Holy Father, the priest was undeterred by the Pope's reasoned decision. "*Holiness, forgive me, but I don't see that parable as being applicable! You yourself have said that the greatest persecution of the Church arises from sin within the*

Church.—*Holiness, don't you have a responsibility to at least try to pull the weeds out?"*

At last, the Holy Father was provoked to give vent to his anger at the priest's stubborn insistence on excommunication as a sovereign remedy.

"Father—that is enough from you! Say no more! The Gospel parable clearly indicates that *the Lord* believes more harm will be done by trying to remove weeds from His field than by leaving them in place until the harvest. Even if I could infallibly divine which were weeds and which were wheat, I would follow His lead."

Fr. Santorelli then realized that not only had he failed to persuade the Pope, he had been far too presumptuous. "Oh! I see that my words have given great offense, and I apologize from the bottom of my heart, Holiness. It's just that I'm right down on the ground myself, and I see so many good shoots of wheat being snuffed out by the overgrown weeds. It almost happened to me. *Please, I truly need to understand—tell me how your trying to pull them up could be worse than letting them go on growing . . ."*

The Pope slumped back in his wheelchair, exhausted by their heated exchange. Gathering his strength for a final effort to communicate, he said, "All right, Father, I *will* tell you! You confuse the provisions of canon law with the *real* power which is given to me *by the consent of my subjects.* On paper, I do have the power to uproot those whom you disparage as 'weeds'—and I have done so in the past as you should know, with one here and another there. But, unlike weeds, they have the power to resist—to get up and walk away. Even if you are not a student of Church history, you must be aware of the unfortunate schisms caused by individual cardinals, bishops and even priests, in your own lifetime. Those painful breaches in our common unity have cut off many people from the life of the Church. *To avoid precipitating another one, I am determined to exercise my powers sparingly, before I am carried away to my end—whether by them or others I know not . . ."*

Fr. Santorelli was deeply touched by the pathos of the situation. He said, simply, *"Holy Father, if I were able to, I would gladly let them carry me off and die in your place."*

"I know you would, Father," said the Pope. *"That is why I have been so patient with you. Now, let me hear no more from you about excommunications!"*

*   *   *

After Fr. Santorelli had left, His Holiness reflected upon their disturbing conversation. It crystallized his thinking about the holy but impetuous young priest. He put in a call to a Capuchin friar in a remote village, and, following that conversation, he summoned Cardinal Zanier.

"Eminence, you know about the recent portentous events and Father Santorelli's significant role in them. What you may not know is how he came to be assigned as a prison chaplain in America. I will relate the affair to you, as it has a bearing on what I will ask you to do."

When the Pope finished his brief summary of Fr. Santorelli's career, he told the Cardinal about the medical examination made of the priest at the Gemelli, and gave his own witness that the stigmata, which Cardinal Zanier had not seen for himself, were genuine. "The reason I am telling you all this is that, for many reasons, including Father's own unfortunate rashness which flows from his total honesty, he will become the target of evil schemes once I am gone from the scene. He is still incardinated in the Topanga diocese of California, and if he were forced to return there, I would fear for his sanity, if not for his life."

"Accordingly, Eminence, I have decided that it is necessary for him to be officially transferred here immediately—incardinated as a priest in the See of Rome, with his full priestly faculties. I realize that even this step may not provide protection in the event that my successor is either Cardinal Malapensa or Cardinal O'Melveny—but, it is all I can do. Also, because of the jealousy on the part of others here, which you have alerted me to, it would be prudent for Father to take a leave of absence. To that end, I have made arrangements with the Father Guardian of the Capuchin convent at San Giovanni Rotondo to shelter him for the present—a recuperative leave, you might say. I would like him to have his full faculties also while he is there, in the Diocese of Manfredonia."

"What I ask of you, Eminence, is that you draft an appropriate *Motu Proprio* for me to sign, tomorrow, if possible, addressed to all the affected parties to carry out the steps I have just described. When it becomes effective with my signature, please transmit it to those parties immediately, by telecopier, not through our usual pouches. I don't know how much time I have left."

"And would you be so good as to personally assist Fr. Santorelli in getting on the train the following day? I cannot overstress the importance of the message he brought to me, and his insightful suggestions, in guiding me in responding to the visions. I encourage the two of you to stay in communication in the coming days. And I pray that he will be of great service to you, as he has been to me."

— 5 —

Rome

Cardinal Zanier was of mixed mind as he knocked on the door of
Fr. Santorelli's room in the Domus Sanctae Marthae after supper.
The Pope was right—the priest had to go, for more reasons than
one—but did he have to be sent away just at the most critical
time? It was a dead issue, though—the Pope had already signed
the Motu Proprio which the Cardinal had drafted.

Hearing a "Come in," he entered, to find the room dark except
for faint light coming through the sheer-curtained casement window at the far end. He could barely make out Fr. Santorelli, lying
flat on his back, head at the foot of the bed, which stuck out into
the room at right angles to the left wall.

Fr. Santorelli called out, "There's a light switch by the door."
When the light went on and he saw who his guest was, he added,
"Eminence! What a surprise! You're welcome—please come in and
have a seat," and he struggled to sit up. "Msgr. Ireland said I
alarmed you by my dark thoughts last week.—I'd like to stress
again that they were solely my own musings, and *not* any message
divinely given to me."

"Father," said the Cardinal, "please—lie back. You don't need
to sit up for me.—Yes, I admit that your thoughts did alarm me,
but you were careful to disclaim any divine source at the time, so
you didn't mislead me."

The room was small and spare, with white walls and a floor
that was bare except for small area rugs. On one side of the head
of the bed was a night stand; on the other side, a straight-backed
chair, on which the Cardinal seated himself after pulling it closer
to the bed. He guessed that Fr. Santorelli, who was wearing black
pants and a T-shirt, had been lying in the upside down position so
that he could focus his attention on the crucifix which hung on
the wall over the head of the bed.

"Were you meditating on the Passion?" he enquired.

"That where I started, Eminence," Fr. Santorelli replied. "I
always do at night. Then I get distracted. Sometimes it's my
wounds. *They throb constantly.*—Have you ever been in a berth on

a ship where you *felt* as well as heard the rhythmic groan of the ship as it beat against the sea—and were kept awake because the beat never stopped?—I'd like to fancy that underlying what I'm feeling is the throbbing of Jesus' heart, but I'm sure if you lined up ten people and hooked them up to a machine that could take their pulse simultaneously, their heart beats wouldn't all coincide with one another. So, the beats are just my own system.—Maybe as the years go by I'll become so used to them that they'll stop driving me crazy ..."

Cardinal Zanier politely allowed the priest's soliloquy to taper off into silence. He was about to bring up the purpose of his visit when Fr. Santorelli spoke again.

"No matter how hard I try to center my thoughts on His wounds and remain on them, my mind drifts away. *Last week, a very holy priest told me that, so far, I was only a servant who suffered—in contrast to a Suffering Servant—capital 'esses'—like Padre Pio.* He was right, you know. I try to excuse myself by saying that I'm in the middle of a battle. The EU and Malapensa and O'Melveny have their conspiracies going, and God only knows who else is out there plotting against the Pope. I can't get out of my mind the coming catastrophe—the shepherd will be smitten, and the sheep will be scattered.—As for that," he added, "I guess by now you've heard about my audience with the Holy Father, when I begged him to weed the episcopal garden ..."

Cardinal Zanier cleared his throat. "Yes—well—Father, that's the reason why I came to see you tonight. His Holiness did apprise me of that audience. Even righteous anger at third persons does not justify you in speaking intemperately to a superior. You are something of a 'loose cannon,' to use one of your American expressions.—It is necessary for you to leave the Vatican, but, to preserve your usefulness to the Church, the Holy Father has already reincardinated you in the Diocese of Rome, by a *Motu Proprio*. And to protect you further, he has decided to send you on a recuperative leave to the friary of the Capuchin Franciscans at San Giovanni Rotondo. At His Holiness's request, I'll come for you in the morning at a quarter to seven to take you to the train station—you'll be leaving with his profound gratitude, and mine."

An "Oh" came out of Fr. Santorelli's mouth, like the air escaping from the neck of a balloon.

The priest managed to pull himself to a sitting position on the side of the bed. "I'm *so* sorry.—*I've failed the Holy Father.* Right in the middle of the crisis.—You know I didn't mean to!—I was determined to stick with him here to the end ... Eminence, would you *please* pass on to him my *abject apology*? I'll write him a note to the same effect tomorrow."

In his remorse, Fr. Santorelli started to cry.

"An apology *is* due, Father," said the Cardinal, "for your presumptuous speech, but *not* for failing him.—He told me that he's grateful to you for your help, and anticipates that you will be of use to his successor. You have many years of service to the Church ahead of you. Look, here—I've brought you a cell phone with my own cell phone number programmed in. If you ever have any thoughts about events that you want to pass on to me, please don't hesitate to use it. And feel free to use it to remain in touch with Msgr. Ireland—I know he's going to miss you. When I leave you now, I'll inform him of your transfer."

*   *   *

Msgr. Ireland was devastated to hear from Cardinal Zanier that Fr. Santorelli was going to be whisked out from under him the next day.

"Eminence, I can't defend him for what you've told me he said to the Holy Father. It was uncalled for and offensive—still, couldn't you have discussed his transfer with me, first?"

"No, Monsignor. The Holy Father asked me to do it this way. He expected you would plead to have Father remain, and he'd made up his mind."

"It's a real blow to me to lose him. I was hoping that Father could be assigned as a Consultor to Cardinal Latoya's Congregation—which His Eminence had agreed to."

"I understand, Monsignor, but in light of the upheaval which Father himself expects to occur here, the Holy Father decided it would be safer to send him out of Rome now, to a remote location. If he remained here, he'd be a lightning rod for criticism about anything having to do with the visions. And, given Father's charism as a stigmatist, you can see that the friary at San Giovanni Rontondo was a natural choice. Don't worry—he'll still be available to you on the cell phone I gave him tonight, and if he's needed, he can be driven back here for a meeting the same day. *He* probably feels he's being exiled, but it's for his own good."

Msgr. Ireland sighed. "He had some sort of romantic notion about sticking close to the Pope in the hope that he would be with him when 'they'—whoever 'they' might be—came to carry the Pope off.—Not that he could have put up any physical resistance, what with his wounds. I don't know what he *thought* he could do—maybe he was going to try calling down fire from heaven, like an Old Testament prophet. At times he seems to act like one—and, believe me, I've warned him about that ...!"

Cardinal Zanier smiled. "That just may have been his plan! Anyway, I've seen to it that the security people are on high alert against any attempt to kidnap the Holy Father. I don't think anyone is going to be carrying this Pope off, not without sending tanks rolling through the Square!"

*　　*　　*

Later that evening, Fr. Santorelli was surprised to hear the new cell phone ring.

"*Tony,*"—it was Msgr. Ireland's voice—"*what in the name of all that's holy have you gone and done now?* Cardinal Zanier just told me of your removal—I can't believe you said what you did to the Pope! What in the world were you thinking of, *badgering the Holy Father*, especially after he made it clear he wasn't interested in excommunicating anyone?"

"I realize now it was wrong, Monsignor, and I've asked Cardinal Zanier to express my deepest regrets to the Pope. I'll send him a written apology when I get to the friary."

His mentor was not appeased. "It pains me to say this, but I'm really disappointed in you, Tony. You know I admonished you to be prudent after your incendiary comments to Cardinal Zanier. I told you to lay low—and I told you the knives were out for you. But for the Pope taking an interest in you, you'd soon be chopped liver at the hands of O'Melveny! I don't understand what kind of a rash spirit you have in you that won't let you keep your mouth shut.—*Now you've escalated matters to the point I can't save your career.* You owe *me* an apology for that! You've been my right hand man, and now you've gone and shot yourself in the foot! How am I supposed to advise the Pope without you there beside me?

...And, I suppose you realize that this puts an end to any hope you had of a teaching career some day ..."

"I beg your forgiveness, Monsignor. I thought I was doing the right thing, but it turned out badly. I'm *so sorry* that *you* got burned too.—If it's any consolation to you, I think the time is running out for this Papacy, so I wouldn't have been much further use to you anyway. But I am truly sorry to have hurt the Pope and you, the two people I admire the most. Will you *please* forgive me?"

The prelate took a while replying. "To be frank, I'm not disposed to—but I suppose I have no choice, unless I can find another one-eyed priest in this land of the blind ..."

Hearing that remark, Fr. Santorelli felt a mite better. His mentor would come around in time.

"I'll look forward to hearing from you, Monsignor—and I'll mail my apology to the Pope to you, to deliver it, so I can be sure he receives it."

*   *   *

Fr. Santorelli's dream was not the only career dream to die that night—Msgr. Ireland's did too.

The Monsignor had hoped that his prize pupil would bring honor to him one day, and in an unanticipated fashion he had just done that, being chosen by the Lord to carry a message to the Pope and help him act on it. But, they both expected that there would be more to the story. Just a week ago, Tony had bright prospects—and the Monsignor did too, as his mentor and facilitator. After all, it was the Monsignor who had called the priest back from prison for the mission to Spain, and it was the Monsignor who had arranged for the appointment with the Pope and then introduced him to Cardinal Latoya. The next step was supposed to be Tony assisting the Monsignor with the work of the Congregation. And *that* might have opened up the next higher level in the hierarchy for the Monsignor—perhaps a titular bishopric as a reward for outstanding service to the Holy Father.

Tony's banishment knocked into a cocked hat those hopes, and did more damage besides. Tony would no longer be present in the Vatican to assist the Holy Father in thwarting the plots against him. If Benedict was somehow pushed out or disabled, and was replaced by one of the plotters, the Monsignor himself had reason to fear the jealousy that Cardinal Zanier had informed him about. He would be in the crosshairs of the new Pope, and liable to banishment to a place far less congenial than San Giovanni Rotondo.

— 6 —

On the train

Cardinal Zanier took Fr. Santorelli to the Termini station, there to board a train to Foggia, which lay due east, almost all the way across Italy. Even without the subsequent hour long bus ride to San Giovanni Rotondo, the priest had more than enough time to read the daily office and meditate on how he came to be heading into exile again. In his breviary, he found this reading from the third chapter of the Epistle of St. James:

> The tongue is a small member and yet has great pretensions. Consider how small a fire can set a huge forest ablaze.
>
> The tongue is also a fire. It exists among our members as a world of malice, defiling the whole body and setting the entire course of our lives on fire, itself set on fire by Gehenna.
>
> For every kind of beast and bird, or reptile and sea creature, can be tamed by the human species, but no human being can tame the tongue. It is a restless evil, full of deadly poison.

He thought back. His tongue had given no one offense all the way through seminary and graduate school, only springing to life when he was given a position in the Topanga Chancery Office. It had wagged then—but not out of malice, which seemed to be the specific sin which St. James decried. Rather, he was only trying to uphold the Magisterium.

Next, he had preached the Word of God fearlessly at his mission church in a slum, and no one was offended, because there was really no congregation to begin with, and the people who subsequently were attracted to his Masses came precisely because he spoke the truth. What he had told the Topanga Times reporter about his parish was true, and he had no idea that she would add material about other parishes, the material which angered the Cardinal. He couldn't blame his tongue for causing that problem either.

He had alarmed Cardinals Latoya and Zanier with some of his speculations of future events, but they had asked for his views, and he had expressed no criticism of *them*.

The private audience with the Holy Father was different. Although he had not spoken to the Pope with malice toward the treasonous cardinals, his tongue had indeed been a "fire." He had been seized by a righteous indignation, and had persisted because the Pope was the only person who had the power to right the wrongs he laid out, the only one who could discipline them. Benedict XVIth himself had once commented that *"priestly ordination means being immersed in Him, immersed in the Truth."* What, then, was *his* guilt in speaking the truth about the noxious actions of those in the hierarchy?

Much as he tried retrospectively to justify his behavior, he knew in his heart that he was in the wrong. It should have been clear to him that the Pope had made a prudential judgment about how to carry out his office, while being fully cognizant of the harmful conduct of certain cardinals. As a young priest, he had no business criticizing how the Holy Father was conducting himself in governing the Church. *It was presumptuous. And presumption was rooted in the sin of self-pride. If that were not enough, he was also guilty of lese majesty toward the Vicar of Christ.* And the only result of his importuning was that the Pope was persuaded to send *him* away!

If the outcome of a confrontation was the test, though, God would not have bothered sending prophets to Israel. The first Christian to be martyred, St. Stephen, had rubbed the noses of the Sanhedrin's members in Israel's history of rejecting God's prophets, with his question to them: "Which of the prophets did your ancestors *not* stone?" Was he himself any more blameworthy for bearding the Pope in his study, than Isaiah, Jeremiah, and the other prophets, for telling the rulers of Israel what they did not wish to hear?

'Whoa!' he had to say to himself.—*'You can't go there. You haven't been appointed as a prophet by God!'* That was true—as he had been forced to admit when he was questioned by Msgr. Ireland. He had been called to a vocation as a priest. He had been called to bear the wounds of Christ. And he had been called to bear a specific message to the Pope.—Not to be an all-purpose oracle.

Apart from the one message he had been given in Garabandal, God had neither told him what to say nor taken control to the point that God was formulating the words and merely using his lips to express them. And so, he resolved that, if the great storm he believed to be coming blew over with only a few drops of rain, he would refrain from further exhortations and withdraw into a great silence.

— 7 —

Rome

On Sunday, a great throng of the Faithful from all over Italy
pressed into St. Peter's Square to show their solidarity with their
Holy Father against the quarantine, which the Italian Prime Minister had announced would be put in place the next morning. It
was an unseasonably mild, blue-sky February day, and the busses
and Metro trains were mobbed with tourists and citizens alike
coming to support the Pope and receive his blessing in return. For
an hour, he rode among them in his Popemobile, responding as
best he could with his limited physical strength to their waving
and chants of *Papa! Papa!*

The people were in good spirits. They had no feelings of
foreboding, for they were unaware of the internecine maneuvering
to unseat the Pope, and they did not expect the diplomatic and
political situation playing out with the European Union and the
Italian Prime Minister would have a tragic ending. It seemed to
them that the spat was like a comic opera whose tragic parts
ended in a triumphant climax. The wisdom of the street was that
both the Pope and the Prime Minister had too much to lose not to
arrive at an accommodation.

When it was time for Mass, the Holy Father was driven inside
the basilica, where he concelebrated from his wheelchair with
Cardinals Zanier and Latoya. In place of the regular readings for
that Sunday in Lent, the Pope had chosen the readings from the
First Letter of St. John, the 2nd Psalm, and the Gospel of Matthew,
corresponding, respectively, to the second, third, and fifth parts
of the message given him—which was still known to only half a
dozen people.

The fifth part, Matthew 24:9–10, was a warning uttered by
Jesus before His Passion: "Then they will hand you over to persecution, and they will kill you. You will be hated by all nations
because of my name."

"I have had these passages of Scripture read to you," the Pope
told them, "so that you will not be taken unaware by what is to
come. *Much evil will soon come to pass here and elsewhere. Rulers*

are plotting against the Lord's anointed, and I will not be with you much longer. As for yourselves, keep in mind the Lord's words that you will be hated because you bear His name. I beg you, dear sons and daughters of the Church, to avail yourselves of the Sacrament of Reconciliation and Penance, so that you will be ready no matter what the tribulation. Be prepared! Then, be at peace, for the Lord has promised to remain with His Church until the end of the world, and Christ has already won for us the victory!"

The Pope would have gone on in that vein, but his words were coming slowly due to his illness and fatigue, and he ended his homily abruptly to save his remaining voice for the Eucharistic celebration. At the end of the Mass, his aides slowly wheeled him down the full length of the nave in St. Peter's as everyone in the pews struggled to photograph or touch their Papa in his time of trial.

*   *   *

Enraged by the public support for Benedict XVI, Prime Minister Genovese decided that an overwhelming show of force by the Government was necessary even before the commencement of the quarantine on Monday. He ordered the Minister of the Interior to send armored units of the Carabiniere to each of the entrances to the Vatican on Sunday afternoon, as an omen of what was coming. The Roma San Pietro Company of the military police had long been providing security for St. Peter's Square and surrounding areas, but had done so silently and inconspicuously. Now, they were instructed to show a mailed fist to the Vatican, which they did, looking and feeling foolish sitting in their armored cars, while the Faithful continued to walk across the Square, peacefully entering and leaving the basilica.

The Vatican Press Officer was astute enough to capitalize on this misstep by the Prime Minister. He staged a made-for-television happening in the barracks of the Swiss Guards. There, the brave young men were shown sharpening their pikes and halberds, and donning their antique metal armor, in preparation for battle. (The camera was careful not to show the racks and racks of submachine guns in their armory.) Their Colonel gave them a short pep talk, calling upon them to defend the Holy Father to the death. Then, the Holy Father himself was wheeled in, and bestowed his blessing on them as they knelt before him.

That night, it was a rare news show that did not feature footage dramatically cutting back and forth between the fearsome Carabiniere with their modern weaponry, and the Pope's quixotic defenders, prepared to die heroically, like the Polish knights on horses who charged invading German tanks at the beginning of World War II. The Italian people wept at the grand spectacle—all that was lacking to make it complete was music by Verdi!

— 8 —

Rome

The barricades went up in St. Peter's Square on Monday morning. Under the Interior Ministry's regulations, anyone already in Vatican City would be allowed to leave at any time, but no one would be permitted to enter, or reenter, except for persons in the categories specified in the new statute. That meant that three large groups normally present during the day would be totally excluded: the Romans who worked in the Vatican as cooks, postal clerks, gardeners and the like; the priests and religious who had official business there such as assisting with Masses, hearing confessions, and working in various offices of the Holy See; and, last but not least, the swarms of pilgrims who came from all over the world to worship at the center of their faith and see the Vicar of Christ on earth.

The Vatican Press Officer arranged to have the Vatican's own TV crew film a special Mass in St. Peter's at noon, celebrated by Cardinal Latoya, for distribution on Vatican TV and any other station that wanted to show it. The main altar was chosen, rather than a side chapel, precisely for the poignancy of showing the vast nave of St. Peter's, which had been filled with an overflow crowd the day before, now totally empty of worshippers except for a handful of clerics.

It quickly became evident that the Pope and the small number of people who actually resided within the Vatican's walls, including the Swiss Guards, were well provided for and quite comfortable in their isolation ward—indeed they were relieved of the burden of accommodating the daily throngs of tourists. Since members of the Curia could travel freely to their offices or to meet with the Pope as necessary, and electronic communications were unaffected, the Holy See's most important business would continue to get done. And those who took care of the Pope's household remained there at their posts. Commentators on the news began to hint at a debacle in the offing—a debacle for the Prime Minister and the European Union. They guessed that the Pope's position would grow stronger as time went on and he would become a latter day "St. Paul in chains."

*   *   *

When he heard on a newscast that bookmakers in London were giving higher odds on the Pope's survival in office than on his own, the Italian Prime Minister called the Vatican's Secretary of State to suggest an urgent private get-together. Where to meet was a problem. The newsmen would no doubt follow the Prime Minister wherever he went during this crisis, and he could hardly be seen going to the Vatican, because that would imply that *he* was backing down and seeking some sort of accommodation. On the other hand, thanks to the barricades around the Vatican, the media would know when the Secretary of State left there, and they would trail *him*. If he went to the Chigi Palace, it would be reported that the Pope had sent him there to discuss capitulation. The Pope would put the lie to that, and Malapensa's duplicity would be exposed.

The Prime Minister vetoed Malapensa's suggestions of a neutral site, because he was afraid they wouldn't be secure from electronic eavesdropping. And so, they were forced to speak to each other by phone, which they did very frankly, in view of their long history of cooperating as members of the freemasons' Cavour Lodge. This was an association which the Prime Minster, too, had to conceal, as secret societies were outlawed by Italy's Constitution.

Prime Minister Genovese began their discussion by venting his frustration. "The way this damn situation has developed, *Ratzinger has the advantage*. I tell you, Seppe, the longer the quarantine lasts, the more heroic he'll seem. The sooner you get him out of there, the better! I thought you had a plan for that . . . "

"Yes, of course," answered the Cardinal. "We're going to send him into retirement in Mentorella, up in the mountains. I've already made arrangements with a private clinic there, for them to care for a high level cleric, though, naturally I didn't say it would be the Pope. But first, I need to get a group together to judge him incompetent and declare the throne vacant. That's taking more time than I expected.—What about you? Can't you say he's violated some law, and drag him out of his palace right now?"

"Not that I know of, or I would have had it done! The masses and the media are in his camp, so I have to watch my step. I had to fight to get the quarantine law through Parliament. As for ousting him as Pope, Seppe, *don't look to me!*—That's up to *you* and *your people.* I've done *my* share of the heavy lifting. Don't ask me to do yours too! What the hell is holding you up?"

Cardinal Malapensa ignored the reproof. "I don't know what's holding them back. Even the ones who complain in private about how he's mishandled the visions are reluctant to make a change. At this point, I'm not sure we can get even a bare majority of them to sign."

The Prime Minister snorted at the Cardinal's inability to handle such an easy political problem. "Seppe! Can't you see? It's simple! You just tell those who are on the fence that you, because of your high position, are privy to Ratzinger's thinking—he's been planning to force them into retirement or even take away their red hats in a purge of all those who haven't supported him 100%. You expect him to take action any day now, so they'd better act swiftly to save themselves! *Either he goes or they go!*"

It was a lie, a bold one at that, but the more Cardinal Malapensa thought about it, the better it sounded to him. The people he would be telling it to knew or at least suspected that they had displeased the Pope in the conduct of their office. The beauty of the stratagem was that even if they had doubts about what Malapensa was telling them, they wouldn't dream of calling the Pope to check it out! "It just might work—I'll give it a try right away, Ercoli," he said. "But if that doesn't do the trick . . . ?"

"You remove him anyway!" the Prime Minister snapped angrily. *"No matter how! Carry him off if you have to! I'll see to it that no one is prosecuted.*—Once it's a *fait accompli,* your fellow cardinals will be quick to sign and you'll wind up with a document you can show the media."

Picking up his glass of mineral water on his desk, the Cardinal raised it in a mock toast. "Agreed! Here's to the soon-to-be-vacant throne of St. Peter!"

Hearing what sounded like a toast from Malapensa, the Prime Minister responded in a like vein—"And here's to the empty boat of Peter the Fisherman."

"So, Seppe," the Prime Minister said, "our associates are counting on you to succeed Ratzinger when he's gone. What are your chances?"

"Very good, my friend," replied Cardinal Malapensa. "The only rival I'm aware of trying to line up votes for himself is O'Melveny, out in California. Not many would vote for an *American*, no matter what. Between that, and support I'll have from cardinals I've done favors for, I'm confident of the outcome!"

After they hung up, Malapensa could scarcely contain his anticipatory joy. As the next head of the Catholic Church, he surely would take his place in the ranks of the secret Masonic rulers of the world—the circle of Adepts!

— 9 —

Rome

Joseph Ratzinger was not a man given to melancholia, but now, looking down on the vast emptiness of St. Peter's Square in the fading sunlight, a feeling of profound sadness came over him. He stood in his study, grasping the handrails installed for him at the window he was wont to open and wave to the Faithful below. How thrilled they always were to see the Pope acknowledge them in that way—they would wave back, and chant *Papa! Papa!* Despite the chill in the air, the Holy Father would gladly have opened the window that afternoon and leaned out, had there been anyone there to look up for his greeting.

The piazza he looked over was immense. During special events, the stone columns, in their elliptically curved setting designed by Bernini, embraced hundreds of thousands of pilgrims. How far back had the area of St. Peter's Square been marked off by the giant colonnades? Four hundred years? Yes, that was about right, he thought. And had there ever been a day since then when the Square was bereft of the Faithful crossing it to worship at the basilica? Probably not, not until yesterday, when the quarantine went into effect.

The man who was the leader of more than two *billion* Catholics was more alone now than at any time in his whole life, isolated both from the Faithful and from many of the prelates in his own Administration. Standing there alone, he wondered how many more sunsets he would see in his Papacy. It was a question made poignant by the message Fr. Santorelli had brought to him.

In one way, it did not matter to him that he would be carried off against his will: he was 87 years of age and he had achieved everything he could reasonably have expected to do in his ten years as Pope, except proclaiming the final Marian dogma—and that he would do on Friday morning, when he was scheduled to announce it in a radio broadcast. The criticism of the American priest, that he had failed to purge the Curia of unworthy prelates, bothered him, but he firmly believed that his refusal to do so was

the right course to take: it was up to the Lord to deal with the
Devil's weeds, interspersed with His wheat.

He sat down and wheeled himself away from the window, took
up his breviary, and turned to a comforting passage from St. Paul's
first Letter to the Thessalonians:

> You are witnesses, and so is God, how devoutly and
> justly and blamelessly we behaved to you as believers.
> As you know, we treated each one of you as a father
> treats his children, exhorting and encouraging you
> and insisting that you walk in a manner worthy of the
> God who calls you into his Kingdom and glory.

Could he not, with justice, say as much? And, like St. Paul, had
he not kept the faith and finished the race?

Yet, his fate mattered greatly to him in another way. He did not
want to see his reign brought to an end in a way injurious to the
Church. That unfortunate possibility was becoming a probability,
due to the actions of Caesar, with help from his own disaffected
associates.

Of course, Caesar was not a single person anymore, but the
hydra-headed bureaucracy of a pan-national government in Brussels, men working in concert with the likeminded Socialist rulers
of most countries on the continent. The bureaucrats of the European Union, like individual Caesars in times past, feared any
religion which they did not control, and so they were carrying out
a campaign to subdue the Roman Catholic Church by pressuring
member states to enact laws and regulations which could not be
obeyed in conscience by Catholics.

There was a folk tale that the way to boil a frog without having
it jump out of the pot, was to increase the water temperature very
slowly until it was cooked, never having realized its peril. The
European Union had been following a similar incremental strategy
for two decades, aimed at Catholics. Everything the EU did was
based upon faith in the continuing progress of mankind, guided
by purely secular principles and policies. It was a fantasy, he
knew, and he had proclaimed it to be such. Progress was by no
means a natural process whereby each generation ineluctably
built upon the bases inherited from the previous one. Rather, each
generation, like each person, had the freedom to reject the good

it had inherited in laws and social institutions, and choose new ways that were evil, even appropriating the scientific progress of the past for inhuman ends.

The Warning visions had been a shock to the EU bureaucrats and to national officials precisely because they put a lie to the propositions that God was non-existent or dead, and that there was no such thing as *sin*, and no Four Last Things. The visions infuriated Caesar, and so a new strategy had been adopted by the European Union for implementation by member countries: to squeeze the life out of the Vatican by means of a quarantine. He understood their goal, and that they could succeed *either* by persuading *him* to give up and reach an accommodation with Caesar, or by convincing *his brethren* among the cardinals to remove him physically and replace him with a Pope of a like mind with Caesar. *To that end, the word was already circulating that they needed to get rid of him in order to save the Papacy and the Holy See.*

He gave no thought to his personal safety—his worry was that a palace coup would greatly tarnish not only the institution of the Papacy, but the entire Catholic Church. It would make the Church's hierarchy seem to be just like an ordinary, tawdry, secular government. The claim of the Holy See to be unique was that it had been founded by Jesus Christ himself, and that it had ever since been under the guidance of the Holy Spirit—whose aid the electors had invoked as they were selecting him to be the Supreme Pontiff. If, however, a group of cardinals could band together to remove him, the Holy See would look to the world like what the Americans called a "banana republic," whose government was subject to change by force for crass motives.

To avoid a public split, he had even considered resigning voluntarily, as Cardinal Malapensa had urged. However, he feared that the next Pope would be chosen from among the cardinals leading the rebellion, and he could anticipate only disaster for the Church if any of them was elected to his office. So, he was resolved to hang on while he could, giving the visions—and God— a longer chance to work a change in people and then in public policy.

— 10 —

Rome

Before the end, which he felt to be so near, the Pope desired to have a final conversation with the journalist he most respected as a writer on religious matters. For that purpose, he had arranged for Arturo Archangelli to enter the Vatican before the quarantine went into effect, and had lodged him in the Domus Sanctae Marthae, there to await the Pope's convenience.

Benedict XVIth had deliberately chosen an unusual setting for them to come together—the Sistine Chapel, now as devoid of pilgrims as the Square. There were several points he wanted to make, congruent with the theology of Michelangelo's heroic size mural, the *Last Judgment,* and he wished to use it as a ready blackboard to explain his thinking.

His personal secretary, Msgr. Waldheim, wheeled him to the far end, fifteen minutes before the interview scheduled for six o'clock, so that he could go over in his mind how he would use the extraordinary visual aid. He knew that Archangelli would have questions lined up based on what interested the journalist, but as Pope, he could lead the conversation where *he* chose, to bring out the messages he wanted the journalist to take away and convey to the public.

*   *   *

While Signore Archangelli was being cleared by the Pope's personal security guards, he was mentally trying out different approaches for beginning his article. Perhaps he would set the scene for the interview by recalling the first time he had the opportunity to question one-on-one the feared Cardinal Joseph Ratzinger, then the head of the Sacred Congregation for the Doctrine of the Faith. They had worked so well together then that several subsequent sessions were held over the years, all of them published to great acclaim. Although Ratzinger's ideas had developed in response to events in the world, Ratzinger himself had not changed significantly. He had always been thoughtful, considerate, humble and

gracious up close, putting forth his thoughts not as pronouncements from on high, but as ideas which he hoped others would
consider—as he considered the ideas they put before him.

But just as a velvet glove can cover a fist of steel, so Ratzinger's
genuine humility overlay one of the greatest minds in the history
of the Church. A random thought occurred to Archangelli. Ein-
stein's brain, upon examination, appeared to be remarkable—not
like ordinary brains in several ways, which led neurologists to
speculate that perhaps it was this endowment that enabled his
feats of mathematical genius. What, then might one see in a picture of Ratzinger's brain? Of course, it was an inane thought. Not
only would the Church never let the body of a Supreme Pontiff be
dissected, but the brain of a man such as Ratzinger could not be
considered apart from his soul, an organ which, not being *of* this
world, was not scrutable *in* it.

Stepping into the Chapel, Archangelli was awestruck. He had
been there a few times during the day covering events, always
under circumstances that required him to pay attention to the
people there, rather than the scene which covered most of the
wall by the altar at the far end. That evening, under the flood
lights mounted on metal railings which ran along the two long
sides of the room, high up under the large windows, the vibrant
hues of the fresco brought all its parts to life, even the scenes of
death.

The only other people in the vast chapel were the Pope and
the Pope's personal secretary, both facing the mural. Able to give
it his full attention as he walked slowly forward, he felt a visceral
impact from the center of the composition, dominated by the
mighty figure of the Risen Christ. Christ was out of place there, by
classical reckoning—He should have been at the top, in Heaven,
in a three-layered schema of heaven, earth and hell. Michelangelo,
though, had located Him in the center, with everything above, on
and under the earth swirling around Him.

Was the artist treating the Son as the center of the universe,
echoing the then-new heliocentric cosmology of Copernicus which
placed the sun at the center of the solar system? Perhaps. Perhaps
not, thought Archangelli, in view of the fact that a highly significant source of Michelangelo's inspiration had come from a round
medal of the Last Judgment, designed many years before, by the
man who had taught him sculpture.

Among Michelangelo's changes to the scheme of the medal was the addition of the Mother of Christ. Preparatory sketches for the mural showed that he went back and forth in his mind as to how to portray her—her pose being dependent on what message he wanted her to convey. Initially, in his drawings, she was shown with her hands together in prayer, pleading for sinners. In the end, however, Michelangelo painted her to Christ's right and slightly behind Him, but not in an intercessory pose. She was turned, deliberately averting her gaze from the damned. The message given was that the time when she could intercede for sinners was past.

And that message dovetailed with the one given by Michelangelo's image of Christ Himself—His muscular, lightly clad body was torqued to His left in the act of rising, with His right arm and hand upraised in the Last Judgment of individuals. Anyone familiar with St. Matthew's Gospel would recall Christ's prophecy of His return in glory, when He would separate the "sheep" on His right from the "goats" on His left, and say to the latter: "Depart from me, you accursed, into the eternal fire prepared for the devil and his angels!"

Coming up to the Pope seated in his wheelchair ten meters from the wall, with Msgr. Waldheim by his side, Archangelli knelt to kiss the Pope's ring, then took the folding chair set up for him close to the Pope. He switched on his tape recorder, and began the interview with no informal preliminaries.

Q: "Holiness, almost twenty years ago, you gave an interview in which you expressed the possibility that in the epoch at hand, Christianity might dwindle to the point that it existed in—to quote you—'small, seemingly insignificant groups that nonetheless live an intense struggle against evil and bring good into the world.'—Do you feel that way now?"

A. "No, not at all. I'm very hopeful about the future of Christianity."

Q. "*Hopeful?* Despite the united force of the European Union countries being brought to bear to force the Roman Catholic Church to change its religious doctrines and make peace with the secular world on the world's terms?"

A. "*Yes, hopeful, because now God is fighting for us on a scale which is unprecedented in history—at least unprecedented in its visibility.*"

Q. "Would you explain yourself, please?"

A. "The visions, which I believe will spread everywhere, could only have come from God. There is no other credible explanation. As I wrote in my Apostolic Letter, *this is a time of grace.* God is showing His hand for all to see, as He did in leading the Chosen People out of the land of Egypt. After Our Lord ascended to Heaven, Christianity was mediated through human individuals, whether or not they were in the Church and whether or not they were clergy or religious. Indeed, it was most often parents, family members, teachers, friends, and so forth—including those who left their testimony in writing, or art or music—who brought God to the attention of each person in a persuasive way. Unfortunately, some people were never touched in this way, and even those who were brought into contact with God could readily ignore Him if they chose. Now, God is contacting everyone directly, wherever the person may be, and whatever language he may speak, so no one can deny that he has received an invitation from the Almighty, an invitation to a journey which ultimately leads to Christ. Many will be converted as a result, and many already living the Faith will be strengthened in it."

Q. "Have you seen much good coming already from the visions?"

A. "Perhaps only a little, unfortunately. Not nearly as much as there should have been. *Many people, I fear, are acting like Jonah, who ran away to avoid doing what God told him to do. I would like to tell these people that they cannot hide from God, even in the belly of a whale! They should take note of whatever He is displeased about in their lives, and remedy it.*"

Q. "Even if individuals *want* to live more Christian lives, Holiness, *how can they* in the face of unremitting hostility on the part of the bureaucracy of the European Union and national governments, which legalize evils such as abortion and euthanasia, and condemn voicing the Word of God in the public square as 'hate speech'?"

A. "It would appear that God is now going over the heads of the secular authorities, taking His message directly to the people of their countries. One would hope that the official persecution of Christians and the repudiation of Christian morality would be halted, as it was in ancient times when a pagan Roman Emperor gave way to a Christian one. When that happens, the pendulum can swing the other way and evil laws can be repealed."

Q. *"In view of the scene right before us, I must ask you about the many voices who claim that the 'End Times' are at hand. Do you put any credence in such prophecies?"*

A. *"None at all. I can only cite the words of Our Lord Himself, who made it clear that no man knows when the end of the world will come. I have no reason to believe that that has changed. Those who agitate the people with talk of the 'End Times' are like the schools of prophets in the days of ancient Israel, who preyed on people's hopes and fears with false prophecies."*

Q. "If you do not sense that the Last Judgment is imminent, how would you explain why it—and this mural which depicts it—is *relevant* to us?"

A. "Michelangelo's *Last Judgment* is a great work of *hope*. Of course, I am not talking about hope directed at earthly things." ... "Do you see the figure of a woman just off to the right of the angels blowing their trumpets?"

Q. "Yes. It looks like she is being pulled down to Hell by demons."

A. "You are right. Her hand is covering one of her eyes, which symbolizes that she only had eyes for what was of the earth, and did not look also up to heaven. Now, the viper of desperation is biting into her, and she is lost. The hope I am talking about is not the kind of hope *she* had, but the hope revealed by the coming of Christ."

Q. "Still, I wonder where you are finding hope in this mural, Holiness, unless you are referring to those figures Michelangelo showed being escorted to Heaven by the angels."

A. "Yes, it is found in those blessed, but also in the figures in the purgative state, who are being beaten by angels even as the angels are preventing them from being dragged down into the fire of Hell. These will attain Heaven shortly. If you look at the figure of St. Bartholomew, to the right as we look at Christ, you'll see he is holding his flayed skin in one hand—and the face on that skin is that of Michelangelo. To understand that imagery, you need to know that in his poetry, the artist expressed the hope that he would be like an old snake that sloughed off its skin and covered its soul with a surer shield. And, finally, I find hope in the figures of the damned."

Q. "Even in the damned?"

A. *"Yes, even in the damned. They show that God's mercy does not totally annul God's justice."*

Q. "It is clear to me that I don't see in this painting what *you* see through the eyes of Faith. Would you be so good as to enlighten me?"

A. "Our Age has been marked by a virulent atheism. Not just agnosticism, but strident atheism proclaiming that there is no God, or at least that, if there ever was one, he is dead now. Part of this can be attributed to the simple vice of pride, hubris, on the part of the intellectual elite. They do not wish to admit that there is an intelligence so much greater than theirs, that theirs is infinitesimal by comparison, and they echo the Devil's words, *non serviam*—I will not serve. For many other people, there is a more respectable, but equally false, reason for denying the existence of God, namely, that there is an incalculable amount of cruelty and suffering in the world, natural and man made. And so, they conclude, like the gnostics, that the world could not have been made by a good God who still cares for us."

Q. "And your answer to them is . . . ?"

A. *"My answer to them is displayed in this work of art. It is that this life is not the end of the story. This life is a period of trial, a limited period of preparation for the next life, which will never end.* The people of today who are mad at God for not stopping crime and wars and sickness and suffering are the same as the people in Jesus' day who were mad at Him when He failed to end the Roman occupation and make Israel an impregnable earthly kingdom. *What this painting says to them is that there will be an accounting one day, and that everything will be made right in a way that no human court or ruler could accomplish. Part of that 'making right' is that the good will be rewarded with the beatific vision, while the evil are eternally punished."*

Q. *"So there is no 'universal salvation'?"*

A. *"There is no universal salvation,* and they who teach that heretical idea sin against those whom they persuade to live without regard to the demands of God's justice."

Q. "In your Mass celebrated in St. Peter's this past Sunday, one of the readings you chose was from Matthew's Gospel—verses about Jesus' followers being hated and killed because of His name. Did you have anything particular in mind?"

A. "Yes. I see hostility to Christians on the part of secular authorities, who will persecute them for failure to conform, just as the pagan emperors of Rome did. And, an even greater hatred against them by jihadists. Christ ultimately will triumph, but the struggle will be much more intense against militant Muslim groups than against the secularists, and it may take centuries to win. The reason is the absolutist thinking of the jihadists, whose members are impervious to reasoning. *I fear that countless numbers of people in Europe will be killed, just as they were in centuries past, resisting the militant thrust of Islam.* But here too, I am hopeful that the visions will have a profound effect on those of the Muslim faith. After all, God saved the life of their ancestor Ishmael, the son of Abraham by a slave woman, and promised to make a great nation of him. I don't imagine that God has abandoned them."

The journalist could see how exhausted the Pope was, so he put to him one last question.

Q. "Finally, Holiness, do you have any special message that you would like me to convey in the article I write about our meeting?"

A. "Yes. *I would like you to undertake the task of urging them to consider carefully the Four Last Things: Death, Judgment, Heaven and Hell. They are all visible right here. Each person will experience the first two—and whichever one of the last two they choose in this life.*"

— 11 —

Rome

Wednesday saw the unfolding of a scheme by one Luigi Finocchio to better his insignificant standing in the reportorial profession. Poor Finocchio—he was merely an ANSA wire service "stringer" who sent in short accounts of minor events as media filler, or acted as a gopher for the details and local color needed to pad the story of a reporter important enough to have his by-line appear.

Determined to achieve sufficient notoriety to rise above his lowly position, he came up with the idea of sneaking into the Vatican so that he could report on what was happening on the other side of the barricades. His coup would be to find out who the *Rasputin* was that Cardinal Malapensa had referred to in the hearing of certain reporters, and what that mad monk was up to! In his mind's eye, he could see the story, with his name on it, as it would appear in *Il Messaggero*, under the banner: "The Pope's Rasputin Unmasked!" Tomorrow he would be famous!

By observing the Carabiniere checkpoint at the end of the Via della Conciliazione for the past two days, he realized he could not get past it unless he was disguised. Members of the press were uniformly being turned back. He thought of bribing a grocery deliveryman and making his run for him, but he saw that all such entrants had their identities checked. On the other hand, the men in purple and red—bishops and cardinals—were courteously waved through. That observation set him off to a costume rental store, where he had himself fitted out in a black cassock with purple piping, and purple sash and zucchetto. Then, he took a taxi close to the entry to St. Peter's Square and waited in it until several bishops passed by on foot, heading for the Vatican. Getting out, he casually fell in line several steps behind them.

Success!!! Just as he planned, the guards waved them all through the gate in the barrier with a friendly smile.

He was ten yards beyond checkpoint when a guard yelled out "Halt!" He and the bishops he was with froze in their tracks. The guard came over quickly, pointed to him, and said, "You are the only one I need to speak with, Excellency. The others may proceed."

Bored TV cameramen, who were waiting around by the gate hoping for some live action to shoot, noticed what was going on, and, in the absence of anything better, started filming the scene.

"Your Excellency, may I see your identity card?"

"Identity card?" asked Finocchio, with a note of outrage in his voice. "Are you blind, Officer? What do you take me for? How dare you ask that I show identification in order to enter my own country?"

"Forgive the imposition, Excellency," the guard said smoothly. "In carrying out the quarantine, we must make sure that no *terrorists* gain admittance to do terrible harm when few people are around to observe them. I assure you, this will take but a moment. Now, may I please see your identity card?"

"Of course," said Finocchio, and he started to fumble through his pockets. "Oh, my! I don't seem to have brought my wallet with me this morning," he said, feigning surprise. "That was stupid! I'll go back to my apartment and get it, and come through again."

As the perspiring newsman turned to leave, he saw that several more guards had come over to block his escape. "Sir," said his questioner to the lieutenant in charge, "as His Excellency passed through, I noticed that instead of wearing proper black shoes, he had on sneakers. That's why I stopped him. In all my years, I've never seen a bishop dressed that way in public. And, it develops that he doesn't have an identity card."

"Well done, sergeant!" said the officer, "We must see what he *does* have in his possession." They found an identity card after all—for Luigi Finocchio, listing his occupation as *journalist*.

A bishop? A journalist? Or, perhaps a *terrorist* masquerading as one or both?

"Excellency!" said the lieutenant, with mock politeness, "forgive the imposition, but for the safety of your church, it is necessary that we unfrock you." And with that, they disrobed poor Finocchio down to his briefs, which happened to be red.

They found no bomb or weapon on him, and inquiries of the databank gave them comfort that the shivering man in front of them was indeed Luigi Finocchio. Still, they had to arrest him for breaking the quarantine, and they couldn't allow him to put his disguise back on. So, they frog-marched him away as he was, past the cameras and the hooting onlookers.

Finocchio got national exposure, all right. Alas, it was not what he had been looking for. He was featured on the television news being stripped of his bishop's regalia, and led away in his underwear by the Carabiniere. "His identity card read 'Finocchio,'" said one commentator, "but maybe it should have been 'Pinocchio', for his nose grew a foot today." This was *opera buffa* at its Italian best, and poor Finocchio was the clown!

With a comedy like that taking place for all to see at St. Peter's, what was there to worry about the quarantine and the political situation at the Vatican?

— 12 —

Rome

Unfortunately, not all the plots aimed at the Vatican and the Pope were as harmless as Finocchio's. On Thursday, a cabal of six cardinals met on the outskirts of Rome at the villa owned by Cardinal Michele Toricelli, who held the position of Papal Camerlengo.

Under the Apostolic Constitution *Universi Dominici Gregis*, promulgated by Pope John Paul II, the Camerlengo was to be in general administrative charge of what transpired in the Vatican during any vacancy in the Apostolic See, before the election of the next Pope. Cardinal Malapensa had engineered Toricelli's appointment to that post two years previously, when Benedict XVIth had accepted the required resignation of Toricelli as the Cardinal Archbishop of Naples on the occasion of his turning 75. Malapensa had thereby won Toricelli's future support for his own papal ambition.

In addition to Toricelli and Malapensa, three of the conspirators were Europeans: Amsterdam's Cardinal Archbishop Gert Van Dijk; Lyons' Cardinal Archbishop Henri de la Tour; and a Spaniard, Cardinal Juan Sandoval, who headed a Curial Congregation. The sixth conspirator was the American Cardinal Seymour Lazard, who attended as Cardinal O'Melveny's proxy. They were the only conspirators willing to confront the Pope face-to-face.

The group had failed to obtain more than a small number of faxed signatures on their manifesto, but they realized that they had to proceed anyway, for news of what they were doing had probably already gotten back to the Pope, from those who had refused their request to sign.

On O'Melveny's orders, Lazard had flown to Rome, to be there for the consummation of the coup. "Malapensa will try to take all the credit for engineering Ratzinger's removal," O'Melveny had told Lazard, "so that *he* appears to be the strongman and the logical choice for Pope. You must go, Sy, and play a highly visible role, so the Europeans will know that *we* are equally responsible. I want you to be an active member of whatever delegation is assembled to deal with the Pope. And when you confront Ratzinger, demand immediate acquiescence. Don't give him time to consider the situation if he requests it—or he'll try to contact the signers and they might back down. Make sure he's hustled out of the Vatican and up to the mountains as fast as possible." Lazard had vowed to carry out those instructions from O'Melveny to the letter.

How were they to present their demand to him? Cardinal Malapensa said he would try to arrange for a Papal audience early the next morning at the Pope's apartment, without relating the purpose of the meeting. If the Pope refused to grant it, as he well might, they would have to barge in on him.

"Can we really do that?" asked Cardinal Van Dijk.

"Of course," retorted Malapensa. "Have you forgotten that I live in the Palace too?"

One of them remembered seeing in the newspaper that the Pope had blocked out time on the Vatican's radio station for a live address the next day at 10:00 a.m., to announce the new dogma about the Mother of God.

Malapensa picked up on that information. "Eminences, we have to act before that happens! It will forever poison our ecumenical relations—even if later we say we are rescinding his pronouncement. So, let's plan our action for 9:00 a.m. We'll head for the first *Sala dei 'Foconi'*. It's likely that he'll do the broadcast from there."

"Where is it located?" Van Dijk asked. "You forget that we don't have access to the Apostolic Palace. I've only been inside once."

Malapensa gave a smile of superiority as he explained, "The room is just off the Raphael Loggia, next to the *Redemptoris Mater* chapel. They used to burn wood there to heat up the Palace in the old days. You'd never know it now from the gorgeous ceiling frescoes. Don't worry—you won't have any trouble getting into the Palace and upstairs, with me with you. We'll have this matter out with him well before the broadcast is scheduled to begin."

As the leader of the group, Cardinal Malapensa then proceeded to lay down the tactics.

"First, I will inform him that he has lost the confidence of the College of Cardinals, and as proof, I will show him our Declaration, stating that we have judged him *incompetent* to hold the offices of Bishop of Rome and Supreme Pontiff, and that therefore, *we have already removed him from those two offices.* I will urge him to go into retirement—one which I have already prepared for him in the mountain village of Mentorella, which he loves.

"I will ask him for the good of the Church to resign and leave quietly, without making a fuss. As an incentive, if he will sign a letter of resignation, which I will have with me, we will tear up the Declaration of Incompetence and Removal. I will also tell him that, if he will not go voluntarily, we will have to make the Declaration public and there will be a schism. I am absolutely confident that he will want to avoid that at all costs. He knows the damage the Church suffered in the schism at the end of the Avignon Papacy, when some Cardinals elected one man Pope, while others elected his rival. For forty years no one was quite sure who was the head of the Church. That sort of rupture might never be healed if it occurred now, and I will make him feel it's *his responsibility* to avoid it by resigning."

"Do you really think that will work?" asked Cardinal Van Dijk.

"Yes, of course!" said Malapensa, annoyed at being challenged. "Ratzinger is nearly 90 years old and is in ill health. How much longer can he expect to live? And, what can he hope to accomplish in that time? The Church is under siege right now, and he's not the man to defend it. He knows how devastating it would be to have open warfare between our *majority* of the Cardinals, and the *minority* still with him. Having come this far, *we* aren't going to back down. So, all *he* could do is be a dog in the manger. I'm sure he'll see that the role would not become him."

"I'm so relieved to hear that we have *a majority* of our brethren with us!" Cardinal Sandoval commented. "I hadn't heard how your efforts were coming."

"We don't have a majority—yet—but *he* doesn't know that," Malapensa answered him curtly. "I've dressed up the Declaration with signatures I've copied from other documents. He won't be able to check them out on the spot—he'll have to assume they're genuine."

"Still, I want to know what we should do if he refuses to go." That came from the "nervous nelly" of the group, Cardinal Henri de la Tour.

"I will put the case for resigning to him *most persuasively,*" replied Cardinal Malapensa, with confidence. "*Unity* has been a major theme of his pontificate. Don't you remember him repeatedly stressing the need for the Church to be united, in his unsuccessful attempts to bring the Lefebvrists back into the fold? Moreover, Eminences, the Holy See cannot do without the financial support of many of the rich dioceses in America and Europe, ones whose Ordinaries are in league with us—or so it will seem to him from the signatures I've appended. *Pecunia omnia vincit!"*

"Yes, I agree that money does conquer all—usually—," said Cardinal de la Tour, "but still, Eminence, *what are we going to do with him if he doesn't agree to go quietly . . . ?"*

There was silence. Malapensa's increasing disdain for Ratzinger coupled with his own vanity had blinded him to the need for a *"Plan B"* to deal with a completely intransigent Pope.

"Why do we need to do *anything?"* one of the group asked. "Once we tell him he's been removed, suppose we just go ahead and elect a new Pope . . . "

Cardinal Malapensa pointed out the defect of that suggestion. "That would not work, Eminence. As long as he's here at the Vatican, wearing his white cassock, the world will treat *him* as the Pope, and they'll consider us to be *schismatics. We must physically remove him from the premises and keep him incommunicado,* at least for a period of time."

"Can't we just bind and gag him and carry him off in a limousine?"

Perhaps that was what the Prime Minister had in mind the day before, when he said that he would protect the cabal from prosecution, but, stated that baldly, Malapensa decided that tactic was too risky. "No," he said. "We can't tie him up. His security detail would spot that and stop us before we got him out the gate."

Thinking furiously as he spoke, the Cardinal said, "I have a different plan!—I've heard that Ratzinger had some sort of fainting spell two weeks ago.—I'll hire a private ambulance and ride in it in the front seat, right into the Cortile del Belvedere. I'll tell the guards at the Sant'Anna Gate that I'm hoping to persuade the Pope to go the Gemelli for some tests, and if he goes, we'll use the ambulance to keep his absence from the Vatican secret."

"In the *unlikely* event that he won't come with us voluntarily after I've done my best to persuade him, a couple of you will need to distract his private secretary momentarily while I hold a handkerchief with ether on it up to his nose. I know a pharmacist who will provide me with a vial without asking questions. That ought to put him to sleep quickly, in his condition. Once he slumps down, we'll all gather around him, push him in his wheelchair around the loggia and into the elevator, and then out to the waiting ambulance. We'll cry out that it's an emergency!"

"Seeing the Pope ill, the guards won't challenge me—after all, I *am* the Secretary of State! I'll ride away with him until we're out of sight of the Vatican, then get out. The attendants will keep him well sedated all the way to his new home in the Alps, one that I've already arranged."

Cardinal Malapensa proceeded to outline the final steps of his plan. "An hour after Ratzinger is gone, His Eminence the Camerlengo will go on television and say that, when we met with His Holiness about recent events of concern to us, he admitted that he was no longer competent to lead the Church, and agreed to go into retirement. Immediately thereafter, he took ill, and has been taken to a place where he can spend his last years in peace. Finally, the Camerlengo will summon the Cardinal electors to a conclave to elect a new Pope. The people will see this is a *fait accompli*, so they'll have no choice but to accept it. And all of us will be calling other cardinals to see if we can persuade them to have their names added to the Declaration, so we can release it to the press later if we have to."

Cardinal Malapensa's impromptu scheme had far too many holes in it to succeed, as he himself would have realized if he had had the time to reflect on it. However, he had never had to plan an assault before, and this was the best he could concoct on the spur of the moment to hold in line those Cardinals whose worries might otherwise have caused them to pull out of the joint action.

Having no alternative of their own to offer in its place, the others acceded to Malapensa's plan, comforting themselves with the thought that it was only a backup anyway—if Cardinal Malapensa was correct in predicting that Ratzinger would resign in order to avoid a schism, no use of force would be necessary . . .

Before they left Toricelli's villa, Malapensa had some chilling words of wisdom for them. "There is an old maxim which says, 'He who shoots at the King, must kill him.' If we fail to remove the Pope, we will be excommunicated and banished from the clerical state. *Therefore, Eminences, failure is not an option. We must do whatever—and I emphasize whatever—is necessary to remove him tomorrow!"*

— 13 —

Rome

Having been denied an audience with the Pope, the conspirators joined up with Cardinal Malapensa at nine in the morning in the Cortile del Belvedere, a large, fully enclosed courtyard almost adjoining the Apostolic Palace, used as a parking lot for Vatican officials. They followed Malapensa up into the Papal quarters, where they found no one in either of the two *Sale dei "Foconi."* They proceeded on from room to room clockwise around the floor, becoming more and more agitated by their fruitless quest for the Pope. Finally, they went through the Papal Library and the *Sala Clementina*, arriving back in the *Raphael Loggia*, where they had started. At that point, Malapensa decided to risk calling Vatican security, which informed him that the Holy Father was up at the Marconi Radio Station.

"Why didn't you think of that first, since it's a radio broadcast?" demanded Cardinal de la Tour, as they hurried down to the parking lot in the courtyard, and got into the private ambulance which Malapensa had hired to spirit the Pope away.

"Because he's only broadcast from there once—ten years ago," Malapensa snapped.

The station was in a sizeable three story building set well back into the western corner of the Vatican City State, next to a tower topped by a modern radio transmitting antenna. It was just to the east of St. John's tower, a section of the old Leonine Wall, and the helicopter pad. To get to it, one had to ascend the hillside on which the Vatican's extensive botanical gardens were laid out, with fountains and special buildings such as a grotto replicating exactly the one at Lourdes. The driver had never been in that non-public area, and so at every twist and turn Malapensa had to point the way. By the time the vehicle arrived at the station, His Eminence was inwardly raging.

As the cardinals climbed out of the ambulance they were greeted by the head of the Pope's security detail, who eyed it suspiciously as he saluted them and asked, "Is there anything going on, Eminences?"

"Nothing to concern *you*," replied Cardinal Malapensa in a high handed manner, judging correctly that he could bluster his way past security.

Malapensa rushed inside, going directly into the elevator, followed closely by Cardinal Toricelli and Cardinal Lazard. The elevator was so tiny that Lazard's bulk precluded anyone else from getting on, forcing the other cardinals to use the adjacent staircase.

Up they went to the top floor. Malapensa was sure that the Pope would, for sentimental reasons, be proclaiming the final Marian dogma from the room where the first Papal radio broadcast had taken place. Pope Pius XIth, with Marconi, the inventor of radio, at his side, had made history in 1931. The microphone used on that occasion was still there, in front of the window, preserved in a lucite block.

That room too was empty! So Malapensa led them across the hall to the large recording studio, a room where small concerts were sometimes recorded. They could see at a glance a Bösendorfer concert grand piano in one corner, a Steinway grand in another, a harpsichord in the middle, and drums off to the side—but no people. Disappointed once again, the plotters turned their attention to the room in the middle on that floor. It was a chapel—beautiful, peaceful, and empty.

Descending, they finally found the place where the action was— the Nuova Regis 3 studio, where the Pope and Msgr. Waldheim were seated at an angular stand, something like a counter, before microphones. It was before ten o'clock, and it appeared that the Pope was reading out loud, practicing his address.

By now, Cardinal Malapensa was uncharacteristically rattled, and he failed to see that in the corner there was an unattended TV camera with a small glowing red light, focused on the Pope.

The time had come for Malapensa to persuade the Pope to resign. He was about to give his little speech, and he was holding a copy of the Declaration of Incompetence and Removal—also the letter of resignation he was going to ask the Pope to sign as an alternative way to make his exit. Momentarily, he juggled the papers, freeing one hand and opening his handkerchief to have it ready for the vial of ether in his pocket if the Pope refused to go quietly.

That was a fatal mistake, for while he was thus engaged, Cardinal Lazard unexpectedly pushed past him.

Mindful of Cardinal O'Melveny's exhortation to him to take the lead, Lazard went right over to the Pope, and, with no preliminaries, grabbed the text of the Apostolic Constitution out of his hands, and tore it to shreds.

"*We don't need any more pronouncements from you, Joseph,*" Lazard said, in a haughty manner. "*The College of Cardinals has judged you to be incompetent to run the affairs of the Church—and we have removed you as Bishop of Rome and as Pope. The chair of Peter is now vacant!*"

The Pope, and his personal secretary, sitting at his side, were thunderstruck. Even the other Cardinals with Lazard were stunned. They had not planned to begin in such a contentious and disrespectful way.

Before anyone could react, Lazard added, "We're here to take you off into retirement."

The Pope found his tongue. "*This is an outrage!*" he said, with all the vigor he had left in him. "*In obedience—I command you to leave at once!*"

"In obedience?" asked Lazard, mockingly. "We owe you no obedience, Joseph, because you are no longer Pope. The throne of Peter is vacant, I tell you. Read this if you care to!" With that, he thrust down the one-paragraph declaration to which faxed pages were appended interspersing the signatures of the few cardinals who had signed, with the forged signatures of the many who had not.

The Pope took one very brief look at it and then put his left forearm down over half of it, to hold it in place, while with his right hand he tried to rip the document itself down the middle. "*This is totally illicit and invalid!!!*" he said. "*Now leave, before you are excommunicated!!!*"

Cardinal Malapensa pushed to the fore, and tried to take charge and set a different tone. However, he was forced to adopt Lazard's demeaning form of address, as he could not afford to address Ratzinger in a way which would concede that he was still Pope.

"*Joseph,*" he said, "*we urge you to accept the judgment of your brothers—a majority of the Cardinals—that the Church needs new leadership. You have the power and the responsibility to avoid cre-*

ating a schism, by resigning and going off into retirement quietly.
By resigning, you would moot our need to remove you. We have
prepared one of your favorite retreats, Mentorella, as a place
where you can spend your last days in peace. We've come to take
you there now."

Benedict XVIth would give them no satisfaction. *"The schism is
on your heads! I am still Pope—and here I stay until I die!"*

At that, Cardinal Malapensa pulled a tiny vial of ether out
of his pocket, intending to implement his contingency plan for
subduing Ratzinger, but Lazard again acted first.

"All right," said Lazard, "if we have to carry you out, we will."
And with that, he pulled the Pope's wheelchair backward to ma-
neuver it out the door. As the Pope tried to get out of the con-
trivance, Lazard shoved him back down by the shoulder. At that,
the Pope let out a cry and collapsed, hitting his head on the edge
of the stand, before falling to the floor.

Lazard expressed no concern for the fallen man, and tried to
lift him under his armpits. "Someone take his legs," he directed,
"I've got him up here."

Malapensa and two other Cardinals pushed aside Msgr. Waldheim, who was rising to the Pope's rescue, blocking him from
assisting his fallen leader.

Malapensa tried again to assert control. "Get him back in his
wheelchair," he ordered.

They struggled to do so, until one of them cried out, *"He's not
breathing!!!"*

That threw them all into a panic. They felt for a pulse, but
there was none.

"He's dead!!!" cried one in a stunned voice. *That was not in
their plan ...*

*"Oh S***!"* ... *"What do we do now?!"*

He might have gotten an answer if Cardinal Malapensa hadn't
happened to look into the control room, and seen a face peering
at him through the tinted glass.

"Shut up! All of you!" he commanded, pointing into the other
room.

One of the Cardinals ran into the control room. "Stay off the
air!" he ordered. "Cancel the broadcast!"

The broadcaster found it hard to speak. "I can't. We're live,"
he croaked.

"What do you mean?" the Cardinal asked, frantically. "The broadcast's at ten!"

"He came early to practice—He decided to go ahead while his voice was strong—We went live at 9:30 ... "

Then, the broadcaster gave out a wail from the bottom of his gut, *"You killed him!!! You killed Papa!!!"*

Cardinal Malapensa tried in vain to give instructions to shut off the recording: "Cut the power!" he roared.

No longer held down, Msgr. Waldheim rose up and screamed at them—*"You murderers! Get out! Get out!"*

And the dogged Cardinal Lazard, not knowing what else he could do to show leadership, started to drag the Pope's body out the door by the feet.

In the pandemonium, the out-of-the-way TV camera remained unnoticed.

At this point, Cardinal Toricelli stepped to the fore. *"Silence! ... All of you!"* he commanded. *"I'm the Camerlengo! I'm in charge now!"*

"You!" he said—pointing at the Pope's personal secretary— *"Out! Leave us alone."*

Cardinal Toricelli was indeed the Camerlengo, but Msgr. Waldheim, who had lionized the late Pope, was not to be cowed. He stood there, refusing to leave.

"Get out yourself, you traitors! ... You're all excommunicated! You raised your hands against the Pope!"

They were old, and he was comparatively young. Not being confident that they could physically manhandle him, they left, despite their fury at him, stepping over Benedict's body, and making threats against the Monsignor as they did so.

When they were gone, Msgr. Waldheim got down on the floor, cradled the dead Pope in his arms, and cried.

PART V

The Smoke of Satan

February–March 2015

From some fissure, the smoke of Satan has entered
the Temple of God.

Pope Paul VI (June 29, 1972)

— 1 —

Rome

Out the door of the radio station ran the engineer, screaming
"Papa's dead!—They killed him!"
    In rushed the Vatican's internal security detail, pushing past
the cardinals as they were trying to exit the building. The first
ones in dropped to their knees beside the Monsignor and bent
over the body to verify that the Pope was dead. Then they called
for a gurney from the Vatican's hospital to remove him, and looked
to the Pope's secretary for orders.
    Unbeknownst to the plotters, two other pairs of eyes had seen
the indignities they had visited upon the Pope. One of these was
in the transmission control room of the Vatican Television Center,
housed in a small building inside St. Anne's Gate, next to St.
Pellegrino's Church. The announcement of the new encyclical was
not being carried live on TV, but it was being recorded for future
broadcast, both by the Vatican's TV station and by Radiotelevisione
Italiana, Italy's state owned public service broadcaster. As was
its practice, Vatican TV was cooperating in covering the Pope's
doings inside the Vatican by sending its signal live to RAI.
    The events had played out in real time on one of the many
screens on the wall in front of the Vatican's transmission engineer.
Dazed, he phoned his counterpart. *"Did you see what just happened
in our radio studio?"*
    "Jesus, yes!" the man at RAI said. "I wouldn't have believed
anything like that could happen these days, if I didn't see it myself.
This is radioactive! I'm calling our news people right now to inter-
rupt programming on all our channels. I'll set it up so they can
replay the whole encounter, from the time when those cardinals
walked in on the Holy Father. The pictures speak for themselves.
We'll come up with the commentary later."
    "Good man!" was the Vatican engineer's response. "The only
way to make sure nobody covers it up is to make it public immediately!"

                    *   *   *

Not long after the security people had wheeled the late Pope's body into the hospital, bells could be heard starting to toll in Rome, in response to reports from viewers of the RAI's breaking news telecast. In the Vatican City itself, there was dead silence. None of *its* bells, which should have been the first to sound, was ringing out. Cardinal Toricelli, as Camerlengo, was supposed to have given the order for that obsequy. Indeed, he also should have remained with the body until the official procedures for verifying the demise of the Supreme Pontiff had been carried out—but he was already engaged in holding a council of war with his co-conspirators.

He sat at the head of a conference table in an office in the Medieval Palace, a large building situated between the Apostolic Palace and the Sistine Chapel. Bitter words had been exchanged within the group on their way from the radio studio. Now he cautioned them—"Mutual recriminations will get us nowhere, Eminences. It is more important than ever that we work together. This morning did not go according to plan, but Ratzinger's death works in our favor—he can't serve as a center for any opposition to rally around. The only problem facing us is what happened in the broadcast room. No doubt the sound track will be broadcast on radio a number of times during the next few days. But, the public won't be able to tell who's doing the talking, and they'll tire of hearing it."

"They're going to make a martyr out of him," moaned Cardinal Van Dijk, avoiding eye contact with the others. "Wait and see the crowds at his funeral ... "

"His funeral—ah, yes," said Cardinal Toricelli, improvising fast. "You are correct. We *would* have reason to be concerned about the crowds and popular fervor, *if* Ratzinger's funeral were held here. An occasion for maudlin sympathy could be turned into support for the reactionary elements. Which is good reason to move it elsewhere."

"Do you mean Munich?" asked Van Dijk, referring to the See which Cardinal Joseph Ratzinger had held before he became Prefect of the Congregation for the Doctrine of the Faith.

"No, Eminence. Munich is a large, easily accessible city. It too could be the site of a mass protest. I think it better to send his body to Regensburg. I'll justify it by mentioning that at one time he taught at the university there. I'll give orders to have

Ratzinger's body dispatched tonight, and instruct the Bishop there, who supports our program, to bury him tomorrow. As for the populace here, I'll ask the Prime Minister to keep the quarantine in force until the body is gone. Then, as they say—out of sight, out of mind. In the meantime, I'll call for the papal conclave to begin next week. That'll cut short the time for any opposition to us to develop."

"But, Eminence, we are required to follow the *Ordo Exsequiarum Romani Pontificis*." The objection came from Cardinal de la Tour. "It specifies a nine day period of mourning ..."

He didn't get to finish his point. Cardinal Toricelli interrupted him with a wave of his hand. "That's exactly the sort of ostentatious ceremony we are committed to doing away with, Eminence. It's as out of date as that chair which they used to carry the Pope around in, lifted up on poles over peoples' heads." Here, the Camerlengo paused for a moment to give his next words added emphasis. "Provided we remain united, we can persuade the people that now is not the time for archaic regulations. We have a pressing matter to attend to—electing the right man as Pope ..."

De la Tour wasn't quite satisfied. "What about Waldheim? Won't the Pope's secretary make trouble for us?"

"Let him try!" said Cardinal Toricelli, very confident of his powers. "He's a mere monsignor. *I'm the Camerlengo!* What authority would *anyone* have to challenge my decision not to follow the *Ordo*?—Now, I suggest that all of us remain here in this room while we call our supporters around the world, and reassure them. The message we need to convey is that no matter what they may hear from the media, we are firmly in charge here and we expect them to come in for the conclave to begin on Monday, with a new, plenary Council to follow immediately thereafter!"

*   *   *

While the plotters were thus engaged, Msgr. Waldheim ordered that Benedict's body be officially examined so that his death could be certified, and then he called Cardinal Zanier to ask his advice about how to deal with Cardinal Toricelli, the Camerlengo. As it turned out, Zanier was then inside the Vatican, visiting a prelate from his country over at the guest house.

Waldheim told him the story of the Pope's demise, then posed the question very much on his mind. "Eminence, over at the radio station, I told the plotters that they were excommunicated. Was I right? And if so, do I need to follow Toricelli's orders, nevertheless?"

"I believe you were right, Monsignor," replied the Cardinal, "based on the scene you described. But that determination is not up to you—or to me either, for that matter. An official decision on Toricelli's status can only be made by one man, and that's Cardinal Brooke—the Cardinal Major Penitentiary. As far as I know, he's visiting his family in America right now, so unless and until he returns and declares that Toricelli is excommunicated, whether we like it or not, Toricelli's legally in charge."

Desiring to pay his own last respects to Benedict XVIth right away, Cardinal Zanier left the guest house. As soon as he stepped outdoors, he heard a great commotion coming from the Square, where a mob was even then on the move.

When a Pope died, it was customary for the Roman populace to gather immediately in St. Peter's Square out of respect. However, on that day, the people streaming down the Via della Conciliazione toward the Square were blocked by the police, who were still enforcing the quarantine. The situation quickly became dangerous as the sidewalk cafés lining the route were raided for bottles. When these started to rain down on the officers, they responded by lobbing tear gas canisters at the people.

The police had not contemplated any such mass disturbance, and their line across the mouth of the broad entrance to the square was only one long row of wooden barriers and thirty officers. Since they were unwilling to shoot live bullets at the thousands of their fellow citizens pressing forward, they gave way, and the crowd rushed into the square right up to the steps of the basilica, with the TV cameras which had previously been stationed at the barricades rolling forward along with them.

Seeing the approaching horde, the Swiss Guards hastily locked all the doors of St. Peter's basilica, and took up their positions across the front of the church and at the entrances to the Vatican enclosure, visibly brandishing hefty SIG and Steyr submachine-guns. An unruly crowd might turn to looting or other mayhem if they forced their way into the enclosure. The situation was tense, for mingled with the heartfelt cries of "*Papa! Papa!*" there were more threatening ones of "*Death to the Murderers!*"

Cardinal Zanier hurried to the front of the basilica and peered around the Swiss Guards, quickly sizing up the situation. He sensed that the people needed some release from the tension, some official response which would give them comfort—otherwise they might eventually give vent to their frustration and anger and start rampaging through the streets.

He asked the head of security to find a crowd-control megaphone for him, and being given one, he passed through the Guards and walked down the center of the steps until he was only a few feet above the heads of the crowd. They instantly recognized who he was—the only black Cardinal in Rome—and word spread back through the mass of people. The TV cameras were able to focus in on him with their zoom lenses and directional microphones. The crowd quieted down, and people with portable radios turned up the volume to catch his words, while those with cell phones picked up the streaming Internet feed.

"My brothers and sisters in Christ! You good and faithful people of Rome," he began, "you did well to come here as soon as you heard the dreadful news. Our chief shepherd, our *Papa*, has been struck down unexpectedly and in a despicable way. You are right to honor his memory, and we all need to band together for protection until a new chief shepherd is chosen.

"We must pray together for three things. First, for the soul of Benedict XVIth, that it may already be with Jesus and His Mother and St. Joseph in Paradise. Second, for those who have the duty of choosing, before God, the person best qualified to succeed to the throne of Peter, that they may carry out their duties faithfully. And third, for those who raised their hands against the Holy Father, that they may seek and receive forgiveness."

Cardinal Zanier pulled out his rosary and held it up high. "For now, I ask you please to join me in praying the Sorrowful Mysteries of the Holy Rosary, which I will lead."

*   *   *

If the black plague had struck every other country in the world that day, the story would have played second fiddle in the Italian media to the twin bombshells which had exploded in the heart of Rome—the death of the Pope, and the attempted palace coup which had brought it about.

Work all over Italy ground to a halt by midday, except for those covering the news. Everybody had to see the film shot at the Vatican, as it was put together by the networks. It began with a half minute clip of the Pope serenely reading the text of his Marian pronouncement. That was cut short by the violent intrusion of the Cardinal from Miami, ripping the papers out of the startled Pope's hands. Other indignities were seen being visited upon the frail old Pope. Then came the death scene, rebroadcast in slow motion, with the unseen broadcaster's poignant wail off screen, "*You killed him!!! You killed Papa!!!*" Following that was the obscenely ghoulish sight of Lazard trying to drag the Pope out by his feet. The commentators likened him to a giant dragon lizard with its prey—and thus the Cardinal Archbishop of Miami became enshrined in infamy as *Cardinal Lizard*.

The death scene would have been horrific enough to stir compassion in an atheist's breast. But there was more—the TV camera recorded the set-to between the Camerlengo and the brave Monsignor, catching the cardinals in the act of stepping over the Pope's body as though it were a log, and, finally, the Monsignor reverently paying his respects after they had left.

Whether one belonged to a party of the right or a party of the left was immaterial—all the people of Italy felt themselves offended, soiled, by the disrespect shown to the person of the Pope and to the institution which had been part of their national heritage for 2,000 years. The scenes were so unbelievable that most people watched them more than once, on different channels, as if still not quite believing that such events could really have happened. They were hypnotized by the scene, just as they had been when they watched over and over again the films of the airplanes flying into New York's World Trade Towers on 9/11. The switchboards of radio call-in shows lit up with calls from citizens, many demanding that the six conspirators be prosecuted for murder.

*   *   *

By the time Cardinal Toricelli phoned the Bishop of Regensburg, the latter had watched the tape of the coup several times on TV, saddened by the clumsy way the plotters had gone about removing the Pope, and angry that they had shown so little respect for the man whom he knew to be a holy man.

When his secretary announced that the Camerlengo was on the phone, he guessed that he might be invited to the funeral due to Benedict's ties to Regensburg. He was totally unprepared to be told that the Camerlengo planned to dispatch the body of the late Pope that night to *his* cathedral, for burial the next day. Like Cardinal de la Tour, he raised the dictates of the *Ordo* for the Pope's funeral rites, only to be brushed off as the Cardinal had been. "I see, Eminence," he said, "you are giving me no choice in the matter."

"That is correct, Excellency. Try to avoid publicity until after the burial has taken place.—Oh, and be sure that we will take your cooperation in this delicate matter into account when the new Pope takes office!"

The Bishop of Regensburg was accustomed to accepting orders from his superiors without challenge, but one does not get elevated to the episcopal rank without learning something about "the fine Italian hand" which unseen pulls the strings in the opposite direction from what was ordered. And so, he now placed a call to the Mayor of Regensburg.

"Your Honor," he said, "I have momentous news.—His Eminence, Cardinal Toricelli, the Camerlengo, has decreed that our late Holy Father will be buried here in Regensburg, in a simple ceremony, in remembrance of his love for our town." After convincing the Mayor that this was not a bad joke, he continued. "The reason I am telling you this is that we will need to have an official burial permit, and more important, a force of police to keep order if news of what we are doing leaks out in advance. No doubt, many of our townspeople will wish to touch his casket, leave flowers, and so forth, and we must keep order as we do in Germany—not the way the Italians do it. When I hang up with you, I will be calling the Rector of the University, as undoubtedly some members of the faculty and students will want to pay their respects too."

Having obtained promises of assistance from the Mayor and the Rector, he sat back to await developments. It was inevitable that both of those worthies would call a number of other persons with the news, and the result was that it was picked up by the local radio and TV stations, and then by the media in Rome. A new wave of indignation swept the capital at the insult to the late Pope and to the citizens of Rome, who felt entitled to be present for the Pope's funeral. They demanded that this "body-snatching" be blocked by the Government.

Commentators on the evening newscasts suggested that the Prime Minister was ultimately at fault—after all, he was the one who had demanded that a quarantine be imposed. That had set in motion the whole train of events. An angry mob gathered outside his apartment in the Palazzo Chigi, shouting insults and threats.

For the first time in his life, Genovese was on the receiving end of a fiery demonstration—instead of the giving end—and he was forced to ask for protection from the riot police. An hour of the chaos was enough. He phoned a concession statement to the media: the quarantine was no longer necessary and would be ended immediately, and the Pope had better be buried in Rome, *or else the civil authorities would concern themselves with the manner of his death . . . !*

— 2 —

Rome

Cardinal Zanier became a media darling when he stepped forward
and calmed the crowd in St. Peter's Square. That night, they all
had his name on their short list of *papabile*—cardinals who might
be elected Pope. And he drew nationwide coverage for the news
conference he called on Saturday morning.

The Vatican's Press Office was located just outside St. Peter's
Square on the north side of the Via della Conciliazione. The press
room could hold over a hundred correspondents comfortably in
blue upholstered auditorium chairs, and that morning every seat
was taken. At one end of the room, there was a blue covered dais
and chairs for speakers, in front of the end wall which consisted
of an articulated series of panels covered in a grayish cloth. High
up on that wall, in the center, was the Papal coat of arms in gold,
flanked by large screen TV sets. Unobtrusive light came from the
high ceiling.

The only speaker that morning was Cardinal Zanier, who read
a carefully prepared statement about the turbulent events of
the previous day. "Yesterday, I addressed those before me in the
Square as my brothers and sisters in Christ, for so they were. I
also reached out to the good and faithful people of Rome. Today,
I would like to address my remarks even more broadly, to those,
whoever they are and wherever they may be, that are my fellow
sheep in the flock of St. Peter, as well as those of other flocks who
bear us good will.

"My first duty today is to offer an apology. An apology for the
failure of those administering Holy Mother Church to publicly
express the sorrow of the whole Church at the death of so great
as leader as Pope Benedict XVIth. The bells here should have been
the first to toll, and a Church spokesman here should have been
the first to regret his passing and recount the highlights of his life
in the service of the Church.

"For years, he was the good right arm of his predecessor of
happy memory, Pope St. John Paul II, who relied upon him to see
to it that our worldwide Church maintained a unity of doctrine,

one faithful to the Magisterium. As Pope, he continued in his predecessor's footsteps as a teacher, issuing encyclicals which enlightened the world concerning reason, truth and love, and he authored many books which taught sound doctrine. Future generations, recognizing his greatness, may accord him the title, 'Doctor of the Church.'

"Like his predecessor, he encouraged our young people at their special gatherings, and he brought the message of Christ to millions around the world with gentleness and humility. He repeatedly spoke out against the delusions of cultural relativism and the salvific equality of all religions, while at the same time recognizing that all men may be saved through Jesus Christ. He attempted, almost single handedly, to stop in its course the demonic drive to an irreligious secularism in the countries of Europe, a drive fomented at every turn by the bureaucracy of the European Union, as you well know from the quarantine imposed upon our tiny state this week.

"And, how could we forget his efforts to bring together warring factions within the Church which, sad to say, resisted to the end his entreaties? In this pursuit, as you well know, he was criticized from all sides, being treated, as he said, hatefully, without misgiving or restraint. He was reduced to begging for Christian charity, invoking the words of St. Paul to the Galatians: 'if you bite and devour one another, take heed that you are not consumed by one another.' And now he lies dead—a victim of the internecine warfare which he did his best to stop. We owe it to his memory to observe the prescribed nine days of mourning.

"As for the six who plotted to carry him off by force and supplant him in a coup d'état, did they not thereby excommunicate themselves, and disqualify themselves from any participation in the Church, until they receive absolution from the Cardinal Major Penitentiary? For my part, I will do all within my power to see to it that they observe whatever strictures may be imposed upon them ...

"And as for others who lent their names to the meretricious decree which was thrust in front of the Holy Father as a *fait accompli* on Wednesday—they too bear a share of responsibility, and should avail themselves of the Sacrament of Penance, whether or not they had reason to foresee that violence would be used against him.

"Finally, I would remind you of the words of St. Paul to the presbyters of the church at Ephesus, set down in the Acts of the Apostles: *'I know that after my departure savage wolves will come among you, and they will not spare the flock. And from your own group, men will come forward perverting the truth to draw the disciples away after them.'*

"In every age such wolves have been at work, and they are at present seeking to obtain high office by bribery contrary to Church law. I know that from having been propositioned myself!* Yet we should not lose heart, for we know from the visions which we have received as part of a divine Warning, that God is still working toward our salvation. As our late Holy Father said, this is a time of grace, and we will be saved if we repent and believe in the good news of Jesus Christ!

"Thank you for your kind attention—and may God bless you! In the name of the Father, Son and Holy Spirit, Amen!" And with that blessing, he left the room without taking questions from the press.

*   *   *

Cardinal Toricelli watched Zanier's performance on television in stony silence, until mention was made of the plotters as being excommunicated, and requiring absolution. Then he exploded. *How dare he? A black man born in the jungle, presuming to chastise his betters!!!* If it was the last thing he did, Toricelli swore, he would drive Zanier out of the Church!

As angry as he was, Toricelli realized that if enough prelates followed Zanier's lead now, he, the Camerlengo, could be precluded from managing the arrangements for the papal conclave. It didn't take him long to come up with a way to deal with that challenge. So long as the Declaration of Incompetence and Removal remained secret and the signatures on it were not open to scrutiny, he could maintain that Ratzinger had been removed by a majority of Cardinals *before* the group had burst into the radio studio. Since Ratzinger was no longer the Supreme Pontiff when the incident occurred, none of them committed an act which could result in excommunication! His thought was to call a press conference of his own to put out that story, after he touched base with Cardinal Malapensa to make sure they were on the same wavelength.

"Don't give in to the African, Eminence," said Malapensa. "By all means—hold your own press conference. You're the Camerlengo—act the part! Make him stop you if he can!"

Those marching orders suited Cardinal Toricelli to a "T," and shortly thereafter he held a news conference at the Vatican's Press Office, which had been reopened at his request. Without referring to the manner of the Pope's death or his own role in it, and without acknowledging any challenge to his own authority, he announced that, as the Camerlengo, he was scheduling the late Pope's funeral five days hence, with the papal conclave to begin the following day. He also appealed to all the bishops to make plans to come to Rome, for he predicted that the Pope to be elected would immediately call for a new ecumenical council—Vatican III!

When he finished his statement, the first question asked by a reporter was, "Haven't you been excommunicated?"

"Of course not," he replied. "If you are referring to an event this week, Joseph Ratzinger had been removed by action of the College of Cardinals before anyone entered the radio studio. He was no longer the Supreme Pontiff when we met with him, so nothing done there could cause an excommunication."

"How can you claim he was removed? What provision of Canon Law allows for the removal of a Pope?"

"I will answer that if you first tell me what provision of Canon Law provides that a Pope is to hold office for life.—It is a majority of the Cardinal electors who choose a Pope in the first instance, and there is no reason why such a majority should not have the power to remove him. Our Lord Jesus Christ is the only unchangeable head of the Church. All subsidiary Church officials are appointed for her welfare, and when the Pope acts to the detriment of that welfare, the other officials, acting together, can and should remove the Pope. Obviously, the Cardinals who signed the document put before Ratzinger did not think that they were doing a futile act."

"You say Ratzinger was removed by the College of Cardinals," one reporter called out. "Tell us when they met on it and show us any document which they signed."

"That is a secret matter," Toricelli replied coolly. And he said he would accept one more question. It was, "Will you be seeking absolution?"

"Why should I?" he asked rhetorically. "I've just told you that I committed no sin."

There! It was out in the open! He had silenced the commentators and thrown the posturing of Cardinal Zanier back in his face! Let the *African* see what he could make of that!

*   *   *

The response came the very next day—from Cardinal Brooke, not Cardinal Zanier. The Press Office was regularly open for a few hours on Sunday, and Cardinal Brooke thought it was imperative for him to hold a press conference then. He feared that Toricelli's mendacious public statement would gravely mislead the Faithful, to say nothing of misinforming his fellow Cardinal electors, and he wanted to have an official refutation out in time to be carried in the Monday morning newspapers.

Accordingly, at noon, the Press Secretary handed out a document titled, *Declaration of Excommunication for Publicly Witnessed Offenses Against Canon Law*. In it, His Eminence set forth his analysis, as the Major Penitentiary, of why the conduct captured by the TV camera constituted an offense punished by automatic excommunication both for those who actually used physical force against the Roman Pontiff, and for their accomplices.

Cardinal Brooke noted that the conspirators had been duly warned by the Pope himself as they sought to abduct him, and he knocked down the defense that Benedict XVIth had already been removed as Pope, first stating that there had been no attempt by the College of Cardinals to do so, and then citing Canon Law to show that cardinals had no power to do so. And finally, because Toricelli had been excommunicated, Brooke ordered him to cease exercising the powers of the Camerlengo. *That was the first shoe.*

The second shoe was dropped by Cardinal Latoya in a release also handed out at the press conference. He happened to hold a secondary title, as the Dean of the College of Cardinals. As such, it was his duty to take charge if the Camerlengo's position became vacant while there was no Pope. He publicly directed that the required nine days of mourning for Benedict XVIth be observed, with the Mass in St. Peter's Square delayed one extra day to the afternoon of Monday, March 9th, because funeral Masses were not permitted on Sundays during Lent. He further announced that the conclave would begin on March 10th, and he asked all Vatican officials to accept the directions *he* would be giving in the meantime.

— 3 —

Rome

11 Espand 1393 Anno Persico; March 2, 2015 Anno Domini

The time was drawing near for a gathering of Church leaders at the Vatican—a fact duly noted in Tehran. A very special "package" was readied for Ali Hashemi, and he was sent off to Rome with it and a new passport, on Iran Air.

The Italian immigration authorities at Leonardo da Vinci Airport took no particular notice of the man whose papers identified him as "Parvez Firouzabadian." He was, after all, a lowly diplomatic courier, a human donkey who schlepped pouches around from one country to the next. With nothing of his own to declare, carrying a large suitcase plastered with Iranian Government seals, he followed the green line out of the restricted area, and was met by the chauffeur from the Iranian embassy. The chauffeur was surprised that the courier would not let him handle the bag or even put it in the trunk of the limousine.

Hashemi rested with his eyes half closed, not looking at the drab and depressing scenery all the way from the airport, by the coast, to the Camilluccia neighborhood in northwest Rome. There, he observed closely the embassies they passed until he spotted the Iranian flag, and the guard at the gate to the embassy.

"Who provides the guard?" he asked.

"Sir, it's the Italian Army—they guard all the embassies," replied the driver.

"Is there any entrance they do not guard?"

"There is a gate further along Camilluccia which is kept locked. That one they do not guard."

To the left of the main gate, the high wall was brick, with a short metal fence atop it. To the right, the wall was stone, low, but with a tall metal fence. The main gate opened to a driveway that led at an angle to a white, four story structure with an imposing entrance, well set back from the road. The driver continued on the driveway, to the right. As the limousine rounded the corner to the back, he could see the irregular shape of the building and the entrance to the underground garage. He was pleased that no one would see him and the bag there.

In the privacy of the Ambassador's study, Hashemi handed the Ambassador a sealed envelope from the Foreign Ministry, which contained instructions directing His Excellency to provide the "courier" with whatever help he asked for, without asking questions. The Ambassador understood.

"I would like to see some of Rome, especially the area of the Vatican," Hashemi said.

"That will be easy to do," the Ambassador replied. "There are tours every day. We can arrange one for you, or if you want to go around by yourself, we can give you guidebooks."

"Some other arrangement will be necessary, Excellency," said Hashemi. "I cannot leave this suitcase unattended—even here at the embassy. It must remain with me at all times. Which means I will need to be driven around Rome."

"By all means. Whatever you wish," replied the Ambassador, smoothly. He was used to assisting intelligence operatives sent from home.

"I also need to know when the ceremony will be held that will bring the leaders of the Catholic Church from all over the world to St. Peter's."

"The very top leaders, the cardinals, will be together on 19 Espand for the process of electing their new supreme leader, but their subordinates, the bishops, will not be with them at the time. However, the day before, 18 Espand, when the funeral of their late leader will be held, both cardinals and bishops will be together in front of St. Peter's basilica."

"How can I get close to that ceremony?" Hashemi asked.

"Tickets will be required for the rows where the common people stand up front in the Square, behind a barricade. If that is what you want, we will procure one for you."

"That would not do, Excellency. I will need to have my suitcase with me, even there. How close to the ceremony could I get with it in a car?"

That was a strange request. "They will cordon off the Square itself. No vehicles will be allowed inside."

"Will they not invite members of the diplomatic corps?"

"Yes, I already have received my invitation. It's security pro-tected with an embedded microchip."

The agent persisted. "How close will they allow the embassy car to come?"

The Ambassador was getting tired of being cross-examined in this fashion, instead of being brought in on a plan and asked his opinion, but he gave the requested information. "I expect to be dropped off a few steps from the front of the church itself. But, of course, they will be checking documentation further away and they will permit only me, as the Ambassador, to be driven up to the gate. You could not accompany me in the limousine."

"If that is the case," said Hashemi, "I will need to take your place on that occasion, so I can get as close as possible to the ceremony. Of course, I will stay in the car and not proceed to the diplomatic seating, so none of the people who know you personally will be aware of the substitution. I ask that you have a new passport and credentials prepared just for that occasion with my face and your name. And tell the chauffeur to accept my orders without question.—That's all I can think of for now, Excellency."

Standing up, Hashemi added, "*I assure you, you will never regret missing the funeral ceremonies ...*"

His Excellency nodded. Looking at the courier and his suitcase, he felt sure he would not.

— 4 —

Rome

Haim Levy had an occupation that kept him constantly looking around at people, as well as back over his shoulder. He was an agent of Shin Bet, the Israel Security Agency, and his primary assignment was to protect the Israeli airline El Al and its passengers in Rome. The Italian Government's own counter-terrorism forces never could quite manage to keep the city of Rome free of terrorist cells. Years before, the terrorists had been of the homegrown variety—the "Red Brigades." These were eventually brought to justice, but others took their place, including Islamic radicals and the so-called "New Red Brigades," which sought links with them.

One of his duties other than screening passengers boarding El Al flights was reviewing the photographs from security cameras of passengers deplaning flights from Iran and Syria. Italian immigration officers checked the names and passports of arriving passengers, but terrorists traveled on false passports, which is why Haim was tasked with checking the images on the camera discs every day to see if he could spot any of the half dozen high value "targets" wanted by the Israelis. It was an accommodation which Italy afforded Israel.

Up until today, it had been a boring and unfruitful task. Today, however, as he studied the film of a man walking out of the covered jetway from an Iran Air flight, with a large suitcase in tow, he thought the man's face looked familiar. He reviewed a file of photos on his cell phone, and found one that looked like a match. The Italian official he interfaced with brought up on a computer screen the passport and booking information of passengers on that flight from Tehran. Parvez Firouzabadian was a dead ringer for the person known to Haim as the notorious commander of Iran's Qods Force, Ali Hashemi.

According to the computer, authorities had no prior record of "Parvez Firouzabadian" having entered Italy, and he had been added to Iran's list of diplomatic couriers only the day before. Now, *that* was intriguing, thought Haim. It was one thing for a terrorist to travel under a fake passport; it was another thing to travel under a country's official passport, with a diplomatic courier pouch. The responsibility of a foreign state for that person could not be denied. What could be important enough to warrant Iran sending him to Rome? Perhaps the answer lay in the large suitcase he carried. It was brown leather, the kind with external straps around it to secure it, and diplomatic seals to verify that it remained unopened. Diplomatic immunity would have prevented it from being inspected even by a suspicious customs officer.

The way it weighed Hashemi down on one side, Haim guessed it must have been a good 40-plus kilos—hardly likely if it was a real diplomatic pouch filled with paperwork. Haim called his Shin Bet station chief and asked him to come to the airport and have a look at what he had found. The latter saw, and immediately passed it up the line to headquarters.

Jerusalem

The top Shin Bet people were sufficiently confident that Levy's identification of Firouzabadian as Hashemi was correct to do a full workup for presentation to a secret meeting of the Israeli cabinet the following day. They had a fat dossier on Hashemi, of course, and knew exactly what he was capable of. The $64,000 question that they had trouble answering was—what was he doing in Rome?

He certainly wasn't in transit to another country—he could either have gone there directly, or taken a connecting flight as a temporary transit passenger in Rome, without attracting notice. Shin Bet could only conclude that he must have gone to Italy in order to accomplish some very major mischief there—the leadership wouldn't have risked his capture or elimination otherwise. And, there must have been something useful for that purpose in his suitcase, something that he, or the Iranian Embassy, could not have obtained in Italy. That ruled out guns, even automatic weapons. Yet, it must have been something so embarrassing that the Iranians had to cover it with a diplomatic cloak rather than risk the suitcase being opened in a chance inspection. It had to be a weapon of some kind—but the Israelis were at a loss to figure out what it was, since they had to reason backward, starting from possible targets of interest to Iran in Italy.

The Director of Shin Bet was in a difficult position with the Cabinet: he had totally failed to identify any person or group responsible for the hated Warning visions. Now, he felt that he had to appear that he knew what was going on in this case. "We believe," he said, "that in the suitcase was a weapon—either a chemical or a biological one. Of these, the most probable is Sarin nerve gas."

"What would he be looking to do with it?" one Cabinet member asked. "Another attack on El-Al passengers?"

"You mean like the one back in 1985 at the airports in Rome and Vienna?—No, that's highly unlikely. Guns would suffice for that kind of project.—We think that there are only two logical targets for the Revolutionary Guards in Rome: our embassy, and the Tempio Maggiore di Roma—the Great Synagogue of Rome."

They all knew of the latter edifice, for it was a landmark of Rome and the cultural and organizational center for the Jewish community in the city. "And of the two," the Director said, "we believe that the Synagogue is far more likely, because that's where many of our people will be gathered for Passover, which falls this year on Friday night, April 3rd. If Hashemi could set off canisters of Sarin there at that time, it would be a major massacre."

That hypothesis seemed reasonable to the members of the Cabinet, and they readily concurred with the Director's recommendation that that security precautions be strengthened immediately at both potential targets, by bringing in extra personnel, with gas masks.

One of them asked. "Are the Italian counter-terrorism people in on this?"

"No," said the Director, "at least, we haven't asked them for help. If they aren't working with us, we just might be able to pick up Hashemi's trail and find a place where we can kidnap or terminate him without it being attributed to us. If we haven't succeeded in doing that by the middle of March, we'll go to the Italians at that time."

— 5 —

Rome

At the Iranian Embassy the day after he entered Italy, Hashemi pored over photo books of Rome and a street map, asking the Ambassador about various sites and routes. The surroundings of the Vatican were really all that Hashemi was interested in checking out, but on the chance that the embassy's limousine was routinely tailed, he planned an outing which would look simply like a casual sightseeing tour of the major monuments, arranged for a visitor from Iran.

"What has your experience been with the traffic police? Have they ever stopped you?" Hashemi asked.

"They wouldn't think of stopping the limousine with our flag flying, to show I'm in it," the Ambassador replied. "We have good relations with the Italians."

"Very good. The flag will be flying on Friday, when I go to the funeral, and today as we go around the city together. As I've told you, I must have my suitcase with me at all times. I've left the diplomatic seals intact, as a precaution just in case we *are* stopped today, so they won't open it."

The Ambassador found his eyes drawn once again to the large suitcase at Firouzabadian's side. What in the world could be in it? Hashemi caught the glance. It was better for the Ambassador not to know, to preserve deniability later.

Later that morning, Hashemi and the Ambassador were chauffeured from the Embassy south into Rome, wandering around the usual tourist attractions, and finally motoring west along the Borgo Santo Spirito toward St. Peter's. They went slowly around the Bernini colonnades on the south side, up close to the Petriano entrance to the Vatican, and then continued along the outer wall, finally heading back to the Embassy.

Hashemi was confident about his plan. At the Pope's funeral, the embassy's limousine would be stopped at the Petriano entrance, by the corner of the Palace of the Holy Office. At that point he would be less than 50 meters away from the basilica's front steps, separated only by the part of the colonnade structure which held the post office and book store. He could detonate the bomb there, though it would be even better if the car made it through the checkpoint and into the enclosed area of the Vatican along the Via Tunica toward the Plaza of the Roman Protomartyrs. That was to be the drop point for the dignitaries, who would then walk through the Arch of the Bells and up the front steps. *From either point, the entire target fell within the half mile radius of total destruction caused by the bomb he was guarding so closely.*

Having made his preparations, Hashemi could now "go to ground" in the safety of the embassy, until he took his final ride in the limousine, flying the flag of Jomhuri-ye Eslami-ye Iran, the Islamic Republic of Iran. This would be the easiest and most spectacular mission of his life . . .

— 6 —

Rome

Unbeknownst to Hashemi, even as he rode around Rome, he was a person of interest to the law enforcement authorities. The customs official at Leonardo da Vinci airport had written up a report of the possible identification of the Iranian diplomatic courier by the Shin Bet agent. The customs police were under the same parent organization as the *Investigazioni Generali operazioni speciali Antiterrorismo* (known as DIGOS), and so the report had been routed to Lt. Gino Marchetti, a junior antiterrorism officer in the massive gray building on the Via di San Vitale that served as the central police headquarters—the Questura di Roma.

The lieutenant had tasked a sergeant with compiling dossiers on Firouzabadian and Hashemi, including a copy of the airport surveillance pictures which had attracted the attention of the Israeli agent, and having reviewed them, he was ready to discuss the files with his superior, Captain Alberto Francesconi. In his office, the captain quickly scanned what was put before him, then gave his attention to Lt. Marchetti, sitting on the other side of his desk.

"There's more than one mystery here," the lieutenant said, putting down the cup of espresso which he had brought in with him. "They begin with whether the courier really is this guy, Hashemi. As you can see, our file photos of Hashemi are all somewhat blurred—like they were taken at a distance in poor light. Plus, all those Iranians look alike. So, the identification looks possible, but not certain.—Do you want me to ask the Israelis to send over whatever pictures they have of Hashemi? They may well have something that will make the identification positive."

"No, for the time being, let's leave them out of this. We already know *they* thought there was a match," said his superior. "Let's try to think this through here first before we ask for help. If Firouzabadian *isn't* Hashemi there's no reason we should care anything about him. So, for the sake of the exercise, let's make the assumption that Firouzabadian *is* Hashemi.—Now, Gino, what are you going to do about him? Pull him in for questioning?" Captain

Francesconi liked to pick his subordinates' brains, training them in the process.

- - "No, sir. Hashemi is clearly a major terrorist, as head of the Qods Force of the Revolutionary Guard Corps. He's suspected of orchestrating all sorts of bombings, assassinations, and that sort of thing, in other countries, *but* he's never stood trial and there's no outstanding warrant for his arrest. So we'd have no excuse to pick him up."

The captain's eyebrows arched. "What about the fact that if Firouzabadian is really Hashemi, he broke the law by entering our country under an alias?"

"Sir, I thought of that," said the lieutenant, "but, he wasn't using an *ordinary* forged passport. It was an *official* passport and his name had been added to the list of diplomatic couriers the day before. Plus, he was accompanying an oversized suitcase with government seals serving as a diplomatic pouch. *They* must've known who he was when they let him go through their own passport control boarding the plane. So, I figured we would be challenging the Government of Iran if we brought him in for questioning over a passport issue.—They also know what he brought in. I keep wondering what was in that suitcase . . ."

The captain nodded in approval of the analysis. "That's good thinking, but leave the suitcase aside for now, Gino. Tell me why you think he's here."

The lieutenant ran his hand through his unruly black hair. It did not produce a solution to the mystery. "It's easier to think of why he's *not* here. He's too high in the revolutionary structure to waste him on a suicide mission. They have enough other people who are willing to blow themselves up for Allāh. Also, I don't see any indication in the dossier that he's personally been trained to be an assassin, as opposed to being the one to order hits."

"Yes, I think you have a point there, he's a commander of men at this stage of his career. Which leads you to think what, Gino?"

"Which leads me to think that he must be planning to link up with people here."

The captain continued to press him. "Who? and To do what?"

Lt. Marchetti shook his head. "I don't know the answer to either question—if we knew what he was up to, we'd have a good idea of who he was seeing, and vice versa."

Since his superior continued to look at him expectantly, Lt. Marchetti volunteered a suggestion. "He may not even be here to conduct any sort of an operation. He could have come for a high level meeting with a terrorist group to strike an alliance, which perhaps could only be done by him in person."

"Are you thinking of a New Red Brigades group like the Communist Combatant Party, or do you have in mind one of the Islamic groups like Al Qaeda?" the captain asked.

"The former—only because he wouldn't have needed to come to Rome to link up with the latter. Which puzzles me," the lieutenant admitted. "I don't see how a general desire to bring about revolutions could be much of a basis for working together. The revolutions the Iranians are trying to foment aren't the same as the ones the communists are working on."

The captain lit a cigarette, knowing that Lt. Marchetti, the one non-smoker in the unit would be bothered by it, but not caring. After all, rank has its privileges.

"Just taking your hypothesis, for the moment, Gino," said the captain, "don't they both have a desire to hit the Americans?"

"Yes sir, they do."

"In which case, what target do you think they'd be most interested in?"

The junior officer thought about that, then suggested "A military base—Aviano." It was a logical choice. Aviano was a major USAF airbase in northeastern Italy, hosting two squadrons of F-16 Falcon fighters.

"All right, suppose *you* were going to attack it with a commando force of terrorists, how would you do it?"

Chagrin showed on Lt. Marchetti's face. "Well, it's so spread out that, unless I was satisfied with just shooting up some people here and there, the only thing that would make much of a dent would be a tactical atomic warhead."

"You don't think that Hashemi was bringing in a suitcase nuclear bomb to attack the airbase do you?"

That was too wild to consider. "No, definitely not," the lieutenant answered. "*If* they even have such a weapon, I'm sure the first target for it would be the government complex in Jerusalem. Aviano would be well down the list."

"Well, then, Gino, let's turn to Al Qaeda. What do we know about their operations here?"

"We know that Al Qaeda is well entrenched in Naples, with the protection of the Camorra, but as far as we know, Al Qaeda has been moving its operatives from North Africa into other countries in Europe. Naples is only a way station, and to date they haven't attacked targets in Italy."

"I suppose that could be about to change," Marchetti added by way of speculation.

Captain Francesconi was relentless. "And if so, what target would they both like to go after in Italy?"

Lt. Marchetti ran his hand through his hair twice, coming up with an answer: "The most likely is Jewish interests ... their embassy ... or ... the Great Synagogue of Rome."

Captain Francesconi put out his cigarette, while his subordinate finished off his espresso, which had by then grown cold.

"Yes, Gino, *that* is plausible. So, again, if *you* were planning a commando raid for maximum results, which one of the two would you pick?"

"The Israeli Embassy, I assume, must be surrounded by a strong fence and be well guarded. My guess is the synagogue would make an easier target."

"Actually, Gino, they're both well guarded, and they both have walls and fences, but, if I remember correctly, the synagogue does have doors which open directly onto the sidewalk along the Lungotevere Cenci. I think that's where the last Pope entered on a special visit. We had to put on special security."

"And, more important," said the lieutenant, "there would be far more people there for services on some occasion. Maybe hundreds."

"Like on the forthcoming Passover?" the Captain helpfully interjected.

"Yes, like for Passover. And I would either use automatic weapons or ..."

He did not finish his thought, so the captain asked him, "Or what?"

"Or, if this is even possible, something like Sarin gas—which would cause a more catastrophic incident. One which would redound to the credit of the terrorists in their own circles."

"*Poison gas?*" Captain Francesconi asked incredulously. "And where would they get Sarin in our country? Do you think they could go to a compounding chemist shop and ask them to mix up a few litres of poison gas?"

"No sir!" Marchetti replied. "But, I keep coming back to the mystery of that heavy suitcase. It must have been 40 kilos. Maybe what he brought with him into the country in that suitcase was poison gas. You know, in pressurized canisters, ready to throw into a crowded room ... "

Captain Francesconi said nothing immediately, preferring to light yet another cigarette and take the first few puffs in silence.

"No, *I don't know*, Gino ... It sounds like a crazy idea you got from one of those spy thrillers you're always reading."

"They stretch my mind, Captain," replied Marchetti.

"Just be sure they don't cause it to snap!—Why do you go for the obscure when the *obvious* answer is staring you in the face? All those Middle Eastern terrorist groups train with rifle propelled grenades. Isn't that the most likely explanation for what Hashemi had in the suitcase?"

"Yes, sir, maybe so," said the deflated lieutenant. "But," he argued, "they wouldn't get anywhere close to the synagogue carrying rifles."

That prompted more thinking from his superior. "What's right across from the front of the synagogue?" he asked.

"Nothing!" was the immediate answer. "There's just the roadway and the river.—Oh!—I see what you mean. There's the Isola Tiberina, right across the little bridge. I guess someone on the island would be in easy range, with a direct shot."

"Yes, he would, wouldn't he?" said Captain Francesconi. He blew a smoke ring to mark his satisfaction with the morning's detective work. "Well, then, Gino, if we think we have a working hypothesis about why Hashemi's here, what should we be doing about it?"

It was Marchetti's turn to think in silence. More hair ruffs. And, an answer. "If that's what he's up to, he isn't going to spring his deadly surprise on just any Friday night—it *is* going to be the great feast of Passover, as you mentioned. I'll check the calendar but I think that isn't going to be until the first Friday in April. So that gives us some time.—I'll work the surveillance we have in place of known Al Qaeda people in Naples as well as here, to see if he surfaces or if anyone mentions him or the Great Synagogue. Also, I'll arrange for a stakeout on the island, and ask the Army to have their guard at the Embassy's gate let us know immediately if he is spotted entering or leaving the grounds. If we pick up anything, we can bring the Shin Bet people in at that time."

— 7 —

San Giovanni Rotondo

Fr. Santorelli had been ill for days with a fever, which he came down with a week after he arrived at the Capuchin friary in San Giovanni Rotondo. It finally broke, leaving him debilitated, but able to sit up and take a bowl of broth. After he had eaten, the friar who had been looking after him in the guest house for visiting priests, went to tell the good news to Padre Ghiardi, the Father Guardian, who came around, hoping to get answers to the many questions which had been accumulating in his mind.

"You gave us quite a scare, Father," he said. "I gave the order not to take you over to the *Casa*, and I'm very relieved to see that you made it through. If you're prone to high fevers, we'd better find a kind of thermometer that goes above 42°C ..."

While the last comment was accompanied by a smile, Fr. Santorelli was embarrassed that already he had been a problem for them. "Thank you, Padre," he said. "I appreciate very much the good care I've gotten. From time to time I was aware of my surroundings, and the friar here was usually in my room, tending to me or praying. He was a great comfort.—I apologize for the concern I caused you. That was the first fever like that I ever had. I've no idea what caused it."

The Father Guardian excused the friar, and said, "Speaking of the future, Father, we need to have a heart to heart talk. His Holiness only spoke to me for a few minutes about you, and I'm sure that there's a great deal more I need to know. I can't ask His Holiness now ... *He died on Friday, while you were ill.*"

"*Yes,*" said Fr. Santorelli. Nothing more.

"You don't seem surprised at the news ..."

"No. I knew it was coming. I just didn't know when. Who came to carry him off? Malapensa? Lazard?"

Father Guardian had a funny look on his face as he replied, "Why, yes. Cardinals Malapensa and Lazard, and some others. They tried, but failed. He died resisting them. *How would you know anything about that?*"

"That's not an easy question to answer, Father. If you'll allow me to wash and change into clean clothes, I'll be glad to come to your office and answer your questions."

While Father Guardian awaited Fr. Santorelli, he thought back to the brief phone conversation he had had with the Holy Father a week before, in which Benedict had asked him to shelter for an indefinite period an American diocesan priest, newly incardinated in the See of Rome—and with faculties also in the Diocese of Manfredonia. Nothing like that had ever happened before, and it made no sense to him, but he was being asked to do it in obedience to the Vicar of Christ, who had plenary authority in the Church. The Holy Father had told him that the priest had been of great service to the Holy See. He also said that while the priest was a stigmatic who had suffered much, he was not at all like either St. Francis or St. Pio. The Father Guardian had replied, that he would, of course, honor the command of the Supreme Pontiff, and that was that.

"Again, I extend a welcome to you, Father," said Padre Ghiardi, when Fr. Santorelli joined him in his office. "These are very unsettling times, and I know you're privy to information as few others are. The comments you made to me a few minutes ago show that. In view of my responsibilities to you, to all our friars here, and to the millions of pilgrims who come here each year, it would be better if I were not kept in the dark. I would ask you to tell me everything that relates to how you came to be here, at least everything that does not require you to reveal a confidence."

Over the next hour, Fr. Santorelli laid out a great deal: his priestly career, the special assignment from Msgr. Ireland regarding Garabandal, the message he had received from the Lord, the opening of his stigmata, and the thinking that lay behind the late Pope's comments on the visions. Also, his own rashness which was in no small part responsible for his being sent to San Giovanni.

The scope and importance of what he had just learned absolutely overwhelmed Father Guardian. The problems he was used to dealing with were challenging, but of a mundane kind—keeping the friary running well and the pilgrims spiritually attended to. He had neither the experience nor the desire to be involved in affairs of state.

If Fr. Santorelli were simply an ordinary visiting priest, he could be accommodated easily. His charism as a stigmatic was bound to cause problems, but that too could be handled, *if* it were the only challenge. However, Fr. Santorelli had brought with him *major baggage*, which the Father Guardian was afraid might cause turmoil in their small friary.

"There have been sharp exchanges in public between the cardinals who sought to remove Benedict and those who were loyal to him, Father," he said. "Do you foresee that you will have any role with regard to the conclave, which will start next week?—Has it been revealed to you who the next Pope will be?"

Fr. Santorelli managed a half smile. "To answer your last question first, No, Padre, I haven't been told who will succeed Benedict, though it's clear to me who the best choice would be. And, I can't imagine any role for me after the conclave in the continuing administration of the Church, if that's what you're wondering about—other than possibly answering very occasional questions from Cardinal Zanier or Msgr. Ireland, if they continue to play any role in the Curia."

"Forgive the indelicacy of my next question, Father," the Father Guardian said, "but aren't you concerned that the next Pope might issue his own order transferring you back to America?"

Fr. Santorelli considered the question. "Padre, maybe I'm being shortsighted, but, the answer is, 'No.' If we have a Pope in the near future, I expect he'll have more important things on his mind."

Padre Ghiardi's jaw dropped. It was a moment before he could bring himself to ask, "*If we have a Pope in the near future . . . ?* I don't understand. What on earth could you mean by that, Father? Do you expect the conclave to be put off?"

It occurred to Fr. Santorelli that he was in danger of breaking his promise to his mentor not to discuss future calamities. "I'm not saying that at all. I was just thinking that these are difficult times—things are very unsettled. And I'm sure the fathers and brothers here could make a worthy contribution if they would pray for the Church's leaders until a successful conclave is held."

Back in his room at the priest's guesthouse, the coming events at St. Peter's weighed heavily on Fr. Santorelli's mind. He *did* have a sense of impending disaster. A line of Matthew's Gospel kept running through his head. It was Jesus' last words about the Temple in Jerusalem, the prediction that "*there will not be left here one stone upon another.*" But the priest couldn't in any way describe what he feared or expected to happen—other than that it involved an explosion.

Foreseeing no more, he desperately tried to think what kind of warning could he give—*'Watch out for terrorists driving a truck filled with explosives near the Sistine Chapel during the Papal conclave?'* He would be laughed at by the police; Monsignor Ireland would think him disobedient; and Cardinal Zanier would be sure he had a monomania about jihadists. He had better keep silent for now—he couldn't afford to annoy his sponsors to the point that they gave up on him and let him be shipped him back to California . . .

— 8 —

Rome

It turned out that nobody wanted to have anything to do with
the so-called "Gang of Six" who had manhandled Benedict XVIth,
and each of the other Cardinals was questioned by the press as to
whether he had signed the malevolent Declaration, found later in
the studio. Many denied that their signature was genuine—which
cast the plotters in an even darker light. Publicly, the others all did
their best to disassociate themselves from the sordid mess, and
privately, they used it to excuse themselves from the promises they
had already made to support Malapensa for Pope—or O'Melveny
either, for he was seen as the sinister force behind Lazard.

   Cardinals who had been on the sidelines, not part of either
camp, started to discuss Pierre Zanier as someone whom they
might support. He had struck just the right tone in his remarks to
the crowd and his press statement—perhaps he should be the one
to eulogize Benedict XVIth at his funeral Mass? Cardinal Latoya
was glad to extend the invitation, and the press applauded the
move. They even hopped on the bandwagon with favorable stories
about Cardinal Zanier's background, which was unique among
the cardinals.

   Born in the Congo, he had been orphaned as a child by the civil
unrest—seeing his parents being hacked to death by mutineers,
he had run for his life through the jungle and found safety in a
refugee camp. The nuns had recognized him as a diamond in the
rough, and educated him in a school run by Catholic missionaries.
The bright young man was then sent to a seminary in France
by his Bishop, where he braved the racial discrimination of his
classmates and stuck with his vocation. Back in his own country,
he had had a successful pastoral career as a priest and then
a bishop, leading regional social projects to help the millions
of people dispossessed by the ethnic and religious wars in sub-
Saharan Africa. Eventually, he was called to Rome to help with
the worldwide task of evangelization.

The six plotters—now excommunicated—took note of Zanier's name coming to the fore and decided to meet again in Toricelli's villa.

"Eminences," said the host, "we're being pummeled in the media, and we need to decide how to react to Brooke's declaration punishing us. Beyond that, we need to figure out a way to stop the electors from turning to Zanier."

"It is impossible while we remain excommunicated," opined Malapensa. "We have to get over that hurdle first, then we can regroup our own forces."

They looked at him, not challenging his opinion, but not voicing their agreement with it, either.

"I know what you're thinking," he said. "You're afraid that if we go to Brooke seeking absolution, it will appear that we are conceding we've done something wrong. But, we don't have any choice—no one in the media has come out in our favor against what he's done."

"What if we go to him and he denies us absolution?" asked de la Tour.

"*He can't*," Malapensa responded. "As long as we *claim* to be sorry for what we have done, he *has* to absolve us. And once he's lifted our excommunication, we'll have an easier time of persuading those who joined us in removing Ratzinger to sign another declaration, this time *removing Brooke* as the Major Penitentiary and declaring his penalties nullified."

And so, swallowing their pride, they jointly petitioned Cardinal Brooke to remove their excommunication. He agreed to meet with them in his office, one by one, beginning with de la Tour, and ending with Malapensa.

The Major Penitentiary was one of the many Vatican officials who worked outside the limits of the Vatican City State. In his case, his office was in the Palazzo della Cancelleria, a building owned by the Holy See with extraterritorial status, located near the Piazza Navona. The massive, three-story structure, built five centuries before, had a flat marble facade punctuated in the middle by a grand entrance to the inner courtyard, where columns of Egyptian granite formed open loggias on the bottom two stories.

These were not routine confessions, either in what was confessed, or in how each penitent was treated. Cardinal Brooke posed questions to determine relative degrees of culpability.

Whose idea was it to depose Benedict? Who solicited the names
on the instrument of removal? Who offered bribes to signers?
Whose idea was it to carry the Pope off? Who arranged for the
ambulance? Who arranged for the "rest home" for him? What was
Malapensa fiddling with his handkerchief for? The final question
was, *"Are you heartily sorry for your sin?"*

"Oh yes!" each one said, *he surely was*, and he made the traditional promise that, with the aid of God's grace, he would "go and
sin no more." So, the Major Penitentiary absolved them, individually, in the name of the Father and the Son and the Holy Spirit!
And the penance he prescribed was to kneel and pray beside the
papal coffin for an hour, when it was on public display.

That wasn't even a slap on the wrist! They wondered what
they had been worried about. However, as each turned to leave
Cardinal Brooke's office, giddy with relief, he was caught up short
by the words: *"The absolution which I have given you only extends
to the excommunication latae sententiae. I am now going to consider
whether other canonical penalties should be imposed for your grave
sin. As to that, I will make my decision public tomorrow, at the same
time as I announce your absolution."*

None of them wanted to extend the humiliation of the session
by asking what Cardinal Brooke might mean by that. They wanted
to get out and get back to politicking, even though that activity
was forbidden by the Apostolic Constitution before the conclave.
The election would soon be upon them and they had to make up
for lost time!

*   *   *

On the late night TV shows in Rome that evening, a number of
the hosts made jokes about the cardinals who had announced
their absolution after leaving the office of the Major Penitentiary.
One of the hosts was inspired to put on a little skit between a
pretend plotter and his pretend confessor, bargaining as to what
the penance would be—how many Our Fathers, Hail Mary's and
Glory Be's. The press corps was not as irreverent, at least not in
print, about the prospect of absolution for the plotters, but they
expected little of interest to come out at the press conference
which Cardinal Brooke had called for the next day, Sunday, in the

afternoon—unless he was prepared to tell what they had said in their confessions.

By his opening words, Cardinal Brooke disabused them of that thought. "Each of the clerics who confronted our late Holy Father in the last minutes of his life came to me yesterday, seeking the Sacrament of Penance. As you know, that Sacrament is very closely prescribed by regulations, the most important of which preserve the absolute inviolability of what transpires between a priest and a penitent during confession. I cannot and will not reveal what was said then. However, because it would be a grave public scandal for a priest who is known to be excommunicated to receive Holy Communion, it is appropriate that I give the public assurance that each of them has been absolved of the excommunication which occurred automatically as the result of his committing the acts which have been publicly revealed."

To the surprise of the newsmen, Cardinal Brooke had more to say. "That is not the end of the matter. The Church uses the sanction of excommunication as a strong medicine to bring sinners back into the Church and full communion. Under Canon Law, for the proper functioning of the Church, it is contemplated that other, additional sanctions, may be imposed, whether or not the excommunication remains in effect. Considering the gravity of the conduct publicly disclosed, I have found it necessary and appropriate to do so. Therefore, I am now publishing the following decree:"

By virtue of the authority vested in me as Major Penitentiary, I decree, pursuant to Canon 1370 of the Code of Canon Law, that Seymour Lazard and Giuseppe Malapensa be, and they hereby are, dismissed from the clerical state. Pursuant to the same Canon and Canon 1333, I decree that Michele Toricelli, Henri de la Tour, Gert Van Dijk, and Juan Sandoval be, and they hereby are, suspended from the offices of cardinal and bishop, and from all powers of governance and the exercise of the rights and functions attaching to those offices, such penalty to remain in effect throughout their lifetime.

"That is the end of my decree, and this matter is now closed. Thank you for your attention."

Closed??? Hardly! If anything, the matter was opened wider than ever.

The first question called out was, *"Are you saying that all six are no longer Cardinals?"*

"That is one effect of the decrees," Brooke answered, calmly.

"Then they can't attend the conclave?"

"Correct. The conclave is only open to cardinal electors."

"Can't they appeal your decrees?"

"Yes, they can—but only to the next Pope, who may or may not cancel or amend the decrees. In the meantime, they remain in force."

"Don't they have a right to a trial?"

"No. A trial is only appropriate where conduct is disputed. That is usually the case, because there are no third party witnesses. In this case, all the deeds upon which I based my decision to impose penalties were captured by a camera and are a matter of public knowledge."

Cardinal Brooke declined to take further questions, and the news conference was over. Reporters scurried into the adjoining room, where the various news services which maintained a constant presence at the Vatican had their own equipment-crowded cubicles, for composing and transmitting stories. Not long thereafter, it was the turn of the talking heads on TV. They could scarcely get over their astonishment. *Nobody* had been expecting much from Cardinal Brooke—a high level functionary, but one whose work was normally kept secret from the press. Certainly nobody thought that penalties would be levied on any of the plotters, as powerful churchmen often had been allowed to drift off into retirement, rather than being publicly disciplined for their misdeeds in a draconian way.

One of the more reflective TV commentators said, *"You know, I think it's about time that something like this happened . . . "* That remark was passed around until it became a rallying cry for the press. More than one editorial was written around the theme: *It's About Time!*

*   *   *

The six plotters against the late Pope now were *genuinely* sorry—not for what they had done to him, but for having gone to Cardinal Brooke for absolution on Saturday. By submitting themselves to the Sacrament of Penance and then publicly announcing that they had been absolved, they had publicly acknowledged that they indeed had sinned, and that the Major Penitentiary had jurisdiction over their offenses. Had they known that he would impose penalties, they would have continued to try to brazen their way through the situation. It was too late for that now—they were forced to deal with the penalties he had prescribed.

"Cardinal" Malapensa, as he continued to style himself, hoped that he could arrange for a vote of all the cardinals before the conclave, removing Cardinal Brooke from office, and substituting a cardinal who would immediately rescind the penalties—or at least Malapensa's. He began calling his colleagues among the cardinal electors. Most of them had their secretaries tell him that they were tied up and would call him when they were free. One of his longtime friends, the Cardinal Archbishop of Milan, spoke with him frankly.

"Seppe, my old friend, you *know* I agree with your agenda for the Church, and I was going to vote for you in the conclave."

"Yes," replied Malapensa, noting the past tense which his colleague used—'*was* going to vote for you.'

"But, everything's changed now. That *oaf*, Lazard, fouled the nest and you were with him at the time."

"I had no control over him!" Malapensa protested. "You can't think that *I* had him shove Ratzinger around."

"You all went there to carry him away whether he wanted to go or not. You said so yourself. When you lie down with dogs, you take a risk you might wake up with fleas ... "

"*You can't approve of them unfrocking me!*" Malapensa thundered. It sounded like a command. It reminded his hearer unpleasantly of the tone Malapensa had used when he was the Secretary of State.

The Milanese Cardinal paused to let his annoyance subside before he answered. "Don't you see, Seppe, it's not a question of whether *I* approve or not. Look, I have to live with the media here in Milan, and for the most part, *they* agree with the penalties imposed. I would lose my own credibility, if I publicly supported you in any way now. We couldn't keep a vote to remove Brooke secret for two minutes!—Don't worry, though, once the papal election is over, I'm sure your penalties will be lifted by the new Pope. And now, if you'll excuse me, I have things to do to prepare for the conclave . . ."

— 9 —

Rome

It had been a bad day for ex-Cardinal Toricelli. He had been trying, without success, to dig himself and Malapensa out of their pit by asking his former colleagues to join together and remove Cardinal Brooke as the Major Penitentiary. Then came a call from his patron, Don Ricardo, which made his day so much worse.

Pasquale Ricardo was the "godfather" of one of the largest of the hundred-odd clans that comprised the Camorra in the city of Naples. The Camorra was a very widespread criminal enterprise which had existed for at least 200 years, defying all attempts by law enforcement authorities to stamp it out. Criminologists said that its loose, horizontal structure, unlike the pyramidal, vertical structure of the Mafia, made it far more difficult to prosecute, and resilient in bouncing back from the loss of leaders. "Don Ricardo," as he was now called, had clawed his way to the top of the Schiavo clan, which had a major share of the garbage disposal racket in the Compania region. All sorts of industrial wastes, from all over Italy, many of them highly toxic, were mixed with ordinary garbage and dumped wherever the clan found it convenient, there being no more room in authorized landfills.

The Camorra had survived and thrived by establishing strong ties with politicians at all levels of government, and sometimes with Church leaders. Michele Toricelli owed his selection as Archbishop of Naples to bribes funded by Ricardo, who had made a further investment in him when he was named as the Camerlengo, by buying a villa outside Rome for use as his base of operations. In his present state of disgrace, Toricelli was no longer of use to Don Ricardo, and it boded ill that the Don had summoned him back to Naples for a meeting. The unmentioned subject had to be his patron's displeasure at his current predicament. Toricelli would have to think of some way to regain his good graces. There was no "or else" . . .

The one faint ray of hope he had came from the facts that Malapensa was under a deep cloud, and nobody was warming to the idea of an American Pope, particularly since they blamed

Cardinal O'Melveny for Lazard's despicable actions. Therefore, *if* Toricelli could get his canonical penalties lifted, *he* might have a chance to attend the conclave and persuade the other electors to choose him as Pope—or to arrange a political deal where he would wind up as Secretary of State. From either position, he would be able to pay Don Ricardo back in full! He could see that in order for him to be reinstated before the conclave, Cardinal Brooke would have to be removed as the Major Penitentiary by the other Cardinals and replaced by a friend of his, a step which no doubt would be opposed by Zanier. And so, he turned his thoughts as to how Zanier might be cleared out of the way, quickly and decisively.

Naples

Toricelli was met at the airport and driven to the country estate outside of Naples where Don Ricardo lived in style as befitted a man of his standing. He even had his own winery, with countless rows of aglianico grape vines recently renewed by being cut back. Their excellent grapes would become hearty Taurasi wine, a specialty of that district. Don Ricardo's cavernous cellars were perfect for aging the wine as long as twenty years, to make it memorable. Thinking of those cellars, Toricelli shuddered slightly. He had once heard a rumor that Don Ricardo was an admirer of the American horror tale, *A Cask of Amontillado. Who knew what enemies had been walled up there while still alive?*

He was fearful, as he entered the oak paneled study where Don Ricardo held court. Little light entered through the curtained windows, leaving the room to be lit by wall sconces and a small light on the Don's desk. As the Archbishop of Naples, Toricelli had been accustomed to having men kiss his ring as a sign of their fealty to him. In the Don's lair, it was he who was the subservient one.

"Things have not gone well lately, have they *Father*?" asked the Don, showing his strong displeasure by using the rank to which Toricelli had been demoted.

"Not as well as I had hoped, Don Ricardo," was the answer.

"Do you know how much I have spent on your career, Michele?—I'll tell you. Four million euros all told! That's how much. And what do I have to show for it?"

"I always supported you as you asked when I was the Archbishop here," Toricelli replied meekly.

"Yes, so you did, but then, when your position here ended, I financed your elevation and life style in Rome, expecting that one day you would be in a position to repay me."

"All *was* going well. I would have been second to Malapensa when he became Pope—if only he and that imbecile Lazard had not ruined everything."

His patron did not accept excuses. "They were incompetent blunderers, but they owed me nothing. *You did*, and you were equally to blame.—Do you understand why?"

Toricelli could only hang his head in shame like a schoolboy and say, "Tell me, Don Ricardo."

"Your mistake was being there with them. That made it impossible for you to deny you were involved! If a factory has to be burned down, to create a little respect, do you think I'm so stupid as to go there along with my men . . . ?"

"I thought that by my being along, it might convince Ratzinger to go quietly . . . "

"*Well, you thought wrong. Now, you're just a common priest again.—I can buy and sell them, any day, cheap.—Tell me, Michele, how I do recoup my investment in you?*"

That was the opening Toricelli was hoping for. "Malapensa is finished, Don Ricardo. He can't be rehabilitated. The American cardinal, O'Melveny has faded from contention, not that he ever had much of a chance. *I* would now be the logical candidate of most of the electors, except for this stupid penalty Brooke imposed on me. I'm working to persuade them to oust Brooke and restore me to being a cardinal, which will let me attend the conclave. And I think they would do that if they saw me as the best choice for Pope. There's just one real obstacle to that happening that I can see—sentiment for *Cardinal Zanier.*"

"The *black?*" Don Ricardo asked. His disdain for blacks came through without his using any other adjective.

"Yes, *the black*. I didn't think any of those who were going to support Malapensa would vote for him, but I'm not so sure now, with the favorable press he's gotten. For me to have *any* chance, he has to be taken out of the equation *before the conclave begins.*"

"*And you are looking to me . . . ?*"

"*Yes, Don Ricardo. It's my only hope of being able to pay you back in full.*" Toricelli had fear in his eyes. What if his patron said, 'No'?

The Don considered Toricelli's proposal for a while, then asked, "How would one get at *the black?*"

Toricelli had a ready answer. "I had him checked out thoroughly last year. There's nothing to blackmail him with into withdrawing. *He needs to be done away with. Period.* Malapensa hasn't moved out of his quarters in the Apostolic Palace, so *the black* still lives in an apartment building at the corner of Via Cola di Rienzo and Via Terenzio. It's got a doorman and a security system, so a break-in would be hard. However, I learned that he gets his exercise by walking in that neighborhood for about three quarters of an hour most mornings. He usually leaves his residence and starts walking down the Via Terenzio at around six-fifteen. The streets are empty when he sets out, and obviously he'd be unmistakable. Someone with a rifle could easily take him out from a distance and get on a main route north out of the city very quickly."

Don Ricardo dismissed his disgraced minion without giving him an answer, and then gave a derisive snort. 'Take him out with a rifle'—how *stupid* could Toricelli be? That could only be seen as an assassination, and one could not assassinate a high official of the Vatican without causing the Carabiniere to devote major resources, for years if necessary, to finding the killer. And if that weren't bad enough, the Mafia would be doing the same, because the killing was done on their turf without their permission. He had no desire to stir up those two foes of his! No, he would order the hit made *his* way—so it would look like the unfortunate result of an ordinary street crime gone wrong.

— 10 —

Rome

Msgr. Ireland was surprised to receive a phone call from Fr. Santorelli, the first since the priest had left for San Giovanni Rotondo. "How are you doing, Tony?" he asked.

"Just fine," came the reply. "They're treating me well, and I have more time to pray than I did when I was with the high and mighty. And nobody here calls me *Rasputin!*" Fr. Santorelli said wryly.

"I'm glad it's working out, Tony," the prelate said. "And since you called, do you have any further insights for us as to what's going to happen here? We *still* can't see any catastrophe on the horizon.—Apart from that, I've heard about a lot of infighting that I'm shocked about. The cardinals who tried to remove Benedict are angling to elect one of their own in his place—but we haven't lost hope—*Cardinal Zanier is attracting a following!*"

"Monsignor, the reason for my call *is* His Eminence. *I feel it's vitally important that you stay with him until the conclave begins.* And by stay with him, I mean, like glue—even to accompanying him into a public restroom."

"*Why? What in the world are you thinking?*" Msgr. Ireland sounded duly alarmed.

"I can't tell you *why,*" Fr. Santorelli admitted. "I just have the strong feeling that he needs you with him now. It would be only a slight restriction on his movements."

"Well, what if I ask him and he says, 'No'?—I'm not in the habit of giving orders to cardinals."

"Neither am I, Monsignor. Just put it to him that if he has any regard for my instincts, he'll do as I ask. Given your position, it shouldn't be hard for him to explain away your presence by his side.—Please promise me, Monsignor, that you'll call him as soon as you get off the phone with me, and start accompanying him immediately. It'll only be for a few days. If you need me to do it, I'll call him myself.—I just think you'll be more persuasive."

"O.K., Tony, I'll see what His Eminence says."

— 11 —

Rome

Cardinal Zanier was feeling foolish and annoyed that he had given in to Msgr. Ireland's request the evening before, that he be allowed to accompany the Cardinal everywhere. He had allowed the Monsignor to sleep overnight on a sofa in his small apartment, and now, on account of his guest, he was beginning his morning walk almost ten minutes late. He was thinking that he would beg out of the arrangement later that day.

The prelates did not notice the two men coming up the street behind them on muffled Vespa motor scooters. They had arrived a half hour before on a truck from Naples; the truck had already moved around the corner, where it was parked, ready to pick them up when they had completed their mission. The riders discussed a hitch in their plan as they rode.

"S***!" said the leader. "*The black* isn't alone . . ."

"No problem—kill 'em both."

The leader shook his head, No. "The Don said it's gotta look like a robbery. I'll take *the black*. You grab what you can from the other one . . . cut him only if you have to."

The riders increased their speed until they pulled slightly ahead of the prelates and then rode up on the sidewalk, blocking it a few paces away. They hopped off, and each pulled out and flicked open a fearsome looking switchblade knife. The leader quickly stepped in front of the Cardinal, three feet away. " *Hey, you black ******! That's a fancy cross you're wearing. Hand it over!!!*"

Cardinal Zanier didn't argue. He started to take off the cross. When his two arms were up pulling it over his head, the thug said, "Faster!" and took a step toward him. He grabbed the cape part of the Cardinal's cassock with his left hand, to hold the prelate in place for the thrust of his knife upward, under the ribs to the heart. The leader was an experienced knife fighter from the streets of Naples. It would not be the first time he had killed a man that way.

Msgr. Ireland had been walking just to Zanier's left. Without thinking about what he was doing, in a reflexive gesture of protection as Zanier was grabbed, his right arm shot out and up—a split second before the thug thrust with his knife. The fortuitous result was that the point of the knife passed through the palm of Ireland's right hand before it penetrated Zanier's thick cassock. Zanier was wounded, but due to the fleshy buffer, the knife only went part way into him.

No doubt, the two men from Naples would have completed their assignment straight away, had not a bakery truck driver noticed the crime in progress as he was proceeding on his route up the street from the other direction. He had the wits to stop and hold down his horn with one hand as he dialed the police emergency number on his cell phone with the other.

Not only was the leader momentarily distracted by the horn and by Ireland's screams, he had to switch the knife to his left hand in order to hold Ireland's right arm steady while he pulled the knife free from Ireland, and then he had to switch the knife back again to his right hand to deliver another thrust toward Zanier's heart. By this time the Cardinal's arms were down in front of him and he managed to deflect the blade sufficiently that it went into his abdomen, again without finding his heart. When the blade was withdrawn, Zanier collapsed on the pavement. The second street fighter meanwhile had turned his attention to the wounded white prelate, relieving him of his wallet.

The leader considered stabbing the Cardinal again, as he lay on the ground in a pool of blood burbling from his chest. He refrained from doing so only because he knew that that would not be what a *robber* would do. Over the sound of the blaring horn, they could hear the klaxon of an approaching police car in the distance. The leader was satisfied that his target would bleed to death in a couple of minutes. It was enough for him to finish off the "robbery" by grabbing the Cardinal's leather briefcase along with the silver Cross. Then the thugs hopped on their scooters and took off like bats out of hell, leaving the two wounded clerics on the ground.

The police managed to slow their bleeding to a trickle with a special clotting powder they carried in their medical kit. The powder had been developed in America for battlefield use, but civilian emergency crews everywhere found it of great value at accident and crime scenes. The unconscious Zanier, and his companion, were taken by ambulance to Santo Spirito hospital, which was only a few blocks away, just outside the southern colonnades of St. Peter's Square. Then the police turned their attention to the heroic deliveryman, taking down his descriptions of the robbers, for immediate broadcast.

News of the dastardly crime spread all over Italy while Zanier and Ireland were in surgery. The newscasters tried to connect three events. First, the Vatican had been quarantined by the Government, keeping the Faithful away from St. Peter's. Then, Peter's successor had been assaulted and killed by those he trusted. And now, a key aide to the late Pope was fighting for his life in a hospital, having been stabbed by a street thug. All in two week's time.

It was too much to believe that all this had happened by coincidence. Some said it must be the work of the Devil—but even the Devil works through human hands. There had to be a *conspirazione* afoot! Everyone could agree on that. The question was—who was behind it? Bureaucrats at European Union headquarters? A cabal of cardinals seeking to take control? The CIA? The Freemasons? With as many theories as there were parties in the Italian Chamber of Deputies, the only thing to do was to wait and see if the next unwelcome surprise would make things clear!

Naples

On his estate in Naples, Don Ricardo was in a cold rage. What kind of *bunglers* did he have in his employ? Could *nobody* do anything right?

Zanier was not going to be in shape to participate in the conclave, but he was supposed to be *dead*. He could still somehow be elected Pope. And, with the Monsignor and the deliveryman able to describe the assailants, the police would be looking for them all over.—At least, the Don could take care of *that* problem when they returned and reported back to him.

He summoned old Ruggiero Paisano, a stone mason who had been on his payroll for thirty years. "I want you to prepare *accommodations* for two right away." Ruggiero nodded. He started to leave to go down to the wine cellar when Don Ricardo called him back.

"Make it for *three*," he said. Toricelli knew who was behind the attack. If he failed in becoming Pope, or attaining some other high position under the new Pope, he too would be laid to rest near the casks of aging Taurasi wine. Toricelli was an investment for the Don, and when his investments ceased to yield the returns he sought, he did what any prudent manager would do: he liquidated them.

San Giovanni Rotondo

The Father Guardian immediately went to Fr. Santorelli when he learned of the heinous crime in Rome.

Fr. Santorelli took the news hard. "As I told you, Padre, the Monsignor and I go back a ways together. We've grown really close the last couple of months, since he called me to Rome. I phoned him last night and asked him to accompany Cardinal Zanier everywhere. I had a vague premonition of danger to the Cardinal, but I couldn't see clearly enough to keep this from happening.—I failed both of them . . ."

"No," the Father Guardian said, as he put his arm around Fr. Santorelli's shoulders. "The future isn't ours to see. I'm sure you did what you could.—His Eminence may owe his life to your intervention last night.—We'll keep praying for the Church leaders around the clock, as you requested."

*　　*　　*

When Msgr. Ireland awoke after the operation on his hand, and was told that Cardinal Zanier was in critical condition, he called Fr. Santorelli. "Tony . . ." was all he could get out before he choked up.

"Monsignor! I'm so glad to hear even that one word from you. Don't feel you have to talk now. You can reach me tomorrow."

"Tony . . ." This time he was able to continue. "*I'll* be fine. It's *the Cardinal* who may not make it. *We have to pray for him!.*—If I hadn't been there at his side . . . *How did you know?!!!*"

"I didn't *know*. It was just like everything else. I have forebodings, but I don't *know* what's going to happen—that's what makes it so hard. *It's been a curse!*—If I had known what was going to happen, believe me, I would have suggested a police guard rather than putting you in danger too, Monsignor."

"Well, Tony, thanks be to God, I came through pretty well, though I guess we have another tie that binds us now.—With what that thug did to my hand, I can claim to be part-stigmatist ... "

In spite of the gravity of the situation, Fr. Santorelli laughed at Msgr. Ireland's attempt at humor. "That's a good one! I'll do my best to keep you from gaining on me in that regard!"

The prelate had one more thing on his mind. "Tony,—what do you think I should do when they release me?"

Fr. Santorelli had already given some thought to that. "Please come here as soon as you can. If you can leave tomorrow, do so, even if you have to check yourself out. Don't take public transportation. Hire a private ambulance to bring you here. I'll get you a room at the *Casa*."

"*The Casa?*"

"Yes. You know about that huge hospital Padre Pio had built here. He named it the House for the Relief of Suffering, and everyone here just calls it 'the *Casa*.'"

"But, shouldn't I be staying here in Rome to attend the Pope's funeral on Monday if I'm up to it then?"

Back came a quick response from Fr. Santorelli: "Let the dead bury their dead."

"What's *that* supposed to mean, Tony?"

There was a moment of silence. "I really don't know," the priest confessed. "They're words that just popped into my head.—In any event, I'd feel better if you got out of Rome now—I think the worst is yet to come ... "

PART VI

The Cleaving

March 2015

See they not that we come into their land bringing destruction ...? And Allāh pronounces a doom—there is no repeal of His decree, and He is swift to take account.

The Qur'an, Sura 13:41

— 1 —

Washington, D.C.

Hiding somewhere within every intelligence agency in the world there is a mole—maybe more than one. Knowing this, every intelligence agency sets out mole traps. And knowing *that*, moles are very cautious about reporting back what they learn. Sometimes long periods go by without a mole contacting his spymaster, waiting for information important enough that it is worth running the risk of exposure to pass it on.

Of course, in other cases, the organization is so inept at protecting itself that the mole can routinely pass on whatever he comes across. A notorious case of espionage against the United States was that of Jonathan Pollard, a civilian intelligence official at the Navy's anti-terrorist alert center, who spied for Israel in the 1980's, handing over a hundred thousand classified documents which revealed such secrets as the design of atomic weapons, the names of U.S. agents abroad, and the capabilities of American signal intelligence and cryptography. Because of the Pollard case, relations with Israel were strained for decades. Aware that the U.S. was making a concerted effort to prevent further leaks to Israel, an Israeli mole, James Goodfriend, had been lying low for years, while putting in his daily 9-to-5 hours as an analyst at the National Security Agency.

On the first Friday in March, he learned something potentially of great importance to the security of Israel that had been picked up from electronic intercepts of the Iranians the previous Sunday—coded messages sent by government transmitters in Tehran, Natanz and Qom. Any electronic traffic going into or coming out of Natanz was captured if possible by satellites or drones, because a nuclear weapons facility was located there. The most complete fragment of a message retrieved was one sent from Qom to Natanz. As best as the computers at the National Security Agency could decode and translate it, it read:

Supreme Leader approves the separation . . . One package authorized . . . Commander Hashemi.

Fragments of the other messages could be linked by reference to the "separation" or Hashemi, but they added nothing of import.

This information had been considered by the analysts at each of the U.S. intelligence agencies, and they had come up with a variety of conjectures as to what the Iranians had up their sleeves. *The worst possible scenario was that the head of the Qods Guards Force was going to be given control of an atomic weapon for an operation.* Which prompted the questions, Where might it be used? and What was it that they were going to 'separate'? There were three main conjectures.

Iran had tried to assume control of Iraq through the "Mahdī Army" of radical cleric Muqtada al-Sadr, only to be defeated by the surge of American troops. With them now out of the country, wiping out the unifying central government in Baghdad might be possible, opening the way for Iranian forces to work with their co-religionists, separating Iraq into Shi'a and non-Shi'a areas, so that the former could be absorbed into Iran.

Saudi Arabia was also in Iran's sights. The Saudi regime practiced a strict brand of Islam, but it was of the Sunni variety, which the Iranian ayatollahs considered heretical. Hashemi could easily cross the Persian Gulf in a small boat to the Arabian Peninsula. If Riyadh were wiped off the map, the Islamic holy cities of Mecca and Medina would be ripe for Iran's control. Under that scenario, the 'separation' could refer to cutting off the Islamic heretics.

The strong consensus was that 'the separation' referred to the third possibility: cutting the country of Israel in two. In ancient times, it had in fact been divided into two kingdoms, Israel and Judah, with the demarcation being just north of Jerusalem.

But it hardly seemed possible that a single—presumably small—atomic weapon could effect *any* of those three *separations*. Which, in the eyes of the intelligence community, cast doubt on the whole analysis. Perhaps the computers had not correctly cracked the Iranian code. There just wasn't enough information to draw a conclusion that any agency was willing to put its name to—and therefore nothing to alarm a friendly nation about.

As inconclusive as the information was to the top people, to Goodfriend it seemed an easy case for connecting the dots: an atomic weapon was involved, else why the messages from and to Narantz, and Ali Hashemi had the action, meaning a guerilla operation. What target would the Iranians have for an atomic bomb except Israel? After all, they had long and loudly been threatening to wipe Israel off the face of the earth. And where better to set off the bomb than Jerusalem?

The intercept intelligence was the sort of information that should have been passed on immediately to Israel, and if that had been the case, Goodfriend would have had no reason to act and risk exposure. However, the security classifications TOP SECRET-NOFORN showed that the U.S. Government was holding the information close to its chest, not warning Israel of the mortal danger posed by Hashemi. That being so, he saw it was imperative for him to act, regardless of the risk that he would be caught and imprisoned for the rest of his life, like Jonathan Pollard.

After work, he drove from Ft. Meade to his townhouse in Bethesda, Maryland, where he changed into nondescript old clothes, covered by a long overcoat and a cap with a visor, before driving into the District of Columbia. He parked three blocks away from a well known liquor store, and once there, he wandered through the aisles, head down, passing as if by chance the stock from Israel. Seeming a bit lost as he looked over the bottles, he was approached with an offer of help by the person he recognized from a picture as the proprietor.

"I'm fond of the Yarden cabernet sauvignon," he said, "but I wondered if you would have anything older—perhaps even something as old as the 1985 vintage, which I hear was outstanding."

The owner showed no surprise. "Sir, we have only the recent vintages out here, but if you'll give me a minute, I'll take you in the back with me. Perhaps I can find that or another old wine to satisfy you." The owner went to the front, where he flicked a switch to stop the surveillance cameras from recording, and made a mental note to wipe the computer disk clean of that afternoon's images.

Once the door to the back room had closed behind them, Goodfriend told the owner what he knew and what he suspected. They poked around while they talked, in case an employee happened to come in, picking out a suitably old Yarden vintage, though not the one he had mentioned, for long before, it would have ceased to be drinkable—a request for a 30 year-old Yarden cabernet was the password he had been given to use there. They went back into the store together, talking about the bottle in Goodfriend's hand.

He paid for it in cash, put it in his overcoat pocket and left. That was all there was to it on his part.

Goodfriend's message was relayed by the shopkeeper as he walked his dog in a park before dinner, to a Mossad agent. The importance of the information was obvious, as was the fact that it was far too sensitive to run the risk of transmitting it to Israel electronically. *Everything* sent that way in the D.C. area was captured and decoded by the U.S. Government's electronic intelligence program. The only way to pass on the information quickly and without creating a further risk for the mole was for the Mossad man to find a flight he could still catch that evening to Europe, continuing on to Israel the next morning on a different airline and with a different passport.

— 2 —

Herzliya, Israel

As soon as the agent arrived at the Ben-Gurion airport, he was met and driven to Mossad headquarters on a hill in Herzliya, a northern suburb of Tel Aviv. Awaiting him on the eighth floor were the heads of both the Mossad and the Shin Bet, and their top staffers, eager to hear what the Israeli mole had passed on in Washington. The information itself was scanty, yet seemed to point to the conclusion which he tried but failed to deliver in the unemotional tone of voice prescribed for reporting: *"It appears that the head of the Qods Force, Ali Hashemi, is being armed with a suitcase atomic bomb, for use in our country!"*

His information came as a real surprise to them, and the room was silent as he sat down. Shin Bet's Barak Rosen made a response which in turn surprised the agent.

"You did well—very well—to bring us this information imme-diately. *Actually, I'm greatly relieved by what you've told us. There's another whole dimension to this picture you know nothing about.*"

"One of our men at Leonardo da Vinci was alert enough to spot Ali Hashemi deplaning from an Iran Air flight a few days ago carrying a very large and very heavy suitcase. He was using a diplomatic courier's official passport in the name of Parvez Firouzabadian. We're sure he was taken to the Iranian Embassy. Our consensus estimate, which we used in briefing the Cabinet, was that he had come to conduct an operation in Rome and had brought in with him some kind of weapon not obtainable there, possibly Sarin nerve gas. We concluded that his target was most probably our Great Synagogue, on the eve of Passover."

The security chief stopped to consider how to put his new analysis. "Obviously, based on what you've just told us, it's a very different threat than either we, or you, have imagined. You were wrong—Ali is not trying to wreak death *here*. He's in Rome. And if he has a suitcase atomic bomb, as now seems likely to me, we also were wrong. He's not targeting *our interests* there with it. Neither the Great Synagogue nor our Embassy in Rome would warrant running all the risks attendant to using a nuclear weapon. Not to mention it would be like using a cannon to hit a fly. That much is clear, though I'm afraid I don't see what he's up to." He looked to Eli Ereli, his counterpart at the Mossad, for a comment.

Ereli spoke up very reluctantly "I agree that he's not after *our* interests—for the added reason that they wouldn't have risked sending him and the bomb into Italy a whole month early. One target *does* occur to me, although it's off-the-wall."

Rosen encouraged him to speak. "Everything these terrorists do is off-the-wall. Let's hear what you have in mind."

"All right, let me ask all of you,—what of importance will be happening *in Rome* in the very near future."

One of the staffers chimed in, "Nothing—except the Pope's funeral, and then the conclave to elect a new Pope."

Ereli nodded. "Yes, that's exactly what I thought of.—All the cardinals will be there for that conclave, concentrated in one very small area. *If a one kiloton bomb, a size which can be carried in a suitcase, were exploded right there at the Vatican, most of the top leaders of the Roman Catholic religion would be killed at once . . .* "

"*Why* would they want to do that?" the puzzled staffer asked.

"Try looking at this with the mindset of a radical jihadist," Ereli answered. "Their ancestors nearly captured Europe centuries ago. They were blocked only by the military power of the Catholic Church. They still have feelings of rage and inferiority over that defeat and over the course of history during the centuries since then. *They may view this as a golden opportunity to deal the Church a blow from which it will never recover, preparing the way for the Islamization of Europe . . .* "

"*My God!*" said the agent who had come from America. "*The funeral's on Monday! And the conclave begins the next day. We've got to warn the Italians immediately!*"

"*Why?*" It was the Director of Shin Bet who issued the unexpected challenge.

Everyone was momentarily too stunned to talk. They could hardly believe his question.

Ereli gave voice to what they were thinking. "*What do you mean, 'Why?'? Are you crazy? It's obvious! Thousands of people would be incinerated. Maybe tens of thousands!*"

Rosen did not back down. "*So?*"

" '*So*'??? . . . Barak, you aren't making sense."

"On the contrary, I'm making perfect sense. *Ali isn't going to blow up the city of Rome—just a small area with certain people there. And who are they?*" asked Rosen. "*Are they members of the House of Israel? Or even righteous gentiles?*"

"*My God!*" said the agent from America again. "*Does that make any difference to you?*"

Everyone held his breath, waiting to see what Rosen would reply.

"*Yes. Doesn't it to you?*"

There was a deathly silence in the room. They looked to the head of the Mossad to carry on the dialogue. "*Barak, if we can warn them and we don't, what are we going to use for an excuse if this crazy scenario actually comes to pass?. . . Do we say that we thought of the nuclear explosion as a repayment—their holocaust for our holocaust?*"

Rosen shrugged his shoulders. "None of *them* will be in a position to ask that question . . . nor will anyone else. No official notes are being taken of this meeting. It stays with us. Besides, Eli, it's the pot calling the kettle black. Your agency didn't warn the Americans of the car bomb attack coming against their Marine barracks in Beirut in the 1980's—your people even watched it happen. They had the right attitude—*our mission is only to protect our own people.*"

"*Barak, don't you see any difference between two hundred military fatalities and thousand of civilians being killed?*"

"*Of course. But have you forgotten we have grievances against the Catholic Church of far more substance than the Muslims do? Grievances for over 2,000 years of discrimination and pogroms? I ask you—why should we do anything to save them now, when it wasn't that long ago that their Pope, Pius XIIth, remained silent while six million of our people were killed . . .*"

Ereli couldn't have disagreed more. "You can't really mean that! When he died, Jewish leaders from all over Europe gave tributes to his work in saving our people. You must have been reading revisionist nonsense from people who weren't alive at the time!"

"And you must have been reading the apologetics put out by the Catholic Church," Rosen sneered. "They think he's a saint! *Think of that! . . . 'Hitler's Pope' a saint!*"

"Don't you know—that whole lie against Pius XIIth was invented by Moscow and put forward to help the communists in Italy in their attempt to take power there, when the Church was standing against them? The facts show he was a righteous gentile, but they don't square with your feelings, so you ignore them. You're a case of cognitive dissonance at its worst."

"*You, my friend,*" replied Rosen, "*are sounding like a Christian.*"

Ereli flushed. "*No, but my parents were among the children he saved. So you and I come at this from different directions.*"

"All right.—*What about those damn visions that we're all getting, trying to make us out to be bad people. Aren't you upset about them? Aren't they enough to persuade you to let Hashemi go about his business?*"

"*Barak, I would agree with you about letting the Vatican be destroyed if you had one shred of proof that it is behind the visions.— Have you heard one word from anyone on the religious right that they have received a vision calling them to conversion? You know as well as I do that they would have set up a howl if that had happened. Instead, all any of us has seen has been our sins. And, you yourself admitted to the Cabinet that Shin Bet has no idea of who is doing this—at least if we are looking only for human actors.*"

Again, silence reigned, and tempers cooled. Finally, the Director of the Mossad said, in a conciliatory tone, "Look, Barak, we're both civil servants. Whether to tell the Italians is too important a decision for *us* to make. I wouldn't suggest bringing it before the Cabinet in the first instance, because any possibility of keeping it secret would be lost, but I think that you and I should meet with the Prime Minister and lay the whole matter before him." That being recognized by Rosen as a sensible suggestion, which would take them off the hook either way, it was agreed to and promptly carried out.

The Prime Minister came to the Mossad headquarters so that staff members and files would be readily available if he requested to see them. After they had reprised their earlier discussion for his benefit, he made a fateful decision.

"*I say that we should let events unfold as they will—but not for any of the reasons you have put forth,*" nodding at the Director of Shin Bet as he did so. "I want each of you to make a memo of what I have to say, to be kept in the Director's personal file of your agency. One day, if our State survives, history will judge what we do, and I want the record to be clear on my motives."

"The problem is that Hashemi is in Rome on an official passport, with the protection of the Iranian Embassy. We can't flush him and the bomb out of the Embassy ourselves. Nor can we go to the Italian Government and ask them to handle the problem, without laying out all the intelligence we have available. Our own part of the picture would only lead one to a suspicion of a non-nuclear weapon. It's only by putting our part together with the American intelligence that the picture is revised to indicate he's brought in a suitcase atom bomb. And, if we surface the intelligence which our mole has passed on to us, it would certainly get back to the Americans and blow his cover."

"Why is that consideration decisive?—I'll tell you why. We need him right where he is in case the next suitcase bomb the Iranians send out really is meant for us. Think, gentlemen—our American friends didn't say one word about this to us, even though on the surface it must have looked like an attack against us was a real possibility—that's what our own agent thought. We cannot rely on the Americans—therefore, we cannot afford to lose our mole in the NSA. That, and only that, is why I am ordering you to keep hands off, and close the file."

The Prime Minister had one additional instruction for them. "As for the extra precautions which we ordered to protect our Embassy and the Grand Synagogue in Rome, we must leave them in place, otherwise I'd have to explain to the Cabinet why I was countermanding that decision. Besides—how can you be 100% sure that even now you have correctly figured out what those *meshuggeneh* Iranians are up to?"

— 3 —

Rome

Captain Francesconi and Lt. Marchetti were working a rare Saturday shift at the Questura. The Captain stopped by his subordinate's cubicle that morning to check on whether the terrorist had been spotted. "Any news so far about Hashemi?" he asked.

"No sir," his subordinate replied, "and that worries me. I've been meaning to talk to you about him anyway. I had another idea."

After clearing the chair by the lieutenant's messy desk of files that were stacked there, the captain dropped into the seat and waited for his subordinate to speak.

"It's like this, Captain," Marchetti said, "Passover is still more than a month off. I don't see why they would have sent someone as important as Hashemi here so far in advance. That's why I'm not favoring the Great Synagogue hypothesis anymore. Instead, I've been thinking about the possibility that Hashemi's after an American target—other than Aviano."

"Another military base?—The American Embassy?" the captain asked.

"No, something more important than those, for the propaganda effect.—It hit me that the Pope's funeral will be on Monday, and the American Vice President will be there with the other dignitaries. Before Hashemi flew here, the Iranians would have known about the funeral coming up and expected the Americans to send their V.P., or at least their Secretary of State . . ."

This was not going to be a quick conversation. The captain looked around for an ashtray to stub out his cigarette. Finding none, he had to make do with the sole of his black leather boot, throwing the butt into the wastebasket.

"I thought a couple of days ago you were convinced that Hashemi was not an assassin?" he reminded Marchetti.

"Yes, sir. I still think that he's not the man to pull the trigger. But he could be the only one the Iranians trust to arrange the hit and see that it's done right, and then kill the man who did it. They wouldn't want to take any chance that the hit could be traced back to them."

"Does the suitcase fit into that scenario?"

"Maybe it held a sniper's rifle with a laser sight. That wouldn't be readily available here."

"A sniper's rifle has a long barrel, you know. Did you think to compare the barrel length of a gun like the HK PSG-1 with the diagonal dimension of Hashemi's suitcase—which you could have calculated from the film?"

"No, sir," replied a crestfallen Lt. Marchetti, "but, what do you think of the idea?"

"Off hand, not too much, other than you get high marks for imagination.—Look, Gino, you can't just throw an idea like that out without thinking it through first. You may be picturing the Vice President sitting out there in front of St. Peter's, in the open for a couple of hours, but you have to explain where a sniper could be hidden. The only nearby buildings looking down on the steps are the basilica itself and the buildings on either side of it, both of them inside the Vatican's gates. Our NOCS people will be on top of all those roofs and the colonnades—and nobody could manage to use a sniper's rifle in the midst of the crowd in the Square for the Pope's funeral. It's not going to be like the outdoor audience with JP II, where that damn Turk was standing only six meters away with a handgun when the Pope passed by."

"There are some tall buildings south of the colonnades, and there's the Janiculum hill." Marchetti offered.

"The buildings that'll have a view of the funeral from their roof tops will be booked by news organizations, like they were for John Paul's funeral. And he'd have to go all the way up the hill to shoot down over the colonnade—too far for an accurate shot".

Lieutenant Marchetti didn't give up. "The Vice President's also going to be vulnerable during other times in his visit, perhaps going to a meeting, or into a hotel," he suggested. "The funeral isn't the only place where they could try to pick him off."

Now, that idea was worth considering with another cigarette. "To be frank," said the Captain, after he had lit up, "I don't think your new idea is nearly as plausible as your old idea, about a possible attack on the Great Synagogue. I don't see that the Iranians have as much to gain by assassinating the American Vice President as they have to lose in a retaliatory action, but your thought does raise an important point.—There's a lesson which you need to learn early in your career: *Always cover your ass!*"

"Sir?" Lt. Marchetti looked expectantly at his boss.

"Gino, we know that a very important and dangerous terrorist has unexpectedly left the safety of his own country to come to our city. Now, we don't know what his mission is, but we do know that the Vice President of the world's only superpower is on his way to our city for a rare appearance. *If the two occurrences are related and we haven't given a warning, any incident whatsoever could ruin your career—not to mention mine too!* There's absolutely no downside to bringing this to the attention of our special operations division, with the suggestion that they inform the United States Secret Service to be on the lookout for Hashemi while the Vice President is here. They've got their own sources of intel—they can connect all the dots. And when the American's gone back home, Gino, I want you to devote all your attention to safeguarding the Great Synagogue."

— 4 —

Rome

So far, the Vice President's visit had been uneventful, and the members of the Nucleo Operativo Centrale di Sicurezza, the elite Italian anti-terrorism SWAT team, were doing their best to have it continue that way. They took very seriously the warning which Captain Francesconi had passed on to them about Ali Hashemi. Pictures of him had been distributed to all those scheduled to be on guard during the Vice President's visit, and the Italian soldier guarding the Iranian Embassy's gate had been ordered to call at once if he spotted Hashemi leaving the grounds.

A plot by Hashemi to assassinate the American official seemed unlikely, but not *highly* unlikely, and so the NOCS team did its best to imagine how Hashemi might try to pull one off. They concluded that they were well protected against the possibility of a distant shot from a sniper's rifle, and that Hashemi's best chance would be with an automatic pistol at short range, like the attempt made on Pope John Paul II in St. Peter's Square, and the one on President Reagan outside a hotel in Washington, D.C. That type of exposure could be greatly mitigated by literally surrounding the Vice President with agents as he entered or exited his limousine or made similar moves in public—all with the exception of his lengthy appearance in the midst of other dignitaries on the raised plaza in front of the basilica during the funeral.

There would be a good five hundred people up close to the American representative—cardinals, bishops, heads of religious orders, with a few priests to assist them, and diplomats from a hundred countries, various heads of state, and Italian officials headed by the President of the Republic and the Prime Minister. As long as Hashemi did not manage to sneak among them somehow, the Vice President should be safe. To that end, it was decided that all of those people should receive a close, final screening as they entered the area of the steps to take their seats. No one outside that area would be in a position for a pistol shot at the Vice President. With a cordon set up for that screening well before noon, the security people felt confident that even if Hashemi was somewhere out there with assassination on his mind, he would not be able to pull it off.

— 5 —

Rome
9 March 2015 Anno Domini; 18 Espand 1393 Anno Persico

At midday, Ali Hashemi knelt in the Embassy on an exquisite Tabriz, facing Mecca, to say his prayers. After lunch it was time for him to make the final preparation for his mission. He broke the diplomatic seals still affixed to his heavy suitcase, and opened the suitcase for the first time. Inside was a simple bomb, to be exploded by him at ground level. Ali had not trusted a timer for the task of detonating it, for fear that traffic or other contingencies might arise which could delay or even prevent his arrival; he needed to be close to the target for it to achieve the desired results, as it was only about a tenth as powerful as the bomb dropped on Hiroshima.

So, at Natanz the engineers had fashioned a triggering mechanism in the form of a thin cable, which he now ran through a small hole in the suitcase into the fuse before he screwed that in place. The cable was a mechanical plunger—a metal wire inside a sheath, like one photographers use to work the shutter release on a camera for a time exposure. When the wire was depressed, a circuit in the fuse would be closed and batteries would ignite plastic explosive charges; these would forcibly drive the smaller, convex container of U-235 through the neutron deflector, and into the larger, spherical, concave container. Assuming the two parts mated properly, the nuclear reaction would occur in a millionth of a second.

Ali was now ready to assume his final disguise, posing as His Excellency, the Ambassador of the Islamic Republic of Iran to the Italian Republic. The Ambassador was expected to arrive at the Petriano entrance to St. Peter's at 2:30 p.m., to take his place for the funeral obsequies beginning half an hour later. Ali was confident that the security people would not know one ambassador from another among the hundred-odd who would be attending, and that his new passport, plus the security-coded invitation, would be enough to have them wave the Embassy limousine, flag flying, through the checkpoint.

One day, his exploit would surely be known far and wide, and in the meantime, his Uncle Muhammad would quietly honor him with a memorial in the courtyard garden in Qom. He was filled with gratitude toward Uncle Muhammad for obtaining the approval of the Supreme Leader for this special project, and he felt a thrill once again as he recalled his uncle's prediction that this deed of his would hasten the return to earth of the Mahdī—the one who would bring peace and justice to the world!

He carried the suitcase down to the waiting limousine, there to ride covered by a lap robe on the seat beside him. During the planning sessions back in Iran, it had been referred to as "the package," *but to Ali, it was the Sword of Allāh!*

Ali instructed the driver to leave the Embassy grounds the back way, through the unguarded side gate, and to turn left down Camilluccia, so that the limousine would not be seen by the sentry at the main gate. The man had only to drive him on a semi-circular route south through Rome's apartment buildings and shops, to the security checkpoint at the Petriano entrance to the Vatican. He would never know who his passenger really was, or what the suitcase contained. There was no reason why he should, and no reason to pity him for his impending death. He too would be a martyr for the Islamic Revolution.

While Ali was en route, at St. Peter's basilica Pope Benedict XVIth's coffin was being readied to be carried down the steps by the pallbearers, to rest in front of the altar as the funeral Mass was celebrated. Almost all the cardinals, and most of the bishops and other dignitaries, including the Vice President of the United States, were very close by or already taking their places in folding chairs set up to the left and right of the altar. The six plotters too had come there together, in their former regalia, confident that no one would risk a disruption by attempting to eject them. A huge crowd of ordinary citizens completely filled the Square and extended back down the main avenue, watching developments on jumbotron screens.

He knew he himself would be dead shortly and he was surprised by his own detachment, the lack of an adrenalin rush. It was so different from the emotions he had felt when he was under fire from the Israelis in the Gaza strip and in Lebanon.

Ali tried but failed to evoke a memory of his father—killed defending their country against Saddam's invasion, when Ali was only a small child. They would have much to say to each other when they met in Paradise!

Deliberately averting his eyes from the streets crowded with immodestly dressed women, Ali settled back and opened the Qur'an to read for one last time verses from his favorite Sura, number 82, the one titled *"The Cleaving."*

Perhaps if the NSA computers had deciphered and translated two words found in the intercepted Iranian message as "the cleaving" instead of as "the separation," an analyst would have thought of Sura 82, and the import of the communication—and the purpose of Ali's presence in Rome—would have been clear from these lines:

> When the heavens are cleft asunder,
> And when the stars are scattered,
> And when the seas burst forth,
> And when the graves are opened wide,
> Each soul shall recognize its actions from beginning
>   to end.

*   *   *

> Surely amid delights shall the righteous dwell,
> And most surely the impure in Hell-fire:
> They shall be burned in it on the day of doom,
> And they shall not be able to hide themselves from it.

Verily, the time had come for him to cleave the heavens and to scatter the stars! With Hell-fire riding in his suitcase, the Day of Doom was at hand!

When the embassy limousine neared St. Peter's, Ali put aside the Qur'an to pay attention to the last couple of minutes of the drive, in case a problem arose. Because the street which ran south from the Petriano entrance to the Vatican was one-way in the wrong direction, the car had to make a big loop to the south of St. Peter's, finally going north on the Via di Porto Santo Spirito, and then west on the Borgo Santo Spirito. The latter street flowed into the Via Paolo VI, right next to the southern colonnade. St. Peter's basilica was just off to the right, with a checkpoint controlling access to the Vatican at the ten foot high iron gate across the Petriano entrance.

Captain Francesconi and Lieutenant Marchetti were at that very moment looking at that gate from the inside, from where they were stationed at the entrance to the Plaza of the Roman Protomartyrs. Although they were not members of the NOCS unit, which was guarding the VIP's, they were on the near perimeter security detail, scrutinizing everyone who was let off to be admitted to the special seating area, and occasionally looking in the direction of the line of black limousines passing through the checkpoint 100 meters away. Each time, the chauffeur handed credentials out his window to be checked, and the guard peered inside through the chauffeur's window to look at the passenger. Once cleared, the cars proceeded slowly through the gate and up to the plaza where Francesconi and Marchetti stood, there to drop the invited guests, who then walked a short distance to the front steps of the basilica where they were seated.

Lt. Marchetti had been holding his uniform cap in his left hand, while he repeatedly ruffed his hair with the right one, as if seeking to massage an idea out of the grey matter inside his head. Suddenly, he erupted with a loud, "*JESUS!!!*"

Captain Francesconi looked in the same direction as Marchetti, without seeing anything suspicious. "*What is it? What do you see?*" he asked excitedly.

"*Those limousines,—*" said Marchetti, pointing at them, "*that's how Hashemi's going to arrive. He used an official passport at the airport. The embassy's in on this. He'll have phony credentials for the funeral. He'll be here any minute now!—With the suitcase!*"

That was barely possible—but why? A question exploded from the Captain: "*The Vice President???*"

Lieutenant Marchetti turned and grabbed his superior by the arms, looking intently into his eyes. "*Forget him! Hashemi's after the Church!!! They're all here. All the leaders in one spot. He's going to nuke them and everything else!!! That's why the suitcase was so heavy—it's an atom bomb!!!*"

Captain Francesconi recoiled backward, physically staggered at the thought his subordinate had just come up with. He'd never even considered *that* possibility . . .

"*No!*" he said, reflexively. "*It can't be . . . !*" The words were shouted at the lieutenant, as if by dint of volume he could refute the thought.

But, then his mind told him—*It could be!*

He had to check it out. That wouldn't be hard to do—just look in the car—and open the damn suitcase, if it was there.

Suspending his disbelief, he pointed down the street. "*Run!*" he ordered. "*Head him off at the checkpoint!*" That would be quicker than trying to explain the situation to the other police over the radio.

Captain Francesconi started to walk quickly down the street toward the checkpoint, unholstering his Glock automatic pistol as he went. He would stop the limousine with the Iranian flag, one way or another, if it passed through security before Marchetti got there. He was not a praying man, but the thought went through his mind, *Please God—not that!*

Lieutenant Marchetti arrived at the checkpoint as the Iranian embassy car was pulling away from it.

"Who was in the car?," he frantically asked the sergeant in charge of the checkpoint.

"Just the chauffeur and the ambassador sir. His credentials were all in order. He matched his diplomatic passport picture. I checked it out real good, because he looked a lot like that Hashemi fellow."

Inside the limousine, Ali felt only exultation. *He was about to strike with the Sword of Allāh!*

"*Yaaaa Allāh!*" he cried out, "*Allāhu Akbar!*"

Marchetti started to run after the car, screaming "*Hashemi!!! Stop him!!!*"

Captain Francesconi squared into a shooter's stance with his gun pointed at the car.

Seeing that, Ali ducked down behind the front seat and ordered the driver to keep going.

When the limousine failed to stop as it approached, Captain Francesconi opened fire, aiming through the windshield.

As the first bullets hit, showering Ali with glass, he pushed down on the wire in the cable—and the circuit was closed . . .

PART VII

The Choice

March 2015

Today, if you hear His voice, do not harden your hearts as you did at Meribah, as you did that day at Massah in the desert, where your fathers tested and tried Me, though they had seen what I did.

Psalm 95:7–9

— 1 —

Rome

*Hell-fire did indeed cleave the heavens asunder. In a fraction of
a second—less than the blinking of an eye—the mortal bodies of
Ali and everyone else at ground zero vanished, as did most of the
world famous basilica of St. Peter's. The blast energy released by
Ali's bomb, exploding very close to the base of the massive structure,
instantly heated it to the point that the stone and metal and glass
all vaporized.*

    Before Ali set out on his fateful ride, all of Italy and much of
the rest of the western world had been watching TV, awaiting the
start of the funeral of Benedict XVIth. With the cameras focused
on the steps of St. Peter's, the TV commentators had been pointing out the dignitaries being seated there, and offering learned
commentaries about the history of the Vatican beginning with
the days when the area was used by the Roman Emperors as a
circus for chariot racing. Interspersed with history lessons, they
speculated about the forthcoming papal enclave, handicapping
the prospects of the various *papabile.*

    All of a sudden, without warning, a strange sound came from
everyone's TV set, as the screen went black. Every station immediately shifted to a picture of its commentators, generated in
its own studio. Epithets flew from the producers as they tried
to restore the Vatican view, while they cursed the unknown and
unimaginable problem that had occurred—possibly the accidental
cutting of a transmission cable at the site.

    Technicians in Rome's TV studios who were trying to figure
out where the process had broken down were mystified by the
fact that the feeds of *all* the stations from the scene were down,
despite their coming in from different cameras. The Vatican's
own TV station had cameras mounted atop the colonnades. Some
networks had their cameras in the stand built near the Vatican
Press Office at the edge of the Piazza Pio XII. Still other networks
had rented the roofs of nearby buildings to cover the event. No
pictures were coming in from anywhere!

What the hell could have caused that? An electric grid power outage?

They learned soon enough what had happened, for a tall, evil looking cloud visible from miles away rose over the Vatican to a height of 10,000 feet.

No physicist's calculation attempting to equate the power of Ali's bomb with one thousand tons of TNT could truly capture its destructive force, for through nuclear fission it had generated millions of degrees of heat, fearsome winds, and radioactive debris.

The dust which rose to the skies in a horrible parody of incense was not common house dust, but atoms of what had been the finest examples of man's creative genius in praise of God over the centuries—an immense golden dome, a bronze baldacchino, the Pieta finely carved out of marble, and the stained glass Holy Spirit above the Chair of St. Peter. These now unrecognizable motes were intermingled in the cloud with bodily elements of the people who had been gathered there, and something even more precious, the Body of Christ, which had been present in the form of the consecrated hosts reserved in the tabernacles on the altars of the basilica.

A few recognizable fragments of St. Peter's could be seen, shattered and strewn on the ground, along with sizeable stone remnants of the Sistine Chapel and the large Apostolic Palace to the north of the basilica. To the south, the Palace of the Holy Office, the Papal Audience Hall and other Vatican buildings had vanished. Buildings further away, including the church of Santa Maria alle Fornaci, were leveled. To the west, the Vatican's tall walls had enclosed various structures including the radio center and transmission facilities which had fixated Ali—all these were no more.

However, the worst of the horrors lay to the east, in the open area of St. Peter's Square. At Natanz, Iran's bomb makers had built a bomb sufficient to take out the basilica with the several thousand cardinals and bishops they expected to be at the Vatican when the conclave began—while not damaging much else in Rome, in order to minimize the revenge-seeking furor which they feared could ensue. They had no knowledge of how events at the Vatican would unfold and they did not contemplate that Ali would explode the bomb on a day when an enormous crowd of people was nearby, all of whom were vulnerable to the multiple harmful effects of the bomb.

Four hundred thousand people had been standing in St. Peter's Square, and in the adjacent Plaza Pio XII, when all the immense stone columns in the colonnades were knocked over like candlepins by a bowling ball, crushing all in their way. Those who were not squashed under the stones died from the blast or the bomb's thermal effects. Close to ground zero, the onlookers were incinerated by the high temperature, while those slightly farther away were suffocated by a lack of oxygen, or were torn apart by extraordinary air pressures, which generated a 250 mph wind.

Late comers, who were standing well back from the Square along the Via della Conciliazione to the east, expecting to watch the ceremony on jumbotron screens, were temporarily blinded by the flash of the blast and suffered flash burns, first from ultraviolet light and then from gamma radiation. Their exposure was prolonged by the fallout which a brisk wind coming from the west blew over them. More than two hundred thousand people died right there in St. Peter's Square that day, twice as many as had been killed instantly in the wartime atomic explosions at Hiroshima and Nagasaki combined, and another hundred thousand would die within days. It was the most dreadful single-day disaster ever caused by man.

As the initial shock of the TV viewers wore off, everyone who had a relative or friend at the scene tried frantically to contact them by cell phone, to no avail. The survivors at the fringes of the Square heard no ringing, nor could they make outgoing calls. Their cell phones had been "fried" by the electromagnetic pulse given off in the explosion, and the result of a hundred thousand calls repeatedly attempted was to overload and disable all the phone networks in Rome.

Santo Spirito, the oldest hospital in the city, located just outside the Square's southern colonnades, was unable to provide help, as it had been reduced to rubble and its staff killed. Emergency responders who raced to the scene from elsewhere in Rome were too undertrained and too overwhelmed to function efficiently. Such a contingency had seemed so improbable that they had never practiced for one like it, and did not have equipment on hand which could tell them whether an area was too "hot" to enter safely. As a result, the units which responded stood off at a distance which they hoped was safe, and only the more lightly wounded—people with broken limbs and minor burns—were able to drag themselves to help. When the wounded got to the mobile aid stations, they were at first sent off in ambulances, with no attempt at triage. As a result, the hospitals were quickly swamped, and radio announcers began making pleas for all public health and military doctors to come and help determine who could be saved by treatment.

The President and the Prime Minister of Italy, and the Mayor of Rome, had been among the Italian officials present for the fatal funeral Mass. Their demise left a vacuum in civic leadership, and no government official stepped forward with a message of reassurance—however hollow—to be broadcast to the citizenry. The Church too was without a spokesman to provide words of comfort, but fortunately, the Spirit prompted priests to come in from all the suburbs, bringing viaticum with them, to anoint the dying where they had fallen.

A half million Romans safely away from the scene were frightened about what might come next, and they grabbed their valuables and their pets and tried to evacuate the City by car, jamming all the roads. *Anywhere* in Italy seemed safer than Rome at that moment. Their panic was shared by those who remained in the city. They rushed around from one food store to another frantically buying up whatever was available, needed or not, and withdrawing all the cash they could from ATM machines, in fear that the banking system would soon shut down.

San Giovanni Rotondo

In the friary, the Father Guardian had been watching the preliminaries for the funeral Mass on the TV in his office, with a few of the senior friars. The one held for John Paul II had been an extremely moving event, and so he was surprised when Fr. Santorelli politely declined to be part of the group, saying that he wanted to continue praying for the Church in the chapel. For the first few minutes after the explosion, the friars sat transfixed. Then the Father Guardian sent for Fr. Santorelli, and when he came in, pointed wordlessly to the screen, which still showed only a picture of the atomic cloud. Fr. Santorelli sank to his knees, as he looked on aghast.

"*Jesus!*" he said, without really having Jesus in mind. The terrible scene immediately evoked a memory of another cloud, very different in form, but equally stupefying—the one which had arisen as the towers of the World Trade Center collapsed. But the scene then was so different, so very different. The towers had stood for a while, until the raging infernos part way up ate through their structural shells, and then they had collapsed in place, like elevators dropping unchecked in their shafts, or an ocean liner, bow pointed up in the air, sinking into the depths. There was no such agonizing end for St. Peter's—one second the massive basilica with its golden dome was standing majestic and immovable, and the next it was gone. *Gone. With only the column of smoke in its place.*

He had been 19 at the time of 9/11, and he remembered just where he had been at the moment when he learned of the ongoing tragedy in New York City.—What American didn't? And what American was not filled with fury at that moment? The hot fury that spurs one to go out into the streets, ready to break open the head of any enemy at hand. Or the cold fury, such as supports a war that takes years of blood and money to wage. He was a priest now, a man dedicated to spreading the "peace of Christ," but just as then, his anger blazed. He instantly grasped what had happened at the Vatican and who was responsible, and the urge welled up in him to retaliate in kind. Let the jihadists be paid back double! Triple! Let *their* holy cities be destroyed, along with them!

This momentary, reflexive martial fantasy was punctured by the Father Guardian, who could no longer control his anxiety. "For God's sake," he implored Fr. Santorelli, "tell us what's going on!"

Fr. Santorelli replied in a hollow voice, while still looking at the screen. "They will kill you. You will be hated by all nations because of my name."

"What?" the bewildered Father Guardian asked him.

Fr. Santorelli slowly got to his feet and faced his host. "I'm sorry, Padre," he said, in a more normal voice. "Those words of Jesus were from the fifth part of the message I received at Garabandal for the Pope. In a way, it explains what's just happened. This is the work of those who hate the Christ."

Wishing to speak with Fr. Santorelli in private, the Father Guardian asked the friars who had been with him to go and make known to all the others what they had seen, and tell them to assemble in the chapel. When the two of them were alone, he asked, *"Father, is this the Chastisement that was prophesied? You know, the Garabandal prophecy . . . ?"*

Fr. Santorelli gave the Father Guardian a pained look. "I wish I could say, 'Yes, it is,' because this is terrible enough without more. *But, I can't—the Chastisement is supposed to follow the Miracle, and that hasn't taken place yet . . ."*

"Then we will just carry on as best we can for now," the Father Guardian said. "I'll ask the friars to turn their efforts to praying for the dead and the dying, and the poor souls already in Purgatory. Is there anything you would suggest?"

"I think it would be well to begin offering several *requiem* Masses a day, even one tonight if possible, Padre," Fr. Santorelli replied.

"I will arrange for that, Father. It will be hard for us to pray for the murderers, but I will remind the others that they must do that too."

The words of the Father Guardian were a rebuke sent by Heaven, Fr. Santorelli realized—he had better put on the mind of a priest to match his clerical garb. "You're good to think of that at a time like this, Padre," he replied. "You're right—we're called upon to pray that one day they'll see the evil they've wrought, and repent, and somehow be reconciled with God. We mustn't wish that they go to Hell—much as it's a punishment that would fit their crime!"

After he left the Father Guardian's office, a second grace was given to Fr. Santorelli—the grace to understand that something more difficult was expected *of him* than an impersonal prayer for those who had perpetrated the outrage. *He had to pray for the soul of his former superior, Cardinal O'Melveny, who surely had perished in the explosion.*

It was easier to pray for the souls of people unknown to him than it was to pray for the soul of this cleric whom he *did* know, one who had worked much evil in the Church and had grievously wronged him. To pray sincerely, he had to suspend *his* judgment of the Cardinal's culpability—which he had not done since the episode when he was sent into exile back in California. Fr. San-

torelli knelt where he was, folded his hands and by a great effort
of will prayed, *Thomas O'Melveny, requiescat in pace* ...

*   *   *

With that obligation of charity performed, the priest hurried over
to Msgr. Ireland's room at the *Casa*. The bed nearest the door
was empty, and a curtain was drawn around Monsignor's bed. He
could see that the overhead TV set was on, although the sound
had been muted. For a minute he paused to look at the picture. No
longer was it of the rising cloud. Now, the subject was St. Peter's
Square, taken from a distance and a height—probably from a TV
news helicopter. Here too there were elements which triggered
a memory of 9/11. A broken fragment of the Apostolic Palace
reminded him of the iconic picture of a twisted piece of the metal
facade of the World Trade Center rising from the rubble. And
the skyline of Rome was noticeably impoverished, deprived of its
tallest structure, just as New York's skyline had been on 9/11.

Even without panning downward and zooming in, the TV
camera showed a kind of carnage not photographed in New York
City. No one saw the bodies of the jumpers there while the towers
still stood, and when the two buildings came down, no one saw
the bodies of the trapped office workers and firefighters and
policemen crushed under tons and tons of debris. At St. Peter's
Square, bodies were everywhere to be seen—on their backs, on
their faces, on their sides. Some thrown together in piles, up
against stonework, others lying flat in the middle, their remains
resembling the flotsam and jetsam deposited by a great river in a
flooded town.

A muffled sob from behind the curtain brought Fr. Santorelli
out of his reverie. He stepped into the curtained-off area, to find
Monsignor Ireland sitting up, head buried in his hands. Hearing someone enter his private room, the prelate looked up, and
through his watery eyes he beheld his old pupil.

"Oh, Tony!" he said, in great distress. "*Thank God you're
here!—It's gone!—It's all gone!—Everything!—I've lost everything—
my friends—my work—my office—the chapel where I say Mass.—
There's no Pope—no Congregation—nothing's left!*"

Fr. Santorelli remained silent, sensing that there was more to
come from his distraught friend.

Monsignor fumbled for the remote control and turned off the TV. *"Tell me, Tony, how could this have happened? The Lord talks to you.—You must have some idea . . . !"*

In truth, there was no *good* answer to be made. Still, the priest had to say something. "Monsignor, Cardinal Zanier asked me a similar question last month. He wanted to know whether the Warning visions had been sent *now* because we were *worse* than prior generations in God's sight. You'll recall that Jesus judged that the men of His time were an 'evil and perverse generation,' but I have no way of knowing whether the same could be said of the people today. Off hand, I doubt it—the inhumanity of man to man in the 20th century strikes me about as bad as it ever was in recorded history. Even if we *are* worse than they were, I don't see what happened today as being intended by God as a punishment, rather than being just the unfortunate working of evil on a grand scale.

"And as for that," he added, "I take comfort in the fact that God is still in charge. The Lord told me exactly what he told the Apostles—while the Church has much to suffer, it will prevail."

The prelate seemed to be more upset than comforted by what Fr. Santorelli had to say. *"The unfortunate working of evil?—The Church will prevail?—How can you be so phlegmatic? Aren't you at all angry by what's happened? Tony, don't you care about the people who died?"*

Fr. Santorelli nodded. *"Of course I'm angry, Monsignor!* And I mourn for all the innocent people who were killed or injured today. But, you read, didn't you, that great interview which Arturo Archangelli had with the Pope just before he died? *The Pope stressed that our hope lies in the promise of the next world—where an account will be rendered for everything bad that has happened in this life, and justice will be done, and every tear dried.*

"That's a message which needs to be sounded publicly now, lest people become depressed or turn away from God in their anger—and *you* are one of the Church leaders left in Rome to proclaim it, Monsignor. You can see that the Church must organize a massive relief effort for the people of Rome and others directly affected. Can you imagine how many widows and widowers and orphans the explosion created? So many people knocked off their bearings, disconsolate, grieving! Where will they find compassion if not in the Church? *So, take heart, Monsignor, you have much work left to do for the Lord!"*

*   *   *

When Fr. Santorelli returned to his room at the friary's guest house, he prostrated himself on the floor before the crucifix on the wall, and cried out in frustration.

"My God ... why do you treat me like this? ... You rack me with fears ... images of death ... destruction ... I sense calamities coming— but I can't stop them ... Why?..."

He intended his lament as no more than a soliloquy, but a reproving voice, one he well knew, answered him internally.

"Anthony—are you *the clay,* or *the potter?"*

He remained silent, until the voice demanded: *"Answer me!"*

"The clay, Lord."

"Does the clay tell the potter what to make of it, or how it is to be used?"

"No, Lord."

"If I had wished you to prevent the evil done today, would I not have armed you for that purpose?"

"Yes, Lord."

"Then why do you try me, like Job, challenging how I make use of you?"

What could he say but, "Forgive me, Lord."

The Lord was not quite finished with him.

"Anthony—recall that I revealed the events of my Passion in advance to my chosen disciples, so that they would realize that I foresaw and accepted every evil that was to come. Be reassured that those who survived today are sufficient to rebuild my Church ..."

— 2 —

Rome

The disaster at the Vatican continued to dominate everyone's thoughts the following day, especially in the City of Rome, where chaos still reigned. Disaster relief in Italy was a perpetual scandal, an activity never well planned or funded, as was visible to all several times a year, whenever an earthquake occurred. TV crews were on the spot, talking with the homeless villagers by the next day, while it took weeks for the Government even to deliver tents to shelter them. And no thought at all had been given to this type of small scale nuclear attack, based on the assumption that if Italy were attacked with nuclear weapons, there would be no one left in Rome to save.

Triage instructions for the different types of injuries had finally been disseminated to first responders and hospitals, but they were overwhelmed by the number of people who truly were victims, plus those who were merely frightened that they had been exposed to radiation—and others who were tearfully looking everywhere for their missing relatives. Fortunately, doctors knowledgeable about radiation burns and sickness started to arrive, as did medical supplies and blood, from other cities in Italy and around the world.

Haz-Mat teams began to mark off rings around the Vatican, noting "hot spots," which were placed off limits by radiation signs, particularly along the Via della Conciliazione. The city of Rome—the Vatican excepted—had truly "dodged the bullet." No blast or thermal or radiation damage was felt across the Tiber to the east, where the heart of the city lay. The city's good fortune was due to two factors—the small size of the bomb, and the fact that it had exploded west of the river, next to a massive structure on the ground, rather than in mid-air over the heart of the city.

What to do with the remains of the dead? There was no room for them in the morgues, even if the health workers had been willing to risk secondary radiation exposure from the corpses, and so they had to be disposed of immediately and impersonally. Ordinarily, all sorts of pertinent data would have been recorded about the deceased, but under the circumstances, the authorities ordered that they be buried in mass graves without even searching through their clothing for identification. The religious orders called upon their priests to be present at the burial sites, and, in the absence of a bishop, to consecrate the ground, and asperge the bodies as best as they could before the lime and earth covered them. *"Ashes to ashes, dust to dust,"* as the Church's penitential rite had declared only three weeks before, on Ash Wednesday.

While all the attention of the authorities was directed to dealing with the dead, the dying and the injured, the dark side of Italy was rousing itself to grab for spoils. Many stores, apartment buildings and offices had been vacated by people who had been killed or were afraid to remain. There simply weren't enough policemen to guard every location around the clock. The local Mafia was the first to take advantage of the situation, but the Camorra arrived from Naples, looking for a share of the loot. Rome quickly became a jungle. Violent crimes of every sort were committed in broad daylight, from ordinary burglaries and car hijackings, to rapes and murders. The surviving members of the Council of Ministers met to consider the breakdown in public safety. They decided that most of the Carabiniere forces in other regions of the country should be ordered to Rome, for temporary duty, and they requested that the Italian Army assist by lending its military police units and other troops to patrol areas of the City at night to enforce the curfew which they announced.

Jesus' poignant verbal picture of "sheep without a shepherd" applied to the citizens of Rome, and of all Italy—and even the entire Catholic world. They had been rocked by personal visions of their sins, then by the tragic death of the Holy Father, and now by the death, in many cases, of their local head shepherd, and the destruction of the place which had served as the focal point of worship for 2,000 years.

They were desperate for an explanation, for comfort, and for reassurance, and all the Catholic churches were jammed, as extra Masses were scheduled, and the priests were kept busy with lines of penitents making overdue confessions.

San Giovanni Rotondo

The Father Guardian took a seat at the long wooden refectory table across from Fr. Santorelli, who was sitting alone, sipping his coffee and nibbling a hard boiled egg—his usual breakfast. He brought up what was on his mind, without posing it directly as a question.

"Brother Porter spent a difficult night. He tells me he was repeatedly awakened by knocking on the front door. Each time, he would go to the door and open it, only to find that nobody was there. It's unlike pilgrims to play a joke on us—I don't know what to make of it. He really is convinced he heard the knocking."

Fr. Santorelli put down his half-eaten egg, and sat there, thinking about how much he would reveal to the Father Guardian.

"Last night was a difficult one for me too Padre," he said, finally. "I got even less sleep than usual. There was a parade of souls seeking me out. Perhaps they came to the friary first and then moved on to the priests' guest house. Nothing like that had ever happened to me and at first I didn't understand what was going on."

It was the Father Guardian's turn to sit in silence, pondering. He had read of such visits happening to Padre Pio.

"*Souls*, you say? You're quite sure of that?"

"Yes, they were clearly *souls*. I don't doubt it was they who were knocking. And I have to say it was quite cold when they were there with me in my room. I assume Hell is blazing hot, but from last night's experience, it seems to me that Purgatory must be frigid."

As if the subject they were conversing about were no more unusual than the day's weather, the Father Guardian calmly carried on. "What were they seeking, Father—that is, if you could communicate with them?"

Fr. Santorelli seemed to be willing to talk about the experience, now that he had begun. "Oh, they managed to communicate all right, in some internal way. They didn't ask for much, just prayers, Masses, rosaries—things that would release them from Purgatory. They seemed to know what they needed. My Mass book is full for a while!"

"Hmmm," said the Father Guardian, "I wonder if they died in the bomb blast at the Vatican? But, how could that be? That was only yesterday. If that's who they were, they couldn't have been in Purgatory very long . . . "

Fr. Santorelli thought about that. "Maybe," he said, "that depends on how time is reckoned in Purgatory, Padre. If the 'clock' there keeps *kairos* time instead of *chronos* time, they could have put in years of sacred time in Purgatory in one day of our ordinary time."

The Father Guardian had a bemused look on his face. It was a good answer. "Well, I thank you for the explanation, Father. I'll pass it on to Brother Porter. He'll be glad to know he's not imagining things—or if he is, he's in good company with you!"

"By the way," he added, "in case you ever wonder about that large picture of St. Pio behind you, you're sitting right where he used to sit, against the wall at the end of the table."

Fr. Santorelli turned around to look. There were other photos of the friary's own saint in the refectory. "He casts a long shadow, doesn't he, even in death?"

The Father Guardian nodded. "Yes, he does, and we're all conscious of it." He stood up to go, but Fr. Santorelli held him with another thought.

"You know, Padre," he said, "when I suggested that you have requiem Masses said here, I didn't give any thought to the omission of the *Libera Me* from the *ordinary* form of that Mass. That section seems so fitting now: 'Deliver me, O Lord, from death eternal on that fearful day when the heavens and the earth shall be moved, when thou shalt come to judge the world by fire.' The same with the *Dies Irae* section: 'Day of wrath! O day of mourning! See fulfilled the prophets' warning. Heaven and earth in ashes burning!' The two would tie right into the visions which show impenitent sinners what Hell will be like for them! How about using them?"

"But, Father, surely you're aware that those sections were omitted from the vernacular Mass after Vatican II because they were thought to emphasize *judgment*, and not God's mercy."

"Yes, Padre," Fr. Santorelli replied, "I'm very aware of that. But, right now, wouldn't they be fitting? *Yesterday was a day of wrath, and many people died in the fire of judgment.*"

The Father Guardian weighed the suggestion before giving his verdict. "I understand the *theological* reasoning which prompts your suggestion, Father, but, for pastoral reasons, I can't agree. *People don't come to San Giovanni Rotondo to be reminded of ashes and threatened with fire—especially right now, when their fate is very much on their minds. They are seeking a place of hope and uplift. A place where their worries and sufferings are turned over to Jesus and His Mother—and then left here when they return home.* They need no intensifier of their fears."

Fr. Santorelli could see the appropriateness of the Father Guardian's decision. "Very well," he said, "you're in charge. Can I help you with the extra load? I can offer Mass in English, Italian and Spanish."

"That will help, Father. Can you also confess penitents in those languages?"

"Yes, in English and Spanish. Confessions in Italian can be a problem for me. I never got out of Rome much in my student days, and the various local dialects can be almost incomprehensible. In fact, I'm having trouble understanding your friars from around here who speak the Puglia dialect. If necessary, I could try to hear confessions in Italian, but I think it would be very slow going, and not of much help."

"All right," said the Father Guardian, "I'll be grateful for whatever you can do. I'll assign you some Masses, beginning tomorrow morning.—And I wish you a better night tonight, Father," he said, and left the refectory.

Exiting alone, Fr. Santorelli sang in a low voice that no one else could hear the words to a section of his favorite Requiem, the one by Gabriel Fauré, which he had sung in the seminary choir: *"Libera me, Domine, de morte aeterna, in die illa tremenda, quando caeli movendi sunt et terra dum veneris judicare saeculum per ignem. Libera me, Domine!"*

*   *   *

After the noon meal, Brother Campanella, the friar with nursing training, came to see the Father Guardian, with a peculiar request: he wanted the priest to hear his confession right then and there.

"I'm not your regular Confessor, Brother. Can't this matter wait for him?"

"Please, Padre, I need to confess now and to you, not anyone else."

As Brother Campanella had never been in trouble, the Father Guardian was surprised by the request, but he acceded.

The Brother knelt down and began his confession. "Bless me Padre, for I have sinned in disobeying my superiors, and I may be guilty of theft."

The priest was nonplussed. "Tell me the details, Brother," he demanded.

"While I was attending to Fr. Santorelli as you asked, when he was ill, I changed his bandages several times. I decided to keep the old dressings instead of throwing them away, because my aunt Lucia in Foggia has been ill with cancer, and I thought that *maybe* . . . She came to the *Casa* here yesterday to get a second opinion. They gave her all the tests. It was osteosarcoma in her right leg, just as she had been told by her own doctor. They told her there was no treatment for her. Most likely, she had less than a month to live." Brother Campanella choked up and had difficulty continuing.

"*Last night, I took a strip of Father's bloody bandages and wound it around her leg.—This morning I went to see her.— She was standing up. Her leg was as strong as ever . . .* "

He was crying now, but he continued. "The bandages weren't mine to take, and I disobeyed your instructions to all of us about not attempting to cure the pilgrims here with relics. And,—" he added, "*I'm not truly sorry for my sins! I love my aunt . . . !*"

Poor Brother Campanella! The Father Guardian was most understanding.

"*Of the three, Brother, the last sin is the most serious. However, while you say you aren't sorry, your urge to confess shows that at least you are sorry for not being sorry, which under these circumstances is sufficient. I will absolve you of your sins. But please turn over any more used bandages you may have to me, and never try such a thing again.*"

After the Brother left, the Father Guardian put in a call to the *Casa*. "This is Padre Ghiardi. Please, may I speak to a patient by the name of Lucia Campanella?"

A few seconds later, the answer came back, "I'm sorry, Padre, there's no one of that name registered."

"Would you kindly double check that? I understood that the aunt of Brother Campanella was there."

"Oh, Oh! How stupid of me. Forgive me, Padre. Yes, of course, his aunt Lucia was here, but she's already been released. It's quite a story from what I've heard.—She walked out of here on her own two legs. Please pass on to Brother Campanella how thrilled we all are at her cure!"

Poor Father Guardian! He realized that this added a new layer of complexity to his administration of the convent. One that required the discernment of *his* superiors, and advice from anyone who remembered how things were done in the days when Padre Pio was there, with his bleeding stigmata and relic seekers. He thought to himself that he was not the right man to be in charge of the convent at this very problematic time, but there was a blessing even in that—he would be more aware daily of his dependence on the Lord.

Jerusalem

A very somber meeting was held among the Israeli Prime Minister and the heads of the Shin Bet and the Mossad on Tuesday afternoon. Each felt somewhat responsible for the holocaust that had occurred in Rome the day before, and wanted to justify his role. The Shin Bet head broke the awkward silence.

"I had no idea Hashemi would set the bomb off *with that huge crowd of people at St. Peter's*—If it's any excuse, I assumed he'd strike during a day of the conclave when there weren't by-standers ... "

The head of the Mossad, too, tried to justify himself. "I've asked myself a dozen times whether we could have done anything different—I still don't think so. Just the fact the Iranians were willing to do this in Rome proves we were wise to stay focused on *our own survival*. We did the right thing in not saying anything that might jeopardize our mole at the NSA."

Prime Minister Hertzel held up a hand as if to say, 'Yes, I agree, but, enough of that. That chapter is closed.' Looking at the head of the Mossad, he asked, "What does your shop think will happen internationally now?"

Ereli had expected the question, and was prepared with an answer, which was necessarily complex. "Well, Levi, let me begin by using our own country as an example. *We know who did this without a doubt, and we could even prove it, . . . but we can't afford to tell what we know.* We can't accuse Iran, because we can't go public with the proof from our surveillance in Rome and what the mole in America learned. It would expose too much, and besides, everybody would say we were equally responsible with Iran because we didn't act to stop it from happening." The Prime Minister and Rosen both nodded in agreement.

"Then, there are the Americans. By now they've certainly taken another look at the message they intercepted and realized that the Iranians did it. But they can't say anything either, because they'd be revealing the capability of their electronic intelligence operation and the stupidity of their analysts . . . as well as opening themselves up to criticism for not sharing such significant intelligence with those who might have made use of it." They nodded their agreement at this too.

"So, they and we both have a strong reason to accept at face value Al Qaeda's claim that they're responsible, even though we know it's bogus. The press has no way of checking, and if both our Governments leak that we think it's Al Qaeda, that's how the stories will be written."

"That all seems reasonable," said the Prime Minister, "but you left out the Italians. The immigration officer that worked with Haim Levy to identify Hashemi surely remembers the incident and he'll put his superiors on the trail of Iran."

"As a matter of fact," replied Ereli, "he probably reported what Levy discovered, the very same day, and they did nothing. They can't afford to explain their own inaction, can they? Besides, what could they do even if they were willing to voice their suspicions about Iran? They have no atomic weapons of their own . . . they're supposed not to need them because they're under the NATO shield. There's no way that Italy is going to call a meeting of NATO and ask for help because it's been attacked."

"Why not?" asked Rosen.

"Because they'd be afraid that the Americans would jump at the excuse to level Tehran if they pointed to Hashemi. The Italians have made nice with the Muslim world, with that huge mosque right in the heart of Rome. *It's all about petrodollars.* They don't want the U.S. to get them blacklisted by avenging them with a retaliation against a Muslim country. So, Al Qaeda will be an acceptable whipping-boy for them too.—Oh," he added, "of course, there will be another session or two of the U.N. Security Council, but none of the Big Three will want anything done, so I figure activity on that front will die out in a couple of weeks."

"And then—what?" asked the Prime Minister.

In a tone of great discouragement, Ereli answered him. *"Then, we'll be at war with Iran. Mark my words, gentlemen, the Supreme Leader will see that he's gotten away with nuking Rome, and he'll come after us next!—The only question in my mind is whether he'll just go for Jerusalem, by trying to sneak in another suitcase bomb, or whether he'll fire off all the missiles he's got, against our cities."*

The other two sat there pondering Ereli's prediction. They were silent because they did not disagree with his thinking. He had only said out loud what was in their minds too.

"We could strike first . . . ," Rosen suggested.

"No," said the Prime Minister. *"The world will let the Iranians strike first, but it won't give us that option, even in self-defense. If we pre-empted, the only way to succeed would be to go nuclear, and the Russians, or others, would finish us off, in the name of 'world peace.'"*

"But, there's one thing we *can* do," the Prime Minister added.— "It's sending a message to the Supreme Leader, through diplomatic channels in a third country.—I'll tell him that we know Ali Hashemi brought the suitcase atomic bomb into Rome, and that, if *anyone* succeeds in exploding such a weapon anywhere in our country, I will presume *he* was behind it, and I will make sure that, by the end of the day, he and Iran and its Islamic revolution are as dead as the Persian Empire . . ."

— 3 —

San Giovanni Rotondo

Msgr. Ireland, whose hand was healing well, checked himself out of the *Casa* on Wednesday morning and met with Fr. Santorelli and the Father Guardian. The latter graciously suggested that the Monsignor concelebrate the noon Mass, with Fr. Santorelli and himself. Thinking that seeing the Mass would bring comfort to many in the region, the Father Guardian quickly lined up live coverage by the TV station in Foggia.

At that time, San Giovanni Rotondo was jammed with an influx of people who had fled Rome, looking for physical and spiritual sanctuary. So many were there that the Mass had to be celebrated in the new pilgrimage church, which could seat 6,000 inside, with room for five times that many standing in the adjacent amphitheatre outside.

This building was an extraordinary work of architecture and construction, as beautiful in its own idiom as a Gothic cathedral was in its. Approaching it from the square by the friary, one saw a shallow, inverted saucer, whose roof of slightly raised flat sheets was supported by two massive metal arches. The longer arch, part of the exterior wall, held up a giant steel grid on which colorful, space-age fabric panels had been installed next to clear windows. The rectangular panels had been printed digitally in very small squares. Together, they formed a canvas on a massive scale with different scenes taken from the Book of Revelation, most prominently the one of Mary with her child being taken up to heaven to protect them from the dragon seeking to snatch the child away. Even on a cloudy day, when the different images were difficult to discern from the outside, they appeared bright from the inside looking out.

The unusual roof was supported inside by metal struts anchored in equally unusual pillars—arches made of stone, with steel through their cores, arising from a central point behind the raised and free standing altar. These arches were purposely designed to be of different lengths, to suggest that they were outstretched fingers. Below the pilgrimage church was the crypt church, whose walls, like the ramp leading down to it, were covered with exuberant modern mosaics of scenes from the lives of Jesus, St. Pio and St. Francis. It was there that the body of St. Pio had finally come to rest for veneration.

The friars decided to process from the sacristy into the above ground worship space en masse to show the people the continuing strength of the Church. It was a moving event. Some of the worshippers recognized Msgr. Ireland from the pictures which had run in the newspapers after he and Cardinal Zanier were attacked. This was the American who had been wounded defending Zanier! His bandaged right hand proved it! The news spread through the crowd, and they applauded loudly as he passed, happy to see this hero up and about. Anticipation was intense as to what message the Monsignor would bring them about the devastation in Rome, which he had fortuitously escaped.

"My brothers and sisters in Christ, the tragedy which has just occurred was so great that some would term the horror 'unspeakable'— and yet speak about it we must, and think about it we must, and pray about it we must.

"Do not try to put the holocaust out of your mind by saying that it was 'God's will.' *Everything* which happens, good and evil, can be said to be 'God's will' in the sense that He allowed it to happen. *But, God is love, and the true meaning of the words 'God's will' is that which God decrees or wishes to have happen . . . and that can only be what flows from love.* I tell you truly, God did not wish any of those killed yesterday to die. He did not wish any of those injured yesterday to be hurt. He did not wish the glorious tribute to Him that was St. Peter's basilica to be destroyed. Yet, He did allow the death, the injury and the destruction to occur. If you ask me why, I will tell you that you already know the answer.—He has given our race free will, the power even to do what He does not want us to do. And, once again we have seen the tragic end result of free will when it is not channeled by love to do good.

"Our faith teaches us that there is an even more powerful fire than the evil one born of renegade atoms—it is the fire which our late Holy Father was referring to when he said that *'Christ carries in his body and on his soul all the weight of evil and all its destructive force. He burns and transforms evil through suffering, in the fire of His suffering love.'* Unite your great sufferings with His, so that, together, you may overcome this evil.

"Take comfort from the fact that Our Lord told His disciples that not a sparrow falls to the ground without it being noticed by the Father. Take comfort from the fact that Our Lord said that He was going to the Father to prepare a place for His followers, so that where He is, we may be also. Take comfort from the fact that Our Lord promised that anyone who believes in Him, even though he dies, shall have eternal life. *And so, my dear brothers and sisters in Christ, I assure you that however tragic your loss was, it is not final. The ultimate chapter has yet to be written by the One who, in eternity, makes all things new!*"

                    *   *   *

Msgr. Ireland was able to go off alone with Fr. Santorelli for a few minutes before lunch. "There's good news and bad news about our friend Zanier. They transferred him to the Gemelli as soon as possible after his surgery, to give him special police protection. So, he was far from the scene of the blast, but he hasn't improved. He's still in critical condition, in the ICU. I'm going to have the driver take me directly to the Gemelli from here.—Tony, if you have any special pull upstairs, *now's the time to use it!*"

"Apart from that," the Monsignor continued, "the concerns which caused the late Pope to send you here no longer apply— there's nobody left in authority who would be hostile to you—and I think the best use for your abilities would be in Rome, assisting what's left of the Curia. These are perilous times, and your ability to sense what is coming in the future would be a great help. *Tony—the Church needs you—and I need you!*"

"Oh, Monsignor," said the priest, look somewhat pained, "I don't know what to say.—You know how thrilled I've been to work with you—but, the Pope *did* send me here. Maybe this is where *God* wants me, though I admit I don't see why that would be.—Can you give me a little time to discern whether I should move again? I'll pray for a sign one way or the other."

"Have you considered that *He* may be calling you back to Rome, *through me?*" asked the prelate. "*That* may be the sign you're asking for."

"Yes, I know, it *might* be. I need to do some serious discern-ment, Monsignor, and I think there's someone here I should try to see about that. I've heard some talk now and then about an old friar, Padre Mario Lombardi, who knew Padre Pio. I know I haven't fully understood what they've said about him in their dialect, but I gather that although he's blind, he can read souls very clearly. So, I think I'll try to find him, and see what advice he can give me. I'll get back to you soon."

*   *   *

After lunch, before Msgr. Ireland departed, the Father Guardian took him aside and handed him a plastic bag containing a blood-stained bandage. "This," he said, "was worn by Fr. Santorelli. One like it worked a miracle in the *Casa*, where you were, curing the bone cancer of the aunt of one of our brothers.—I'm giving it to you because I expect you might be going to see Cardinal Zanier. If he's not recovering well, you might try this . . ."

*   *   *

That afternoon, when Fr. Santorelli walked out on the veranda of the friary, a spot where Padre Pio had often sat, a voice called out to him: *"Padre 'Tonio?—So there you are at last!"*

A friar whom he had not yet met sat alone in a rocking chair. "Come, sit with me if you have time," he said. "I am Padre Mario."

Padre Mario? He was just the man Fr. Santorelli wanted to meet. The old priest looked like he was in his late eighties, and he wore black glasses over his eyes.

"It's good to meet you, finally, Padre," replied Fr. Santorelli. "I was about to look for you, but I didn't know where to start. Of course I'll join you.—How in the world did you know it was me here?"

"It was the smell of roses."

Fr. Santorelli wondered if he had understood the old man correctly. "Roses?—There are no roses here I can see, Padre," he said, puzzled.

"No, but there are roses I can smell. I guessed it might be you."

That was something to think about later. For now, he had a question to ask. "I've been wanting to meet you especially to ask whether there was anything about the friary or your old companion, Padre Pio, that you think I should know? Perhaps something that would help me adjust to life here."

The rocker went back and forth, back and forth, as Padre Mario thought about the question. "That's a different request than I usually hear . . . Yes, perhaps there is something that would help you. It's about the gift of the stigmata, which I'm told you also have. Do you understand why *St.* Pio's stigmata became visible?"

Fr. Santorelli did not fail to note the gentle rebuke—the appellation 'Padre Pio' had been superseded by 'St. Pio,' even for his former companions. Rather than trying to guess the answer, Fr. Santorelli replied simply, "No. I'd like to hear about it, Padre."

Padre Mario stopped rocking and turned to Fr. Santorelli. "It had to do with *who and what* a priest is. *You know* of course that a priest is an *'alter Christus.'* But if the Faithful thought about a priest as being 'another Christ,' it was only in connection with him acting explicitly *in persona Christi* when consecrating the bread and wine at Mass. That mental picture was true as far as it went, but it didn't go far enough. Being 'another Christ' is not limited to that one particular action—as though, once a priest takes off his chasuble, he is no longer 'another Christ' but an ordinary man again. The limited conception of the priest and the priesthood which the Faithful had before St. Pio became known was wrong because it was inadequate."

Fr. Santorelli hung on every word, as Padre Mario continued. "So, God sent us St. Pio with wounds that proclaimed that *even when he wasn't celebrating Mass*, he was 'another Christ'—a living, sacramental sign of Christ's presence. The message of his wounds was this, Padre: *'Here is a true priest, one who wholly identifies himself with his Master, one who unceasingly offers himself as a victim to assist in the task of redeeming the world.'* I know that it hardly sounds possible to carry *that* cross, *yet that is what all of us priests are called to do*—and since *your* wounds are visible, they mark *you* out as a priest-victim and a sign to the rest of the world that the Lord lives! So, you must never be ashamed of those marks or be unwilling to bear them.—*You wouldn't be that way, would you?*"

"Padre Mario," replied the young priest, "I can tell you're an old fox! It's been a while since I've been able to go to confession. Would you mind hearing my confession now?"

The friar being agreeable, Fr. Santorelli reviewed very briefly his story, and then focused on his confrontation with the late Pope—the anger he had felt against the plotters and other malefactors in the episcopacy, and his presumptuousness in badgering Benedict XVIth to act against them, and finally, his complaint to the Lord.

When he was finished, Padre Mario said: "It seems to me that you have a problem with the sin of pride."

"I really don't think I'm *proud* that I bear the wounds of Christ, Padre, if that's what you're referring to," Fr. Santorelli said.

"No, that's not what I meant. Your pride lies in still wishing to be master of your own destiny—choosing how you would serve God, rather than letting Him choose that for you.—Padre 'Tonio, you are like a horse that tries to carry off its rider down this path, and then down that path—not responding to the reins. God will use you in His great plan, but you need to accept that you will render Him a greater service if you renounce your own plans and desires for your future. Offer them up as a sacrifice and let Him direct your course."

That was advice Fr. Santorelli didn't want to hear. "Sometimes I really don't see what course God is dictating to me, Padre. My mentor, Msgr. Ireland, has asked me to go back to Rome and assist him, as I was doing before the Holy Father sent me here. If I go, I *know* I'll be useful to God—but I can't see any use for me here. Shouldn't I see the hand of God in Monsignor's request now—just as God's hand was clearly involved in his asking me to leave my post in California?"

Padre Mario resumed his rocking for a while, as if he didn't realize there was a question pending. At last he stopped. "The difference, Padre, between when Monsignor asked you to come over to Italy and now, is that *now* you have the visible wounds of Christ. Help your mentor, if you will, long distance, *but remain here and suffer. Suffer for the love of the Lord. All else is secondary now. If the Lord wants anything further of you, He will let you know it.*"

"If I do as you propose, Padre," asked Fr. Santorelli, "do you think I'll finally attain the mystical union of my soul with God?—I've read so much about that goal, but I've never felt it happening."

Padre Mario was silent for a time. "For that to happen, Padre 'Tonio," he replied, "your love for Him must be much greater than it is now. Your soul is a crystal, but a cloudy one that resists the light that is bombarding it. The cloudiness will disappear only as *you* decrease, so that His light can penetrate you fully."

— 4 —

Rome

Richard Symmes, the Cardinal Archbishop of Philadelphia had taken off for Rome on Tuesday evening, having been fortuitously prevented by the flu from flying two days earlier, to attend the funeral. On Wednesday, he had worked his phone all day, contacting as many of the remaining Cardinals as he could. Several had been delayed in traveling, but most of them had not come to Rome for the conclave because they were over 80 years of age, the prescribed cut-off age for voting. He had also reached Msgr. Ireland by phone, and accepted the Monsignor's offer to act as a clearinghouse for the needed ecclesiastical reunion.

When the two of them met on Thursday, Msgr. Ireland gave Cardinal Symmes an extensive briefing on all that had taken place in the previous two months, including his visit to Cardinal Zanier the evening before in the ICU at the Gemelli.

"They asked me to give him Viaticum, which I did. And, I did something else, which I would ask you to keep confidential.—I slipped a plastic bag containing a bandage from Fr. Santorelli's wounds under his sheet. A brother at San Giovanni Rotondo had already obtained a medical miracle by using them . . . " Msgr. Ireland let the thought trail off, in embarrassment.

Since they wanted to assess whether Cardinal Zanier might recover sufficiently to be considered as a candidate for Pope, they decided to pay him a visit together. The police, now viewing cardinals as an endangered species, provided a car to take them to the Gemelli. They found Cardinal Zanier still in the ICU, but ready to be transferred to a private room. He was doing much better—the fever and the other signs of infection had left him Wednesday night, and while he was still very weak, he definitely was on the mend. The hospital staff had kept from him knowledge of what had happened at the Vatican on Monday, expecting that Msgr. Ireland could best give him the sad news when he thought it appropriate.

Cardinal Zanier greeted the Monsignor as warmly as he was able to, propped up in bed with tubes still in him. He would have liked to discuss the fate that had befallen the two of them on the street, but he felt constrained from doing so by the presence of Cardinal Symmes, whom he was very surprised to see.

"Eminence! shouldn't you be in the conclave now?" he asked. "Don't tell me it's over already?"

Rather than answer, Cardinal Symmes looked at his companion. Msgr. Ireland drew up a chair close to Cardinal Zanier's hospital bed, and introduced the subject hesitatingly.

"While you were in intensive care, Eminence, our world was totally altered.—*Totally and irrevocably.*"

"By your faces, I gather it was not for the better. Please tell me—I can take it."

"There's no easy way to lead into this, Eminence," said Msgr. Ireland, "so I'll tell you straight out—*the Vatican is no more ... Gone ... All of it ... St. Peter's too, and everybody who was there for the funeral on Monday.*"

"*No! ...* How can that be?" Zanier asked. "Is the world at war?"

"It was an atom bomb. Someone smuggled one in. It went off right next to St. Peter's," the Monsignor replied. "The authorities think as many as two hundred thousand died—they weren't able to make a count because there were no bodies of those close in. Many of the others were buried in mass graves ... Then, the criminals, the *Mafia*, attacked the City in force."

"*Oh my God! ...* What about Cardinal Latoya?"

"Cardinal Latoya? Gone, with all the other cardinals, and the bishops, and the dignitaries who were there. The President and Prime Minister of Italy, the Vice President of my own country. All gone. May their souls rest in peace ... "

"Who did this?" Cardinal Zanier asked.

"Al Qaeda claimed responsibility, but no one knows for sure. Apart from the Vatican, the City of Rome was spared. It wasn't an attack on Italy. So, the question is who would want to stamp out the Church. All the commentators say it must have been Islamic jihadists."

Large tears rolled down Zanier's face, and he had to stifle a sob.

"My village—after independence was declared, the rebels came one day without warning, out of the jungle. They burned our huts. They started shooting people, and hacking them to pieces with their machetes. I was small. They didn't notice me as I ran into the jungle ... Now it's happened to my home and my family here ..."

He wept quietly, while Msgr. Ireland held his hand. He and Cardinal Symmes both spoke words of consolation, which did not ease the pain he felt, a deeper pain than had been caused by the assassin's knife.

*   *   *

Still progressing well the following day, Cardinal Zanier suggested to Cardinal Symmes the need for holding the papal conclave as soon as possible, and they decided to set it to begin on the following Tuesday, with all the living cardinals invited to attend, irrespective of their age. The location chosen was the Lateran Palace, for in the centuries before the Popes went into exile in Avignon, France, and briefly after their return, the Lateran Palace was where they lived, and the attached basilica was the cathedral church of the Bishop of Rome. That distinction still pertained to it, even though the Popes had made the Apostolic Palace at St. Peter's their home since the 1500's and the basilica at the Vatican had far eclipsed St. John Lateran as a pilgrimage site.

— 5 —

Rome

In keeping with the grieving mood of the city, there was no public fanfare attendant upon the opening of the conclave. Scenes from the past, when the pious and the curious would stand for hours in St. Peter's Square waiting to see whether the smoke which emerged from ballots being burned after each vote of the cardinal-electors was white or black, were just that—scenes from the past. The Square itself was no more, and there was no crowd at the location where the cardinals now met.

The basilica was closed to the public for the conclave, and the cardinals gathered there in the apse, near the exquisite gothic canopy over the papal altar, which was located at the crossing of the nave and transept. The gilded baldacchino, dating back seven centuries, bore comparison in magnificence with Bernini's monumental bronze one over the tomb of St. Peter, destroyed by the bomb. On an upper level, behind a gilt metal grille, it held reliquaries with fragments of the skulls of St. Peter and St. Paul. The interior decorations of the worship space in St. John Lateran were so magnificent that, in its walls, and ceilings, and floors, it was in no wise inferior to what had been the basilica of St. Peter's.

At the end of the apse, a series of marble steps led up to the marble *cathedra*, the chair of the Bishop of Rome, which one of them would succeed to after the election. Above it was a magnificent mosaic. In the vault, against a gold background, there were depicted the Virgin Mary, and Sts. Peter and Paul, John the Baptist and John the Evangelist, and Andrew. And above them was Christ's face, surrounded by angels, looked down upon the Holy Spirit and a jeweled cross from which life-giving waters flowed.

After the 22 cardinals had concelebrated Mass to invoke the Holy Spirit's guidance in choosing a new leader for the Church, they withdrew into the Lateran Palace through two immense doors on the north side of the basilica. The Palace, in the shape of a square with a square courtyard within it, was as large in scale as the basilica. The fourth floor, almost invisible from the outside, was being used by Caritas International, while the third floor was used for offices of the Diocese of Rome. Those floors had been closed for the conclave, and provision had been made to house the cardinals there if the conclave lasted more than one day. The actual meeting area was on the second floor, a wing of a museum corridor populated with busts and portraits of former Popes and eminent cardinals. Light streamed in through the floor to ceiling windows facing the courtyard, supplemented by the lighting designed to show off the frescoes on the barrel-vaulted ceiling.

Most of the procedures which had been formulated in the Apostolic Constitution *Universi Dominici Gregis* to regulate a conclave of over a hundred electors within the Vatican's precincts were omitted, though oaths were taken by the electors as a whole, and by the cardinals appointed to count written ballots. By general agreement, each cardinal was allotted 10 minutes to address the others, stating what challenges he foresaw for the Church, and how he thought they should be addressed. Although the cardinals came from many different countries and had had only limited exposure to one another previously, the unusual circumstances which brought them together had a unifying effect on their thinking about the Church in the changed world.

When it was Cardinal Zanier's turn, he asked their indulgence to speak at greater length, so that he could first relate the events which had occurred at Garabandal and later in Rome, including what Fr. Santorelli had reported that the Lord had told him, and also the seven parts of the message for the late Pope—those fulfilled and those still to be carried out.

They then broke for lunch, which had been set for them outdoors in the Vassalletto Cloister, a peaceful green spot, enclosed by magnificent stonework, at the end of the left aisle of the basilica.

After lunch, they went back into the basilica for the voting. They sat in the chancel area by the papal altar, which they approached one by one with a written ballot in hand. At the altar, before a cardinal placed his ballot on a silver plate in full view of the others, he spoke out loud the prescribed oath: '*I call as my witness Christ the Lord who will be my judge, that my vote is given to the one who before God I think should be elected.*'

Cardinal Zanier was elected by more than the required two-thirds vote on the first ballot, and he chose as his papal name one taken by six Popes before him, that of Paul. He asked them to withhold the news of the election for a short time until they finished some business which he also wanted to have covered in the public announcement.

"My brothers," said the new Pope, "I do not propose at this time to reconstitute the administrative structure of the Church as it was prior to the explosion. We have a window of opportunity to consider whether the Curial congregations, the Pontifical Commissions and Councils, and the other institutions that have grown up over the centuries are the best way to govern the Church in these times. Out of necessity and choice, I hope I can play a role more akin to that of the first Peter, whose primary roles were evangelizing and acting as the touchstone of unity for the particular churches spread throughout the world."

Paul VIIth was surprised and pleased when a number of the cardinals immediately expressed their approval of that audacious proposal, by calling out "Si!" or "Placet!" or clapping.

He continued, "I see a need for far greater emphasis on evangelization—in all countries—than has existed for many years, and to that end, I would like to create new cardinals who would make that their priority. Also, I need two new cardinals immediately to assist me. One to be my deputy in handling administrative matters, and the other to take charge of maintaining the Faith. For those posts, I propose to name Archbishop Tedesco, who has done an outstanding job witnessing to Christ as the Papal nuncio in Brussels, and Msgr. Ireland, who worked very closely with our late Holy Father in responding to the visions—to say nothing of his shedding his own blood in defending me."

These proposals also met with acclaim, and the assembled cardinals suggested other names acceptable to the Pope for elevation to the cardinalate. As the result of that discussion, a total of 10 more new cardinals were named and their territories assigned. Having done a good day's work, the newly elected Pope and the cardinals went outside to where the news media had been waiting.

"Habemas Papam," the joyful, traditional words—"We have a Pope"—were spoken by the senior Cardinal deacon, who then introduced to the world Pope Paul VIIth. The members of the media showed their excitement at the choice. He was a churchman whom they had grown to admire over the past weeks, one who was qualified from every standpoint to lead the Church in very troubled times. They listened respectfully as he gave his first papal address.

"My brothers and sisters in the city and in the world, I greet you with joy in this great time of grace. The world is still beset by dangers, and evil men still plot wars and persecutions, but *the Holy Spirit is more visibly at work than He has ever been since the time of Pentecost!*"

"You are all familiar with paintings of that great event, showing tongues of flame above the heads of the Blessed Mother and the Apostles. *Those tongues of flame are even now above your heads, awaiting being welcomed, so that they may enter into you and set you on fire!*"

"Almighty God has spoken powerfully and plainly through the visions of the Warning. As St. Paul told the citizens of Athens, 'God has overlooked the times of ignorance, but now He demands that all people everywhere repent because He has established a day on which He will 'judge the world with justice' through a man He has appointed, and He has provided confirmation for all by raising him from the dead.'"

"*The primary task now of Christians everywhere is evangelization.* It is for that reason that I have taken the name of the great evangelist, St. Paul. The harvest is ripe, but souls, unlike wheat, cannot be gathered up by machines—human workers are needed to go out into the fields and bring the crop of souls into God's barns, the Christian churches. And we earnestly beseech the governments of countries around the world to provide protection to the men and women who will be bearing the Good News to people who have lived in darkness."

"I look forward to serving as your chief shepherd, and I wish that all of the Faithful might have an especially meaningful celebration of Holy Week this year, for we have seen Christ crucified again in our midst. And now I bless you in the name of the Father, and of the Son, and of the Holy Spirit. Amen."

*   *   *

Later that day, the new Pope phoned Fr. Santorelli. "Father! I'm calling to thank you for making this day possible. How does it feel to have a Pope in your debt?"

"I'm *absolutely overjoyed* with this turn of events, Holiness!" Fr. Santorelli replied. "After all the harm done to the Church in recent days, your election is like a rainbow in the sky—a miracle."

"Speaking of miracles," said the Pope, "I've been reflecting on my narrow escape, and comparing it to that of John Paul II, when an assassin tried to kill him in the Square. The Pope gave the Blessed Virgin Mary the credit for his survival. He said, 'One hand fired, and another hand guided the bullet' . . . I feel the same way, Father. It's hard not to think that the hand of our Blessed Mother guided the knife of that thug away from my heart . . . "

"Not just hard, Holiness—impossible!" Fr. Santorelli replied.

The Pope paused before raising a new topic. "Now that the old order has changed, Father, do you have any plans for yourself? Are you content to stay there at the friary? In which case, would you like me to call the Father Guardian and ask him to continue to extend his hospitality to you? Or, would you like an assignment here in Rome?"

"You're kind to offer that, Holiness, and I thank you for it," Fr. Santorelli said, "but, for once in my life, I'm trying *not* to make plans of my own. I'm just waiting to see what will develop—and if nothing does, that will be O.K. too.—Well," he added, "at least I'll give it a try."

His honesty brought a laugh from the Pope.

"In any event," said the priest, "I promise to pray every day that your pontificate will be gloriously successful!"

Their conversation might have ended on that note, without any shadow falling across the happy occasion, but Fr. Santorelli's last remark triggered a memory, and then a question. *"I'm sure you know the prophecies of Malachy.—What do you make of the one for my pontificate?"*

Fr. Santorelli understood just what a momentous question the Pope was asking him. *Saint* Malachy was an intriguing figure in the Church, now more so than ever, nine hundred years after his death. There was no doubt as to his sanctity—he had been the Primate of Armagh, in Ireland. However, his memory was caught up in contention between those who gave ready credence to mystical events and those who did not. It was all due to what he apparently wrote about the succession of Popes to come, from his own time down through the ages. Those writings were not discovered until four hundred years after his death, so some argued that they were written much later and spuriously attributed to him. In any event, the Latin text had undeniably existed since 1559—itself an impressive antiquity.

Malachy did not attempt to list the given names of the future Popes, nor the formal names they would assume; rather he provided short descriptions of them or their reigns. Scholars were amused and often amazed at the substantial correspondence between the prophecies and the facts which were known about the successors to St. Peter. The public bandied these matters about at the time of each Papal election, and even the highest ecclesiastics themselves were not above acknowledging an interest in them.

The Pope corresponding to Pius XII had been described with the phrase *"Pastor Angelicus,"* and that was what he was to the many he saved from extermination in World War II. When he died and it was time for the cardinals to choose his successor, a joke made the rounds that one of their American colleagues had chartered a boat, loaded sheep on it, and had it motor up and down the Tiber River—all in apparent fulfillment of the prophecy that the Pope to be chosen would match the description *"Pastor et Nauta."* In his autobiography, America's great televangelist Bishop Fulton J. Sheen wrote about his first private audience with Pius XIIth's successor, John XXIII. The latter had asked him if he knew what Malachy had written of him. When Bishop Sheen correctly recited it, the former Cardinal Roncalli, who had been the Patriarch of Venice, said "That is what I was in Venice"—a shepherd as head of the diocese, and a sailor, because of Venice's waterways. And John XXIII had presented him with a small silver gondola.

Then came Paul VI, whose armorial bearings, which showed three fleurs-de-lis, corresponded to the prophecy *"Flos Florum"* (flower of flowers), John Paul I, whose incredibly short reign of about a month seemed to fit the prophecy *"De Medietate Lunae"* (of the half moon), John Paul II whose tireless papal travels around the world fulfilled the prophecy *"De Labore Solis"* (from the labors of the sun), and Benedict XVI, described as *"Gloria Olivae"* (the glory of the olive). The religious Order of St. Benedict had long speculated that this Pope would come from their order, because it is also known as the Olivetans. Although Joseph Ratzinger was not a Benedictine, he did take the name of their founder and proclaim a mission to return Europe to its Christian roots, so greatly nurtured by St. Benedict.

The concern in the mind of the new Pope was that the prophecies of Malachy stretching over perhaps nine centuries were now at an end—the last one being the one applicable to himself. It was an ominous one:

PETRUS ROMANUS

In the final persecution of the Holy Roman Church there will reign Peter the Roman, who will feed his flock among many tribulations; after which the seven-hilled city will be destroyed and the dreadful Judge will judge the people.

Fr. Santorelli carefully considered his response to the Pope's question. With a sigh, he said, "I have two countervailing thoughts, one positive and one negative. Would you like both of them, and if so, in which order?"

"Let's end on a positive note, Father," said the Pope. "Tell me the bad news first."

"I've given a lot of thought to the disaster that took place at the Vatican, and I've concluded that there is no realistic possibility of demonstrating to the Muslim terrorists that they are guilty of a grave sin against God in conducting their jihad. Therefore, the ecumenical dialogue between Christianity and Islam strikes me as an exercise in futility, and I believe that the inherent conflict between Christianity and Islam will inevitably lead to an all-out religious war, unless there is a divine intervention that converts the Muslims to Christianity."

When the Holy Father collected himself, he said with a sigh. "I'm ready for your good thoughts, Father. What might they be?"

"Holiness, it just may be that the calamity foreseen by Malachy has already occurred—although that doesn't seem to fit with the Garabandal prophecy. We've been spared seeing the whole seven-hilled city destroyed, but the ecclesiastic heart of it was wiped out, and hundreds of thousands of people have gone to meet the dreadful Judge."

The Pope had one more question for Fr. Santorelli. "Do you have *any* idea why Malachy's prophecies ended with my pontificate, nine hundred years later, other than that they had to end at some point in time?"

Fr. Santorelli took a moment before answering that one. "Possibly I do, Holiness, this time emphasizing the Garabandal prophecy. The visionaries seemed to think that its fulfillment would mark the end of an age. As I told my mentor, that was not to be the end of time, but the end of some period in our history. I'd suggest that you ask our friend *Cardinal* Ireland for his thoughts. He taught a course in eschatology that might shed some light on the question you ask."

"All right, Father, I'll follow up with him. Again, you have my lasting thanks and blessing for all you've done for me and the Church."

— 6 —

San Giovanni Rotondo

The day after the conclave, the Father Guardian invited Fr. Santorelli in for a talk in his office. They shared each other's happiness at the selection of Cardinal Zanier as Pope, and then took up what the Father Guardian had on his mind. "You've been here about a month, Father," he said, "but I've hardly had a chance to talk to you about how you feel you're fitting in with us, and what you see yourself doing in the future."

The question was asked in a friendly tone, and Fr. Santorelli took it that way. It was understandable that the Father Guardian might be apprehensive about the significant role that his guest had continued to play regarding events in Rome, an involvement which had served to disconnect him from the life of the friary.

"As far as fitting in, Padre," he replied, "I'm happy here, and I'm still grateful to you for taking me in without hesitation or strings attached. These have been an extraordinary few weeks in my life, and I apologize if I've upset anyone's settled routine. As to your question about what I foresee for myself, the fact is that I'm totally in the dark. I've never been able to anticipate my own situation correctly."

Fr. Santorelli gave his host a brief summary of his career, concluding with an admission: "In my prayers, I keep sending up to God elaborate blueprints of the future I think would be best—but He keeps sending my blueprints back down to me in tiny pieces, like confetti!"

They had a good laugh together. "God can do that to our plans, can't He?" said the Father Guardian, knowingly.

"As for what comes next," Fr. Santorelli continued, "two holy priests, one at the Vatican, and one right here, have told me in no uncertain terms that my vocation is to be a Suffering Servant. On the other hand, Msgr. Ireland recently asked me to return to Rome and assist him with the affairs of the Curia. And this afternoon I had a long talk by phone with our new Holy Father, in which he too extended an invitation to go back there. I didn't give him an answer, thinking I would first ask the Lord for a sign. Well, I didn't get one from Him, but just before you sent for me I got one from the other side. I was in the garden out back when the Devil or one of his minions appeared, *impersonating you*, and telling me I wasn't wanted here and I ought to go back to Rome. So, I figure that if that's what the *Devil* wants me to do, *God* must want the opposite."

"That's quite a story!" said the Father Guardian. "I don't know how it happens, but you have more unusual spiritual encounters in a few weeks than most of us have in a lifetime . . . "

"Believe me, Padre—I'm not out there seeking them!" the priest replied. "In any event, if I do stay here long term, I think I'd feel strange remaining a diocesan priest incardinated in Rome. I wonder if I should be exploring whether I have a late vocation in your Order.—Which brings to mind a number of questions, like, how long does it take to become a Capuchin? And, would I have to grow a beard?"

The Father Guardian smiled at the latter question. "Beards are optional here, but very traditional. All of us *love* having a beard—as did St. Pio. As to how long it takes to become a Capuchin, our novitiate is one year, and then for three years, one takes one-year vows. It doesn't sound long, but *I have to stress that the important thing is to feel a vocation as a Capuchin.* A person either has that conviction or he doesn't—and given your vocational decision many years ago to become a diocesan priest rather than an order priest, my *guess* is that our Order is *not* for you. But," he said, not unkindly, "I wouldn't want to stand in the way of the workings of the Spirit.

"And, if you're determined to discern the right course, why don't you try to get a better feel for our life by moving out of the guest house and into a cell in the friary? A few are vacant right now. Also, Father, I've observed that you usually only eat breakfast, but the midday and supper meals are times when we gather as a community, and I think it would be good if you could make it a point to join us then, as well as for morning and night prayers."

"I'll be glad to do that, Padre," said the priest. "And I suspect I'd attract less attention as I went around the friary if I didn't dress in my black clerical garb.—Would you think it improper if I wore a Capuchin robe around here?"

The Padre Guardian pondered the idea. "Well, maybe a bit," he allowed. "But, I'll discuss it with my superiors, and under the circumstances, I think they'll approve. For the time being, feel free to put one on if the Spirit moves you."

Fr. Santorelli happily began to carry out the new plan, but his guess about his future was, as usual, not very good. *A cloud was about to shower down blue confetti upon him.*

Jerusalem

That same day, the editors of the Jerusalem Post reluctantly published a major exposé of government activity, even though they foresaw that the appearance of the story could have seriously negative consequences for the State of Israel. They did so only because the project they had uncovered was certain to touch off a war if it was attempted.

The newspaper had learned of Prime Minister Hertzel's promise of support for an ultraorthodox plan to construct the *Third Temple*, at long last.

The *First Temple* had been built by King Solomon on Mt. Moriah, a location considered sacred by the Jews because it was there that Abraham had erected an altar to sacrifice his only son, Isaac, as commanded by God. That Temple had been destroyed by the Babylonians. The so-called *Second Temple* was built on the same site centuries later by the Jewish King Herod the Great. It was the one which Jesus worshipped in and the Romans destroyed in 70 A.D. The orthodox and ultraorthodox had long desired the construction of a *Third Temple*—which could not be built anywhere else. Indeed, it had to be located precisely where its predecessors were, so that the most sacred area within it, the "Holy of Holies," where the Ark of the Covenant once rested, would be exactly where it had first been positioned by Solomon.

What made the project so explosive was that, in order to carry it out, it would be necessary to raze the Dome of the Rock—an immense, golden-domed seventh century Muslim structure on the Temple Mount—and the nearby Al Aqsa mosque. When ultranationalists had concocted a plot many years before to blow up the Dome, the government had cracked down hard. Yet here it was condoning the same idea now, for reasons of domestic politics!

The outrage throughout the Muslim world at learning of the plan was instantaneous. Sunnis and Shiites were united on this: if the Israelis went ahead, there would be war! Naturally, an emergency session of the U.N. Security Council was called, to force the Israelis to retreat.

— 7 —

Qom, Iran

At the United Nations, on Thursday morning, all the Security Council member nations—including the United States—voted to condemn Israel. The vote was greeted with joy by Iran's Supreme Leader, for it appeared to show that Israel had antagonized its only protector, the United States, and was now all alone in the world. It was a propitious time for Iran to strike!

Henry Kissinger, perhaps the most insightful Secretary of State in American history, once commented that "Iran has to make a decision whether it wants to be a *nation* or a *cause*." His point was that nations usually act in their national interest, while causes can be irrational, unmanageable, and even inimical to the survival of the nation which engages in one. But Iran had remained ambivalent about which it was. It was not just a 'republic', but an 'Islamic republic', and its Chief of State was also the leader of the Islamic Revolution, a cause which it sought to export to other countries against their will.

Under the Supreme Leader, Iran had pursued a three part military strategy: 1) destabilize the region with jihadist guerilla actions; 2) develop atomic weapons; and 3) develop ballistic missiles which could deliver atomic weapons at great distances. Work had proceeded well on the latter two fronts, despite concerns expressed by many nations which, collectively, were irresolute about stopping Iran. Iran's own scientists and engineers were greatly helped by technology supplied by the Chinese and North Korean regimes, both of which needed money and had no concern for whatever evil the Iranians might cause in someone else's backyard. The missiles, under the control of a special Revolutionary Guard air force (known by the acronym AFAGIR), had long been capable of reaching Israel with a conventional payload.

Success had recently come to the project of mating atomic warheads with the missiles, and the Supreme Leader finally felt confident that he could direct a fatal strike at Israel—provided that his missiles got off the ground. The Iranians had not developed hardened sites like the ones the Americans and Russians had, and so their missiles were vulnerable to a pre-emptive first strike by the Israelis. The only way to get around this vulnerability was to strike first.

Three factors were now added to the equation. The first was that there was reason to believe that the world would not act against Iran if it attacked Israel—for neither Italy nor its allies showed any interest in probing into who had caused the atomic explosion in Rome. The second was American anger at Israel, possibly compromising the American military protective shield. It was the third factor, though, which was decisive—leaked accounts in the Israeli press that the Government was considering launching a pre-emptive strike of its own now that Iran was building a force of nuclear tipped Sajjil-2 medium range ballistic missiles.

Now seemed a propitious time to carry out a policy goal long publicly articulated—*the destruction of Israel*. To that end, the Supreme Leader approved a plan for a massive atomic strike against Haifa, Tel Aviv, Netanya, and the Israeli base near Zechariah—Jerusalem, the seeming prime target, had to be spared, so that the Mahdī could one day rule from there. The Supreme Leader chose the date of the 14th of Farvardīn, the eve of the Jewish Passover, thinking that a strike then might catch the Israeli defenders off celebrating. And, as a first test of the readiness of the AFAGIR's rockets for that "final solution," he ordered that several firings of Sajjils be conducted two days later, on Saturday, to celebrate New Year's Day in Iran.

— 8 —

Jerusalem

The adverse vote in the U.N. Security Council was bad enough, but what set the Prime Minister reeling was what he learned in an urgent meeting called by the heads of the Mossad and the Shin Bet on Friday morning.

The only Mossad mole in Iran's defense establishment had just made his first ever report. There could have been no more chilling news: the Supreme Leader had authorized a strike against Israel with nuclear missiles on the eve of Passover.

The electronic report had been picked up by an Israeli satellite—and likely by the Iranians too. The sender was probably even then fleeing for his life, if he had not already been caught. In any event, there was no way that he could be queried as to his source or the exact details of what he had learned.

"How do we know the message is really from your agent?" the Prime Minister demanded of Director Ereli.

"It used code words only he had. Even if the Iranians had found him out and tortured the code out of him, I'm sure *they* wouldn't have sent us *this message.*"

"Do you think it's for real?"

"Why would he make up such a thing?" Ereli asked. "*The fact that the Iranians nuked the Vatican tells me that they're willing to use their atomic weapons—unlike every other country, including ours.* Besides, the date chosen makes sense—they think they'll catch us off guard then."

They knew exactly what he was referring to: in 1973, Egypt and Syria had attacked Israel on Yom Kippur, the Jewish High Holy Day, and had caught the Israeli defense establishment by surprise. Disaster had only narrowly been averted.

"No," said the Prime Minister, "I wasn't questioning the message in that way. I meant, are you sure our source is in a position to know this? As opposed to just hearing a rumor? He didn't send any message about Hashemi, you know . . ."

"He's in a different unit of the Revolutionary Guards than the Qods Force. Our man is in their special Air Force—they operate the missiles. He wouldn't have known about the suitcase bomb operation. Sending this message risked his life, so I think we have to accept it as accurate and go from there."

"That's what I was afraid you'd say. I'll arrange a conference call with the Defense Minister and the service heads." They were located at the headquarters of the Israel Defense Forces in Camp Rabin, which was within HaKirya, an area in central Tel Aviv.

When the group was all on line, after the Mossad Director had related the agent's message, the Prime Minister asked, "*If we go on the assumption that the message is correct, do we have any alternative other than striking first?*"

"If the Air Force could assure us that our missile defense system is a hundred percent effective, I suppose we could shoot their missiles down and figure out then what to do next," replied the Defense Minister.

"You know I can't guarantee that," said the Air Force chief, "and if they got lucky and landed a big one on our Sdot Micha base, that might take out a real chunk of our retaliatory force."

The Prime Minister challenged him: "I thought the Jerichos there were hardened."

"We have three squadrons in total. Many are. Others are only sheltered in rock caves and tunnels. They're all defended by Patriots in close, but I don't know if we can count on the Patriots if the Americans aren't with us."

"You mean, if we pre-empt, they might actually not arm the Patriots—leaving us vulnerable to retaliation?" the Prime Minister asked.

The Defense Minister had a caution. "I'm afraid that may be the case. *Whether we strike first or second, the Patriots are going to be necessary at short range if the Iranian missiles get past our Arrows. I don't see any way out of sharing this intelligence immediately with the Americans and finding out, if we can, the extent to which they'll help us deal with Iran . . .*"

Since no one objected to that recommendation, the Prime Minister said he would have the Israeli Ambassador ask for an emergency audience with the U.S. Secretary of State. And, at the suggestion of the Defense Minister, he authorized the immediate recall of all essential reservists, and the updating of existing contingency plans for a first or retaliatory strike on Iran as early as the following day.

"Do you want to work from your office over here for the time being?" the Prime Minister was asked.

"It probably would be a good idea for me to move sometime next week," he responded. "We've still got two weeks to go before Passover, and I have meetings over here over the next few days. But, line up everything for me at your place, including the bunker—we might really need to use it this time ... "

Washington, D.C.

Secretary of State Howe was still annoyed with the Israelis for having caused him to be tied up all Thursday morning at the U.N. on account of their crazy Temple Mount scheme. They must have known it would bring down the wrath of a united Muslim world—were they counting on God to protect them, no matter how reckless their policies were? Nevertheless, he granted the Israeli Ambassador's request for an urgent meeting in Washington on Friday afternoon, presumably to discuss Israel's consternation at America's support for the resolution passed by the Security Council.

He was shocked when the Ambassador divulged the actual purpose of his visit: to discuss the message the Israelis had received from their mole in the Iranian Revolutionary Guards. His first thought was that the communication was fabricated—a put-up job, to justify an Israeli pre-emptive strike. If so, then the meeting had been called for the purpose of tricking him into condoning what the Israelis wanted to do.

"*Is your Government contemplating a first strike on Iran?*" he asked the Israeli Ambassador outright. Better to get that issue openly on the table, so that no one had an opportunity later to claim that he had approved any such action implicitly.

The Israeli Ambassador wouldn't have dreamed of answering that question. "My Government has contingency plans for every circumstances imaginable. Of course, that is one of many *possible* actions we would consider, depending on future events. What we actually will do will depend on many factors, including what help our allies are willing to render in our defense.—Obviously, Mr.

Secretary, we're vitally interested if your people have picked up any intel that would support or contradict this message."

"None that they've told me about," replied the Secretary, quickly.

Even though the Secretary seemed to be genuinely taken aback by the message, the Ambassador only half believed his answer. After all, the Americans had not passed on to Israel what they knew about Hashemi and his suitcase bomb mission.

Secretary Howe followed up his denial with a strong statement. "I would ask you to tell your Government, Mr. Ambassador, that my Government would find it *unacceptable* if your Government launched a pre-emptive strike, especially on the basis of such *scant* intelligence. We have been trying ever since your country was born to prevent a cataclysmic war in your region, and so far we've succeeded. If you launch missiles at Iran, the war you start would certainly wipe out tens of millions of people, and perhaps a number of countries—*quite likely including your own.*

"We will do nothing to encourage such a first strike by your Government. Consider yourselves very fortunate that we will make the Patriot batteries available to defend your country against a first strike by another country—but only in that case. We will not make them available if Israel strikes first—is that clear?"

That was indeed clear . . . and exactly what the Israeli military feared was the U.S. position. The Ambassador tried to squeeze some concession out of the Secretary of State. "*Do you expect us to be sitting ducks, Mr. Secretary? Have there not been situations where the U.S. has itself launched a pre-emptive strike?*"

"Yes, and we have later regretted doing so, Mr. Ambassador. *And, I would hardly call Israel a sitting duck behind its Aegis-Arrow-Patriot missile defense shield, especially against an enemy untested in such warfare.* Also, I trust that you will not forget that any war with atomic weapons would engender immense problems of aid to surviving populations and the physical reconstruction of what remained of Israel. And only the United States would consider helping you with that—at least if your country had been struck first."

That was the end of the audience, one which the Ambassador would describe in his message to the Israeli Foreign Secretary as a "full and frank exchange of views," diplomatic language for total disagreement.

As soon as the Ambassador left the Secretary's office, the information he had brought was shared with the entire U.S. intelligence community and the Department of Defense. The operations officer for the Joint Chiefs of Staff thought the Iranian threat was more real than the State Department believed it was, and so he encouraged the Chief of Naval Operations to take immediate action. The CNO decided that it was a propitious time to send a cruiser and a destroyer armed with Aegis antimissile missiles, then cruising in the Mediterranean south of Cyprus, to stations just off the Israeli coast, one near Haifa and one near Tel Aviv—full speed ahead. The CNO also alerted the naval task force in the Persian Gulf, not far from the coast of Iran, which included half a dozen ships with the Aegis Weapon System. The orders sent to them and the Patriot batteries laid out in detail the terms of engagement for the U.S. units, based upon different scenarios as to which party was pre-empting and which was retaliating.

*   *   *

A worried White House Chief of Staff consulted with Mel Lawton, the Secretary of Defense. The question in Bernie Cohen's mind was whether the Israelis would actually launch a pre-emptive attack, in response to the supposed intelligence from their mole in Iran. Lawton was firmly of the opinion they would not.

"Israel's problem is that Iran is far too big a country and has too many targets for any sort of a surgical strike. Israel was able to take out Syria's nuclear reactor years ago, because the target was only one site. Iran has nuclear facilities and military bases all over the country, some of them hardened, some of them in populated areas. The only way Israel could make itself safe from Iran would be to destroy the whole country with atomic weapons, making it impossible for Iran to rebuild and rearm. I very much doubt that the Israelis have the capability of doing that without sustaining unacceptable retaliation in the process. Moreover, I'm sure that if they pre-empted, the world community wouldn't stand for it—and they know that. So, they have no choice but to live day to day at the mercy of that crazy Grand Ayatollah."

"And up to right now," he continued, "we've figured that Iran would not initiate a war with Israel by a direct attack. We've assumed that when it was ready to make things hotter for Israel, it would foment a proxy war, probably by giving Syria weapons which would pose a threat to Israel's ability to protect itself. I'm not talking nukes, you understand—I'm talking long range missiles, and anti-aircraft and anti-ship missiles. Supplying those armaments in quantity probably would draw a major attack by Israel, making *it* appear to be the aggressor, and opening the way for Syria's ally Iran to retaliate with atomic bombs against Israel. That's not a pleasant prospect, but it's one we might be able to choke off because it would develop in stages over time. The prospect you've just hit me with—a nuclear strike out of the blue—is much more worrisome. At the moment, I don't have any advice to give you."

"What do you think the odds are that he'll give the order to attack?" asked the Chief of Staff.

"Bernie," replied the Secretary of Defense, "nobody who's in his right mind would give odds on what a man who *isn't* in his right mind will do."

— 9 —

Jerusalem
March 21, 2015 Anno Domini; 1 Farvardīn 1394 Anno Persico

The Israeli Air Force reservists who had been called back to duty unexpectedly on Friday were still grumbling about it. They had long been giving up one day a week for military training, and they were already fully proficient in the American X-band radar located in the Negev desert, which they were counting on to give Israel several minutes warning of an Iranian rocket attack. They had also participated in firing the Arrow II interceptor missiles made by Boeing and an Israeli manufacturer, in simulated exercises. The reservists knew that international relations were very tense at the moment, but they *always* were tense for the Israelis—and these men and women were given no reason why they had been unexpectedly called away from their families and livelihood for an indefinite period.

Early that morning, the Iranian Minister of Defence issued a press release that the Air Force of the Army of the Guardians of the Islamic Revolution (AFAGIR) would be conducting test firings of missiles, as part of the Iranian celebration of Nowrūz, the Iranian New Year's Day. The Israelis knew that Nowrūz was a great holiday in the Persian calendar—traditionally a time for wearing new clothes, eating a meal of rice with green herbs served with fish, visiting members of the family and friends, and, of course, for the women, the occasion of spring cleaning. But missile firings??? That was something that was done on Revolution Day, which had come and gone over a month ago.

There was no hint from the Iranians that they would be conducting anything more than routine tests. However, in light of what the Israelis had learned from their mole, their Air Defense people anxiously monitored the pictures from their two Ofek 8 spy satellites, which took turns crossing over Iran every thirty minutes. Soon, satellite pictures showed the set-up preparations at Semnan, Iran's space center, for a solid-fueled Sajjil-2 rocket. It had a range of 1,200 miles, more than enough to target Israel. This one was fired, but not in their direction.

The success of the launch, and assurances of success from his generals, who were afraid *not* to give the Supreme Leader assurances, now emboldened him to give the orders for an immediate nuclear attack on the three large cities of Israel and its missile base previously marked out as targets for a strike on the eve of Passover.

Two hours later, a dozen more rockets were simultaneously readied for launch, from different locations in Iran. To the surprise of those watching the pictures from space, these were all fired off within a five minute period. Some of the launches were first picked up by the S-band SPY-1 radars on board U.S. Navy ships in the Persian Gulf. Shortly thereafter came the alarm from the X-band radar in Israel. *That was the first notice the Israelis had that missiles were heading straight for them!!!*

As soon as the Iranian IRBM's were within range, the first flights of Arrows, and the Aegis SM-3 anti-missile missiles from the ships off Israel's coast, were launched. They were tasked with intercepting the Sajjils in the high stratosphere, which they did with considerable success—blasting nine of them out of the sky by exploding close to them. That still left three descending, one on Haifa, one on Tel Aviv, and one on the Sdot Micha base. Now it was the turn of the Patriot PAC-4 short range missiles, built to kill with kinetic energy, by directly hitting an incoming warhead.

The Iranians had thought that they would not be employed, given Washington's recent coolness toward Israel, and, in any case, had regarded the anti-missile missiles lightly, given the limited success of Patriots in protecting Israel from SCUDs during the U.S. invasion of Iraq. Fortunately, the whole Patriot weapon system in use then had undergone a series of major upgrades to its capabilities, and the U.S. was willing to have them used to meet an Iranian first strike. The new Patriots did their job superbly—the three remaining enemy warheads fell to earth in pieces.

A nuclear attack against major population centers had been launched and repelled in just minutes, before the world became aware it was happening.

The war was over almost as soon as it began!!!

Or was it?

*   *   *

That was not a simple question to answer. While the enemy's missiles were incoming, there was no time to think, only to react as one had been trained. Now, the thinking came, fast and furious.

Iran was believed to have perhaps a dozen more nuclear-armed Sajjils in its arsenal. Would there be a second wave of missiles fired at Israel? If so, right now would be the best time for Israel to retaliate—hoping to catch all of the senior leaders of Iran off guard with a flurry of Jericho-3 missiles. Even if Iran planned to withhold its remaining missiles for now, it could never be trusted again. *Better to destroy the country now!*—Besides, an immediate response could be justified to the world community by the fear of a continuing attack, but the longer a response was delayed, the less urgent the problem would appear—and the greater the pressure by the international community on Israel to refrain from military action.

If the Israelis did retaliate now, without American approval, would the Americans consider that to be the equivalent of an Israeli pre-emptive first strike, and withhold their support against any further Iranian launches? The American Aegis and Patriot defense systems had already been of vital help in warding off harm. Would Israel be safe with only its own Arrow anti-missile missiles?

And, what would the world think of Israel if it went ahead and totally destroyed Iran? Would the Muslim world—perhaps with an anti-Israeli champion like Russia—join in trying to annihilate Israel?

These were the sorts of considerations whirling in the minds of the Prime Minister, the Minister of Defense, and the armed service heads of Israel, linked by a hotline within minutes of the action. The military was unanimous in their advice: "If you give the order immediately, we are sure of striking them before they can set up the next round of Sajjils. They've already taken their best shot at us. *By taking out Tehran, Natanz, Qom and Semnan, and all their known missile and nuclear sites, we can prevent any further attack by Iran for generations to come!*"

The Minister of Defense was worried about the reaction of the United States, especially after the chilly meeting the Israeli Ambassador had with the Secretary of State the day before, and so, before making a decision, the Prime Minister put the conference call on hold and phoned his Ambassador in Washington.

While waiting for the Ambassador to come to the phone, he was startled by the appearance of another person in his office—one who had not walked through the door.

"What . . . ???"

"*Do not give the order to fire!*" said the figure, a tall man in the brown robe of a friar. "*You must refrain from retaliating!*"

The Prime Minister was momentarily too shocked to respond.

The intruder continued. "*It was with the help of the Lord God that Israel has been preserved. Now, He commands you not to launch an attack of your own.—Your strength is in the name of the Lord God, and you must rely upon Him. If you act contrary to His command now, He will abandon you to destruction. Therefore, choose life, not death!*" And with those words, the figure faded from view before his eyes.

"Levi . . . Levi . . . are you there?"

The voice of the Israeli Ambassador brought the Prime Minister back to his senses. "Yes, Dan, I'm here.—A few minutes ago, the Iranians fired a dozen Sajjils at us. We shot them all down. The Americans helped. We're trying to figure whether we should wipe out the Iranians right now. If we retaliate, will the Americans stand by us?"

"*You're telling me we escaped unscathed from the Iranian attack . . . ?*" Hearing no contradiction, he answered the question. "I strongly doubt they'd support us in whatever follows from our retaliatory strike. And the more time that passes, the more likelihood there is that they'll be on the phone telling you to hold your fire."

"*Then, what help do you think we'd get out of the international community, if we do hold up? Will they come together and force Iran to give up its nukes?*"

"*No chance of that, I'm afraid,*" replied the Ambassador.

"So, your advice is what . . . ?"

"*My advice is that, unless you're confident we'll have the same success against their next attack, you have no choice except to hit them hard. They opened the can of nuclear worms in Rome. Let them eat some themselves . . . !*"

That advice accorded with Prime Minister Hertzel's own instincts. "Never Again!" was a cry deeply ingrained in him. The Iranians had caused one holocaust already, and just now they had done their best to cause a much greater one. *They had to be stopped once and for all, and there was only one way to do it.* He hung up his call with the Ambassador, and reached for his other phone to give the order to launch a massive retaliatory strike.

The friar appeared before his desk again, holding up his hands in a STOP signal.

"Do not disobey the command of the Lord God! Do not retaliate! If you do, innocent blood will be on you and your people! Again, I tell you to choose life, not death!"

The Prime Minister reached in his desk drawer, pulled out an automatic pistol, and pointed it at the figure, who stood his ground a few feet away. The Prime Minister fired once, aiming right at his chest. The friar showed no reaction other than a look of sadness before he faded away.

Hearing the shot, the Prime Minister's aides rushed in, to find him alone in the room, gun in his hand. They assured him that no one had entered or left the room, and he told them that he was quite all right.

Then he picked up the phone and gave the orders to fire the Jerichos at all the previously chosen targets in Iran, and also to sound the civil defense sirens nationwide, calling all Israelis to take shelter wherever they could.

Within a few minutes, death began raining down from the sky as it never had since God destroyed the cities of Sodom and Gomorrah.

The Israelis employed three different types of nuclear weapons—one to destroy hardened underground facilities such as Iran's nuclear weapons facilities, one to destroy their above ground military and atomic installations, and one to create an electromagnetic pulse that would knock out all electric and electronic equipment in a wide area under the aerial atomic burst. The latter was used for the Iranian cities.

The Israeli attack brought to the world's attention the nuclear war then being waged. The world was horrified, and condemnation of Israel was voiced along with the first reports of the conflict, despite the fact, which was never mentioned by the media in many countries, that Iran had attacked Israel first.

Something much worse than condemnation was on its way.

Iran was a large country, and Israel had not known of all the locations where its missiles were hidden. Even though Iran's central military command and many key sites had been annihilated, there were still other undestroyed bases where the local commanders readied and launched their missiles at Israel—again excepting the city of Jerusalem.

Once more Israeli Arrows were sent aloft—but this time the U.S. Navy ships had been ordered not to fire their Aegis missiles to defend Israel. Again, most of the incoming IRBM's were destroyed, but not all, for the Patriot batteries too were silent—the Pentagon had sent an electronic signal to block them from firing.

And so, the second and third largest cities of Israel, Haifa and Tel Aviv, were destroyed in nuclear fireballs.

Now, the war was really over, two hours after it had begun.

Or was it?

*   *   *

Once again, that was not a simple question to answer, though the decision tree had shrunk significantly.

The cities and military sites of Iran were done for—cooked by atomic bombs. The Israeli Prime Minister's concern was no longer incoming missiles, but the possibility of an invasion—three invasions to be accurate—by Israel's enemies on the north, the east and the south. They had invaded once before, in an effort to smother the Jewish state at its birth, and he feared they might be tempted to do so again, now that it was gravely weakened by the loss of so many people and facilities.

On the hotline, the Prime Minister sought the advice of his council of war in their bunker. "Can we afford to stop at this point? Or do we have to take out all our enemies, no matter what the consequences may be?"

"I assume you're thinking about Syria, Jordan, Egypt, Lebanon and the Palestinians in Gaza," the Air Force Chief of Staff responded. "Or do you have in mind the Saudis too, Levi?"

"Can our people be safe anywhere in the world as long as the Muslims are on a jihad? You know the Wahhabi sect of the Saudis is the most anti-Semitic form of their religion.—I'm thinking of making a clean sweep."

That brought a protest from the Minister of Defense. "Aren't we able to beat back any invasion with tactical nukes—or even firing our remaining missiles at other capitals, if we're invaded?—*Why do we have to decide now?*"

The Air Force Chief of Staff answered him. "Given what's happened so far, the Russians might try to make themselves heroes in the Muslim world by exploding a few large ICBM's of their own high over us, to set off electromagnetic pulses that would destroy our remaining electronic infrastructure and our capability to defend ourselves. We could wind up making our last stand defending Jerusalem with machine guns and hand grenades, unless we knock out right now everyone who might invade us."

The Army Chief of Staff agreed with him. "We have to reduce the populations around us to the point where they're no longer a threat. They've always wanted to drive us into the sea—they've just been biding their time. I say, let's clear them off the table while we still can. *Ein breira*—there's no choice."

"Give me a couple of minutes to think about this," said the Prime Minister, "meanwhile, prepare the orders you would give for an across the boards strike with everything we have—missiles and planes."

As soon as the Prime Minister hung up the phone, the intruder appeared out of nowhere.

"Now listen to this word of the Lord God, you rebel.—Your name has been blotted out of the Book of Life.—The blood of a million of your countrymen, and of tens of millions more in Iran is already on your head. If you give the order to strike against all your country's enemies, the Lord God will not shield any of your countrymen. They will all perish with you! This is your final warning!"

The specter faded leaving the Prime Minister alone in his office. He sat there, spooked, almost in a trance, until the Air Force general called to ask for his decision. He linked everybody with the hotline, and said, "There's something I have to tell you.— Before I gave the order to attack, something strange came over me. I thought I saw a friar standing right here by my desk—you know, the kind that goes around in a brown robe with a rope around his waist. I had no idea how he got in. He told me that the Lord God commanded me not to retaliate, and if I did anyway, the blood would be on me and my people. I pulled out my pistol and shot him from a distance of four feet—right in the chest. I couldn't have missed. He just stood there, like it didn't hurt him, and then he sort of disappeared. My staff found the bullet in the wall—it had gone right through him ... "

"That isn't all," he said, as the others remained silent. "He appeared just now—said if I ordered this next attack, it would kill everyone in our country too. He just faded away again. I know he didn't come or go through the door . . . "

They waited for him to continue. When he didn't, the Minister of Defense spoke up. *"I think what you saw has to be tied in with those damn visions we've all gotten. I don't know who's been sending them, but I've disregarded mine.—A Catholic religious is the last person in the world I'd listen to—I'd do the opposite of whatever he said!—I say, Levi, don't pay any attention to this phantom, and tell us what you want us to do. Nothing matters now except the survival of our people . . . !"*

"In that case," said the Prime Minister, *"I'm ordering you to strike all our enemies, including the Saudis. If we don't take them out too, with their money they'll buy whatever they need from other countries to finish us off. Coordinate the attacks among the three services, and strike as soon as you are ready."*

Over the next hour, the Israelis dispatched nuclear armed fighter-bombers and more flights of Jericho-3 missiles, as well as missiles from their three submarines. The initial reports were that the attacks were succeeding, but the Israeli defense command never heard further. It was wiped out by one of the multiple warhead Russian ballistic missiles targeting Israel. By the end of the day, more than fifty million people were dead and half a dozen countries had permanently ceased to function, Israel among them.

Finally, the war truly was over.

But, only that war.

PART VIII

The Beggar

March–April 2015

God is not being loved and honored as he should by the race he has elevated to the sublime dignity of adopted sons. There is a gap, and God is looking for someone to stand in the gap before him on behalf of this race and beg that he may not destroy it.

Mother Teresa of Calcutta, *Jesus, The Word to Be Spoken*, 89
(Servant Publications 1998)

— 1 —

Washington, D.C.
March 21, 2015 Anno Domini; 1 Farvardīn 1394 Anno Persico (cont'd)

A call from the President of the United States might have dissuaded the Israeli Prime Minister from ordering a strike on Iran,
but, at the news of the first Iranian missile launches against Israel, the Secret Service had whisked the President off to a secure
location. It was in the critical minutes when the President was preoccupied with being moved to safety and getting reports from the
Pentagon that the Israeli Prime Minister decided to retaliate. After
that, the atomic genie was out of the bottle, not to be recaptured.

Bernie Cohen was left at the helm of a nearly deserted White
House. Ordinarily the most rational and stable of men, he became highly agitated after each side had fired off its first wave
of rockets. The second strikes temporarily unbalanced him, and
when he learned that a Russian IRBM had obliterated Jerusalem,
he roamed aimlessly through the empty corridors venting his an-
guish by sporadically shouting out, "Is everyone ******* crazy???"
. . . "Why the **** did they do it???"

Half of his brain was thinking about the ruined homeland of
his people, while the other half was worrying that the Russians
were out of control and might attack America next. What should
he advise the President to do? Go from DEFCON 2 to DEFCON 1,
which would cause the ICBM's to be readied for firing, and the
bombers to be sent aloft to wait in holding patterns for a possible
order to attack Russia? Or should he suggest that President Gardiner call the Russian President on the hot line?—It was an idea
which he considered, dismissing it only after he realized he would
not be able to answer the President's obvious question: 'What
should I say to him?' Russia's action was an egregious provocation
to the United States, one requiring a well thought out response.

An assistant who had remained with him took the initiative
of getting the Secretary of State on the line. With his years of
international experience, the Secretary was a reassuring counselor.

"Take a deep breath, Bernie.—The Russians aren't threatening
us at the moment, thank God!—They've never cared for the State

of Israel or their own Jews. I suspect the reason they wiped out Jerusalem is that they wanted to remove any last capability the Israelis had to launch more planes or missiles against Iran."

Secretary Howe's steady voice calmed Bernie down somewhat. Enough to process what the Secretary had said. "Launch more missiles *against Iran*? I don't understand, Bill,—how does that make sense?"

"*You'll see, Bernie.—The Russians will be moving into Iran soon in a big way. And we should be moving into Saudi Arabia, as fast as we can! What it's come down to now is a race to control the oil fields.—You better tell the President to make that the priority for our armed forces in the Middle East. I'd suggest that the Joint Chiefs meet on it immediately.*"

New York

Is there a Jew who does not carry in his soul the Psalmist's threnodic lament for the city of Jerusalem?

> *By the rivers of Babylon we sat mourning and weeping when we remembered Zion . . .*
>
> *If I forget you, Jerusalem, may my right hand wither! May my tongue stick to my palate if I do not remember you, if I do not exalt Jerusalem beyond all my delights!*

Written in exile after the fall of Jerusalem to the Babylonians, those verses of the 122nd Psalm did not cease to be chanted when the captives were allowed to return and rebuild their holy city. Nor after it was again destroyed, by the Romans, and the inhabitants were led away in slavery, never to return. For millennia it continued to be thought of as the city to which the tribes of the Lord had gone up to give thanks to His name.

They would always remember it—but never again return, now that it was a radioactive waste. No more would Jews in the diaspora raise the toast of anticipation, "Next year, in Jerusalem!" They wept openly without consolation . . .

San Giovanni Rotondo

Back—wholly—in the friary, Fr. Santorelli knelt in his cell, gasping
for breath and fighting back a scream of protest as he tried to
control his emotions, so that he could make some sense of the
ordeal he had just been through. At the beginning of the incident,
he had been conscious of a sensation of blacking out, as if his
brain was not receiving sufficient oxygen. Before he could move,
he found himself in the office of the Israeli Prime Minister. Not
that he would have recognized the man from newspaper photos,
but he saw the Israeli flag and had infused knowledge of the
whole situation—not only where he was and the identity of the
man he was facing, but what had just happened, and what the
man was contemplating doing.

And then, he found himself speaking words. Not exactly like a
ventriloquist's dummy, because the muscles of his mouth were not
manipulated—but the words he spoke he did so under compulsion,
they were words that were put into his mind.

Everything about what had happened baffled Fr. Santorelli.
God had shown Himself to be personally involved in the battle by
aiding the Israelis in their defense—and then interjecting *him* into
the conflict to warn the Israelis against retaliating against Iran.
Nevertheless, when His warning was rejected, He had allowed
the greatest slaughter in the history of mankind to be perpetrated.
Tens of millions of people must have been killed—that much he
knew from being thrust back into the Prime Minister's office to
warn him against a further attack, after the first atomic bombs of
each side had already exploded.

What was he supposed to make of the momentous events?
Had the cataclysmic battle of the End Times begun?

Ever since he had been given the message for Benedict XVIth
at Garabandal, the priest had been meditating on part six—the
citation to the third verse of the third chapter of the Book of the
Prophet Joel. It was a prophecy of the actions of God in the End
Times: *"I will work wonders in the heavens, and on earth, blood,
fire, and columns of smoke."*

It struck him hard that it was the exact same prophecy as was
quoted in the apocalyptic flyer which he had found in the airplane
seat pocket on his way to Rome—the flyer which linked Joel's

prophecy with eclipses darkening the sun and turning the moon blood red. He had thought the whole idea was utter nonsense then, and he still wasn't disposed to credit it. Yet, the coincidence was eerie, and the possibility could not be dismissed out of hand.

Following the destruction of the Vatican, he had prayed that that dire event would prove to be the complete fulfillment of the sixth part of the message. His prayers had now been revealed as unavailing. Columns of smoke had risen in the Middle East, and he feared that they would not be the last to be seen on the face of the earth.

The only matter as to which he had been somewhat enlightened was the Lord's words to him at Garabandal: *"Through your mouth I will offer many the choice of life or death."* That had happened in Jerusalem, and the Israeli Prime Minister had chosen death—not once, but twice—*and the consequences had been immediate and catastrophic.* Hadn't the official believed him? How could he *not* have, once he saw that his shot had no effect? And given the result, what was the point of Fr. Santorelli's intervention?

The priest felt a desperate need to unburden himself, and the name that came to mind was not that of his mentor, but Zanier. So it was to the new Pope that he turned for help. His plea over the phone for an audience the next day was granted, and the Pope graciously offered to send a car to pick him up at the friary.

— 2 —

Iran

On Sunday, the Russian Army began to move, just as the Secretary of State had predicted. Russia had long coveted the oil fields of Iran, which were estimated to contain over 100 billion barrels of oil, and also access through Iran to the Persian Gulf. It saw a way to attain both objectives without even having to force its way through a third country. All it had to do was transport its tanks and troops from a staging point at Groznyy across the Caspian Sea, landing in Iran. From there, the Russian Army headed toward the oil fields along the Persian Gulf, meeting only light, disorganized resistance from survivors along the way.

What could the United States do about Russia's aggression in Iran? Realistically? Nothing.—Nothing except take advantage of the situation to secure control of the even vaster Saudi Arabian oil fields. The U.S. Navy, already present with a task force in the Persian Gulf, landed Marines at Dharan, the headquarters of the Saudi oil network, just north of Bahrain. The American government broadcast a radio message to the survivors in that country—leaderless now that the Saud Dynasty and all government ministries had been destroyed by the Israelis—assuring them that the Marines were there to protect what was left for the Saudis, and that America would pay for all the oil it took.

In the animal kingdom, the large animals kill and eat their fill, leaving carcasses for the smaller animals and birds. In the nuclear war fought on Saturday, it was the small animals that had fought each other to the death—and now the big animals had moved in to feast on the remains.

Washington, D.C.

The lengthy editorial in the N.Y. Times on Sunday morning was almost incoherent, veering between grief and anger over the past, and concern about the future. One of its targets was the United States Government.—*How had it happened that the Iranian missiles*

succeeded in destroying Haifa and Tel Aviv? How could the Russians
be punished? And, what was the U.S. going to do to aid the Israelis
who had survived in scattered places, such as Dan and Elat?

These were questions being pressed right now by the Jewish
members of Congress, and the Administration had to decide how
much to reveal of its defense strategy and its dealings with Israel.
The Secretaries of State and Defense were united on this issue,
advising the President that full disclosure was in the best interests
of the United States.

From the perspective of the Secretary of State, it was important
that the world understand that while we would stand by an
ally under attack, we would not support an ally launching an
unnecessary attack that we had cautioned against. *We were not*
to blame for Israel's decision to attack, as it was taken against our
advice, and without reliance on our protection.

The Secretary of Defense wanted our enemies to know that our
anti-missile missiles worked perfectly. Together with the Israelis,
we had successfully defended our ally against an attack by nuclear
armed ballistic missiles. The reason our ally was destroyed was
that our missiles defenses were not made available to it after it
had retaliated against Iran.

And Congress was determined to use the grim occasion to
announce a new policy—the U.S. was no longer going to be the
automatic provider of disaster relief without regard to where
and why it was needed. Congressmen of both parties expressed
their opposition to sending any aid to Israel. It had, they said,
brought this calamity on itself. Besides, the need for relief was
even greater in the countries which Israel had attacked—were we
going to rebuild them too? Enough was enough. It was time, they
said, for Uncle Sam to stop playing the Good Samaritan to the
world.

— 3 —

Rome

Fr. Santorelli met the Holy Father in the Lateran Palace, where he
now both lived and worked. While the third and fourth floors of
the Palace were being readied for his full time occupancy, he was
sleeping and working in a two-story appendage where the late
Cardinal Vicar of Rome had lodged.

The Pope came out from behind the desk in his office, greeting
the priest warmly, and then sitting beside him on a sofa.

"My dear friend," said the Pope, "if you don't mind my saying
so, you look terrible.—Are you in pain from your wounds?"

"My wounds? Oh, *those*—why, yes, Holiness, but they're not
what's gotten me down. To explain, I have to begin with a confession: *after the bomb went off at the Vatican, I rashly reproached the
Lord for ill-using me—for giving me premonitions about onrushing
calamities such as that one, but only fragments of the picture, not
enough to enable me to prevent the harm.* As I might have expected,
*He in turn reproved me for playing the part of Job, in challenging
His actions and demanding an explanation.*—So, I'm trying hard
not to complain to Him now about what's just happened, but . . ."

Fr. Santorelli then proceeded to lay out the story of his bi-
location to Jerusalem and his failed attempts to head off the Israeli
Prime Minister from ordering nuclear strikes. It was nothing the
Pope could have thought of in his wildest imagination.

"My God!" the Pope exclaimed. "Is what you're telling me
true?" He was nonplussed. He knew that many books about St.
Padre Pio included reports of his bi-locating, and that a very few
other saints in history were reported to have done so, but, like
Fr. Santorelli's mentor, the Holy Father had not thought of the
young priest as being in a league with the great saints. If anyone
but Fr. Santorelli himself had told him the story he just heard, he
would have dismissed it as a jest. As it was, he knew the priest
well enough to be satisfied that the events had indeed occurred
as stated. The Pope made a mental note that he would have some
meditating of his own to do when Fr. Santorelli left, about God's

intervention in human affairs, but for now, he needed to try to understand how God was using the priest.

"Yes, Holiness, every word. So help me God!"

"How did you get to Jerusalem and back?"

"I don't know. I didn't have any sensation of splitting in two, or going through the air or some kind of a tunnel, if that's what you mean. I felt like I was blacking out in the friary, and then like I was coming to in the Prime Minister's office. That obviously wasn't the case—the *bodily* me was in the friary, and whatever was in Israel was some sort of phantom, like a holographic presence in an amusement park feature. The transfer in *my perception* of where I was happened instantaneously, and without warning. I returned the same way—without any thought or control on my part."

"Did you do anything to insert yourself into that situation, Father," asked the Pope, "even thinking about it mentally?"

"No, Holiness. I had no idea that a war had started. I wasn't thinking of the Israelis or the Muslims at all. Somehow, though, when I found myself in the Prime Minister's office, I knew everything—it was infused knowledge. I didn't use it though. I didn't think about what I should do or say—words just popped into my head and I spoke them, like a robot." Fr. Santorelli paused for a moment, then continued with regret in his voice. "Maybe the fact that the words were His was for the best—I'm kicking myself around now for failing, but at least I know it wasn't because I was tongue-tied or didn't say the right thing . . ."

The Pope quickly grasped the problem. "Why ever would you think that *you* failed, Father?" he asked. "Consider the opposite outcome—if the Prime Minister had refrained from ordering retaliation, would you have thought that *you* had brought that result about?"

Fr. Santorelli thought about the Pope's point, then nodded in agreement. "Yes, you're right, Holiness—Much as I might have wanted to, I couldn't have taken any credit for a successful outcome."

The Pope pressed his line of reasoning. "Not only that, Father, don't you think that God *knew in advance* that your intervention was going to fail?"

Another slow nod by the priest. "Yes, I guess He must have. But, that only adds to my perplexity.—*Since He knew that my*

*speaking the words I did would not persuade the Prime Minister,
why did He bother to involve me?* I mean, He could have made
His plea directly by giving the man a locution or a vision, or by
sending an angel to him.—Or He could just have done nothing at
all, and wound up with the same result."

The Holy Father permitted himself a small smile. "Well, He *did*
choose to use you, and it seems unlikely that He was giving you
pilot training, so to speak, in bi-location. *So, I can only guess that
He's trying to leave you with a memory for the future to teach you
something.—Perhaps, it was a lesson about how only God can defeat
the Devil's schemes—for man alone, it's impossible.*"

Fr. Santorelli smiled grimly. "He didn't need to go to all that
trouble, Holiness, to teach me *that*. I've never doubted it."

"I'm sure you haven't Father, but maybe He's expecting the
experience you just had will cause you to *act* on that knowledge
in a particular way in the future."

"What do you have in mind, Holiness?" asked the priest.

The Pope began to answer the question in a roundabout fashion. "Do you remember the story in the Book of Genesis about
Abraham, and the cities of Sodom and Gomorrah?"

"Yes, of course. God was about to destroy them because of
their wickedness, and Abraham pleaded with God not to do so
if there were some righteous men left in them. I think the final
number he bargained for was 10, and God agreed to it."

"And do you remember," the Pope persisted, "what the Book
of Exodus records as happening when Moses came down the
mountain with the tablets of the Law and found that in his absence
the people had made themselves a golden calf to worship?"

"God was going to destroy them all, but Moses pleaded with
Him, and God relented. Why do you ask?"

"I ask because perhaps He wants you to play a somewhat
similar role—begging Him not to destroy the whole human race."

"I don't understand your idea—what you're driving at,
Holiness.—Why do you think that might be called for?"

"It's not *my* idea, Father," replied the Pope, "it's Mother Teresa's.
Or part of it, anyway. *She said that 'God is not being loved and
honored as he should by the race he has elevated to the sublime
dignity of adopted sons. There is a gap, and God is looking for
someone to stand in the gap before him on behalf of this race and
beg that he may not destroy it.'*

"Now, I'm going to tell you something that I'm sure you don't know. When Benedict XVIth asked me to make arrangements for you to go to San Giovanni Rotondo, he ended by quoting to me those words of hers. And, what's more, he told me: *'Fr. Santorelli may be that man.'*"

Fr. Santorelli had never been so shocked in all his life. Not even when his stigmata burst forth. The Pope gave him time to collect his thoughts.

"*Me?* ... I can't believe *that*—begging your pardon, Holiness. Only weeks ago I was a prison chaplain, far from here and forgotten in a corner of Hell. It took a long chain of coincidences to bring me here today."

"*Coincidences, Father? —I think not*," said the Pope.

"Still, Holiness, you know me well enough to know I'm not fit to be mentioned in the same breath with Abraham and Moses—they were Patriarchs ... "

"You've read the *Divine Mercy Diary* of St. Kowalska, haven't you, Father?"

"Several times, years ago, Holiness."

"Perhaps you should reread it again now, especially the part where the Lord told her that He was going to cause a chastisement like the punishment of Sodom and Gomorrah to fall upon Warsaw—and asked her to offer His Blood and His Wounds to the Father for that city, for seven days at Mass in expiation for its sins. At the end of the period, Jesus told her that *for her sake*, he was blessing the entire country."

Fr. Santorelli remained incredulous. "*You think He is looking to me to beg on behalf of the world?* Holiness, please, say you're not serious!—If any such plea were wanted, surely, *you* would be the right person to make it. You're His Vicar on Earth—our Chief Priest ... "

After a period of silence, the Pope responded. "Father, I think you know the story of what happened to my family—my village. I've prayed on my knees every day since that massacre for peace. Peace in my country. Peace in Africa. Peace everywhere. And, I can't say I've seen any sign that my prayers have been heeded. Perhaps He's looking for something special from someone else. *Something from you. Something you can give Him that I can't ... *"

Fr. Santorelli again tried to brush off what the Pope was saying. "*I have nothing to give Him, Holiness, at least nothing beyond the service that I render as one of His priests."* He thought further. *"Well, I suppose that if it's bearing the stigmata for 50 years as St. Pio did, He already knows I'm willing to do that if that's what He really wants.—But, you know, He doesn't need anything. Never has. Never will . . . "*

His Holiness was patient with the priest. He understood that he was not trying to teach the Pope basic theology, only trying to express his own lack of comprehension of what the Pope was saying.

"I didn't mean that you have something *He needs*, Father.— Rather, that you have something *He wants*. Does a mother really *need* the violets that her little daughter picks and brings to her in her hands, all crushed? Of course not. But does she *want* them? You know she does, for the love that the gesture signifies . . . Now, Father, my advice is to go back to your duty station at the friary and try to understand what it is that He wants you to do. *And, out of love for Him, and for all our sakes—please do it!"*

— 4 —

Manoppello, Italy

On an otherwise ordinary morning in March, Fr. Santorelli saw the face of Jesus.

After resting overnight in Rome in a room at the Lateran Palace, the priest was being driven back to the friary at San Giovanni Rotondo, when, without consciously thinking about them, the only lines he had ever memorized from the *Divine Comedy* came to mind: "*Segnor mio Ies Cristo, Dio verace, or fu si fatta la sembianza vostra?*" What was Dante referring to? Ah yes, he was making an allusion to someone looking at the Veil of Veronica and asking Jesus whether it truly was His semblance depicted on it—a question Dante left unanswered.

The Veil of Veronica was one of the most precious relics in the Church's possession—perhaps second only to the Shroud of Turin in importance. By tradition, a pious woman watching Jesus carrying the Cross on His way to Calvary had run out to Him and wiped His face with her veil—and for that act of kindness she was rewarded with an imprint of the Lord's visage on the cloth. Thereafter, in legends, she was known as "Veronica" (true image). A legend—but one which drew credibility from the nature of the veil itself.

It was like no other fabric relic in the world, for it was woven of *sea byssus*, a very rare, costly and incredibly fine silk harvested from fan mussels. The veil was so gossamer that it was virtually transparent from the backside when held up to a light. Yet there was on it a very well delineated, and finely shaded, face of a bearded man who had obviously been bruised. And the face had been imprinted on the cloth in some way scientists still could not explain, for examination with ultraviolet rays revealed no trace of paint whatsoever. That was the relic that Dante had presumably seen for himself when it was displayed in Rome during the Holy Year of 1300.

The seven by ten inch rectangular fabric was prized so highly by the Popes that when the construction of the dome on St. Peter's basilica began in 1506, one of the four pillars on which the gigantic dome was to rest was built with a safe receptacle to hold the ciborium in which it was kept. During the construction process, however, the veil disappeared, only to reappear a century later in the village of Manoppello, in the Abruzzo region of central Italy, where the Capuchins eventually took custody of it.

Fr. Santorelli recalled that Benedict XVIth had made a pilgrimage to see it in Manoppello, and, being curious as to what he himself would make of the relic, he asked the driver to make a short detour en route. As the car approached the town, the basilica with its campanile stood out against the verdant hill behind it. The flat facade was beautifully decorated in an unusual design. Thick armed Greek crosses of variegated red marble were set in a geometric pattern interlocked with white crosses potent—crosses with a small bar at right angles at the end of each arm. Above the central door was a mosaic of the Risen Christ, and a small rose petal window was set in the middle of the facade.

Inside, the priceless treasure was kept under glass in a silver frame, which in turn was sealed in a glass reliquary on the Holy Face altar. From a pew at a distance, he could look right through the back of the veil to the mullion of the window at the end of the apse. After he said a prayer, he approached the altar and went up a side staircase to a landing. There he could view the veil from the front at close range, and see the distinct facial image.

He was overwhelmed, as he had been when he saw the Shroud of Turin during the exposition of 2010. The verdict was undeniable: *It is as it was!* This was indeed a "vera icona" depicting the human face of God.

The face of a mature man that stared out from behind the glass had a broad, high forehead, slim, curved eyebrows, and widespread eyes whose whites, under the irises, indicated that He was looking slightly upward. His skin color appeared to be a very soft, pale yellow, lighter than the hair—but probably that was the intrinsic color of the sea byssus. His nose was long and abraded, and His slightly open mouth was surrounded by a thin moustache and beard. The whole made a powerful impression, most particularly through the light brown eyes which were not only open, but alive. The priest had the sensation that as he was looking at Jesus, Jesus was looking back at him.

It was a gaze at once piercing, knowing, and sad—the sadness of resignation, as of a person abandoned by his friends in the hour of his need.

At the same time, the eyes were asking a question of the one who looked into them. There were words of His which exactly fit that look. Words forming poignant questions which Fr. Santorelli now meditated upon as they occurred to him:

"Do you also want to leave?"

"Judas, would you betray the Son of Man with a kiss?"

"Will you lay down your life for me?"

On his own, Fr. Santorelli might have remained there for hours, waiting to see if the Lord was going to tell him exactly what was wanted of him. However, his driver had grown impatient at the delay, and motioned that it was time to get back on the road. And so, the priest left before he had arrived at his own answer to the last question, or received the guidance he was seeking.

— 5 —

San Giovanni Rotondo

A weak sun shown through the early morning mist over the face of Monte Castellano a few days before Holy Week. At the mountain's base, by the basilica of Our Lady of Grace, a priest on a personal pilgrimage was kneeling in prayer in front of the bronze statue of Padre Pio, whose right arm was extended, as if to bless him. A brown-robed figure passed by him, heading up to where the Way of the Cross began.

The Way, an ancient Christian devotion, was laid out on a grand scale up the forested slope, using fourteen stops, or "stations," each of which commemorated a specific event in the Savior's Passion, Death and Resurrection—events drawn either from the Gospels or from Tradition. After the last station, which depicted Jesus being laid in the tomb, a sculpture of the Risen Christ had been added in the Square of the Resurrection.

The kneeling figure called out—"Padre!—May I join you, please? I'm a stranger here." Although the stone staircase upward at times overflowed with thousands of pilgrims, in the cold of that early hour it was barren except for the two men.

Fr. Santorelli turned to look at the man, who stood rubbing his bare hands together for warmth in the icy wind coming down the mountain. He was clad in a black overcoat and fedora, with a clerical collar showing—the standard garb of a diocesan priest. Since he had spoken in fractured Italian—mixing in words of Spanish—Fr. Santorelli answered him in Spanish, thinking that might be a better language in which to converse. "Si. Bienvenido, Padre—we will make the Way together."

They walked up the staircase to where there was a monumental marble statue of the Blessed Mother displaying the infant Jesus. After saying a Hail Mary, they proceeded upward again in a straight line until a meandering footpath crossed at a landing. They followed it into an area with tall pine trees, and there came to the first station. It consisted of a large, square bronze plaque, nicely framed in stone and raised off the ground about four feet. The scene depicted was of Jesus standing in front of Pontius Pilate, who was deciding whether to condemn Him to death. According to the Gospels, Pilate had asked Him—"From whence hast thou come?" A question which Jesus did not answer—an affront to the Roman ruler of the territory, who had the power either to crucify Him or to release Him.

It was this moment of pregnant silence which the sculptor captured in their eyes, eyes which do not meet. The gaze of the uncomprehending, worldly official, is on his prisoner, while the gaze of the all-knowing Man-God is not on his captor. Although their faces are shown as being but a few feet apart, Jesus is looking through and beyond His human antagonist. Perhaps He can see His real opponent, the Devil, there, invisible to Pilate, or perhaps He is contemplating the path which He will shortly take to Calvary, for He knows what the outcome of the interrogation will be—what it *must* be in order to achieve the Father's purpose.

At that point, Fr. Santorelli began the ritual which they would go through at each of the fourteen stations: the announcement of the event commemorated, followed by the same verse and response, spoken out loud.

"The first station: Jesus is condemned to death." Kneeling, he continued by saying, "We adore You, O Christ, and we praise You." To which the other priest gave the prescribed reply: "Because by Your holy cross, You have redeemed the world."

They rose and walked slowly on together along the path. Since his companion was a clergyman, Fr. Santorelli thought to share his meditation on that station with him.

"Consider, if you will, that most of the religious and civil authorities who condemned Our Lord did not believe that they were being unjust. They thought they were doing the will of God, or at least what was needed to keep the peace. And yet, we know that they convicted the One who was *Truth itself* of *untruth*, for claiming to be both man and God . . . We sometimes find ourselves judged unfairly—if not by the authorities, then by those who know us, or perhaps those who have only heard of us. Whether their judgment is fair or not, Our Lord asks us to accept such a cross, just as He did, without complaint."

As they approached the second station, the visitor said, "Padre, I know what you mean. *I was judged—by my Bishop.* I still have my priestly faculties and act as a tour group chaplain, but I'm forbidden to return to my diocese. I've been living in Europe for five years—like the man without a country. It's been a real cross."

"Then we're *compadres*," came the reply. "I was exiled by *my* former Bishop—he sent me to be the chaplain in a prison among 4,000 violent criminals ..."

When they arrived at the plaque for the second station, Fr. Santorelli announced: "The second station: Jesus shoulders His cross.—We adore You, O Christ, and we praise You."

Back came the response: "Because by Your holy cross, You have redeemed the world."

Continuing on the Way, Fr. Santorelli gave the next meditation. "Jesus said, 'If you would be *My* follower, you must take up *your cross* and follow Me.' ... When we follow the Lord, we find that a cross has been assigned us. We need to accept it as the burden that God has chosen for us—not wishing that it was a different cross, or a lighter one. Intellectually, I *know* that, but it still is difficult for me to *accept* it."

At the next stopping point, Fr. Santorelli again broke the silence: "The third station: Jesus falls for the first time. We adore You, O Christ, and we praise You."

"Because by Your holy cross, You have redeemed the world."

He shared another meditation. "Jesus fell repeatedly under the heavy weight of the Cross, due to the terrible scourging he had been subjected to. *We* fall repeatedly, not from physical causes, but tripped up by our sins. We *must* get up again—if we stay down, we'll die in our sins. And, there's no excuse to stay down, since we have the rite of reconciliation to help us back to our feet."

Thus they proceeded up the Way as it zigged and zagged through the pine trees, and crossed here and there the steps which linked the top directly with the base. Fr. Santorelli paused for a long time in front of Station XI, which showed a muscular man with hammer upraised, in the process of nailing Jesus' feet to the Cross. An expression of great pain was on the face of Christ, and the priest could imagine an agonized cry coming from the Savior's open mouth.

Finally, they completed all fourteen stations and reached the Square at the summit, bare except for a monumental bronze statue of the Risen Christ affixed near the top of a thirty foot tall stone wall in the shape of a tombstone. It was at that point that the visitor asked to sit down, so they could talk for a few minutes.

Looking down at his feet, rather than at Fr. Santorelli, he said, "Oh, Padre—there's something I have to tell you.—I came to San Giovanni because it's been years since I made a full confession. I made a partial one in December, but I've got still more to get off my chest. I've heard there's a new friar here who's a stigmatist.— Do you think he could help me?"

Fr. Santorelli decided in favor of discretion in replying. "I know the friar you're referring to quite well, and I can assure you that *he's no Padre Pio*, if *that's* what you're thinking. He has absolutely no charism for reading a person's secret sins and bringing them to light.—But you shouldn't need that. You're a priest—you should know what you've done wrong. —Why don't you tell me what it was that caused your Bishop to bar you from his diocese?"

The man hesitated, but then sighed, and, with head still bowed, began his tale. "I did confess *that* sin, to another bishop no less, but since it's part of the story, I'll tell you too. I tried to be a good pastor—really I did, and I think the people of my flock loved me. Unknown to them, I was stealing from the collection plate to support my lifestyle—which was not what it should have been. It's why I was turned out and banned from the diocese. Then, as a tour chaplain, I earned so little that I kept the alms which pilgrims gave me for the needy—that is, until what happened to me in Garabandal, a few months ago."

Fr. Santorelli's gasp was not noticed by the other priest. So, this was the man about whom the Bishop of Santander had written! Without revealing what he knew, Fr. Santorelli nodded at him to continue. "What was that . . . ?"

"I was the chaplain for an American tour group at the time. Many of us were overcome by visions there—me first. No one was really expecting anything like that to happen, despite the apparitions of Our Lady many years before, prophesying that a Warning would be sent to everyone someday. I was so terrified by what I saw—the warning I got—that I went straight to the Bishop of Santander. I was in tears, and . . . and . . . I confessed to being a *thief* . . . I would have confessed my other sins too, but he really didn't want to hear them—he said I could find another confessor after the pilgrimage was over. Then, right after I had left him, the Lord spoke to me. *I'm sure it was the Lord!* He said He wanted to use me and would strengthen me—and He has!—*Believe me, Padre, I'm cured of that sin. I would die rather than steal again . . . !*"

"I do believe you, Father," said Fr. Santorelli, without hesitation. "And there's no good reason why you can't confess your other sins to me right now, and go down the mountain a new man."

Within ten minutes, close to the statue of the Risen Christ, the visitor had made his confession and a good act of contrition, and had received complete absolution at long last.

"I'm very grateful to you, Padre," the visitor said, as they began their descent. "I think a great weight has been lifted.—I wonder if you would do me the added favor of arranging for me to spend a few minutes with the stigmatist, since you know him.—I'd like to ask him for guidance as to what I should be doing now. I'd would like to leave this itinerant life and work in a parish again."

Still without identifying himself, Fr. Santorelli replied, "Perhaps your Bishop was one of the many Ordinaries who died in Rome. And even if he was not there for the Pope's funeral, he may feel a need for another priest in these turbulent times. You need not discuss with him the sins of your past—you've been washed clean. My advice to you is to return to Utica, beg forgiveness for your faults there, and ask to be reinstated. I will pray for your success in that endeavor."

The man looked at Fr. Santorelli wide-eyed. "*Utica?* I never mentioned Utica . . ."

"You *are* Fr. Martinez from Utica, New York—the one who saw Judas Iscariot in a vision—*aren't you?*"

The visitor, dazed, could barely whisper, "Yes.—*How. . . ?*"

Fr. Santorelli understood what the man was asking, but he chose to answer a different question.

"How did we come together here?—I have no idea. Sometimes God delights in arranging things we can't even dream of for His prodigal sons.—*He is our Father*, you know . . ."

— 6 —

San Giovanni Rotondo

Fr. Santorelli had planned to spend this Friday, the final one in Lent, in his cell, except for when he was adoring Jesus in the form of the Sacred Host in the friars' chapel. However, in the morning, he was summoned by Brother Porter. Some pilgrims who knew him had come to San Giovanni and were asking for him.

He went down to the parlor, and was greeted by a former classmate from seminary, whom he had not heard from since his friend had dropped out. They had quite a bit of catching up to do, as Fr. Santorelli could see when the man introduced his wife. And there was a second lady with him—his ex-classmate's sister, Maeve, as beautiful as she had been on the seminary's Christmas break when he had met her years ago.

She broke the ice. "Tony!—I'm so glad to see you again—I've missed you so much ... " She turned her cheek, as if expecting a kiss of recognition from him. As he drew closer to her, undecided what to say or do, he detected an odor. It was not that of perfume— quite the opposite. It was more like raw sewage. His train of thought was broken and a new one began.

"Friends," he said, "before we sit down for a talk, do me a favor—please—all of you say, *'Jesus Christ is Lord.'*"

All of a sudden, the three of them uttered snarls, and disappeared. The room was empty except for himself, though the smell lingered.

Fr. Santorelli wondered what Brother Porter would say when he didn't see the three visitors leave the friary—but, then, perhaps it wasn't really Brother Porter who had let them in and fetched him.

*   *   *

In mid-morning, the Father Guardian came to see him with a request. "Father, we make do every year with a wooden crucifix for the Veneration of the Cross. Your wounds show that you are a living embodiment of Christ. I think it would be very meaningful for the friars if you were to stand there by the altar next Friday at the devotion, and let them kiss the wounds in your feet, in place of kissing the crucifix."

Fr. Santorelli tried not to show how repulsed he was by the suggestion. "Really, Padre, I wouldn't want anyone to be venerating *me* instead of Christ. I don't think it would be at all proper!"

"Whatever you think, Father," the Father Guardian replied sternly, "I am asking you to do it to reciprocate our hospitality."

Something didn't feel right about the whole situation. Fr. Santorelli bowed his head and prayed silently. Then he responded, "All right, I will do it, Padre, provided that you first say, 'Jesus Christ is Lord.'"

As with the three visitors earlier, there was a loud, animal-like snarl, and the demon impersonating Padre Ghiardi vanished, leaving behind a sulfurous odor.

*   *   *

Fr. Santorelli bled even more profusely from all his wounds on Friday than on other days of the week, so he was pleased when the Brother with nursing training showed up at his cell to aid him in rebandaging them.

"What's in the container you've brought?" he asked.

"Oh, just a little coffee. Father Guardian thought you would be losing a lot of blood and should replenish your body fluids."

A grim smile appeared on Fr. Santorelli's face. "And I suppose he forgot that today we are fasting on bread and water?"

"Oh, Father," replied the brother glibly, "you're ill, and ill friars are exempt."

"Get out of here, Satan!" Fr. Santorelli commanded—and his visitor disappeared in a "Poof!" along with the coffee.

*   *   *

Leaving his cell to go downstairs for an hour of Eucharistic Adoration in the chapel, he passed the Father Guardian in the hall.

"You don't look well, Father," Padre Ghiardi told him.

Fr. Santorelli looked hard at the friar and tried to sniff the air without being obvious about it. This person seemed to be real. "I've had an interesting morning of it, Padre," Fr. Santorelli replied.

"I'm beginning to see how trying it was for St. Pio to have visits from the Devil."

He would have liked to have prayed for the whole hour vigil in the form of the Cross, with his arms outstretched, but he found that he did not have the strength to keep them up for more than a few minutes at a time. The throbbing in his wounds was so intense that he feared he would collapse, calling unwanted attention to himself. A great thirst came over him, as it had over Jesus from the loss of blood. It was all he could do to resist the urge to slip out for a quick drink of water. All the while, he was making deposits in the Church's treasury of merits, merits which he would have liked to apply to his own sins, but which he surrendered to the disposition of Our Lady, Mediatrix of all graces. Some one's else's merits, he hoped, would meet his needs.

*   *   *

At the end of his Holy Hour, he walked with difficulty back to his cell, looking forward to lying down to regain his strength. As soon as he entered, however, he saw a horde of ugly demons, part human and part animal, waiting for him. He knew he was in for another session of torment.

They took off his shirt and beat him all over with rods until he was sorely bruised. Fr. Santorelli kept calling on his Guardian Angel for help, but the little fellow didn't come until it was all over.

"What good are you?" Fr. Santorelli angrily demanded.

His angel looked abashed, but replied, "I can't interfere with what's meant to be."

When the devils had finished with him, he didn't have enough strength to get off the floor and onto his bed. As he lay there on his stomach, he saw the door open and someone enter. The person bent down—it was none other than his friend Fr. Justin Casey!

"Why, Father!" said the visitor, "I didn't expect to find you on the floor like this—but I can guess what happened. Devils must have been working you over! They're horrid things—they do it to me too. Take it as a sign that you are greatly disturbing their master!"

Fr. Santorelli managed to roll onto his left side. "Why are you here, Father?" he asked, in a weak voice.

"The Pope sent me with a message for you. You were sent here to protect you from what Cardinal O'Melveny might do to you. There's no need for you to be stuck up here in this friary now that O'Melveny is dead, and the Holy Father needs you. You're still a priest of the Diocese of Rome, and he wants you back there now."

Fr. Santorelli was suspicious. "Did the Holy Father say why he wanted to make this change?"

"Why, yes," Fr. Casey answered. "After you've assisted him for a while, he intends to send you back to America and make *you* the Archbishop of Topanga. He said no one served that man Jesus better than you! *Think of that, Father. You, heading O'Melveny's diocese!* He'd turn over in his grave if he had one. All you have to do is say goodbye and leave with me."

'*That man Jesus*'? The phrase was the tip-off. It was just as Fr. Santorelli suspected. "*Go to Hell, you liar!*" Fr. Santorelli told his visitor—who did so, with a shriek.

*   *   *

Then, the Brother whom he had chased out earlier came into Fr. Santorelli's cell, bearing a supply of bandages.

"What? No coffee this time?" Fr. Santorelli asked him. "Why do you keep tormenting me, you devil? You should be ashamed of yourself, pretending to be a Capuchin! Off to Hell with you!"

The Brother was flustered. "Why, Father, is there something wrong with you?"

Fr. Santorelli, still lying on the floor, took another look at the Brother. "Say 'Jesus Christ is Lord,'" the priest demanded.

"Jesus Christ is Lord!" came the reply.

"Oh, thank God!" Fr. Santorelli said, and he cried with relief, apologizing profusely to the Brother. "When you came this morning, it was the Devil in disguise. Please forgive me, Brother. It's been like that all day ... "

— 7 —

Washington, D.C.

The effects of the Middle East War were continuing to roil the geopolitical situation worldwide. The staff of the National Security Council had been consumed with trying to foresee its many ramifications, especially for further jihadist activities against the West, and hostile activity by Russia, which had shown itself willing to use nuclear weapons. Russia's renaissance as an "evil empire" was quickly demonstrated not only by its takeover of Iran, but by a threatened invasion of the Republic of Georgia, an independent country once part of the old Soviet Union, situated on Russia's southwestern flank.

At an emergency meeting of the NSC's Principals Committee, the top defense, foreign policy and intelligence officials heard reports from the staff on what had been picked up by satellites and aerial reconnaissance. Russian troops were massing in the South Ossetian Autonomous Region and the Abkhazian Autonomous Region. These were areas of the sovereign nation of Georgia which Russia had torn from it in the war of 2008. Added to that threat, the Russian Black Sea fleet was now positioned off Georgia's coast, presumably to block any attempt by the west to come to Georgia's aid by sea.

On Thursday, Secretary of State Howe had allowed himself a glimmer of hope about the international situation because the Russian Foreign Minister had readily agreed to meet with him in Washington, the following Monday, to discuss matters in dispute between the two countries. His disillusionment came on Friday, when the Russian Army invaded Georgia. The capital, Tbilisi, fell quickly, and resistance proved futile. Before the day was out, Russia had formalized its territorial aggression by proclaiming that Georgia had been annexed as part of the Russian Federation, and would thenceforth be defended against all third parties.

That was bad enough. What was worse was that the Russian Black Sea fleet, no longer needed along the coast of Georgia, did not return to its home ports of Novorossiisk in Russia, and the base at Sevastopol in the Ukraine, which was being used pursuant to an agreement with that country. Instead, those warships moved into the Crimean area, taking up stations that would enable them to blockade the Ukrainian Black Sea fleet at Sevastopol and at Donuzlav. Not only that, but Russian tanks slowly began to mass along the Ukraine's eastern border. These were very inauspicious omens for a peace conference . . .

— 8 —

Washington, D.C.

The members of the National Security Council Principals Committee were called on Sunday morning by the President's National Security Adviser. The troop buildup on the border between Russia and the Ukraine was continuing, and Russia had formally declared a blockade of the ports where the Ukrainian Black Sea fleet was based. The President of the Ukraine had immediately denounced these moves and had requested an emergency meeting of the U.N. Security Council. He had also ordered a mobilization of the Ukrainian armed forces, and phoned the Secretary of State, begging for whatever military help the U.S. could provide.

At a morning meeting in the White House Situation Room, the Principals Committee heard a briefing from an Army colonel sent by the Joint Chiefs of Staff. He first explained the ethnic divisions in the Ukraine, showing the percentage of citizens of Russian heritage in the various regions. They were concentrated in the east and in the Crimean Peninsula, the only area with a majority ethnic Russian population. Citizens in the west of the country wanted stronger ties with the European Union, while those in the east wanted stronger ties with Russia—but only the diehard Communists were publicly calling for a Russian invasion.

"If that's so, Colonel," asked White House Chief of Staff Bernie Cohen, "why would the Russians invade?"

"Sir, there are several different reasons," said the Colonel. "Although the Russians would claim they were invading to protect the ethnic Russian population, that would only be a smoke screen. There are three very substantial reasons. The first is to prevent NATO from militarizing the Ukraine, which, as the Russian Foreign Minister noted, has a border only 300 miles from Moscow. In these days when ballistic missiles can cross continents in minutes, it may seem unreasonable to be paranoid about missiles next door, but that's the Russian mindset. The second reason is that they covet the industrial and agricultural production of the Ukraine. And third, they view the Ukraine as the potential point of a spear directed at the heart of Europe."

"It sounds like you're about to answer my next question," Cohen interjected. "Which is, *why would it matter to us if Russia took over the Ukraine?*"

The Colonel put another slide on the screen.

"Sir, Please look at this map. The Ukraine is a country of almost 50 million people right in the heart of Eastern Europe. If the Russian Army moved into the Ukraine, it would immediately threaten the independence of the countries on the Ukraine's border—most notably Poland, but also Moldava, Romania, Hungary, and Slovakia. Close by, across the inland Black Sea, which Russia controls, there are also Bulgaria and Turkey. The invasion of the Ukraine would also create an expectation of Russia's annexation of the three Baltic States. All of these countries, Turkey excepted, were part of the Soviet Empire. Following Russia's recent successful annexation of the Republic of Georgia, governments in Europe have expressed concern that Russia is bent on reconstituting the former Soviet Union. *The Joint Chiefs believe that the United States has a strong interest in preventing a new Iron Curtain from being rolled out across Eastern Europe.*"

"Bill," said Bernie Cohen, turning to the Secretary of State with his next question, "I'm sorry to put you on the spot, but is the strategic interest which the Colonel has just outlined sufficient to warrant meeting a Russian invasion with military force of our own?"

Everyone in the room looked intently at Secretary Howe, and waited for his answer, not at all sure what it would be.

"*That may be like asking,*" said the Secretary, at last, "*whether I want war now—or war down the road.* All of us in this room were born after World War II was over, but we've read countless times of how Hitler could have been stopped, with relatively little loss of life, at the beginning of his conquests, and we surely don't want to be the ones to allow Russia to march through Europe, one country at a time, with us always feeling that it isn't worth going to war over *one more country.* The President of Russia was a Communist *apparatchik,* and I for one don't see any way to dissuade him from trying to reassemble the old Soviet empire, unless we show that we are willing to fight to stop that from happening.

"There's something else that's hanging over us, and the whole world, that I think needs to be added into our analysis. And that is the Russian missile attack on Israel. That country was our *client* country. We were its ultimate protector. I'm not second guessing now our decision not to provide an anti-missile shield when it went off on its own suicide mission. What I am referring to is the fact that we've done nothing, *nothing*, in response to the Russian attack. I think the countries in Europe are wondering if we are prepared to resist the Russians—*if we are really willing to put our own lives on the line in confronting Russia.*"

He paused before delivering his summation.

"So, I would say, to answer your question—*Yes*—*our strategic interest in the Ukraine is sufficient to warrant militarily resisting the Russians, and I would recommend military action to the President, provided—and it's very big provided—that we have a good chance of achieving some meaningful success—which may be less than preserving the status quo.* Since I'm not in a position to speak to our military capability, I trust the Colonel will enlighten us . . ."

The Colonel had been patiently waiting the opportunity to do just that. He began by pointing out that since the Ukraine was surrounded on three sides by Russia and the Russian controlled Black Sea, any aid America sent would have to go through Poland. He next reviewed the Ukraine's defenses in comparison to the Russian invasion force shown by satellite reconnaissance, expressing the Joint Chiefs' opinion that, in view of the overwhelming superiority of Russian forces and the very short supply lines needed by the Russians to reach and hold major cities in the eastern part of the Ukraine, there was *nothing* that the U.S. and the Ukrainians could do to stop the Russians from overrunning the country if they were really determined to do so—short of all out nuclear war with Russia.

"So, the situation is *hopeless*?" asked the President's National Security Advisor.

"Not necessarily, Ma'am," came back the answer, "unless the Russians are determined to prevail no matter what the cost. The Joint Chiefs believe that strong resistance involving the U.S. militarily—which bloodies the Russians and stops them temporarily in their tracks—*might* bring them to the negotiating table. There's even a small possibility that we could scare them into negotiating rather than invading—though I've been instructed not to imply that the Chiefs think it's likely."

"We'd certainly like to hear about those possibilities," the Advisor said. "And whatever specific force levels the Joint Chiefs would propose with respect to our involvement."

The Colonel was ready with an answer. "Yes, ma'am. Speed is critical. Within 48 hours, we could send one atomic artillery brigade from the U.S. to Kharkiv, a major city very close to the Russian border. Also we could deploy two squadrons of jet aircraft to Dnipropetrovs'k, which is centrally located in the Donets Basin. One would be A-10C Warthogs—they're tankbusters—from Germany. The other would be F-16C Fighting Falcons—they're fighter-bombers—from Italy. The shells fired by the Warthog's canon are made out of depleted uranium, to make them hard enough to pierce armor, and the Falcons would be armed with tactical atomic weapons including ERW's."

"ERW's?" Bernie Cohen asked, "What are *they*?"

"Sir, they are enhanced radiation weapons, sometimes referred to in the public press as the 'neutron bomb.' They're low yield atomic weapons designed to emphasize the production of neutron radiation rather than blast and heat. Their purpose is to kill people in tanks and other armored vehicles by giving them a lethal dose of radiation. Years ago, we dismantled all such weapons in our arsenal, but in view of the Russians' development of a new, heavily armored main battle tank, we recently started production of improved ERW artillery shells and air to ground missiles.

"The other necessary deployment would be sending the 1st Fighter Wing of F-22A's to Germany for air-to-air exercises there. The Raptor is our top air superiority fighter—the Russians have nothing to match it—and they would see that we were serious about providing protection for our other aircraft.

"If the Russians cross the border, our strategy would be to attack with nuclear weapons the concentrations of Russian armor massed *on the Russian side* waiting their turn to get on the roads leading directly to Ukrainian cities like Kharkiv, or stalled at whatever roadblocks the Ukrainians could throw up inside their country along the way. Use of ERW's would lessen the long term environmental degradation of the Ukrainian territory, compared to what would happen using normal atomic weapons."

"Under what scenario might the Russians not even invade, Colonel?" Bernie Cohen asked.

"We might be able to scare them off before they cross the Rubicon, by publicizing our deployments, albeit giving misleading statements as to our intent. We would announce that we were sending the forces I mentioned on a 'training mission,' just as soon as they were on their way. The Russians would, of course, see through that fiction, and understand that their real purpose was to help in the Ukraine's defense. They would also know that those forces, with atomic shells and bombs, could do serious damage to their invasion force. Perhaps more important, they would worry that our involvement would escalate when they reacted by attempting to destroy our artillery and aircraft. While the Russians are ready to take on the Ukrainians, they may not be willing to start a war where *we* have signaled that *we* will fight them, by putting significant forces in harm's way.—At least the Joint Chiefs believe there's a *chance* of that positive outcome. It's the same 'tripwire' strategy that has led us to station troops in Europe and South Korea."

"It sounds like you're proposing a high stakes game of 'chicken,'" protested the National Security Advisor. "If we use atomic weapons on the Russian side of the border, I think they're certain to retaliate with atomic weapons somewhere on U.S. territory! You saw how quickly the situation in the Middle East spiraled out of control. The same could happen here. We could be bringing disaster on our own country in a vain effort to save the Ukraine!"

The Colonel took her objection in stride. "The problem, Ma'am," he replied, "is that we don't want a repeat of the experience during the Korean War, where the Chinese troops and aircraft had a sanctuary beyond the Yalu River. You'll recall that General MacArthur was relieved of his command for protesting the restriction on his conduct of the war. If we can't fight the Russian invaders wherever we find them, our chances of prevailing will be much lower—and the Russians will know that."

The smartest man in Washington made up his mind quickly. "I think it's vitally important to make a *limited* effort to try to stop the Russians, even one that puts our military in harm's way. Obviously, no one wants to get into a full scale war with Russia, so let's assume that we will *not* attack across the Russian border *to begin with*. Our field commanders can assess the situation if we *don't* deter the invasion, and the President can decide whether to change the rules of engagement based on how the war is going.

That's what I'm going to recommend to the President now—and the National Security Advisor can go with me if she wants, and argue the case against intervening to him."

The President, flattered by being compared by Bernie Cohen with John F. Kennedy, who had risked nuclear war in resisting Russian aggression during the Cuban missile crisis, accepted Cohen's recommendation, and U.S. forces were ordered on their way to the Ukraine, with fanfare.

— 9 —

San Giovanni Rotondo

Fr. Santorelli went out on the veranda after supper, hoping to find Padre Mario—and there he was, sitting in a rocker, saying his Rosary.

"So, we meet again, Padre 'Tonio?" Padre Mario inquired as the priest approached.

"You knew it was me?"

"Yes. It was the roses again . . . I heard you were sent for by Rome—I'm glad you returned."

"Your advice was decisive, Padre Mario!" Fr. Santorelli replied. "And I'm planning to stay here indefinitely. You may be surprised to hear this, but I'm even sticking my toe in the water to test whether I have a vocation to be an order priest. As a diocesan priest, I promised my chastity and obedience, so all I would be adding is a vow of poverty, which wouldn't be hard to do, since I have no money or possessions anyway!"

Padre Mario smiled at what his companion had said. "You Americans pride yourselves on being self reliant, on earning whatever money you need. Aren't you somewhat bothered by being totally dependent on others to provide for you now?"

Fr. Santorelli's silence answered that question.

"And," Padre Mario continued, "if you think that the vow of poverty only pertains to *material* poverty, you're mistaken. There's another whole part you need to consider—poverty of spirit."

"I take it, you don't think I already have that?" asked Fr. Santorelli, somewhat hurt by the comment.

"I haven't been with you long enough to form a judgment as to that, Padre 'Tonio," came the reply. "But, if *you* think you have it, try being inactive for two weeks. No trips, no phone calls—nothing but communal meals, Mass, the daily office, and your own devotions. See if you can be content with that sort of inactivity. You've always led an active life by choice, from what you've told me—setting an agenda for yourself. Poverty of spirit is more often associated with passivity."

"Forgive me if I don't fully agree with you, Padre," Fr. Santorelli said. "Take even your revered Founder, Father Francis—was he not a man of action, going to the Pope to get his proposal for a new order approved, and then crossing the sea to evangelize the Sultan?"

"I see I did not make myself clear.—What I meant by passivity was letting the Lord direct all your actions, instead of having an agenda of your own. Letting Him push you and pull you as He wills—or even leave you sitting inactive for a long period of time, just meditating on His glories, or consoling Him for His sorrows. *Do you think you could accept that?*"

"Maybe not," Fr. Santorelli admitted, "but I'm willing to give *your spirituality* a try while I'm here, surrounded by you Capuchins.—Maybe the effort will help me to figure out what it is that God wants from me. The Holy Father said he was sure God *does* want something in particular, but he didn't know what it was, nor do I. As I told you before, at one time I just assumed God wanted me to teach, but He's done nothing in years to indicate that's what it is.—On my way back here earlier this week, I stopped off in Manoppello to see Veronica's Veil. I thought He might say something to me in the basilica there, but He didn't.— Is it possible that *you* have an idea what He wants, Padre?" Fr. Santorelli asked, hopefully.

Padre Mario rocked for a while. "I think He wants your hands, Padre."

"*My hands?—That's crazy!* Whatever do you mean by that, Padre?"

"I can't say."

It was Fr. Santorelli's turn to think. "They're a bit large even for someone who's as tall as I am. When I was a kid, I tried a number of things to see what I could do with them. I could reach a ninth on the piano, but I didn't have the hand-eye coordination necessary for playing music. I could pick up a basketball with one hand, but I couldn't dribble well enough to make the team, even in high school. And so on—I never found any special use for them except giving strong handshakes—which I did until the stigmata came internally. So, Padre, I don't see how *my* hands would be more useful to God than those of any other priest."

"Nevertheless, Padre 'Tonio, I expect that He will make special use of them in His good time."

And that was all Fr. Santorelli could get out of his aged companion on that subject.

A thought occurred to the priest. He hadn't noticed anything out of the ordinary about Padre Mario—no foul smell, no coldness like a soul from Purgatory—except he did have an *unearthly* air about him. Was this another imposture of the Devil?

"I'll leave you in peace, Padre," the priest said, "but before I go, please bless me in the name of the Father, and the Son, and the Holy Spirit."

It was the Padre's turn to smile. "I would be glad to," he replied, smiling, and he raised his right hand for the benediction.

— 10 —

Washington, D.C.

Monday's meeting in a conference room on the top floor of the State Department building was held between only two men—the U.S. Secretary of State and the Russian Foreign Minister—though their subordinates were standing by in the anteroom in case their expertise was wanted. Perceiving that the United States had "blinked first," by seeking the meeting, the Russian official came in so confident that he had no hesitation in making territorial demands from the outset.

"Mr. Secretary," he said, "the present *untenable* situation of the Ukraine is attributable to the fact that *your country* has played a destabilizing role in Europe twice in the past 30 years. First, your country succeeded in destroying the fraternal unity of the soviet socialist republics, and now you are seeking to force the Ukraine into the NATO Alliance.

"*My Government is determined to regain control of all the areas of the former Soviet Union and integrate them into the Russian Federation. You were wise not to resist us when we did so with the Georgian Republic!—I am here today to apprise you of our next step, so that your country can again stay out of the way and avoid being drawn into war in the Ukraine through an unfortunate miscalculation.*"

"Mr. Minister," the Secretary of State interjected, "*I'm shocked at what you are saying!*" That was true. Not because the Secretary didn't expect the Russian to say what he did, but because he understood what a great threat Russia's territorial ambitions were to world peace. "*Mr. Minister, territorial aggrandizement of the sort you have just described cannot be reconciled with the United Nations Charter, or with any hope the Russian Federation has of peaceful coexistence with the other democracies including mine.*"

The Russian coldly dismissed his protest. "*You* are lecturing *me* about territorial aggrandizement? *After your troops have just taken control of Saudi Arabia? Let's not play games, Mr. Secretary— posturing is dangerous. What is necessary is for both of us to look at the world realistically.*

"The reality is that our nations have natural spheres of influence. Your country's extends to the two American continents. My country's extends into continental Europe, and into Asia, up to the Chinese sphere of influence.

"I ask you to suppose that American citizens in Mexico living in retirement communities were threatened by the violent crime in that country, and the local government was unable to protect them.—Can you tell me with a straight face that your country would not send in its troops—as it has done in the past? Just so, my country will act as necessary to ensure the safety of ethnic Russians who are threatened in countries on our border, including the Ukraine."

The American official shook his head from side to side, indicating disbelief. "You are proposing that we accept your country's domination of smaller countries in your sphere of influence, in return for which your country will do the same for America in our sphere of influence? *That's totally contrary to the ideals of American foreign policy.*"

"*Really? Since when, Mr. Secretary?*" the Russian taunted. "*I am well familiar with the Monroe Doctrine, which contemplates America's overlordship of the countries to your South. Have you ever counted how many times your country has intervened with its military? In Mexico—Colombia—Panama—Nicaragua—Cuba— Guatemala . . . Shall I go on, Mr. Secretary?*"

"It's true," Secretary Howe replied, "that we have intervened in the past, Mr. Minister, but we've always withdrawn our troops, and those countries are not in any way controlled by us now. Our actions were in great contrast to how it was with the countries in the Soviet Union, where Soviet troops were continually employed to subjugate the local populations, until President Gorbachev refused to continue to hold the Soviet Empire together by force."

The Russian was tired of the jousting. "Enough of generalities, Mr. Secretary. We will not convince each other with them. *I will return to the subject of the Ukraine, and the dangerous situation America has brought about by promising NATO membership for that country. Its eastern border is less than 300 miles from Moscow. It is unacceptable for us to have so little land as a buffer between our capital and the armies of the NATO Alliance.*

"Moreover," he continued, "for us, the Ukraine is 'Little Russia,' where the Russian and the Ukrainian peoples are thoroughly intermingled. You have just seen how we acted to protect the Russian population of Georgia, by annexing that territory. *We are committed to bringing Little Russia back into the Russian Federation, by whatever means it takes.*"

Russia's immediate goal was as dangerous as the Secretary of State had feared. "*Surely you are not going to attempt to subjugate that independent country, Mr. Minister! You know that if your country tried to do so, it would bring nuclear war very, very close to your capital.*"

That issue was a two edged sword, and the Russian turned it on the American. "*Mr. Secretary, we both know that the Ukrainians have no nuclear weapons. If any are used in war there, they could only be weapons introduced by NATO, and we would not hesitate to respond in kind.*"

"Mr. Minister, any legitimate issues Russia has with the Ukraine Government, whether about the treatment of Ukrainians of Russian descent or otherwise, must be settled by negotiation. *Anything else would be a clear threat to world peace, one unacceptable to my Government.*" That was a counter threat, albeit a veiled one, unlike the Prime Minister's.

The Russian, who had been growing increasingly hostile, now exploded. "*It is the imperialist policies of the United States that are threatening world peace. What business is it of yours how the Russian and Ukrainian peoples resolve their affairs? Who appointed America to be the world's judge and peacekeeper? We are moving close to nuclear war, due to the meddling of your country in other countries' spheres of influence. It is your country that will be responsible if there is a nuclear war in Europe . . .*"

The Russian Foreign Minister glared at the American Secretary of State. Perhaps it was a theatrical device, for, after a moment, he replaced his angry look with a less threatening one, and changed his tone of voice, so that it took on a conspiratorial cast.

"Look," he said, "we are both *men of affairs*. Let us put aside threats, and talk about how our countries can both benefit from certain situations. In the Middle East, *we* took over the oil fields of Iran, and *you* took over the oil fields of Saudi Arabia, all without firing a shot at each other, or even making a diplomatic protest. *There are other areas where we should be able to cut up the goose together—to use one of your American expressions.—That's exactly what your President Roosevelt did with our supreme leader and*

Churchill at Yalta, and it facilitated joint cooperation in the war against the Germans.—Bring over, if you will, Mr. Secretary, the globe you have over there, and let's look at where we can draw some lines to our mutual advantage . . . "

The Secretary of State was uneasy with the suggestion, but thought it only prudent to hear out the Foreign Minister so that he would be able to report to the President exactly what the Russians were proposing. He carried the large globe on its floor stand and set it down next to where they were sitting. "Exactly what are you proposing, sir?" he asked.

The Russian foreign minister was deeply engaged in drawing lines across the map of Europe with his index finger, and the American Secretary of State was arguing with him as he did so, when a startling event occurred.

A figure in a brown robe suddenly appeared in the room, ten feet away from them.

The two men looked up, amazed at the sight of the tall intruder.

"Peace!" the man said, raising his right hand, palm facing them in the traditional gesture. *"Peace from Our Lord and Savior Jesus Christ. It is a peace which you cannot achieve by the territorial aggrandizement you are considering."*

The Russian froze in his seat. *"Who is that???"* he exploded angrily.

"Security!!!" Secretary Howe shouted out, without waiting to hear more. Within seconds, two guards from the Bureau of Diplomatic Security dashed into the room, guns drawn.

"Take him!" called out the Secretary, pointing at the figure.

The guards looked all around. "Take *who*, sir?" the senior one asked.

"Him!" said the Secretary, pointing.

The guards looked where he was pointing. The senior one said, with deference, "Sir, I don't see anyone. I see only the two of you in the room, and the two of us guards."

"Damn it! He's right in front of you now," said the Secretary, his voice showing his anger. "Walk straight ahead." The guard walked straight ahead, all the way to the window. As he came up to the image that the two officials were looking at, they saw it disappear, and then reappear when he had passed.

"S***!" said the Secretary. He wondered if the image was a hologram, being projected from an unknown source. "When was the last time security swept this room for any electronic devices?" he asked.

"Right after lunch, sir," came the answer, "and we've guarded it at all times since. No one was allowed to enter except you and His Excellency."

"*They're useless. I'm invisible to them. Tell them to go,*" said the figure, "I will leave peacefully as soon as I have delivered the Lord's message to you."

"*There, just now, did you hear him speak?*" Secretary Howe demanded of the guards.

"*Who, sir? I didn't hear anyone speak.*"

"All right," the Secretary said, reluctantly, "leave and stand right outside the door, in case I call for you again."

"Thank you," said the specter, when they had left. "Your Excellencies, last week, the Lord sent me into the office of the Israeli Prime Minister immediately after all the incoming Iranian missiles had been destroyed *with the help of the Lord.*—In words the Lord had me say, I begged him not to retaliate. I told him that the Lord would protect Israel if he refrained, but that He would not do so, if the Israelis retaliated. *I offered him the choice of life or death.* Again, I appeared before the Prime Minister ordered retaliation for the second time, explicitly offering him the same choice. *As you know, he chose death once again.*—The result is that Israel is no more . . .

"The Lord now offers Your Excellencies the same choice for your peoples. *Each of your countries is well endowed with every resource it needs to make its people prosperous. There is no need to subjugate other nations such as the Ukraine, and your threats to wage wars are contrary to the will of God.*"

The intruder paused just slightly to look intently at each of the officials, before he made his final plea, with arms extended beseechingly. "*Your Excellencies, the Lord sends you this message: If you refrain from territorial aggrandizement, the Lord will give you peace and prosperity. If however, you attempt to carve the world up into spheres of influence to control, and you begin wars of conquest to enforce those spheres, your countries will be destroyed. I put before you now the choice of life or death, and I beg you—choose life!*"

With those words, the specter again made the sign of peace, and his image faded away.

"*Security!!!*" Secretary Howe called out, this time with less urgency than before. The two guards rushed into the room again.

"Did anyone just leave the room?"

"No, sir! We've been standing right outside the door, as you ordered."

"Thank you," said the Secretary, "you're dismissed again."

When they had left, Secretary Howe had the inspiration to see if he could make good use of the unexpected message from the phantom. He turned to the Russian Foreign Minister and said, "*Well???*"

"I don't know how you managed to pull that off," said the official, trying as best as he could to appear unimpressed, "but if you think you're going to persuade me to abandon the legitimate aspirations of my country by some parlor magic trick you worked here in your office with a hologram, you are very much mistaken. I did not come all the way here for a Disneyland show. I call upon you, Mr. Secretary, to be serious, and respond to the demands I have put on the table . . . "

San Giovanni Rotondo

When the bi-location ended, Fr. Santorelli came to his senses back in his cell. As before, he understood fully where he had been and what he had said, and he began to pray on his knees, arms extended in the form of the Cross, that his intervention would prove successful.

While he was thus engaged, his visual plane was filled with a vision of Jesus, though not the real, living Jesus. It was a stylized Christ in Majesty, right arm and shoulder uncovered, with the rest of His torso clothed in a blood red robe—and the priest recognized it as the depiction in the enormous mosaic covering the dome of the north apse of the Shrine of the Immaculate Conception in Washington, D.C. That Christ, a sight unavoidably intimidating to all who walked down the long nave toward the altar and the apse beyond, was truly fearsome. He had a look on His face which was in sharp contrast to the portrayals of His merciful Mother in the many side chapels lining the shrine dedicated to her. His look said unmistakably: *"The time for my mercy is past.—I have come at last to judge the world."*

Fr. Santorelli was frozen in place by the sight. Then, he heard the inner voice which he recognized as that of the Lord.

"Anthony,—the leaders of Russia are about to choose death. They are preparing even now to invade the Ukraine. The war they begin will spread until it has destroyed their country and yours, and the rest of the world as well."

At those words, Fr. Santorelli fell forward on his face, so that his forehead touched the floor. Prostrated thus, he silently formed the words of a response. *"No! It can't be! It isn't time yet!"*

When he realized how foolish his thought was, he tried again. *"Lord—remember the rainbow—the sign that God will never again destroy mankind!"*

A response came back immediately. *"It is men, not God, who will deal out Death."*

Fr. Santorelli tried a different plea. "Please, Lord, you have just pruned your Church severely, and the Holy Spirit has guided us in the choice of a new Pope. *Surely, you don't want the world to be destroyed now!"*

"In My mercy, I do not wish it, but in My justice, I will permit it to happen." Then the image faded and his sight temporarily failed him.

"Lord," Fr. Santorelli pleaded, *"without your aid, we are doomed.—What is it you want from us?"*

"I want the love and honor which I deserve from the human race. You have seen how I am so often ignored, mocked, blasphemed ..."

Fr. Santorelli was quick to protest. *"But, Lord, you have many servants who love you. We would even die for you!"* The words came to his lips quickly, without any thought of what they might lead to.

"Would you really, Anthony?" asked the Lord in a tone which suggested He did not fully credit the priest's glib assurance. "Right now, you are begging Me to prevent the world from being destroyed by evil men. *In return, what are you willing to offer for your part in the redemption of the world?"*

"Lord, my life is in your hands. If that's what you want, take it!"

" 'Take it'?—A gift given under compulsion is no gift but a tribute. You're better than that."

"You're better than that"—a memory flooded in unsought. That was what his mother had said when he had joined a bunch of boys in toilet-papering the tree of a crotchety old neighbor who was wont to turn his garden hose on them when they cut across his front lawn. He had cried then for having disappointed her, and he did again now.

"You know everything Lord," he said. *"I offer you my life* in atonement for my sins and those of the whole world."

That prompted a warmer response. *"Anthony, are you willing to suffer My fate—being led away bound, being mocked and tortured—and then crucified?"*

Fr. Santorelli felt as though all the wind had been knocked out of him. It was more than anyone else was asked to give.—No, not really. His closest friends, the Apostles, had been treated similarly, as well as the martyrs in every age . . .

"Try to understand what it is that He wants you to do—and out of love for Him and for all our sakes—please do it." Those words of the new Pope came to mind. They were easier said than done. But, how could he justify refusing what the Lord asked of him?

The Lord waited patiently for Fr. Santorelli until He heard the priest say, *"Yes, Lord. I am even willing to suffer your fate . . . "*

Fr. Santorelli heard the voice no more. A different mystical experience took place—a consciousness of the inner sweetness of the Lord, as he had known it back in his student days in Rome. His sight returned though his surroundings were bathed in light too bright for him to see more than blurred shapes of winged things he could not identify. At the same time, he was emotionally uplifted by the sound of a children's choir singing the *In Paradisum* section of Fauré's *Requiem*: "May angels lead you into paradise; may the martyrs receive you at your coming and lead you to the holy city of Jerusalem . . . "

It took a while for the glare to fade from his eyes and the harmonies from his ears.

Fully back in his cell, mentally and physically, he took that shining moment as a sign his offer had been accepted, and that the menace foretold by the sixth part of the message for the late Pope—blood, fire, and columns of smoke—had now run its course. The threatened world war would not occur—He was sure the Lord would uphold *His* end of the bargain. *What he wondered was whether he was strong enough to do likewise ...*

*   *   *

That night, Fr. Santorelli called Pope Paul VIIth, and told him every last detail of what had happened that day. His Holiness listened in silence, and at the end said, simply, "I will pray that you succeed in carrying the cross you've accepted. It's an extraordinarily heavy one, but Our Lord would not have asked you if He didn't know that you could carry it with His help ... Father, I thank you from the bottom of my heart for what you've already done for the Church, and what you've committed yourself to do now."

Fr. Santorelli was touched by the Pope's expression of gratitude. "It was a privilege to be of assistance to you, Holiness. And I'll be praying for *you*, that your reign may never experience the Chastisement ..."

A final thought occurred to the Pope. "Father, do you have any family members that might need taking care of with you gone?—Perhaps a parent?"

"No, Holiness. My parents are long dead. I have no family, other than those in the Church. And no property to leave to anyone. If you ask them to do it, the friars would probably bury me here ..."

"Well, then, Father, please stay in touch as long as you can, and I again extend to you my Papal blessing."

— 11 —

Monte Sant'Angelo, Italy

Built of the local gray-white limestone, the town of Monte Sant'Angelo was spread out along the southern side of an east-west mountain ridge, high enough up that the sea off Italy's Adriatic coast could be seen in the distance. Despite its remote location in the region known as the Gargano, the town had been a noted pilgrimage destination for fifteen centuries, thanks to the Archangel Michael. He had appeared to the local Bishop there several times shortly before the year 500 A.D., on one occasion miraculously saving the town from attack by a neighboring town. According to the Bishop, the Archangel himself had placed an altar in a large cave and had dedicated it, and left his footprint in stone, promising that there the sins of men would be pardoned and what was prayed for would be granted. Those promises had drawn not just credulous commoners, but celebrities, crowned heads, and even St. Francis of Assisi and various Popes, to the cave and a basilica built there later.

Feeling the attraction of that hallowed site, Fr. Santorelli took the bus which shuttled between San Giovanni Rotondo and Monte Sant'Angelo, alighting near the octagonal bell tower of the multi-layered basilica. He entered through one of its two Gothic arched portals. A tympanum on the facade held in a niche the first of many sculptures he would see there of St. Michael slaying the dragon. Passing by a modern oratory in honor of St. Benedict, the priest slowly descended to the grotto by an ancient staircase whose steps, hewn in the rock, turned and twisted downwards. As he went, he observed many items of interest—frescoes and sculptures from the distant past, as well as the deplorable graffiti of modern times.

At the bottom, he went through a Romanesque portal with beautifully incised bronze doors into the "celestial basilica," the space chosen by the Archangel. Above the portal, workmen in ages past had carved in the stone an inscription which Fr. Santorelli read as saying: "In all the space of this cavern the sins of men are forgiven. This is a special abode where all guilt is washed away."

The forepart of the large space consisted of the vaulted Angevin Nave, built with bricks in the 13th century, and embellished repeatedly since then. The remainder of the area was the original grotto—a natural cavern in the calcereous rock. Standing at the entrance, he was amazed that there was so much to see. The cave spread out laterally and encompassed a number of different altars, all under an arched, irregular rock ceiling, which at its high point was no more than twenty feet above the flat, tiled floor. To his left was the 18th century Chapel of the Holy Cross, containing numerous relics. Straight ahead were altars of the Most Holy Sacrament, St. Peter, and the Crucifixion. But it was off to the right of the entrance that the major altars were located.

Turning in that direction, the priest saw, back in a far recess, the elaborate altar of Our Lady of Perpetual Help. Closer, and to the right of it, was the altar dedicated to the Archangel Michael. Here was the main attraction of the grotto: a three foot high Carrara marble statute of a curly-headed, fey-looking Archangel, metal sword in his upraised right hand, as he trampled on a piteous little monster. It wasn't even a proper dragon: the face was that of a monkey, the thighs were those of a goat, and the tail was that of a serpent. Attached to the Archangel's back were wings of gold, and the whole sculpture was set inside a silver and crystal urn, like a reliquary, on top of a marble slab.

Fr. Santorelli sat on a pew near the altar, looking at the numerous depictions of St. Michael, ignoring the overly ornate one in front of him. He couldn't help thinking of the last time *he* had been face to face with the saint! It was back in Garabandal, when the little wooden statue in the church had come alive. The numerous dragons in the grotto—manifestations of Satan—prompted the priest to repeat with feeling the famous prayer of Pope Leo XIIIth. That Pope had a vision of dire calamities befalling the Church in the future, and so he had prescribed that a prayer for divine help be said at the end of each Mass:

> *St. Michael, the Archangel, defend us in the day of battle. Be our safeguard against the wickedness and snares of the Devil. May God rebuke him, we humbly pray, and do thou, O Prince of the Heavenly host, by the power of God, cast into Hell Satan and all the evil spirits who prowl through the world seeking the ruin of souls.*

Why had that prayer been dropped in the liturgical changes made after the Second Vatican Council? Certainly not because Satan was any less powerful or less aggressive. Probably, Fr. Santorelli thought, because of a diminished sense of the existence of Satan and Hell on the part of some in the hierarchy—perhaps even embarrassment that they were still elements of Catholic theology.

Fr. Santorelli was privy to the current scheme of Satan— causing Doomsday to come *now*, prematurely, by prompting men to launch a nuclear war that would destroy the whole world. And the priest knew he had been assigned a role in thwarting that plan—yet he found himself on the sidelines in San Giovanni Rotondo, far from any possible field of battle. While he sat there in the cave, an idea occurred to him—he would put St. Michael to the test. The Archangel had promised that prayers said there would be answered, so he decided to pray that if God needed him elsewhere now, St. Michael would find a way to get him to where he was needed—immediately, if not sooner!

— 12 —

Washington, D.C.

The U.S. Secretary of State was a man of broad knowledge and experience, yet nothing he had ever done, or even heard about, had prepared him for the bizarre experience in his conference room two days before. He had gone into the meeting with the hope that if his visitor refrained from making territorial demands at the outset, they could have a reasoned discussion about reducing tensions in the world. When, however, the very first words out of the Russian's mouth were territorial demands, coupled with threats, he had little room for diplomacy and even less prospect of his efforts at it succeeding.

The appearance of an intruder out of nowhere had initially unsettled him. He could hardly believe what he saw, yet the fact that his visitor also saw the man helped persuade him to suspend his disbelief. In any event, he was forced to do so by the inability of the security people to rid the room of the specter.

Hearing what the intruder had to say, he himself had been caught up in the moment, wondering if God was coming to America's rescue. Perhaps the stranger was being inserted unexpectedly into international events by God—like the *deus ex machina* in a Greek tragedy by Euripides, where a "god" or a person was lowered to the stage by a crane to cause a happy ending to the play. Seizing the opportunity, he had been quick to try to use the intervention to his advantage. Unfortunately, the Russian Foreign Minister had been equally quick to reject the intruder's plea out of hand. So, there was to be no *deus ex machina*—no salvation in that way . . .

He had never been confronted with failure like he was now. He was flat out of ideas as to how to reverse the flow of events which were drawing America into a European war, one which could spiral out of control.

*   *   *

Frantic efforts were made to discover who the intruder had been, not the least because the Russian Foreign Minister had made it clear before he left that he did not appreciate having his country threatened with destruction by someone who, he said, must have been an *actor* conveying a message dictated by the Secretary of State. The specter's garb indicated that he was a Franciscan friar of some kind. That might be a red herring, but it was logical to start by looking in the F.B.I.'s files of all known priests and religious brothers who had been arrested for protesting at a Government site, especially peace protesters at military installations and recruitment offices. None of the descriptions from that review matched the one given by Secretary of State Howe.

By happenstance, one of the F.B.I. agents was a devout Roman Catholic and an admirer of Padre Pio. As he had been fruitlessly working on the peace-protester hypothesis, he had been nursing a far-out-of-the-box idea, that the man had bi-located into the meeting. It was the sort of inspiration that either made one's career or, much more likely, resulted in it being ruined by ridicule, so he had kept it to himself.

Rereading the Secretary's statement again Wednesday morning, he happened to notice the observation that the man's right hand, when he raised it in greeting, seemed to be bandaged. The agent knew that Padre Pio's hands had been bandaged because of his stigmata, and that he had had the charism of bi-locating. That prompted the agent to search the Internet for information on any living stigmatists or stigmatics.

Bingo! His search brought forth a very recent article in a newspaper whose bent was to present the views of the very liberal wing of the Church, which had been headed by the late Cardinal O'Melveny:

The Late Pope's "Rasputin" Uncovered

During the last days of Benedict XVIth, a shadowy figure came to have great influence over his actions. That figure was Anthony Santorelli, a young priest who had proven himself disobedient to his direct superior, Cardinal Thomas O'Melveny, to the degree that His Eminence felt compelled to assign him to the lowly duty of a prison chaplain. Not withstanding this, and without the permission of his superior, Fr. Santorelli

left his post and decamped for Rome. By claiming to
be a stigmatic, he won a private audience with the
late Pope, who was fascinated by this alleged charism
and allowed Fr. Santorelli to remain close to him, giving ear to him instead of to Cardinals with years of
experience.

In the several weeks before the Pope's death, according to Vatican insiders, Santorelli had the presumption to recommend many actions to the Pope,
even coaching him on what words to use in his procla-
mations. Instead of focusing on the reforms needed
in the Church, the Pope was distracted by Santorelli
into dealing with the ephemeral, soon to be forgotten visions, and composing another unwanted Marian
dogma.

Just before his death, the Pope awakened from
the spell cast by this "Rasputin," and exiled him to a
remote monastery, San Giovanni Rotondo. A recent TV
broadcast of him concelebrating a Mass there showed
him wearing gloves, presumably to further his masquerade as a stigmatist. And he was attired in the robe
of a Capuchin friar—which he most certainly is not.
This whole episode would be comical if it were not
so tragic. It points up the need to elect a new Pope
who will have his eyes firmly fixed on the problems
of this world, and not be led astray by mystical ideas
and charlatans.

The agent immediately asked his international section to obtain a copy of the tape of the Mass from the Italian TV station.
That was done and it was streamed to Washington. Fr. Santorelli
appeared to fit the description, and so the agent took the career-
risking gamble of suggesting that a picture of the friar be shown
to Secretary Howe.

It was he!!!

Once his name, Anthony Paul Santorelli was ascertained, other
information cascaded in. He was a priest of the Topanga Diocese,
who had recently resigned his employment as a prison chaplain at
the California State Prison in Lancaster, California. Santorelli had
exited the United States through LAX on January 19th, on a flight

to Rome. There was no record with Customs and Immigration of his re-entry—which, of course, was consistent with the bi-location hypothesis.

While everyone was patting the agent on the back for his success in identifying the intruder, behind his back they were rolling their eyes and making jokes at the thought that he believed bi-location could be real. Somehow, the priest must have flown back from Italy, possibly into Canada or Mexico, and crossed the U.S. border without detection—and then repeated the process to return to Italy. *Anything was possible but bi-location.* At least, that was the thinking among the career people at the Departments of State and Justice.

However, the top people in the Department of Defense and the CIA were not ready to dismiss a possible paranormal aspect of the event so readily. After all, even if the priest had somehow slipped back into the country and then out again surreptitiously, they were intrigued with the question of how he had been able to enter and exit the closely guarded conference room undetected, and make himself selectively invisible to the people in the room.

The Secretary of Defense, accompanied by the Director of the C.I.A., came over to meet with the Secretary of State. The two visitors had no idea of how the man had done what he did, but they were in accord that the ability to project oneself through walls, and become invisible at will, would be an incredible technology to use in warfare. Even if the person so projected had no physical substance and could not fire a real weapon, he could spy on anything, anywhere, with impunity. It was imperative that whoever had done this divulge the secret so that the Defense Advanced Research Projects Agency could develop it into a useful military weapon! *The urgent plea of the two high level officials was that Santorelli be brought back to America by whatever means it took—ASAP—before the idea of getting to him occurred to the Russians.*

"Damn it," said Secretary Howe, "we can't just call the Agency's station chief in Rome and ask him to kidnap this renegade priest today and put him on a government plane back here. That sort of thing is exactly what got us into a ****load of trouble when the Agency grabbed an Egyptian cleric in Milan years ago. You remember, don't you? An Italian judge convicted a couple of dozen of our agents, *in absentia*, of the kidnapping.—I'm not going to let us get caught pulling a caper like that again ... "

"OK, Bill, then, what do we have to do to get him back here for questioning?" asked the Secretary of Defense.

"We have to do it the *legal* way, even though that takes a little longer. I'll ask the Attorney General to have him indicted by a grand jury today for whatever crimes they can think of, and then work up a warrant for his arrest and run it through Interpol. Once that's done, the Agency's station chief and someone from our embassy can go with the Carabiniere and pick him up, nice and legal, and fly him back here under guard.—Don't worry, we'll get our hands on the *wizard* tomorrow for sure ... "

PART IX

The Suffering Servant

April 2015

Our faithful God, who has set apart his chosen ones for close union with himself, when he sees that their life is not conducive to that, visits them with quick and terrible suffering. By that means, whether they will it or not, they must partake of his beatitude, and that is a trait of fidelity in God that we should be exceedingly thankful for.

Fr. John Tauler, O.P. (14th century German Dominican priest)

— 1 —

San Giovanni Rotondo
Holy Thursday

After Fr. Santorelli had said his morning Mass in the basilica of
Santa Maria della Grazie, Brother Alessandro approached him
with a suggestion.

"It's such a fine day out, Padre, why don't you accompany me
to the cemetery. I'm going there to lay some flowers on the grave
of a friar who died a year ago today."

Fr. Santorelli being agreeable, they drove to the far eastern
end of the town, and went into the cemetery, to the section where
the Capuchins were buried together. Brother Alessandro stopped,
knelt down at a grave, and carefully arranged the bouquet of
flowers.

"That's strange. They put the wrong name on his grave," said
the priest.

"Whatever do you mean, Padre?"

"It says 'Mario Lombardi.' But, he's not dead. At least he wasn't
as of a few days ago.—Or has there been more than one Mario
Lombardi at your friary?"

"Oh no, Padre. There was only one, and a very holy man he
was. He knew everything that was going on, even though his eyes
had failed him. I was there when he was buried."

The priest looked aghast. "I see," said he, but he didn't.

"Is something upsetting you, Padre?" asked the Brother.

Fr. Santorelli answered him reluctantly. "Padre Mario has been
giving me advice, out on the veranda—even confessing me. I
thought something wasn't quite right when he said that the Lord
wanted my hands. Now, I have to wonder if my mind has been
going—if I've been having hallucinations. And, if so—which of
my experiences recently have been real?"

"I see," said the Brother, but he didn't either.

They stood there in silence until Fr. Santorelli spoke again.
"Brother, leave me here to think about what's been happening.
Please—go on back to the friary. When I'm ready to leave, if no

one else offers me a ride, I'll call you and ask if you can pick me up."

As soon as Brother Alessandro returned, he reported to the Father Guardian what had happened at the cemetery. "Thank you for letting me know," was all Padre Ghiardi said. Brother Alessandro left his office even more in the dark than before, for the Father Guardian had expressed neither surprise nor curiosity at what he had been told.

*   *   *

In mid-morning, a Mercedes luxury sedan with darkened windows pulled up in the small square in front of the friary. The driver, attired in chauffeur's livery, got out and went to the door. A very large man also emerged from the car, and waited by it, holding a rear door open. The chauffeur requested that Brother Porter ask Fr. Santorelli to come out to speak to him about an emergency in Fr. Santorelli's family back in the United States. He explained that the family had sent him in the hope of driving Father straight to the airport for a quick visit home "before it's too late."

"I'm sorry, sir," Brother Porter replied, "but Padre Santorelli is not here at the moment. I expect that he's still at the cemetery, on the east end of town. I left him there this morning. Of course, you are welcome to wait for him here." With thanks, the chauffeur hurried back to the car and the men drove off.

*   *   *

After Brother Alessandro went back, Fr. Santorelli wandered aimlessly among the graves, trying to figure out what was real and what wasn't. Was he going crazy? Or worse—had he gone crazy some time ago? Padre Mario had seemed real, and his blessing proved that he was not a trick of the Devil. What then, was he? And which of the other locutions and visions the priest had experienced were real? The bi-location episodes surely were—weren't they?

As he left the cemetery, mind in a daze, he was approached by two men who had been standing by a car in the otherwise empty parking lot. One was small and in livery, the other had on a suit that barely contained his large, muscular body. "We've finished

our visit here, Father," said the chauffeur. "Can we offer you a ride
back to the friary?"

Something made him reject the offer, with thanks. They came
closer anyway, and the giant went around in back of him and
pinioned his arms with a bear hug, while the small man injected
him with a powerful sedative. Then they carried him to their
limousine and sped away—over to Manfredonia on the coast, and
then southwest to Foggia, where a hospital plane awaited them.
For an appropriate bribe, the officials at the Gino Lisa Airport did
not require a passport for the sedated invalid in a hospital gown
who was being strapped to a stretcher and taken aboard for a
flight to Belgrade, where he was to receive medical care arranged
by "his family."

In Serbia, where he was off-loaded for his flight to Moscow,
there was no need to pretend that "the patient" was a voluntarily
passenger.

*   *   *

In mid-afternoon, a police car with a Carabiniere officer and
two gentleman in suits appeared, also looking for Fr. Santorelli.
"Please take me to him immediately," said the officer. "I have an
international warrant for his arrest."

Brother Porter reeled back in shock. "*Arrest? Padre Santorelli?*
That's not possible ..."

"Here is a copy of the warrant to give to your Father
Guardian.—Now, we need to see Fr. Santorelli immediately!"

"Officer, I'm sorry, but I left him at the cemetery this morning.
He didn't call me to pick him up, as I expected. Maybe he went
off with the people his family sent for him."

"*What? You say his family sent someone this morning?—What
are you talking about, Brother?*"

Brother Porter's recounting of the short incident that morning
brought curses in Italian from the officer, and profanity in English
from one of the others: "Sonofabitch—they beat us to him!" And
off they roared in the police car, siren blaring.

Brother Porter hurried inside to find the Father Guardian. He
handed over the arrest warrant, and related the two strange visits.
A badly shaken Padre Ghiardi decided that he needed to tell the
Holy Father of the developments.

*   *   *

Paul VIIth took the call from the Father Guardian, who outlined what had happened that day, with Brother Alessandro filling in the details as necessary.

"Something here doesn't ring true, Padre," said the Pope, "*beginning with the fact that I know that Fr. Santorelli has no family.*"

He paused to think. Then asked, "Would you please read me what Fr. Santorelli is being accused of?"

"Certainly, Holy Father," replied Padre Ghiardi, who looked at the words for the first time. "According to what this document states, *he is accused of international terrorism, acts of terrorism transcending national boundaries, threats against foreign officials, and assault on the head of a Cabinet department.*—Holy Father, I can't imagine how we were tricked into sheltering a *terrorist!* He seemed to all of us to be such a holy priest!"

"Don't be too quick to judge him, Padre," said the Pope. "Let me ask you to look at the warrant again, and tell me *when* and *where* he is supposed to have committed those crimes."

Padre Ghiardi read through the warrant more carefully this time. "Why, it says that he did these things in Washington, D.C., on March 30th—just three days ago. But . . ."

"But he was there with you then—is that what you were going to say, Padre?" the Pope asked.

"Oh, yes, Holy Father!" came the reply. "He's been here ever since he came back from visiting you. I swear that to you!—*I don't understand* . . ."

What the Father Guardian did not understand was clear to the Pope—if the American authorities were after Fr. Santorelli for bilocating into that high level meeting in Washington, the Russians must have been too—and they must have scooped him up first and carried him off.—"*Family*" indeed! The Pope felt certain that Fr. Santorelli would never be heard from again, and he surmised that there was nothing he could do other than offer Masses for the priest—dead or alive.

"I *do* understand, Padre," said the Holy Father. "Bad people in two countries were trying to take him away to use him for their own purposes. *He has done nothing wrong, and I can assure you that he is as holy a priest as you thought he was.* He has been a great help to me, both before and since my election."

"Well, I thank you so very much for your reassurances, which I will make known to the others here," said a greatly relieved Father Guardian. "If there's anything further I can do for you, Holy Father, or for him, please let me know."

After a pause, the Pope said, "There *is* something, Padre, that I would be grateful to you for doing. Kindly gather up *everything* of his—clothing, reading material, diaries, notebooks, letters, anything like that—even used bandages—and preserve them under lock and key until I give you further directions. Will you do that for me?"

"Right away, Holy Father! I will see to it myself, and I will await your instructions."

— 2 —

Moscow

By that evening, Fr. Santorelli was incarcerated in Moscow's notorious Lefortovo prison. Like people, prisons are known by the company they keep, and the old, five story building had kept its share of famous political prisoners, including the Swedish diplomat Raoul Wallenberg, and Soviet dissident Aleksandr Solzhenitsyn. Some had never been seen again.

The unconscious captive was first medically examined to determine if there was any electronic device implanted in him which could communicate or be used to track him—or any novel device which might explain his feat in Washington. The medical people found nothing, and turned him over for interrogation.

When his sedation wore off, Fr. Santorelli found himself lying shivering on the floor of a small cell, alone, naked and bloody. A very dim light bulb hung well out of reach, and there was a pail in a corner. He was disoriented, but he began at once to pray for strength to accomplish God's will. While he was thus engaged the black mastiff which had attacked him in Rome manifested its presence by jumping on his back and sinking its teeth into his neck. When he feebly tried to roll over in self-defense, it let go of his neck and gave a bite to each of his wounded hands and feet. Then it disappeared, leaving him crying out in pain.

After a while, his body told his brain that he couldn't remain sprawled on the cold floor. Standing up was not much better. Without clothes, he was continually losing body heat. Like generations of prisoners in the cell before him, he hit upon the best solution: sitting on his haunches with his back resting against a wall, with his legs encircled by his arms and drawn up to his chest. At least that minimized the exposure of his skin to the chill air.

What day was it, he wondered? That information was meaningless, but it was a point of contact with reality, something that would help his mind regain control of the situation—as would knowing where in the world he was. There was no outside light to give him a clue, and he couldn't tell how long they'd kept him drugged. He was bleeding noticeably from his unbandaged wounds, which might indicate that it was Friday, though that might just be due to having had his wounds probed—which is what it felt like, as they were throbbing far more strongly than usual.

Wounds aside, it was hard to make his mind think about something other than being cold. He could do it—but his thoughts jumped around and did not last long, interrupted, as they were, by shivers.

He had talked with Jesus only a few days before, offering himself up as a living sacrifice. He hadn't imagined then that he would be taken up on his offer so soon, or how it would come about. Judging from the Slavic accent of the men who had kidnapped him, he guessed he was in the hands of the Russian security organization. Between spasms of shivering, his mind functioned well enough to allow him to guess that they wanted to interrogate him about how he had managed to appear and then disappear in the meeting at the State Department in Washington.

Yes, that was it! They wanted to ask The Invisible Man how he did it! Quite a nice trick it was—and one very useful for spying and making war. That's what they were interested in—not the message he had delivered. Fine. They should be able to tell quickly that he had no knowledge of how the bi-location had happened, and no control over it. The same for the Warning visions, if they were interested in them.

Jesus had asked him if he were willing to be *crucified*—but, it made no sense to him that the Russians might end up doing that to him. Even Aleksandr Solzhenitsyn, in recounting the many horrors of the Gulag, didn't describe that as one of the punishments inflicted on enemies of the state—if that's what he was, for crossing the Russian Foreign Minister.

A hope crossed his mind that maybe Jesus had pressed him in the last spiritual encounter just to see how completely he was willing to put himself into the Lord's hands. Maybe, having agreed then to whatever suffering came, even crucifixion, he would be spared that last sacrifice.

Yes! That was logical! He was Isaac, having submitted to be bound by his father, Abraham. He was already laid out on the altar of sacrifice, yet God could still prevent the slaughter from occurring, as He did for Isaac.

That comforting idea slowly evaporated. He realized that his mind was trying to assert itself, against his will. *He had already agreed to undergo the Cross, and now he must truly embrace it, instead of seeking to flee.*

A Latin phrase wandered into his consciousness. *"Quo vadis, Domine?"*

It was fitting. He recalled the tradition about St. Peter, who, having been condemned to death, somehow escaped his captors and was making his way out of Rome, when he encountered the Risen Christ on the road, *going toward Rome.* "Where are you going, Lord?" Peter had asked Him. "I am going to Rome to be crucified again," was the answer—and that shamed St. Peter into turning around and returning to jail, to suffer his ordained fate of crucifixion.

His mind was back under control by his will, but precariously so, assailed by the fears which kept returning, redoubled. If they did crucify him, would they make use of the stigmata he had already received, or would they bore new holes through his flesh? ... Would they flagellate him first? ... Would they hang him upside down, like St. Peter? ... Would he be left hanging alive on the cross for days?—He'd read that had sometimes happened in Roman times, which is why the leg bones of the thieves crucified with Jesus were broken, to make sure they died and were taken off their crosses before the Passover began that evening.

Now he felt a little less cold—or was it his imagination? He had read somewhere that people who were freezing to death actually felt warm, even to the point of taking off their clothes in below zero weather. He would much prefer death by freezing, considering the alternative ...

Why were they waiting to start questioning him? Maybe it was night and the interrogators only worked during the day? Maybe they wanted him to be weakened first by cold and hunger and thirst? Or, maybe someone in authority was just now looking over his file and deciding that they had been stupid to bother with him. They might take him, blindfolded, somewhere out in the countryside, so he wouldn't know where he had been, and release him ...

"Jesus!" he said aloud. *"Forgive me!"*

Once again his doubts and fears had overpowered his will. He could tell he was driving himself crazy, thinking about himself and his plight. He needed to focus his mind on something outside and put his mind to good use. He had to pray for his friends Zanier and Ireland!

They had already been attacked once—and now that their profile was even higher, they would have more enemies. This might be the last chance he had to pray for them. He would try to focus on saying five decades of the Rosary for each of them, on his fingers, before he was taken away for interrogation. The last five decades would be for his captors. He was certain they didn't know what they were doing.

After he made it through the Rosary, a comforting thought occurred: *God had taken charge of his fate.* He no longer had the possibility of fleeing, of running away from his commitment. He was in a stronger position even than that of St. Peter and the other Roman martyrs, for in their final hours they had to resist the temptation to live, by apostasizing. *His* captors were not interested in getting him to worship the Emperor—he was sure they wanted information on how to accomplish supernatural feats. Even if they promised to let him live if he gave them that information, he didn't have it to give. He no longer had the power to go back on the offer which he had made to Jesus, the offer of his life, to head off worldwide nuclear war. He couldn't fail the Lord now!

That was another reassuring thought which did not last long. True, he could not flee *physically*, but he could still flee *mentally*. He could be like Jesus, in praying that the bitter cup would pass Him by—without reaching the vital conclusion of Jesus' prayer, "yet not *my* will, but *thy* will be done!" The stigmatic nun whose mystical visions he had taken to heart had seen Christ kneel by His Cross and kiss it, before it was put on His shoulder. He had to do the same, in spirit, accepting his own cross, when it was ready for him.

— 3 —

Moscow
Good Friday

In an interrogation room at Lefortovo prison, Fr. Santorelli, still naked, was strapped into a heavy wooden chair, with his forearms extended and his hands resting on small tables. The lights shining on his face were so bright that he had to keep shutting his eyes. Wires were clamped onto his genitals—he could not see where they went, but he knew it must be to an electric generator. His interrogator also was hidden by the glare.

Ivan was not the interrogator usually used on English speaking prisoners. That one spoke fluent English, having served a tour as a guard at the Russian embassy in Washington; his drawback was his modus operandi, which was methodical, wearing a prisoner down over days or weeks of relentless questioning, with only occasional acts of brutality. Ivan, by contrast, was a brute of a man who had himself once served time in a prison camp for assorted robberies and assaults. His knowledge of English was only rudimentary, barely sufficient for the purpose, and his technique relied heavily on torture.

He was the one chosen by the head of the prison to work on Fr. Santorelli, because of the extraordinary pressure being exerted by a Special Deputy Assistant to the Russian President, to have the priest talk, and talk very quickly. There was no time to squeeze the tube of toothpaste slowly and methodically from the bottom up; it had to be squeezed hard in the middle to start it coming out. Once that happened, the more fluent interrogator might be brought in, with a scientist to hear the American's answers and provide new questions. In any event, there was no worry about having to keep the man alive, or having to render an account or apology to American authorities for mistreating one of their citizens.

Ivan, having read a summary of the report by the Russian Foreign Minister and the meager file put together about the prisoner, decided to begin with the "reasonable man" approach. It sometimes worked with intellectuals who were physically soft and dreaded pain, once they understood just how much suffering he could inflict on them.

"You charch man. You know wat *true* and wat *no true*," said Ivan, in broken, heavily accented, but understandable, English. "I want *just true* from you. You charch man—must say *just true*—yes?"

Fr. Santorelli recognized it as a rhetorical question and did not answer.

"*I say you true—you dont go from here alife. It simpel—say me true fast, I shoot you in back your head, no pain.—You no say true, you die slow, you ask to die.—You make choise . . .*"

Ivan walked over to his prisoner. "Pain—tree levels—forse you good talk."

Now that his adversary was out from behind the lights, Fr. Santorelli could see that he was a muscular man dressed in black. And that was all he saw before Ivan took a backhand swipe at his face, hitting the priest hard enough to break his nose.

"*Level one—usual pain,*" Ivan said in a matter-of-fact voice, and walked back to his seat.

After a minute's wait to let the lesson sink in, Ivan turned the rheostat dial on the electric shocking device. Fr. Santorelli's body contorted in a spasm, straining against the straps which held him down.

"*Zis pain level two—agony.*"

Ivan waited until the priest came to his senses before proceeding.

"*Now level tree,*" Ivan said. He walked over to Fr. Santorelli again, a knife in his hand, and stuck it through the stigmata in the priest's left hand. Fr. Santorelli screamed and fainted.

"*Now you know it!*" said Ivan, with enthusiasm in his voice, when Fr. Santorelli had been revived. "*Level tree pain—you tink you die.* You lose your sense? O.K. Ve vake you!" Ivan sounded pleased with the workings of the system. It was time to begin the interrogation.

"You vas in Vashington—in Monday. How you come zere?" asked Ivan.

Fr. Santorelli briefly weighed trying to remain silent, but he knew he couldn't hold out in the face of torture, and he also apprehended that truthful answers would give witness to Jesus Christ. And so he answered.

"I wasn't there. I was in Italy then."

Ivan gave Fr. Santorelli a brief electric shock.

"*No true.* Forein Minister see you in Vashington, hear you talk.—How you come zere?"

"I don't know. I wasn't there. Something that looked like me was sent to Washington. I was in Italy."

"You fly on airplan in Vashington?"

"No."

"How you come in Vashington?"

"I didn't. My body was in Italy. Just something like a picture of me was in Washington."

"How picture sent in Vashington?"

"I don't know."

"*No true.*" Another electric shock, this one longer. "Who send your picture in Vashington?"

"God."

"How God make it?"

"I have no idea. You can ask him yourself."

Ivan walked over again and struck Fr. Santorelli's forehead a glancing blow with a kind of whisk made of sharp, thin, flat wires. They scored the flesh, and blood started to drip down from the ribbons of flesh into his eyes. The priest could see little now, due to the lights and his bleeding. It was like having a blood-letting crown of thorns.

"Picture vas, how you say—'hologram'?"

"No. It was bi-location."

"Bi-location?" Ivan had trouble repeating the word. "Bi-location? Wat it mean? Explain."

"It means being in two places at the same time."

"How it heppen?"

"I can't make it happen. Only God can make it happen."

"Who know zis *bi-location?*"

"*Your priests know.*"

Another shock to his genitals.

"How bi-location heppen?"

"No one but God can make it happen," Fr. Santorelli said in exasperation. "I can't control where I go in bi-location—or when.— I can't control what I say or do when I'm somewhere else, or when I return."

"So—it heppen before? Say me."

Fr. Santorelli haltingly related the episodes of bi-location into the office of the Israeli Prime Minister in an attempt to stop the war.

"How you know wen go see Primer Minister?"

"I didn't decide when.—I was sent there then."

"Who send you?"

"God."

"How you know wat say Primer Minister?"

"God put the words in my mouth. I didn't think them up."

"You say Israel Primer Minister shoot you. *No true.* You no have bullet wund."

"He shot what he saw, what looked like me. The bullet went through my image, into the wall.—My body wasn't there. It was in Italy."

"'Bi-location' in Vashington . . . ?"

"The same.—My body stayed in Italy. Something like me was in Washington.—When it was over, I was back together in Italy."

"You know wat say Forein Minister?"

"Not before I went there. I understood what he was demanding only as God gave me a response to speak."

"How you receve vords? Wat mashin?"

"*No machine.* They just popped into my head. God put them there. He used my mouth to say them."

A longer shock. Once again the priest's body convulsed savagely.

"Wich mashin move you in Vashington?"

"No machine."

"*No true.* Wich mashin send picture like hologram?"

"No machine."

"You say me or my peopel go in Italia. *Find mashin or shoot charch man.*"

Fr. Santorelli rashly vented his exasperation. "Stupid! If it existed, the machine would be in Washington."

Ivan walked over, stuck his knife in the hole in Fr. Santorelli's right hand, and twisted it. After Fr. Santorelli was revived from his faint, Ivan resumed the interrogation.

"Say about visions. Who cause?"

"Only God causes them—I don't know how."

"*No true.*" Ivan gave Fr. Santorelli another electric shock before he tried again. "Wich mashin make visions?"

"No machine. God does it."

"How visions go acros air?"

Fr. Santorelli foolishly thought it was worth trying to cut through the nonsense. "I don't know. Why ask me? Ask your own scientists. They should know."

His punishment came swiftly in the form of a shock strong enough to make him pass out again.

"If sientists know," said Ivan, "no need ask you.—*You* say visions from God. Sientists not know it. You charch man. *You know.*"

Silence from Fr. Santorelli.

Ivan walked over to the prisoner again and struck him full in the mouth, bashing in some teeth. Then, he sat back down and recommenced the interrogation as if nothing had happened.

"I not believe dat you not know how 'bi-location' and visions made."

"*It's true,*" Fr. Santorelli managed to say, with his mangled mouth.

"*True?*" Ivan snorted.—"*No true wich I want.—True I want you say wich mashin used, how mashins work, where mashins, who use mashins . . . You say me now—den I kill you—no more pain.*"

When the priest remained silent, at Ivan's order, a team of men entered, unstrapped him, and hung him by his wrists from a metal pipe in the ceiling, so that his feet were off the floor. Two of them, with whips, took turns lashing his back and chest until they were badly cut up. Each time he fainted from the blows, they brought him around by throwing a bucket of cold water in his face. After they had worked him over to Ivan's satisfaction, they tied his hands behind his back and suspended him by roping them to the overhead pipe before they left.

— 4 —

Moscow
Holy Saturday

The President of Russia, a man as cold blooded as any reptile, was in an icy fury over the obstacles suddenly cropping up to his planned annexation of the Ukraine.

The 4th and 10th Guards Tank Brigades of the 20th Army had been deployed close to the eastern border of the Ukraine, awaiting the order to invade. With supporting infantry and air forces, their two hundred new T-95 main battle tanks were easily enough to punch through the weak Ukrainian defenses and take the first group of objectives: the cities of Kharkiv in the north, and Donets'k, Luhans'k, and Kramators'k in the east, thus menacing Kiev, the Ukrainian capital, and putting the whole of the heavily industrialized Donets Basin in Russian hands. The Black Sea fleet had already blockaded the Ukrainian navy in its ports, and the Russian amphibious vessels were prepared to land troops at the neck of the Crimean Peninsula, thus bringing that territory too under Russian control. Together, these steps would show the central government in Kiev that they could not expect help from the West, and had no alternative but to agree at once to become part of the Russian Federation.

His grand strategy was now endangered by the unexpected deployment of U.S. planes and artillery to the Ukraine. The story was that they were there for "training." Given their nuclear armament, which had been disclosed, he recognized that "training" was a diplomatic fig leaf to cover their real purpose—helping the Ukrainians resist the coming invasion. With them in the picture, the Russian tank forces no longer looked invincible.

And, he suspected that the Americans would not be foolish enough to join the battle with those few aircraft. There was nothing in the press release about American stealth aircraft also being sent to the Ukraine, but they might fly in at night as needed to bomb Russian positions. He knew he could prevent the American planes from being a factor—but only by initiating a first strike with missiles on airfields all over the Ukraine. The quick, surgically precise and almost bloodless invasion that he had expected to command, with no risk to Russia, could become the type of confrontation that had escalated into a full blown nuclear war in the Middle East just days before.

The other problematic factor was not a tangible one. It was the bizarre event at the U.S. State Department, namely, the appearance and disappearance of a talking ghost. He suspected that the Foreign Minister had seen a *maskarova*—an elaborate show, designed to mislead him. Yet, the state security apparatus had actually found an American priest, living at a Capuchin friary in Italy, who exactly matched the description given by the Foreign Minister, and who, under interrogation, had admitted that he had been present at the meeting in Washington and had indeed threatened both countries. His story matched that of the Foreign Minister exactly!

Being a confirmed atheist, the President did not believe for a minute that there was a God somewhere out there who had offered his country a choice between life and death. Nor did he credit the priest's story about "bi-location." Religious nonsense like that was for grandmothers in babushkas. No doubt the U.S. Government, not God, was behind the whole affair, and the man was an actor using a script prepared for him. That still left one loose end: the fact that the man apparently could make himself invisible at will. *If* that had really happened, the only rational explanation which occurred to the Russian President was that the man had been employing a new secret weapon of the Americans.

In exploring that possibility, the Russian President had learned that American scientists had presented papers on what they termed an "invisibility cloak," made of metamaterial that had negative light refraction. The prisoner must be made to reveal everything about how such a cloak worked, and whether it could be used to render invisible something as large as a tank! Being somewhat unsure whether such invisibility was a new type of stealth weapon system in the American armory, and whether the Ukraine was more heavily defended than it had appeared a few days ago, the Russian President was temporarily paralyzed with indecision, and anxiously looked for further results from the interrogation of the priest.

*   *   *

At Lefortovo prison, Ivan was frustrated at not being able to start in on his interrogation again in the morning, especially given the order he had received to get answers immediately, no matter what he had to do. It happened that Ivan also had his own motive for abusing the prisoner. He was angered by the fact that this man was only a lily white 'charch man'—not the sort of man inured to harsh treatment—and yet, he had resisted every torture Ivan inflicted on him. The result was that when Ivan was not pleading with Fr. Santorelli to be reasonable and end his suffering, he was inflicting ever greater cruelties on him. When the prisoner had finally been lowered to the ground, he was in very bad condition. The doctor who examined him was of the opinion that he was on the verge of going into shock, and would shortly die unless he was given intravenous feeding and a blood transfusion. Ivan did not receive clearance to go back to work on the priest until it was evening.

As he had been ordered, Ivan now began to ask questions about an "invisibility cloak," whatever that was, for Ivan had never heard of one before.

"No such thing—never had one," said Fr. Santorelli, prompting Ivan to give him the first of many electric shocks that session.

"How you make invisibel?"

"I didn't do it. God did it."

"*No true.* Wich mashin make you invisibel?"

Back and forth Ivan went over the same ground, getting the same answers, or none at all, as Fr. Santorelli increasingly lost his ability to focus his mind on Ivan's questions or to speak when he could.

Feeling the pressure to make the prisoner talk without further delay, and enraged that he was not able to break him even with third level pain, Ivan hit upon the idea of crucifying the 'charch man.' He ordered that a wooden cross be constructed, with an iron base to hold it upright. Then, he let his assistants drag the man back to his cell, after first telling the 'charch man' what his fate would be in the morning if he did not give Ivan the answers he was seeking.

— 5 —

Moscow
Easter Sunday

The apparatus ordered by Ivan was ready at dawn, a dawn that did not penetrate the windowless interrogation chamber.

Once the cross had been set up in its heavy base in front of Fr. Santorelli's eyes, Ivan was ready to speak his cruelest words of persuasion.

"You have littel marks in hands and fit.—Littel marks make just littel pains, charch man." Ivan said, contemptuously. *"Cross make big pain! ... Masels spasm ... You no briz ... Open mouth—no air."*

Ivan moved right in front of his seated prisoner, spread his arms wide and assumed a look of agony, pretending to gasp for breath. *"Uh—uh—uh ... !"*

When his pantomime was finished, he said, "You live until say me *true* about mashins—and invisibility cloak." Ivan stumbled again over the last two words, still wondering what they meant.

Fr. Santorelli had nothing to say in response. His mind mostly wandered on its own now in the intervals when he was conscious. Terrible pains in every part of his body prevented him from deliberately thinking about anything for more than a few seconds at a time.

His silence angered Ivan. *"You understand?"* Ivan thundered. *"I have power crucify you!!!"*

Fr. Santorelli tried to look at Ivan, still behind the lights, but his eyes were clotted with blood. The words 'Crucifixus etiam pro nobis, sub Pontio Pilato' welled up from a deep font, though he could no longer have explained their meaning. They were submerged again as a semi-lucid thought hovered briefly: *Pontius Pilate had the power to crucify him.*

He struggled hard to respond, managing to gasp out an answer. *"Power— comes from—God."*

"No true!!!" Ivan knew where *his* power came from, and it wasn't God. It was time for pain beyond 'level tree.' He gave an order, and Fr. Santorelli was hauled to the crucifix lying flat on the floor.

The priest's hands were nailed to the crosspiece. Then, his arms were tied on at the wrists and elbows, and his body under the armpits. After that, his feet were nailed to the upright.

The nails were larger in diameter than the stigmata, and as they were hammered in, his blood spurted out on his executioners. Somehow he had enough energy left to scream loudly as it was happening, then he immediately lapsed into unconsciousness when they raised the cross with its living corpus. His torso sagged despite the roping, as his shoulders had been dislocated.

When the prisoner was revived, Ivan continued his questioning, going over the same issues as before, time and again, frantically seeking to force him to reveal the mechanism behind the visions and the bi-location, and the "invisibility cloak" that his superiors were so interested in.

Fr. Santorelli reached the final state of hypovolemic shock and exhaustion asphyxia. He looked at Ivan, and gasped out a barely audible, *"Forgive—you ... "*

Et inclinato capite, emisit spiritum.

The charch man's words of forgiveness unleashed a torrent of abuse from Ivan, who did not notice the slight change in his victim's condition.

An idea came to him—he had not yet inflicted pain at the site of the wound in the charch man's side. Maybe digging into the wound there would finally make him talk ...

He inserted his knife between the fifth and sixth ribs on Fr. Santorelli's right side. When the priest failed to respond in any way, Ivan increased the pressure, until the knife slipped and the blade went in further, piercing the side of the heart. Serous pleural and pericardial fluid spurted out and ran down Ivan's arm, followed by blood.

Enraged that the priest had died before he talked, Ivan rammed the knife up as far as it would go. The black dog in the shadows, which Ivan never saw, wagged its tail in approval before it disappeared.

*   *   *

The Russian President was greatly displeased to learn that the American prisoner had died before giving the answers he was looking for. While his uncertainties remained, he couldn't just hold the invasion indefinitely in abeyance. An internal political dynamic had been set in motion with the military deployment. He could not afford, for domestic reasons, to look weak by pulling back the troops and armor with nothing to show for the exercise. He decided he would go ahead with the invasion, first ordering missile strikes to wipe out the airfields in the Ukraine, and then sending the tanks across the border.

Although he was still somewhat worried about the possibility of an "invisibility cloak" being an American secret weapon, he convinced himself that it was likely a figment of his imagination. After all, the proof that it existed in workable form was merely that an intruder had magically appeared and disappeared in a Washington conference room, and the only outsider who had seen this was his Foreign Minister, who might have been duped by a hologram. True—the priest had claimed, in the course of being interrogated, that he had also bi-located into the office of the Israeli Prime Minister during the Middle East war—but, there were no living witnesses to that appearance, so the claim was probably just part of the *maskarova*.

Such were the thoughts of the Russian President when he was suddenly immersed in his own vision, one totally unlike anyone else's.

He found himself an unseen observer in the State Department conference room, where his Foreign Minister and the American Secretary of State were poring over a large globe. He noticed, before they did, a figure materialize in the middle of the room—it was the American priest dressed in a brown habit. Everything then unfolded exactly as the Russian official had said—and the American had confirmed under torture—until the priest had spoken his piece, and disappeared as strangely as he had come.

Finally, the President understood what had happened! The explanation was that the Americans had invented a novel mind-effects machine, able to project images into men's minds at a great distance! It was probably circling the earth in one of those secret satellites the Americans had launched several months before. That would account for the reports of people in many countries seeing visions. He had dismissed the reports as mass hallucinations. Now, though, he had seen a vision for himself—and he understood they were a real phenomenon.

It occurred to him how visions aimed at the Russian troops by this secret weapon could completely undermine the invasion and lead to heavy losses. If even he and his Foreign Minister could not resist the power of the vision machine, his men could certainly be tricked into regarding their comrades as enemy soldiers, and turning their weapons on each other!

It was necessary to rethink everything once more . . .

There was a chance that an invasion would not be necessary, if he could gain sufficient concessions at the negotiating table. The bottom line demands from his perspective were that the Ukraine not become a member of NATO, and that offensive weapons not be stationed east of the Dnieper River, which ran north to south, splitting the country roughly in half. If, in negotiations, those objectives could be achieved, together with an agreement protecting the ethnic Russian populations in the Crimea and the eastern areas of the Ukraine, that would sufficiently serve his interests and those of Russia, and allow him to call off the pending invasion without loss of face.

He had nothing to lose by trying that tactic first. And so, he summoned his Foreign Minister, and instructed him to call the American Secretary of State and suggest that the two of them meet with the Ukrainian President in Kiev on Tuesday, to see whether an agreement to resolve tensions could be reached in a three-party high level session.

— 6 —

Washington, D.C.
Monday of Easter Week

Secretary of State Howe had been greatly relieved when the Russian Foreign Minister called to propose immediate three party talks in Kiev. Now, only hours later, on board a U.S. Government jet taking him to Kiev, he thought back to his last meeting with his adversary. The one at the State Department, where the priest posing as a Capuchin had popped into the middle of the room out of nowhere, lectured them, and then suddenly disappeared without a trace.

What a stunt! How in the world had he managed to pull it off? The security people would give their eye teeth to find out. Well, he was no doubt paying dearly for it now! The poor fellow was bound to be in a Russian prison, where they were offering *him* the choice of life or death, to get him to talk.

The Secretary sighed. He had been silly to hope momentarily that the intruder was a heaven-sent *deus ex machina*, there to bring about peace between the United States and Russia. Fortunately, *realpolitik* had succeeded where mysticism had failed. President Gardiner had the courage to risk nuclear war by making a show of force in the Ukraine—and *that* had brought the Russians to the negotiating table.

— 7 —

Moscow
Friday of Easter Week

It should have been a good day for Igor Mikhailovitch Ivanov, what with the news reports of a breakthrough in the negotiations being conducted in Kiev. It looked as though there would be a peaceful resolution of the dispute with the Ukraine, which is something that he was very grateful for, being a man of God—an Archbishop in the Russian Orthodox Church.

Instead, it was starting out as absolutely the worst day of his life. He stood, with a great deal of dread, looking up at the building he was about to enter—Lefortovo prison. He had unexpectedly been summoned to present himself at No. 3 Energeticheskaya Street, the entrance used for witnesses to be interrogated. He had no reason to believe that he was going to be detained there, but one never knew in Russia. A chilling uncertainty as to purpose and outcome was a concomitant of all encounters with the state security apparatus. That had not changed since the days of the Czars.

The summons was highly unusual on three accounts. To begin with, this day was Good Friday on the Russian Orthodox calendar—celebrated one week later than the Roman Catholic Church celebrated the same sacred day. That it was a religious holiday could not have gone unnoticed by the person whom he was to meet, a Special Deputy Assistant to the Russian President. That too was a surprise, as was the place chosen for the meeting, for, of course, the official did not have his office at the prison.

He was aware that the official, Viktor Vladimirovitch Federenkov, had been a colonel in the old KGB, now the FSB. So, it was obviously a security matter of some importance that would be discussed. The Archbishop could think of nothing that he himself had done against the Russian state, but it was possible that someone had falsely accused him, or that a complaint had been made about one of the priests under his supervision. He worried that one of them might have been arrested.

He arrived early and was kept waiting. He knew that was done to increase his apprehension, and despite knowing that, it succeeded in doing so. For an hour he sat alone in one of the interrogators' offices opposite the entrance—a room empty except for a table and two chairs. The official finally entered, carrying a small parcel wrapped in white paper, like butcher paper, which he casually dropped on the table before they shook hands and sat down.

Coming straight to the point, the official brought up the *modus vivendi* which had been arrived at between state security on the one hand and the Russian Orthodox Church on the other hand, in the time of Patriarch Alexius II, and continued since then: what was Caesar's would be rendered unto Caesar, and what was God's would be rendered unto God. One of the corollaries of that understanding was that priests would refrain from acting in the political arena. There had indeed been a transgression years before, by a priest who made inappropriate remarks at the funeral of a newspaper reporter, implying that the Government was behind his murder. The priest had been arrested and beaten, but then turned over to the Church, which had punished him severely canonically and exiled him to the eparchy of Vladivostok.

The case now at hand was somewhat similar, said the official, in that a priest had acted inappropriately in the extreme. He had somehow intruded himself into a negotiating session of the Russian Foreign Minister with the United States Secretary of State, and he had proceeded to make threats against their two countries because of their policies. After offering them the choice of "life" or "death," he had disappeared. How he had gained access to the meeting in Washington, D.C., was a mystery still under investigation. In any event, it was clear that his corporal body was not in the United States—it was in Italy at the time. He had subsequently been located there and brought to Moscow—to that very prison—for interrogation, during which he had maintained that he had "bi-located" into the meeting.

At this, the Archbishop could not keep himself from protesting, "He *surely* was not one of *ours*, Viktor Vladimirovitch."

"You are correct—he was not one of *yours*. You are *very fortunate* in that ..."

The churchman sighed audibly with relief.

"He was a priest, an American by birth who was living in a Capuchin friary in Italy. *I am bringing this case to your attention only as a warning that if any of your priests ever has a similar thought to try this 'bi-location' trick, whatever it may be, he had better watch where he goes and not intrude into matters which do not concern the Church.* To emphasize that point, I have brought you something which I request that you display to all the priests of the Eparchy of Moscow as an object lesson to them."

With that, the Deputy untied the string and unwrapped the paper, revealing two large severed hands, dry and graying.

Archbishop Ivanov recoiled in horror. There was no question about what they were. Without thinking, he blurted out, "*The holes in the palms . . . ?*"

"Ah yes.—The records state that the man was what some call a stigmatist. Of course, the holes may have become enlarged during his interrogation . . . " He shrugged his shoulders as he spread his hands, as if to say, 'Those things happen here.—What can one expect?'

"So," the Deputy continued, "now that you've seen them, you may rewrap them and take them with you."

Screwing up his courage, the Archbishop asked, "And the rest of his remains . . . ?"

The official looked at him coldly. "As you know, we don't provide burials for enemies of the State."

"Yes," the Archbishop said, "I understand." And he did, for it was known that in the bowels of the prison there was a giant meat grinder used, at least under the "old regime," to grind up the bodies of torture victims before they were washed into the sewer. He would have liked to ask the name of the priest, but, given the official's last answer, he was afraid of seeming too interested in the case.

His command appearance having concluded, Archbishop Ivanov left the prison as quickly as he could, in a trance, numbed by the horror of it all. He must tell his superior, the Patriarch, about the meeting right away, and ask him how to carry out the instruction he had been given.

On the way back to Church headquarters, a marvelous thing happened to him: he was surprised by Truth.

A recess of his mind had been turning over what he had learned from the official about the dead man. Information which the State credited. *It meant that stories which he had read about men of God who bore the marks of Christ—and others who bilocated—were not merely pious tales of hagiography . . . They were true!*

And as with Jesus, all the authorities could do was kill the man—they could not manage to suppress the evidence that God did exist and had acted through him!

The Archbishop smiled as he thought of how he could—very carefully and subtly, to be sure—use the display of the severed hands to teach his priests lessons quite different from the one the official intended! Lessons about how God was still using men to show His glory and do His bidding! And he would do this with information that came from Caesar!

*   *   *

The Patriarch heard the Archbishop's report of the meeting, saying as little as possible, and nothing by way of protest or condemnation, for the walls, even in his office, had ears. Feeling obliged to see the grisly parts himself, he asked the Archbishop to unwrap them.

It was an experience that the Patriarch would remember till his dying day.—The hands were not gray as he expected, but pink, as though they were still alive, and blood began to ooze in drops from the grossly distorted stigmata. But, what most caught his attention at the time was a strong, fragrant smell.

He sniffed audibly, then gave his subordinate a questioning look, as if asking him, *'Do you smell what I smell?'*

The Archbishop nodded. *"Roses,"* he said.

Then and there, the Patriarch resolved that after the hands were displayed as ordered, they would be preserved reverently.

A thought occurred to him. His Church had never properly reciprocated the grand gesture of Pope John Paul II in returning the most sacred icon in all of Russia, that of Our Lady of Kazan, which had come into the Roman Church's possession after being stolen and smuggled out of Russia a century before. One day, in the course of his ecumenical rounds, he would surely pay a fraternal visit to Paul VIIth in Rome, and he would need a holy gift to present, a token repayment of sorts.

It would be a worthy gesture to give the new Pope, in a reliquary of crystal and gold, a hand of this unknown Roman priest— *martyr* and *saint*.

THE END

About the Author

HURD BARUCH received degrees from Hamilton College, Yale Law School and Columbia University Graduate School of Business, and was elected to membership in Phi Beta Kappa, the Order of the Coif and Beta Gamma Sigma. He practiced law for more than forty years, in the fields of corporate and securities law and litigation, with particular emphasis on investigating corporate wrongdoing in this country and abroad. He served as an official in the Office of the Secretary of Defense (1962–1964), and at the Securities and Exchange Commission (1969–1972). He has authored *Wall Street: Security Risk* (Washington: Acropolis Books 1971; Baltimore: Penguin Books 1972), a book about the near collapse of the brokerage industry at that time, and *Light on Light: Illuminations of the Gospel of Jesus Christ from the Mystical Visions of the Venerable Anne Catherine Emmerich* (Maxkol Communications 2004), a book summarizing and commenting on the detailed visions of the daily life of Christ by a stigmatic German nun, who has since been beatified. Mr. Baruch now writes in retirement in Tucson, where he lives with his wife.